American Social Character

American Social Character

MODERN INTERPRETATIONS
from the '40s to the present ☆ • ☆ • ☆ • ☆ • ☆

Edited with Introductions and Commentaries by
RUPERT WILKINSON

IconEditions
An Imprint of HarperCollins*Publishers*

In grateful memory of
Marcus Cunliffe

HarperCollins books may be purchased for educational, business, or sales promotional use. For information please write: Special Markets Department, HarperCollins Publishers, Inc., 10 East 53rd Street, New York, NY 10022.

FIRST EDITION

Designed by Barbara DuPree Knowles

LIBRARY OF CONGRESS CATALOGING-IN-PUBLICATION DATA
American social character : modern interpretations / edited with
  introductions and commentaries by Rupert Wilkinson. — 1st ed.
    p. cm.
  Includes bibliographical references and index.
  ISBN 0-06-438877-8—ISBN 0-06-430979-7 (pbk.)
    1. National characteristics, American. 2. United States—
Civilization—20th century. I. Wilkinson, Rupert.
E169.1.A4825   1991
973—dc20   90-56402

92 93 94 95 96 CC/HC 10 9 8 7 6 5 4 3 2 1
92 93 94 95 96 CC/HC 10 9 8 7 6 5 4 3 2 1 (pbk.)

Contents

Preface

This anthology features the writing of seventeen important analysts of American (United States) character and culture—from Margaret Mead and David Riesman in the 1940s to Robert Bellah in the mid-1980s. The book is designed for courses on American culture and identity, and for students and scholars interested in American social thought since World War II. For further study in these topics, the volume ends with a long, bibliographical essay that shows how different trains of thought intersect. It provides a reading guide to ideas of American character, problems of defining and researching it, the intellectual background of key writing on it, the relationship of national character to cultural pluralism, and international comparisons.

American character has attracted writers from a remarkable variety of intellectual backgrounds. By no means are all of them social scientists, but in discussing them, my introductions and commentaries refer to a number of sociological schools of thought. Students may find this useful as a way into the social sciences.

The main topic, however, is the question of American character itself: how to describe it, what has shaped it, whether it has changed. Twenty years ago it was said rather sniffily that American national character was a passé subject, academic vintage 1940s and 1950s. This is still sometimes said today, but those who say it have not looked under their noses. Since the late 1970s, a stream of books has poured forth on this topic. While often focusing on middle-class attitudes and values, they have supplied a *unifying corrective* to much of American

Studies today, which is often more concerned with the *differing* experiences of minorities and under-groups. (Of course, many people in American Studies would put it the other way: they see themselves as providing a corrective to excessive generalizing in the past about an "American consensus.")

Despite the continuing output on American character, there is at this time no anthology in print that gives a sample of the literature. Michael McGiffert's anthology, *The Character of Americans* (1964, rev. ed. 1970), has been out of print for some years, and his selections only go through the 1960s.

McGiffert's book is still useful, all the more because it differs from this volume in several respects. His selections start with Crèvecoeur in the 1770s, whereas I begin with Margaret Mead in 1942 and end in the 1980s (the Bibliography goes to 1991). I have fewer selections, but I put them in a more chronological order, and I say much more about each author and each reprinted text.

All writing on American character, indeed almost *all* writing, is a conjunction of three things: the author's personal background and development; the times he or she wrote in; and a changing intellectual tradition—a *procession* of thinking and writing by others—into which the author's work fits. This volume's general introduction, "On American Character," and the specific introductions to each piece recognize all three. Where the piece is excerpted from a book, I give some idea of the book's overall argument and purpose. Each selection is followed by a critical commentary. This commentary is not an exhaustive critique; it is more a contentious guide to some issues that arise, with further remarks here and there on background.

To reduce repetition, defects common to many studies of American character are noted in the general introduction. All works referred to or quoted in my introductions and commentaries are in the bibliographical essay of the corresponding section.

Finally, in choosing the contents of this anthology, I have occasionally changed the pace by putting in something that is more of a story than a solid chunk of exposition. I have done this partly to entertain and partly to remind ourselves that 'American character' is about real people in real situations.

Preface

In writing the chapter introductions and commentaries, I have used some passages from my previous book, *The Pursuit of American Character* (Harper & Row, 1988). The original idea for both books came from Cass Canfield, Jr., at HarperCollins. I am indebted to him for his support, as I am to David Riesman and Fred Greenstein who, many years ago, helped me yield to the temptations of studying American character. As I near the end of this vein of work and turn to other fields, I also realize how much I owe to the wide, untutored reading and open, speculative mind of my mother, Lorna Wilkinson—far more than she realizes.

For various kinds of advice, information, and encouragement that helped me construct this anthology, I thank Christopher Gerry, Christopher Brookeman, Roger Thompson, Richard King, Richard Gillam, Paul Pickrel, Daniel and Helen Horowitz, Craig Comstock, Tony Lanyi, Mary Wilkinson, and the book's copy editor, Robyn Bem; my colleagues at Sussex University and students in my Sussex course on modern interpretations of American social character; and the library staffs of Sussex University, Smith College, and the Chicago University archives.

This book is dedicated to the memory of my beloved friend and intellectual master, Marcus Cunliffe (1922–1990), who was founding Professor of American Studies at Sussex. He needs, however, no such memorial; his own writing supplies it.

RUPERT WILKINSON

A Note about Editing and Style

Each author's reference notes, if any, are at the end of the author's text. Occasionally I have rearranged them, and I have edited the citations to follow one style. Notes in square brackets are my own additions.

Throughout my own text, double quotation marks are used for quotations from specific writers. Single quotation marks usually denote colloquialisms or revealing clichés.

INTRODUCTION

On American Character

$\mathbb{S}$ince the 1930s a remarkable procession of writers have attempted the bold task of identifying a modern American character. They have argued that, for all the nation's famous differences of region, ethnic group, 'life-style,' and so forth, Americans tend to share a distinctive bundle of values, attitudes, and feelings about themselves. Even when the claim is confined to 'middle-class' groups, as it sometimes is, it still covers an awesome range of people, from Miami merchants to Seattle nurses.

These writers are not stupid: they do not mean that all Americans, middle-class or otherwise, are identical. They take for granted a lot of variation between individuals and groups. Nonetheless, they maintain that Americans *tend* to be different psychologically from other people.

Which other people? For some writers on modern American character, the main standard of comparison is the character of non-Americans, usually Europeans. For others, the main comparison is with a *past* American character: they are interested in how Americans have changed (usually for the worse; Jeremiah is alive and well in this writing). In explaining the change, they often point to forces of modernization that are not peculiar to the United States, but these forces usually seem to be particularly advanced and dominant in America (consumer capitalism, for example) and to engage with American traditions such as various kinds of individualism. The result, as these writers portray it, is a distinctive American mix.

I explain in my previous book why American character has attracted so much attention, from foreigners as well as natives.* What-

---

*Rupert Wilkinson, *The Pursuit of American Character* (New York, 1988). This book gives its own account and background of postwar writing on American character and relates it to four fears in American history. All writers referred to in this introduction are in the Bibliography (p. 331). See the Index of Names at the back.

ever the reasons, the literature on the subject is essential for students of American culture. Even when its conclusions seem too generalized and unsubstantiated, it provides arresting insights along the way. And it deals in ideas that are themselves part of American culture, central to the way in which Americans have talked about themselves and their society.

———

Discussion of American character goes back to puritan New England and the early Republic. Religious and social thinkers wondered if the people would show the qualities Providence required of them for their special tasks in the New World. In the nineteenth century, European visitors and émigrés joined native moralists in depicting American traits; they were fascinated—sometimes horrified—by what had happened to their own kind when they were set loose on a raw continent to realize a bourgeois democracy. Then, at the turn of the century, worries about the 'passing of the frontier' and the flooding of big cities by polyglot immigrants stimulated new efforts to define a traditional American identity.

After World War I, literary writers such as Sinclair Lewis and H. L. Mencken sank some barbed shafts into American character. They reacted against small-town intolerance while debunking the urbanite scramble to look smart and modern. As merchandisers increasingly used the psychology of fashion and appearance to sell their goods, it seemed that the great American freedom to move up the social ladder was bought at the price of conformity—copying the status-group sitting on the next rung.

In the 1930s and early 1940s, social scientists largely took over the pursuit of social character. They asked many questions about the individual's place in modern society, where huge organizations seemed to dominate an atomized mass of people, uprooted from traditional ties of neighborhood and kinship. A related interest was the psychology of mass movements, including fascism. Some writers, influenced by the German neo-Marxist 'Frankfurt School,' worried that mass organization annihilated and swallowed up the individual self.* The sociologist Robert Lynd, however, took an almost opposite line, applied more specifically to the United States. In Lynd's view, America's strong tradition of individualism, based on acquisition and competition, thwarted the inner need to accept oneself regardless of how much money one made. Based on private property, American individualism also conflicted with the expanded role of government and the ethos of collective responsibility needed in the modern state.

All these worries were to return in later writing on American character. In the 1930s and 1940s, however, the most immediate influence on the writing came from anthropologists of 'culture and personality' who adapted Freudian ideas in their fieldwork on Polynesians, North American Indians, and others. Led by Ruth Benedict and **Margaret Mead** among others, the 'C and P' school attacked racist-biological notions of group character by declaring that culture affected personality and vice versa.† Genes might create some individual differences, but what made a tribe or nation behave and think differently than another tribe or nation was its culture, its social rules and way of life, not its biological 'stock.' A key to understanding a culture lay in the kind of child-rearing it enjoined. This produced a prescribed personality type that in turn shaped everything the society did. Culture, in Ruth Benedict's words, was "personality writ large."

Benedict and others were important in reshaping the concept of national character; they were working at a time when the whole notion had been discredited among liberal academics because of the Nazi passion for classifying people by race. The cultural anthropologists built an alternative to racism by generalizing about group character.

Throughout the 1930s anthropologists pretty much confined their studies to 'primitive' (preindustrial) cultures. Margaret Mead did compare Polynesians with Americans in her first book, *Coming of Age in Samoa* (1929), and continued to do so in the 1930s. (As a later anthropologist said rather sourly, Mead "went to Samoa and discovered

*The 'Frankfurt School' refers to scholars associated with the Institute for Social Research (Institut für Sozialforschung) attached to the University of Frankfurt; it moved to Columbia University, New York, in 1934.
†Boldface type denotes the first mention of an author of an essay or book excerpt reprinted in this volume.

3

Connecticut.") But Mead was unusual here, and her main research was not on modern Americans. It took World War II to focus anthropology on the national character of modern peoples. As part of the social-science war effort, Mead and others studied the social character of Americans, their allies, and their enemies for a variety of reasons—to work out how to impose food-rationing, how to stop amorous GIs from offending the British, how to get the Japanese to surrender.

After the war, anthropologists continued to influence social-character writing—some practiced the trade themselves, some criticized it—but a variety of other spirits entered the field. Of the seventeen authors of the studies reprinted in this book, one is an anthropologist, six are sociologists, and four are historians. The remainder consist of a psychiatrist (with a Ph.D. in history), a philosopher, a journalist, a survey-research director, a political scientist, and a hippie-ish law professor.

———

Between the early 1940s and late 1980s, writing on American character made a U-turn. It began by stressing the group pressures on people to conform. Then, in the early 1970s it shifted to claims that Americans had lost a sense of community and had become egocentric. The literature thus started by challenging the 1930s picture of atomized individuals and returned, with a different language, to that picture in the 1970s and 1980s. It returned with less abstract theory about modern 'alienation' and more specific references to American styles and institutions. As we shall see, however, an underlying concern about alienation ran through much of the literature in both phases.

At the start of the first phase, writers such as Margaret Mead and **Ralph Barton Perry** showed in the 1940s how competitive individualism could coexist with social bonding and pressures to conform. Subsequent writers like **David Riesman, William Whyte,** and **Gregory Stone** made less of contemporary individualism and more of conformity, which became a popular middle-class issue in the 1950s.

To some extent conformity could be attributed to postwar consumer spending, the spread of standard brands and suburbs, and the continued growth of giant bureaucratic corporations. Well before this,

4

however, Margaret Mead in the early 1930s and David Riesman in the 1930s and early 1940s had given careful thought to the social psychology of "standardized" consumption. In doing so, they were responding to trends well established by the 1920s—the development of a consumer culture and bureaucratic marketing organizations. When 'conformity' became a buzzword in the 1950s, it was a delayed response to these trends, which the depression and war had eclipsed but not stopped.

The postwar boom in American-character writing came to a head in the early 1960s, when a number of essays took stock of the literature—especially Riesman's work—and offered revisions. **Seymour Martin Lipset**'s essay in this volume is a good example. Since that time, political comments on American-character literature of the 1950s have often described it as a product of the Cold War. I believe this to be overstated, and the matter warrants a little discussion.

The 'Cold War' thesis runs like this: Because communism was seen as an ideological challenge as well as a dire military threat, liberal intellectuals felt they had to affirm an American consensus of values and play down group differences. At a time when radicals who wrote of class conflict and oppression in the United States were ridiculed and harassed, the notion of a common American character was politically safe and attractive because it implicitly denied that 'American values' might be just a quasi-official line put out by business and government elites and imposed on groups with different inclinations. (Even those theorists of American character who attributed changes in social attitude to changes in the economy believed that American character and culture had changed profoundly on a wide front; people were not simply manipulated into their styles and beliefs, or semblances of belief, by bosses and advertisers.)

When one looks at individual writers, however, it is difficult to attribute much of their thinking to Cold War biases. David Riesman, for example, was an anti-Communist liberal, but he was also antimilitarist and an early campaigner against the A-bomb; in the early 1950s he believed that "Stalinism" was an international danger, but he also warned against the social repressions of a "garrison state." William Whyte's famous book, *The Organization Man* (1956), came in part from earlier writing with slightly Cold War overtones: he was concerned that

American business was not selling itself effectively at home and abroad. *The Organization Man* itself, though, did not mention communism or the Cold War, and it actually attacked personnel managers for denying that conflicts of real substance might exist between employees and management. **David Potter**, author of *People of Plenty* (1954), belittled and oversimplified socialism, and favored the export of U.S. know-how overseas, but he also rejected American assumptions of moral superiority in the world, and he disliked the U.S. advertising industry for debasing taste and demeaning women.

If it is true that American-character writing of the 1940s and 1950s, like other writing of the time, was particularly apt to play down class differences and class power, this was due less to Cold War defensiveness than to the spread of abundance, which really did seem to be making American society more equal as well as uniform. But then Americans had long tended to exaggerate their classlessness, and social-character theorists have always been drawn (not just in the 1940s and 1950s) to middle-class psychic problems rather than issues of economic deprivation and class power.

All this said, anticommunism and the Cold War probably did have a secondary influence on American-character writing. One thing it provided was money. The belief that U.S. civilization was 'on trial' fed the notion that the United States needed to inventory its values and spiritual resources as well as its economic ones—hence the Eisenhower and Rockfeller commissions on "national goals" in the late 1950s. At Yale University a decade earlier, the Committee on National Policy, which funded (with Carnegie Corporation money) books on the oil industry and military procurement, also supported David Riesman's research on how Americans formed opinions and why they showed political "apathy"—work that later became *The Lonely Crowd*, Riesman's celebrated book on American character (many committee members, however, found it too unscientific).

In Chicago in 1950, David Potter's lectures that became *People of Plenty* were part of a series funded by drugstore magnate Charles Walgreen, a keen anticommunist: the Walgreen Foundation for the Study of American Institutions was created to teach a better appreciation of the American way of life. Strictly speaking, however, the Walgreen endowment was not a Cold War product. It was made during a Red-hunting campaign by Hearst newspapers in the 1930s.*

───────

On a more popular middle-class level, the Cold War probably supplied readers and publicity for American-character writing by reinforcing (not creating) concerns about conformity, consumer softness, and loss of individualism. Were Americans losing the special spirit and vigor they needed for leading the 'free world'? John F. Kennedy campaigned in 1960 on this very theme, but even as he spoke, some writers on American character were moving away from the obsession with conformity. As political liberalism and the civil rights movement gathered force, essays by **George Pierson** and David Potter portrayed overlaps and shifts between conservatism and dissent, conformity and self-expressiveness, communities and loners.

Later in the 1960s, the youthful 'counterculture' produced a more radical view of a 'technocratic' America that dehumanized its subjects. Shriveled by competitive and grasping relationships, albeit veneered by 'plastic' smiles, Americans were out of touch with themselves and each other. Two works on the national character published at the end of the decade reflected this view: **Charles Reich**'s *Greening of America,* with its hippie vision of past, present, and future Americans, and **Philip Slater**'s 'New Left' book, *The Pursuit of Loneliness.* Writing in the wake

*In 1935, Walgreen's niece, a University of Chicago student, spun yarns to him about professors who promoted communism and "free love." Her family withdrew her from the university (though she went on attending a class until she got a note from the dean of students asking her to leave or pay up!). Walgreen made charges against the university which the right-wing press was delighted to publicize. In a subsequent Illinois state senate investigation, the university was exonerated and Walgreen was embarrassed. Robert Hutchins, the university's charismatic president, upheld academic freedom (more or less) while making friends with Walgreen and persuading him to create a foundation at the university for public lectures and other academic benefits. (Walgreen's daughter enrolled at the university.) Walgreen Senior died two years later, but his son and successor, "Chuck" Walgreen, kept an eye on the lectures. Lectures scheduled for 1950 by the renowned economist Joseph Schumpeter on "How Capitalism Created and Destroyed a Civilization" caused some anxiety among university officials, but Schumpeter died before he could give his series (Potter may have been a fill-in). The Walgreen lectures included some criticism of U.S. policy and performance, such as George Kennan's lectures of 1951, which became the book *American Diplomacy.*

of assassinations, riots, and escalations of the Vietnam War, Slater was one of several commentators who suggested that American character itself had deeply violent strains.

In general, though, the late 1960s and early 1970s saw a lull in writing on American character. That enterprise had always been something of a classy deviance, largely practiced by 'name' scholars and writers but never considered sound enough to be established as an academic subject: rarely could one take a degree in it. Now, however, the whole notion of an American consensus of attitudes went out of intellectual fashion as scholars followed the spotlight given by reformers and militants to minorities, underdogs, and social conflict. By the early 1970s, if 'American character' was mentioned at all, it was likely to be ridiculed as an elite construct, a value system that well-placed white males propagated via the media to other groups—how successfully, the critics did not agree. When books on social character did reappear, its authors sometimes claimed that they were writing not about social character but about "the way we clothe ourselves in certain social roles and emotional robes" (Michael Kammen) or a "psychoculture" of "shared meanings" and "inner processes" (**Daniel Yankelovich**). Such language merely reminds us that social character can be studied on a number of psychological levels, reaching into the unconscious.

The "Me Decade," Tom Wolfe's famous phrase for the 1970s, caught some of the tenor of American-character theories that began surfacing as the decade wore on. Well before then, the 1960s counterculture had subsided into a wider-based but less political movement for self-expression and self-awareness. As the economy fell into 'stagflation,' it was generally accepted that you couldn't solve social problems by 'throwing money at them.' Although Watergate had produced a reform-minded reaction against 'wheeling and dealing' in politics, this did not reach very far into everyday life. On campus, 1960s idealism was out and a new generation of students appeared to be taking over, ruthlessly grade-hunting to get a good job afterward. As the divorce rate continued to rise and more adults lived as 'singles,' obligations of family seemed to be in headlong decline.

Against this background, many commentators saw a new "egocentrism" at large in the culture, though they did not agree on its precise nature or on its history: how recent it was and what caused it. **Christopher Lasch**, Daniel Yankelovich, and **Robert Bellah** exemplify such writers publishing between the late 1970s and mid-1980s. These and other authors differed about the extent to which Americans still showed 'caring' qualities and attachment to community.

In the late Reagan and early Bush years of big fortunes and widespread debt, a flurry of books about the American middle class struck variations on the old theme of individualism. Herbert Gans paid qualified respects to middle-class self-reliance. Others found an anxious greed and what Barbara Ehrenreich called "the fear of falling." Sharp as these writers sometimes were, they were playing with stale notions. A few authors in the 1980s developed a fresher line, focusing on specific attitudes that previous works on American character had only touched on. Joseph Epstein's book on the changing attitudes to ambition, my own book on "the tough-guy tradition," David Bertelson on sexuality and American character, **Carol Stearns** and **Peter Stearns** on anger—all represent this new development.

My own view is that much more needs to be done on the relationship between *subcultures* and national character—on the way in which a specific group departs from some mainstream values and styles while subscribing to other mainstream values in its own fashion. **Peter Lupsha** essentially does this in his study of organized criminals. His approach is not new. It goes back through studies of Southerners, black Americans, and youth gangs to some almost-forgotten writing by anthropologists on class and region in the late 1940s and 1950s. It is time it was revived.

Despite the changes and differences in what they saw, postwar writers on American character shared common concerns. These revolved around the effects of mass organization, mass media, and a consumer culture. Again and again scholars declared that the 'Protestant ethic' of achievement through hard work and saving was dead or dying—as if nobody had said this before. Nearly all the writers were concerned, one way or another, with the nature and health of American individualism. Although writers from the 1970s were more worried about the atomizing effects of individualism, the earlier writers who stressed conformity sometimes conceded that social bonds between Americans were not deep. Riesman's book of 1950 was called *The Lonely Crowd*, and William Whyte's *Organization Man* (1956) was about suburban "transients" who held back from deep attachments to their neighbors since they knew they would be moving on.

Behind the concern with individualism and community lay a basic interest in social ethics. I said that just one of the authors in this book was a professional philosopher (Ralph Barton Perry), but two others have backgrounds in philosophy and comparative religion (Daniel Yankelovich and Robert Bellah), and David Riesman is really as much a social philosopher as a sociologist. The question 'How should we live?' is an underlying theme in much of the writing of the others too.

––––––

Writers on American character in the past five decades have also shared a common intellectual parentage, though their paths to the subject were very much their own. It is often impossible to prove the source of a thinker's ideas: respectful references by writer B to writer A do not necessarily mean that B's train of thought came from A. Nevertheless, four historic figures largely framed the concepts that have been used, modified, and debated in the modern literature.

The first was J. Hector St. John Crèvecoeur (1735–1813), the versatile French émigré (soldier, farmer, consul, writer) who on the eve of American independence asked his famous question, "What, then, is the American, this new man?"—and answered it more subtly than is often realized; he recognized different regional characters as well as a national one. Crèvecoeur established what is now called the 'exceptionalist' view of American culture and character, the belief that Americans were essentially different from other peoples, though he also recognized the carryover of customs from different old-world nationalities.

The most referred-to figure is Crèvecoeur's fellow countryman, Alexis de Tocqueville (1805–59). Since his time, different writers on American character have dwelt on different aspects of his complex masterpiece, *Democracy in America* (published in two volumes, 1835 and 1840). Tocqueville exaggerated the extent of equality in 1830s America, and he attributed too much to it (though in one brief chapter he feared that industrialization would produce a degraded underclass). He observed, nonetheless, many features of American character that sound strikingly modern: mobile, restless, ardent for "material gratification," yet also religious; without strong ties of class or extended family; isolated by self-reliance, yet frequently getting together in projects and civic affairs; appreciative of "the affection of their neighbors" and subservient to public opinion, yet quick to seize on petty privileges to distinguish themselves from the mass. These and other paradoxes of Tocqueville's Americans can be reconstructed from what modern writers have said. The main difference, according to several of them, is that Tocqueville's Americans struck a better balance between individualism and society.

The third intellectual 'parent,' the historian Frederick Jackson Turner (1861–1932), was, curiously, the only one who was a native-born American. In his famous paper, "The Significance of the Frontier in American History" (1893), Turner claimed that the frontier "called out" the American "traits" of dynamism, restlessness, inventiveness, "a masterful grasp of material things," and "a dominant individualism, working for good and for evil." "Let us see to it," he said in 1903, "that the ideals of the pioneer in his log cabin shall enlarge into the spiritual life of a democracy where civic power shall dominate and utilize individual achievement for the common good." Turner was writing at a time when powerful new business barons were ranged against 'Progressive' reformers, but his sense that American individualism could be selfish or public-spirited, could destroy or could build, is no less relevant today when Americans must mesh their traditions with new concerns for the environment.

Finally, Erich Fromm (1900–1980), the German-born psychoanalyst and social psychologist. He is probably the least recognized of our four classic framers of thinking on American character, in part because he wrote about 'modern man' rather than Americans per se. Nonetheless he had an enormous influence, especially on David Riesman, who in turn is the most cited of the postwar writers in the field.

Fromm said that the way in which parents brought up their children was deeply affected by the social and economic system in which they lived. Largely because of this, modern capitalism, like other economic systems, produced distinctive types of personality. Fromm's basic position here resembled that of 'culture and personality' anthropologists (see p. 255), but he paid more attention than they usually did to economic change and social class—the experience, for example, of being raised by anxious middle-class parents in an economic depression.

Fromm usually discussed social class in the context of Europe; but what he did for subsequent writers on America was to put together an element of Marx (the notion that stages of economic development shaped attitudes) with an element of Freud (the notion that early child-rearing molded character). Since Marx and Freud, of course, said much more than this, one did not have to be very Marxist or very Freudian to be influenced by Fromm. Fromm did use and adapt Freud's sexual categories of personality (Freud's "anal" type, for example, became Fromm's "hoarding" type), but Fromm made them less inherently sexual—that is, less centered on sexual feelings about oneself and one's parents.

Fromm did not contend, in fact, that society only affected character through child-rearing. In his view the "aloneness" that so often went with the freedoms of individualism in a capitalist society had deeply psychological effects. Fromm depicted these and other aspects of personality in a way that writers on American character could use and modify. His picture of the "automaton" conformist, fleeing aloneness by being automatically like others, and the "marketing" personality, selling herself like a "handbag," were obvious legacies to the American-character field. So, too, was Fromm's struggle to distinguish an *authentic self,* with basic needs for growth and freedom, from the social *roles and masks* that people so often assumed. While usually recognizing that character must be socially conditioned, theorists of American character have often mounted a *quest for authenticity,* trying to identify the real and healthy needs of the self as opposed to social pressures that frustrate those needs and make people false to themselves and to others. (See pp. 239–40 for more on this problem.)

———

Common concerns, common 'parents'—and common flaws. This literature has a number of defects that were, in a sense, avoidable; they are not inherent to the enterprise.

One defect is the tendency to overgeneralize from middle-class groups, especially from the young and trendy. Geography helps to explain this, for during the time of the studies reprinted here, most of the authors were based in five intellectual centers: Manhattan, especially at Columbia; Yale; Harvard and the Boston area; Chicago; and the San Francisco Bay area, especially Stanford and Berkeley. Even when our writers explicitly said they were talking about middle-class groups, they were apt to assume that the values and styles of young cosmopolites would spread through the population. Only David Riesman described outright working-class resistance to middle-class attitudes, and he generally believed that a new upper-middle-class character would spread downward and predominate. In a somewhat similar vein, these writers have been accused of overgeneralizing from *male* character too. They have paid more attention to women's experience than is usually recognized, but only David Potter's essay on "American Women and the American Character" (1962) stressed the differences between men and women.

Another defect of this writing is the tendency to over-'psychologize' institutions and public policies. For instance, because the new *face* of America looked so uniform after World War II, with standard-brand consumption and look-alike suburban houses, it was tempting to infer from this that the *spirit* of America had become conformist. Again, in the 1980s, it was tempting to infer that the antiwelfare, pro-big-business policies of 'Reaganomics' had bred a general meanness and loss of community. I am not saying that the alleged shift in American character from 'togetherness' in the 1950s to egocentrism in the 1970s and 1980s was imaginary: research by Joseph Veroff and others indicates that Americans of all classes became somewhat less communal between the late 1950s and late 1970s. I do believe, however, that the shift was exaggerated by commentators who wished to find a *zeitgeist* in every economic policy or political development.

Such exaggerations can easily occur in a literature that by and large does not rely on survey data, either from interviews or from questionnaires. Of our seventeen authors, only about a third made *some* use of this kind of data; and almost no one cited surveys comparing attitudes in different countries. Interesting comparative surveys have been done, especially in the 1950s and 1960s; but only Seymour Martin Lipset has made a big effort to include them in a theory that *explains* (does not just describe) how American character has come to be the way it is.

In 1977 the British writer Daniel Snowman did publish a systematic comparison of British and American character—*Britain and America.* He argued that the social character and culture of the two peoples were converging from separate traditions, though at some points they had always overlapped. One trouble with such a comparison is that it does not show whether an 'American' tendency or tradition is really *American* or just non-British or non-European. Again, only Lipset has supported his ideas about American values by comparing a range of modern democracies, including Canada and Australia.

These defects do not invalidate the literature on American character; they merely tell us how to view the literature, as a source of ideas and hypotheses rather than hard fact. (Even Lipset, credited here for his methical approach, makes some tenuous inferences.) Taken as a whole, modern writing on American character should be regarded as something between social science and social fiction. It proves nothing conclusively; it illuminates much.

The enterprise deserves our respect for asking big questions that cut across the different disciplines of history, sociology, and psychology. In an age when so much learning has been parceled into arcane specialties, and when American studies has divided itself up between sub-groups and minorities, the *chutzpah* of generalizing about social character is a corrective and a challenge.

MARGARET MEAD

An Anthropologist Looks at America

In the summer following Pearl Harbor, Margaret Mead wrote a book about American character: *And Keep Your Powder Dry: An Anthropologist Looks at America*. It took her just three weeks to write it, and it was published the same year (1942). A 'natural' writer, she wrote poetry as well as tracts; she majored in English and psychology as an undergraduate at Barnard College, and her student clique, the "Ash Can Cats," were avid literateurs. Her poetic interest gave her a sharp eye for a culture's symbolic details. She believed that in a sense everything in a society reflected everything else.

As a leading anthropologist of the 'culture and personality' school, Mead was particularly interested in the way a society raised and molded its young. Her first book, *Coming of Age in Samoa*, which made her famous at twenty-seven, was about adolescent girls; but her interest had started before her own teens, when her live-in grandmother got her to take notes on the development of her younger sisters. *And Keep Your Powder Dry* appropriately has a chapter on "Brothers and Sisters" in America.

In Mead's opinion, the immigrant background of Americans and their frequent moving about were largely responsible for the anxious way in which they raised their children. In the 1920s and 1930s other scholars had produced some important studies of American immigration and population movements; directly or indirectly these may have influenced Mead.

Long before this, however, as a graduate student at Columbia in the early 1920s, Mead had written an M.A. thesis in psychology on the assimilation of Italian-Americans. Partly based on data collected by her mother Emily Fogg Mead for a U.S. government study, the M.A. thesis proved that Italian-American children tended to score low on IQ tests not because they were inherently stupid but because of the lack of English spoken in the home when the parents had come only recently to the United States. Mead's thesis was implicitly antiracist at a time when racist calls for curbs on immigration were mounting. It was also in line with the antiracist theories of Franz Boas, the great Columbia anthropologist who was one of Mead's mentors. Two decades later, during World War II, Mead's spirit of tolerance, channeled into anti-fascism, gave added zest to her work as a civilian warrior. And that work included writing about Americans.

Well before Pearl Harbor, Mead collected and coordinated studies that might bear on problems of war morale and psychological warfare. At the time of writing *And Keep Your Powder Dry*, she was directing research into American food habits and attitudes, to inform the government on such policies as rationing and giving food away as foreign aid. The book was written in part to help Americans understand their strengths and weaknesses in fighting the war and to scotch what Mead saw as misunderstandings of America among European social scientists (including her close friend and protégé, the British anthropologist Geoffrey Gorer). By late 1944, copies of the Penguin edition of her book, retitled *The American Character*, were being issued to British liaison officers attached to American units.

But Mead's book had another purpose, explained in its second half (not excerpted here). A year after its publication, Wendell Willkie, former Republican nominee for president, published *One World*, calling for a new postwar internationalism based on freedom, cooperation, and mutual understanding. Mead was very much of this persuasion; she was what would later be called a 'UN type'—and then some. She wanted Americans to use their aptitudes and control their biases in helping to "build the world new" on a democratic basis. To this end, she believed, Americans were in a position to analyze and orchestrate the world's different national traditions. This picture of Americans as a host of action-anthropologists, a Peace Corps of Margaret Meads, departs somewhat from her main portrait of American character (excerpted below), which suggests a culturally timid conventionalism. The saving grace, in Mead's view, was a Protestant tradition of child-rearing, originally European but intensified in America, which stressed personal responsibility, endeavor, and faith in constant progress. It produced a mixture of moral purpose and practical invention in line with the old American saying, supposedly from Oliver Cromwell: "Trust God and keep your powder dry."

☆ • ☆ • ☆ • ☆ • ☆

What is it that makes it possible to say of a group of people glimpsed from a hotel step in Soerabaja or strolling down the streets of Marseilles, "There go some Americans," whether they have come from Arkansas or Maine or Pennsylvania, whether they bear German or Swedish or Italian surnames?* Not clothes alone, but the way they wear them, the way they walk along the street without awareness that anyone of higher status may be walking there also, the way their eyes rove as if by right over the façade of palaces and the rose windows of cathedrals, interested and unimpressed, referring what they see back to the Empire State building, the Chrysler tower, or a good-sized mountain in Montana. Not the towns they come from—Sioux City, Poughkeepsie, San Diego, Scotsdale—but the tone of voice in which they say, "Why, I came from right near there. My home town was Evansville. Know anybody in Evansville?" And the apparently meaningless way in which the inhabitant of Uniontown warms to the inhabitant of Evansville as they name over a few names of people whom neither of them know well, about whom neither of them have thought for years, and about whom neither of them care in the least. And yet, the onlooker, taking note of the increased warmth in their voices, of the narrowing of the distance which had separated them when they first spoke, knows that something has happened, that a tie has been established between two people who were lonely before, a tie which every American hopes he may be able to establish as he hopefully asks every stranger: "What's your home town?"[1]

Americans establish these ties by finding common points on the road that all are expected to have traveled, after their forebears came from Europe one or two or three generations ago, or from one place to another in America, resting for long enough to establish for each generation a "home town" in which they grew up and which they leave to move on to

*"We Are All Third Generation" and "Parents, Children and Achievements," from *And Keep Your Powder Dry* by Margaret Mead. Text copyright © 1942, 1965 by Margaret Mead. Reprinted by permission of William Morrow and Company, Inc.

a new town which will become the home town of their children. Whether they meet on the deck of an Atlantic steamer, in a hotel in Singapore, in New York or in San Francisco, the same expectation underlies their first contact—that both of them have moved on and are moving on and that potential intimacy lies in paths that have crossed. Europeans, even Old Americans whose pride lies not in the circumstance that their ancestors have moved often but rather in the fact that they have not moved for some time, find themselves eternally puzzled by this "home town business." Many Europeans fail to find out that in nine cases out of ten the "home town" is not where one lives but where one did live; they mistake the sentimental tone in which an American invokes Evansville and Centerville and Unionville for a desire to live there again; they miss entirely the symbolic significance of the question and answer which say diagrammatically, "Are you the same kind of person I am? Good, how about a Coke?" . . .

———

In our behavior, however many generations we may actually boast of in this country, however real our lack of ties in the old world may be, we are all third generation, our European ancestry tucked away and half forgotten, the recent steps in our wanderings over America immortalized and over-emphasized.[2] When a rising man is given an administrative job and a chance to choose men for other jobs, he does not, if he is an American, fill those jobs with members of his family—such conduct is left to those who have never left their foreign neighborhoods, or to the first generation. He does not fill them exclusively with members of his own class; his own class is an accidental cross-section which wouldn't contain enough skills. He can't depend upon his golfing mates or this year's neighbors to provide him with the men he needs. Instead, he fills the jobs with men from somewhere along the road he has traveled, his home town, his home state, his college, his former company. They give him the same kind of assurance that a first-generation Hollywood producer felt when he put his cousins in charge of the accounts—their past and his past are one—at one spot anyway—just as in a kin-oriented society common blood assures men of each other's allegiance. The secretary, trying to shield her boss from the importunities of the office seeker, knows it's no use trying to turn away a man from that little North Dakota college that the boss went to. The door is always open to them, any one of them, any day. And a newspaper headline screams: "Rock of Chickamauga blood still flows in soldiers' veins."[3]

European social scientists look at this picture of American intimacy and fail to understand it. In the first place, they cannot get inside it. An Englishman, who has never been in America before, arriving in Indianapolis and trying to establish relationships with an American who has never been in England, finds himself up against what seems to be a blank wall. He meets hearty greetings, eager hospitality, an excessive attempt to tie the visitor to the local scene by taking him rapidly over its civic wonders, an equally excessive attempt to tie in Uncle Josiah's trip to India with the fact that the guest was reared in the Punjab—and then blankness. But if the Englishman then takes a tour in the Northwest, spends a week in the town where his Indiana host lived as a boy and then returns to Indianapolis, he will find a very different greeting awaiting him, which he may mistakenly put down to the fact that this is a second meeting. Only if he is a very astute observer will he notice how the path he has taken across the United States has the power to thaw out any number of hosts at any number of dinner parties.

The wife of the European scientist, now living as a faculty wife in a small university town in Colorado, will find herself similarly puzzled. She doesn't seem to get anywhere with the other faculty wives. Their husbands and her husband have the same status, the same salary, perhaps the same degree of world-wide reputation. She has learned their standards of conspicuous consumption; she can make exactly the same kind of appetizers, set a bridge table out with prizes just as they do—and yet, there is no intimacy. Only when both have children can she and some faculty wife really get together. She thinks it is the common interest in the children which forms the tie; actually it is the common experience of the children, who have something in common which the two women will never have in the same way—the same home town, which provides the necessary link, so fragile, and from a European point of view so meaningless and contentless, and yet, for an American, so essential. Later, even if they have lived childlessly beside each other, should they meet again in Alaska or Mississippi they would be friends—with no real accession of common interests that the European wife could see. For she does not realize that to Americans only the past can give intimacy, nor can she conceive how such an incredibly empty contact in the past can be enough.

A group of people travel together from Australia to San Francisco: a manufacturer from Kansas City; a nurse from Sydney; a missionary from India; a young English stockbroker temporarily resident in New York; and a jobber from Perth. They form a fair enough table group on the boat, dance together, go ashore together, and separate on the dock without a shadow of regret. Then, to the amazement of the Englishman, he begins to get letters from the Kansas City manufacturer, reporting on the whereabouts and doings of every one of the ill-assorted group. The man actually keeps up with them—these people who shared three uneventful weeks on an ocean liner.

But it is impossible for all Americans who must work or play together to have a bit of identical past, to have lived, even in such rapidly shifting lives, within a few miles of the spot where the others have lived, at some different period for some different reason. Thin and empty as is the "home town" tie, substitutes for it must be found; other still more tenuous symbols must be invoked. And here we find the enthusiastic preferences for the same movie actor, the same brand of peaches, the same way of mixing a drink. Superficially it makes no sense at all that preference for one brand of cigarette over another may call forth the same kind of enthusiasm that one might expect if two people discovered that they had both found poetry through Keats or both nearly committed suicide on account of the same girl. Only by placing these light preferences against a background of idiosyncratic experience—by realizing that every American's life is different from every other American's; that nowhere, except in parts of the Deep South and similar pockets, can one find people whose lives and backgrounds are both identical or even similar— only then do these feverish grabs at a common theme make sense. English or Dutch residents in the colonies will spend hours sighing over the names of the shops or drinks of their respective Bond Streets, creating in their nostalgia a past atmosphere which they miss in the harsh tropical landscape about them. Americans, in a sense colonials in every part of America, but colonials who have come to have no other home, also create a common atmosphere within which to bask in the present as they criticize or approve the same radio program or moving picture actor.

There is also that other American method of forming ties, the association—the lodge, fraternity, club which is such a prominent feature of American life. Lloyd Warner has described our societies of veterans of past wars as comparable to a cult of the dead which binds a community together, with the veterans of the most distant war lowest in the social scale.[4] Seen from the point of view which I have been discussing, each war creates a magnificent common past for large numbers of men. It is not surprising that those who have the fewest ties among themselves—those whose poverty-stricken way of life admits of few associations—cling longest to this common experience.

Social scientists have observed with mild wonder that among American Indians, ranging the Great Plains before the coming of the white man, there was the same efflorescence of associations, that Blackfoot and Omaha Indians were also joiners.[5] But Blackfoot and Omaha, like the inhabitants of Kansas City and Fort Worth, were also newcomers. They came from a wooded land where the rituals of their lives were localized and particularized to the great undifferentiated open spaces where men had not lived before. Like the Palefaces who came later, they needed new ties and based them upon new patterns of group relationship; and those new patterns served at least as a bulwark against loneliness, in a land so great that the myths are full of stories of groups of playing children who wandered away and were never found until they were grown. So the white man, having left his brothers—in Sicily and Bohemia, in New York and Boston and Chicago—rapidly creates new patterns of social kinship, trying to compensate by rigidness of the ritual for the extemporized quality of the organization, so that men who have no common past may share symbolic adoption into the same fraternal society.

Social scientists, taking their cues from Eastern colleges or from Sinclair Lewis, have been inclined to sneer at the American habit of "joining," at the endless meetings, the clasp of fellowship, the songs, the allegedly pseudo-enthusiasm with which "brothers" greet each other. Safe on the eminence of available intellectual ties and able to gossip together about the famous names and the scandals of their professions, they have failed to appreciate that these associational ties give not the pseudo-security which some European philosopher feels he would get out of them if he had to share in them, but very real security. Not until he has been marooned—his train missed, no taxi available—and driven sixty miles across bad roads in the middle of the night by someone who belongs to another chapter of the same national organization does he begin to realize that the tie of common membership, flat and without content as it is, bolstered up by sentimental songs which no one really likes to sing but which everyone would miss if they weren't sung, has an intensity of its own; an intensity measured against the loneliness which each member would feel if there were no such society.

———

If this then, this third-generation American, always moving on, always, in his hopes, moving up, leaving behind him all that was his past and greeting with enthusiasm any echo of that past when he meets it in the life of another, represents one typical theme of the American character structure, how is this theme reflected in the form of the family, in the upbringing of the American child? For to the family we must turn for an understanding of the American character structure. . . .

By and large, the American father has an attitude towards his children which may be loosely classified as autumnal. They are his for a brief and passing season, and in a very short while they will be operating gadgets which he does not understand and cockily talking a language to which he has no clue. He does his best to keep ahead of his son, takes a superior tone as long as he can, and knows that in nine cases out of ten he will lose. If the boy goes into his father's profession, of course, it will take him a time to catch up. He finds out that the old man knows a trick or two; that experience counts as over against this new-fangled nonsense. But the American boy solves that one very neatly: he typically does not go into his father's profession, nor take up land next to his father where his father can come over and criticize his plowing. He goes somewhere else, either in space or in occupation. And his father, who did the same thing and expects that his son will, is at heart terrifically disappointed if the son accedes to his ritual request that he docilely follow in his father's footsteps and secretly suspects the imitative son of being a milksop. He knows he is a milksop—or so he thinks—because he himself would have been a milksop if he had wanted to do just what his father did.

This is an attitude which reaches its most complete expression in the third-generation American. His grandfather left home, rebelled against a parent who did not expect final rebellion, left a land where everyone expected him to stay. Come to this country, his rebellious adventuring cooled off by success, he begins to relent a little, to think perhaps the strength of his ardor to leave home was overdone. When his sons grow up, he is torn between his desire to have them succeed in this new country— which means that they must be more American than he, must lose entirely their foreign names and every trace of allegiance to a foreign way of life—and his own guilt towards the parents and the fatherland which he has denied. So he puts on the heat, alternately punishing the child whose low marks in school suggest that he is not going to be a successful American and berating him for his American ways and his disrespect for his father and his father's friends from the old country. When that son leaves home, he throws himself with an intensity which his children will not know into the American way of life; he eats American, talks American, dresses American, he will be American or nothing. In making his way of life consistent, he inevitably makes it thin; the overtones of the family meal on which strange, delicious, rejected European dishes were set, and about which low words in a foreign tongue wove the atmosphere of home, must all be dropped out. His speech has a certain emptiness; he rejects the roots of words—roots lead back, and he is going forward—and comes to handle language in terms of surfaces and clichés. He rejects half of his life in order to make the other half self-consistent and complete. And by and large he succeeds. Almost miraculously, the sons of the Polish day laborer and the Italian fruit grower, the Finnish miner and the Russian garment worker become Americans.

Second generation—American-born of foreign-born parents—they set part of the tone of the American eagerness for their children to go onward. They have left their parents; left them in a way which requires more moral compensation than was necessary even for the parent genera-tion who left Europe. The immigrant left his land, his parents, his fruit trees, and the little village street behind him. He cut the ties of military service; he flouted the king or the emperor; he built himself a new life in a new country. The father whom he left behind was strong, a part of something terribly strong, something to be feared and respected and fled from. Something so strong that the bravest man might boast of a success-ful flight. He left his parents, entrenched representatives of an order which he rejected. But not so his son. He leaves his father not a part of a strong other-way of life, but bewildered on the shores of the new world,

23

having climbed only halfway up the beach. His father's ties to the old world, his mannerisms, his broken accent, his little foreign gestures are not part and parcel of something strong and different; they are signs of his failure to embrace this new way of life. Does his mother wear a kerchief over her head? He cannot see the generations of women who have worn such kerchiefs. He sees only the American women who wear hats, and he pities and rejects his mother who has failed to become—an American. And so there enters into the attitude of the second-generation American—an attitude which again is woven through our folkways, our attitude towards other languages, towards anything foreign, towards anything European—a combination of contempt and avoidance, a fear of yielding, and a sense that to yield would be weakness. His father left a father who was the representative of a way of life which had endured for a thousand years. When he leaves his father, he leaves a partial failure; a hybrid, one who represents a step towards freedom, not freedom itself. His first-generation father chose between freedom and what he saw as slavery; but when the second-generation American looks at his European father, and through him, at Europe, he sees a choice between success and failure, between potency and ignominy. He passionately rejects the halting English, the half-measures of the immigrant. He rejects with what seems to him equally good reasons "European ties and entanglements." This second-generation attitude which has found enormous expression in our culture especially during the last fifty years, has sometimes come to dominate it—in those parts of the country which we speak of as "isolationist." Intolerant of foreign language, foreign ways, vigorously determined on being themselves, they are, in attitude if not in fact, second-generation Americans.

When the third-generation boy grows up, he comes up against a father who found the task of leaving his father a comparatively simple one. The second-generation parent lacks the intensity of the first, and his son in turn fails to reflect the struggles, the first against feared strength and the second against guiltily rejected failure, which have provided the plot for his father and grandfather's maturation. He is expected to succeed; he is expected to go further than his father went; and all this is taken for granted. He is furthermore expected to feel very little respect for the past. Somewhere in his grandfather's day there was an epic struggle for liberty and freedom. His picture of that epic grandfather is a little obscured, however, by the patent fact that his father does not really respect him; he may have been a noble character, but he had a foreign accent. The grandchild is told in school, in the press, over the radio, about the founding fathers, but they were not after all *his* founding fathers; they are, in ninety-nine cases out of a hundred, somebody else's ancestors. Any time one's own father, who in his own youth had pushed his father aside and made his own way, tries to get in one's way, one can invoke the founding fathers—those ancestors of the real Americans; the Americans who got here earlier—those Americans which father worked so very hard, so slavishly, in fact, to imitate. This is a point which the European observer misses. He hears an endless invocation of Washington and Lincoln, of Jefferson and Franklin. Obviously, Americans go in for ances-tor worship, says the European. Obviously, Americans are longing for a strong father, say the psycho-analysts.[6] These observers miss the point that Washington is not the ancestor of the man who is doing the talking; Washington does not represent the past to which one belongs by birth, but the past to which one tries to belong by effort. Washington represents the thing for which grandfather left Europe at the risk of his life, and for which father rejected grandfather at the risk of his integrity. Washington is not that to which Americans passionately cling but that to which they want to belong, and fear, in the bottom of their hearts, that they cannot and do not.

This odd blending of the future and the past, in which another man's great-grandfather becomes the symbol of one's grandson's future, is an essential part of American culture. "Americans are so conservative," say Europeans. They lack the revolutionary spirit. Why don't they rebel? Why did President Roosevelt's suggestion of altering the structure of the Supreme Court and the Third-Term argument raise such a storm of protest? Because, in education, in attitudes, most Americans are third generation, they have just really arrived. Their attitude towards this country is that of one who has just established membership, just been elected to an exclusive club, just been initiated into the rites of an exacting religion. Almost any one of them who inspects his own ancestry, even though it goes back many more generations than three, will find a gaping hole somewhere in the family tree. Campfire girls give an honor to the girl who can name all eight great-grandparents, including the maiden names of the four great-grandmothers. Most Americans cannot get this honor. And who was that missing great-grandmother? Probably, oh, most probably, not a grand-niece of Martha Washington. . . .

———

In old societies when the extended family or the clan is still an important part of the way of life, the child moves easily among many relatives, many of whom bear his name, with some one of whom he can almost certainly find a community of interest and even a common physique. But in America, with the family whittled down to father and mother, a child may often feel he is like neither of them. The fact that two parents are all the anchors he has in a world which is otherwise vague and shifting, over-emphasizes the tie and brings it into question. And so the phantasy of adoption develops, the fear which grips so many children's hearts that they are adopted, that they don't really belong anywhere at all. The day comes when both father and mother seem strange, forbidding figures, enforcing some meaningless moral code in a meaningless world. At first it gives a fine feeling of rebellion to say: "I don't care what you say. I am not your child anyway. My father and mother were a king and a queen and you are nothing but gypsies who carried me off," or: "I won't listen to a word you say. I am not your child. I don't look like you. I don't think like you. I don't feel like you. And I won't come out from under the bed," but afterwards, when the anger has worn off, the child is left with a terrible fear that maybe the words spoken in stubborn rejection are true. The children who are adopted, the children who have feared they were adopted, all serve to exaggerate for each American child his dependence on his father and mother, of whom there is only one edition in the whole world. From broken homes come our delinquents and our neurotics; from unbroken homes come the ordinary Americans, terribly impressed with the fragility and importance of those homes which made them into regular fellows, not children about whom other children whispered and whom teachers and neighbors commiserated.

From this curious structure of the American family, from the fact that two young people, often of quite diverse backgrounds, are sent out into the world together to make a way of life, with no oldsters by to help them, with no guides except the movies, the pulp magazines and the fumbling experiences of those very little older than themselves, it follows also that each child's experience will be different from each other's. However much his mother may study the daily specials, may deck his baby carriage in the type of tailored cover in style this year, and dress him in the most approved sun suit or slacks, beneath the outward conformity there lies always the mother's sense of difference. How does her marriage compare with that of the other women who stroll beside her with their impeccably dressed babies? She doesn't know, she doesn't dare to ask, even if she had words in which to ask such a question. The questions themselves might betray her, might betray some peculiarity in her own make-up or some inadequacy in her husband. The endless query: "Am I happy?" can in part be translated into the question: "How close am I to what I should expect to be?" Back of her lies her single experience with family life—her view of her own parents. She lives in the only other experience she may ever have. She cannot know how her worried version of life compares with the average, with the normal, with those who are "really" happy. And her voice is sharp as she admonishes her child if he deviates from the public behavior which is common for all of the children of the block, if he fights when they don't or fails to fight when they do. The basis of her life, her membership in her new family, like her membership in her old one, is secret, and probably deviates in a thousand ways from that which others would respect and envy—if they knew. To compensate for this, she insists on conformity. Their house, their car, their clothes, their patterns of leisure time, shall be as much like other people's as possible. Her face cream, her powder, her lipstick, shall be publicly validated. But inside the walls of that home, there is no one to tell her, or to tell her husband, whether their expectations are too high or too low, no one to quote from the experience of other generations, no yardstick, no barometer.

Some of this desperate uncertainty is conveyed to the baby, as she dresses him to take him out, as she undresses him when she brings him in. Just as virtually no American family is completely certain of its social antecedents, or can produce a full complement of unblotted escutcheons, so also no American family is sure of its position on an unknown chart called "happiness." The mother anxiously searches her baby's face. Are his "looks" something which should make her happy, is his health something which shows she is a good mother, does he walk and talk early enough to be a credit to her, to prove to others and so prove to herself

27

that she has a right to be what she wants to be—happy? From the day when self-conscious fathers stand outside the glass-walled hospital nursery and anxiously compare the shape of their own babies' heads with those of the other babies, the child is valued in comparative terms, not because he is of the blood and bone and "name" of his parents, but because of his place on some objective (but undefined) rating scale of looks and potential abilities. In his parents' every gesture, the child learns that although they want to love him very much, although they hope they will love him very much—for loving your children is one of the things that books say parents do—they are not quite sure that he will deserve it, that when they check him up against the baby book and the neighbors' baby he will come out A-1 and so worthy of complete blind love. . . .

So while the child is learning that his whole place in the world, his name, his right to the respect of other children—everything—depends upon his parents and on what kind of a house they have been able to build or buy or rent, what kind of a car they are able to drive, what kind of toys they are able to buy him, he also learns that his own acceptance by these parents, who are his only support, is conditional upon his achievements, upon the way in which he shows up against other children and against their idea of other children. To the anxiety with which small boys in many if not all cultures of the world view grown men and wonder if they will ever be as tall and strong, is added in America, for both boys and girls, the anxiety as to whether they will be successful in keeping their parents' love as children. American girls of college age can be thrown into a near panic by the description of cultures in which parents do not love their children. Against the gnawing fear that their personal achievement has made them unworthy of love, they have placed a vague persistent belief in "mother love," a belief that somehow or other their parents won't be able to get out of loving them some—because they are parents, and theirs. Any evidence that destroys their faith in this "maternal instinct" is profoundly disturbing. They know they are not worthy; if the modicum that was to be theirs forever, even without worthiness, is taken away— what is there left of which they can be sure? Their own children? No, because what if they are imbeciles? The brightest people, college professors especially, have imbecile children. "If your skirt turns up in back, your mother loves you better than your father. If your skirt turns up in front, your father loves you better than your mother." "She loves me, she loves me not," is a game that Americans do not wait to play until they are in love. . . .

. . . [T]he further the child goes from standards that his parents know, the greater is his need for success. He is leaving them, he is giving up every concrete thing which they did, he will neither eat like them, nor dress like them, nor have the same standards as to what is appropriate to say to a girl or how he should plan his life insurance or where he should take his vacation. In big things and in small, in all the habits of life through which they taught him what the world was like, he will leave them, he will in a sense betray them. All he can offer in return is success. As a high school principal said recently to the parents of the graduating class: "They lay their success, their achievement, before you, a thank-offering for all that you have done for them."

When we see this situation dramatized in the immigrant father, himself with no book learning and hardly an English word, pathetically delighted because his son has won some academic honor, we are touched with the pity of it, of the father who cannot, himself, realize the inward-ness of what his son has done. We can sympathize with the young research chemist who is offered a job as the president of a small college—"Presi-dent! Now that is something my father and mother would understand. They don't get this sort of thing I am doing at all. But a title, a limousine, to live in a big house called the President's house. They'd know I'd made good then." And he hesitates and goes back not quite happy to the research work which his fine mind is so perfectly fitted to do, not able to be gay in the rejection of the conspicuous role which would have made sense to his less schooled parents. These seem to us extreme cases, part of the drama of immigration, of the rapid rise from generations of peon-age to a place in a free world. But they are only extreme cases of what happens to almost every American parent, no matter how successful his son.

NOTES

1. I owe my understanding of the significance of these chronological ties to discussions with Kurt Lewin and John G. Pilley.

2. Margaret Mead, "Conflict of Cultures in America," in *Proceedings of the 54th Annual Convention of the Middle State Association of Colleges and Secondary Schools* (Philadelphia, 1940), pp. 30–44.

3. [A Civil War reference to Union general George Thomas, whose defensive fighting in the Chattanooga campaign ("we will hold the town till we starve") won him his nickname, "the Rock of Chickamauga."]

4. W. Lloyd Warner and Paul S. Lunt, *The Social Life of a Modern Community*, Yankee City Series, vol. 1 (New Haven, Conn., 1941).

5. Robert H. Lowie, "Plains Indian Age-Societies: Historical and Comparative Summary," in *Anthropological Papers of the American Museum of Natural History*, vol. ii, part 13 (New York, 1916), pp. 877–984.

6. I owe my classification of the American attitude toward the "founding fathers" to a conversation with Dr. Ernst Kris, in which he was commenting on the way in which Americans, apparently, want a strong father, although in actual fact they always push their fathers aside.

☆ • ☆ • ☆ • ☆ • ☆

Mead's account is a graphic and pioneering analysis of the way in which American society transmits achievement values to the next generation. Her writing is still relevant fifty years later, at a time when there has been much talk of 'fast-track' parents anxiously programming their tots for success. The pace at which she wrote the book adds to its verve, but it also may have magnified its flaws. It is difficult to tell how much of the book's problems come from hasty writing, and how much from a conflict between her crusading hopes for the United States (inflamed by wartime morale-boosting) and underlying doubts about American character.

As Mead herself later claimed, she was the first anthropologist to describe a complex modern culture in the same way that she had generalized about small, "primitive" societies. This was part of her bold determination to see a culture whole, be it the New Guinea Manus or the United States. In describing Americans, however, she confused her comparisons, many of which were with Europe, especially the England described by her British husband, anthropologist Gregory Bateson. Sometimes, though, the comparisons shift to the preindustrial world such as New Guinea. This shows what is modern and western about the United States but not what is distinctively American. Mead also may have exaggerated the difference between modern Americans and traditional non-Westerners by deliberately *not* studying a New Guinea village, where the people lived quite far apart and did not seem to have—in her words—a "rich ceremonial life."

Mead's first book, on Samoa, was impaired by underestimating class differences in attitudes and behavior. The same is true of her handling of classes, regions, and ethnic groups in the United States. As I said in the general introduction, many writers on American character do not properly deal with group and sectional differences. Here and there in her writings Mead showed she was well aware by 1942 that different American regions and social groups had different styles; but when it came to generalizing about American character, she overrode these differences without any qualification. Despite her dislike of cultural snobbery, she tended to see in the average American the educated Episcopalian WASP that she herself was.

Except that she more often saw a boy. By the 1940s Mead had thought a lot about the different characters that a society often prescribes for males and females, but she was particularly taken with what she saw as the curiosity and skepticism of twelve-year-old American boys. Perhaps, too, the war atmosphere encouraged her to write more about masculinity. *And Keep Your Powder Dry* has a whole chapter on boys and aggression.

War conditions, with their stress on teamwork, may also also have made Mead more favorable to "the American habit of 'joining' " fraternities and lodges—no mention here of color bars, or the subtler but cruel exclusiveness she found among sororities at her first college, DePauw. If the war, however, made her too kind to American styles, she could also be too harsh. Her theory of "conditional love," insisting that American parents withheld their *love*—not just their *approval*—from children who did not match up, was extreme and unsubstantiated. (Children may not always perceive the difference between conditional love and conditional approval, but Mead did not get into that.)

In her discussion of children and forebears, Mead's claim that "we are all third generation" is not completely clear. Most Americans, she means to say, are like the grandchild of the immigrant; they are expected to go beyond rather than reject their parents, but they are supposed to do so in conventional ways that their parents can measure: "a title, a limousine . . . a big house." Yet elsewhere in the book Mead briefly mentions a "fourth generation" type, especially prevalent in California, whose drive is more open-ended: "to master an unknown future." Mead seems to hope that most Americans will become this, but one wonders how they will do so, especially since Mead says that Americans have become too passively dependent on technical gadgets.

Mead was also unclear and contradictory on the new world order that she hoped American character would help build. On the one hand, she wanted in a very American way to foster *individual* freedom and development; on the other, she sought tolerance for different *cultures*, though some would surely restrict the individual more than others. Her ideals, in short, were in conflict.

RALPH BARTON PERRY

The American
Cast of Mind

L ecturing at the University of Indiana in 1938, the Harvard
philosopher Ralph Barton Perry gave a vivid comparison of two famous philosophers, no longer alive, whom he had known at his university. William James and Josiah Royce—colleagues, neighbors, and
close friends—were almost perfectly opposite in their backgrounds and
temperaments. Born into a distinguished, well-to-do Boston family,
William James moved with ease and pleasure in the company of others.
Raised by a poor, frontier family in California, Josiah Royce was a
loner; he talked well but he was awkward. In their philosophies,
though, "each man idealized his opposite" in many complex ways.
James stressed, among other things, that society needed loners, eccen-
trics, creative individualists; Royce, that individuals needed community, solidarity, and a sense of common human values.

Ten years later, lecturing at the University of Michigan, Perry
addressed both outlooks in his analysis of American character. That
character, he said, was an amalgam of opposites. Its essence was a
"collective individualism," a mixture of competitive, individual dynamism and sociable conformity. In his lecture series at Michigan, Perry
went on to explore the American nature of various institutions and
spheres of life, from politics and sports to education, religion, and
philosophy. The lectures became a book, *Characteristically American*
(1949), and its first chapter, "The American Cast of Mind," is excerpted
here.

A prolific author (his books occupy three large pages of the Library of Congress printed catalog), Perry was an authority on William
James and wrote some technical philosophy; but he was also a layman's philosopher, writing readable books on philosophical problems
of society. During World War II, like Margaret Mead, he was a "One

World" internationalist: he dedicated his book, *One World in the Making* (1945), to Wendell Willkie (see p. 16). As one might expect of a philosopher, Perry's discussion of peaceful internationalism and America's role in it dealt with theoretical issues and problems more rigorously than Mead's. Perry was keenly interested in American history and also wrote *Puritanism and Democracy* (1944), a long, wartime discussion of America's many-sided puritan past and its relevance to modern American values.

In "The American Cast of Mind," Perry placed himself among those writers who related American character to the growth of government and economic planning in the New Deal and the war. Margaret Mead had feared that big national organizations, both business and government, might smother individual and local initiative. Perry, by contrast, respected the creative power of large-scale organization and believed it to be compatible with traditional American individualism. Long before the New Deal, he said, Americans had shown a capacity to conform as team players. The conformity did not worry him too much. Here and there he had some criticisms of American character, but his mood was mainly that of an early postwar optimist, writing just before the main clouds of the Cold War rolled in. At home and abroad, it was a time when U.S. economic prowess promised to make life better; Marshall aid to Europe was winning over political isolationism. 'We can do it' is a motto for Perry's Americans and for Perry himself.

☆ • ☆ • ☆ • ☆ • ☆

There is no more teasing and baffling task than the definition of national characteristics.* Just as we love to talk over our friends, whether in a kindly or in a malicious spirit, and put their indescribable peculiarities into words, so we turn again and again to such complex and unanswerable questions as, "What is the distinctive genius of the Englishman?" "What is particularly French about Frenchmen?" "What are those German traits which have brought disaster to Europe?" "What is that dark Russian soul on which the future of mankind so largely depends?" These are delightful subjects for discussion because almost anybody can have an opinion without impertinence. There are no experts who have the answers.

What of ourselves? What is it to be American—in thought and deed and feeling? The fascination of such questions lies not only in the uncertainty of the answer, but in its paradoxes. Each nation appears to be a compound not only of many characteristics, but of opposite characteristics. Start with any formula and you will shortly be reminded not only that it is incomplete, but that it is contradicted by what it omits. The Englishman "muddles," but he "muddles *through*"; that is, he gets results. The Frenchman is logical, but he is obsessed with *"l'amour."* The German appears to be a mysterious blend of romanticism and technology, of kindliness and cruelty. The Russian is both autocratic and socialistic. And, similarly, America is, in the same curious fashion, both harshly competitive and humanely idealistic. What is needed, then, is some idea or set of ideas that will not only cover the complex manifestations of American life, but resolve its paradoxes.

A mere enumeration of characteristics does not suffice. Thus Henry Pratt Fairchild, pleading for restricted immigration, in order to preserve that "spiritual reality," that "complex of cultural and moral values" which constitutes Americanism, has listed certain traits on which there would be general agreement: "such things as business honesty, respect for womanhood, inventiveness, political independence, physical cleanliness, good sportsmanship, and others less creditable, such as worship of success, material-mindedness, boastfulness."[1] But how do these and other characteristics *go together?* What is the underlying idea which expresses itself in this aggregate of items and in their paradoxical balance of opposites?

It might be supposed that the continental vastness of America, and its unparalleled variety of climate, natural resources, race and creed, would make such an inquiry both impossible and unprofitable. But the fact is that identity is more easily traced when it dwells amidst variety. It is because there is something common to life in New England and California, Montana and Florida, in the arid deserts of Arizona and the lush Mississippi and Ohio lowlands, in great cities and small towns, that it is possible to find a meaning for Americanism. It is because this thing which is common within our boundaries stops so abruptly at the Mexican border, and so unmistakably though less abruptly at the Canadian border, and begins when one disembarks either at New York or at San Francisco, that it can be detected and set apart from the rest of human life, however similar this life outside may be, taken item by item. It is because Americans are English, Scotch, Irish, German, French, Spanish, Jewish, Italian, East-European, Asiatic and African that their common Americanism is something else again, something discernible and recognizable, however indescribable. The melting pot has not merely melted: it has cooked a broth with an unmistakable flavor of its own.

In conveying this pervasive and identical character of the American mind it is impossible to make any statement to which exception may not be taken. There is no indivisible Platonic essence of which America is the unique embodiment. There is no American characteristic which is not exemplified elsewhere, or which some Americans do not lack. All that one can possibly claim is that there is among the people of this half-continent taken as a whole, a characteristic blend of characteristics. The cast of the American mind is not a simple quality—but a physiognomy, a syndrome, a form of complexity, a contour, a total effect of the distribution and comparative densities of elements. Nor should one be expected to say on this subject anything that has not been known before. Any claim of original discovery should be distrusted. For America has not hidden its face; its character is not mysterious, but palpable—there are those who would say, flagrant.

Of what elements does a national character, mind, or soul, consist? Not of ideas in the strict sense of the term. The acceptance of attested facts, or of some portion of the body of scientific truth, does not go to the heart of the matter. No doubt most Americans believe that $2 + 2 = 4$, and that the Pacific Ocean is larger than the Atlantic, and that matter is composed of atoms. But Americanism consists not of what Americans believe to be true, but rather of what they believe *in*—their attitudes, their sentiments, their hopes and resolves, their scruples and maxims, or what are sometimes called their "valuations." It is here that Gunnar Myrdal, for example, looks for "the cultural unity" of America—"the floor space upon which the democratic process goes on." He finds such a common ground and sanction in "the fact that *most Americans have most valuations in common* though they are arranged differently in the sphere of valuations of different individuals and groups and bear different intensity coefficients."[2]

How America came to be American is a story that has been often told, and a story that can properly be told only by the historian. The present study is an interpretation of America, and not a history. Nevertheless, it is well that it should include a brief summary of the major influences which have formed the American mind and given it its peculiar cast or bias.

In the first place, America developed from a group of colonies. It began as the child of Europe, and while it has achieved maturity and independence it has never lost its parentage and ancestry. Its culture was transplanted after having flowered on other soil. Its thought, therefore, is rarely indigenous, and has always retained something of provincialism even in the manner and tone of its self-sufficiency. It diverged from the main stream of European culture in comparatively modern times, and in the realm of fundamental ideas it still imports more than it exports, thus reversing the balance of trade in the realm of commerce.

Therefore great importance attaches, in the second place, to the ideas which the colonists brought with them, or which were imported during the early formative period of the nation's history. These consisted of mediaeval European thought; of the literature and science of the Renaissance, and especially of Elizabethan England; and of the "new philosophy" of the Seventeenth and early Eighteenth Centuries, comprising Newton, Locke, Hutcheson, Berkeley, Adam Smith, Descartes, Malebranche, and the broad currents of thought, and especially of political thought, known as the Enlightenment.

In the third place, the colonial mind of America was moulded by Protestant Christianity and in the main by Puritan and Evangelical Protestantism. Except for Maryland, the Catholicism of colonial days was peripheral; and the Catholicism of the later migrations not only came after the main characteristics of the American mind were already crystallized, but did not as a rule reach the upper economic, political and cultural levels of American society.

Fourthly, since the colonies which combined to form the United

States were British colonies the institutions of the new nation were fundamentally British. The American Revolution was not a social revolution, or even a political revolution, but a war of liberation, in which the new entity retained the structural characteristics of the parent organism. The very principles invoked to justify the overthrow of British authority were themselves British—Magna Carta and the "higher law," the Common Law, representative parliamentary government, the rights of the individual, the pursuit of happiness. While these original social and institutional forms, together with their associated habits and sentiments, were modified in the course of time, they were never repudiated, but became the heroic memory and sacred legend, the ceremonial symbols, the norm of self-criticism, the core of conservatism, the dream of the future.

Fifthly, the original settlers of America, and many later immigrants, were products of the advancing capitalistic economy. They were yeomen, tradesmen, artisans, professional men, or small landowners, already emancipated from a feudal past—"rising men," jealous of authority, and seeking an opportunity under more favorable conditions to prove the capacity which they felt within themselves. Such men were neither hopeless nor self-satisfied, but ambitious to improve their condition and build for themselves a new society corresponding to their ideas and hopes.

Finally, the philosophical, religious, cultural, and social ideas brought or imported from Europe were modified by the experience of settlement. A sparsely inhabited area of wide expanse, rich in natural resources, presenting formidable but not insuperable obstacles, both stimulated and rewarded effort, and generated a sense of man's power to master nature. The temperate but variable climate, the freedom from economic pressure and congestion, the rugged and primitive life of the frontier, and the mixture of ethnic types produced men of physical robustness and energy who felt a contempt for the effeminacy and softening luxury imputed to older civilization.

Through the operation of these and other influences the American mind came to possess a specific character which, despite an immense variety of local, ethnic, and economic differences, pervades the whole from coast to coast and from border to border, is recognizable to visitors from abroad, and is sufficiently strong to stamp its imprint on successive generations and waves of immigration.

If one were limited to a single word with which to characterize America, one would choose the word "individualism"—used, however, with reservations. If individualism is taken to mean the cult of solitude, or the prizing of those personal traits which set one man apart from his fellows, or are the effect of retreat from the world, then no word could be less appropriate. American individuality is the very opposite of singularity. The people of the United States are highly gregarious and sociable. The individual who holds himself apart, who will not "join," who does not "belong," who will not "get together" and "play the game," who does not "row his weight in the boat," is viewed with suspicion. Americans find silence hard to endure, and if they develop an oddity, they make a fad of it so that they may dwell among similar oddities. Their individualism is a *collective* individualism—not the isolation of one human being, but the intercourse and cooperation of many.

At the same time, there is a tonic quality of American life that imbues men with a feeling of buoyancy and resourcefulness. They believe that they can improve their condition, and make their fortunes; and that if they fail they have only themselves to blame. There is a promise of reward, not too remote, which excites ambition and stimulates effort. It is this prospect of abounding opportunity which constitutes that appeal of America abroad which attracted immigrants in colonial days, and still in 1949 causes multitudes in all parts of the world to look wistfully toward our half-closed doors. However harshly America is criticized, foreigners, including the critics themselves, come to America of their own free will. Seen from afar America is a land of promise; and that vision is never wholly obliterated by closer acquaintance, but remains in the form of gratitude and love of country. It is to be assumed that those who come find confirmation of this hopefulness in the reports received from those who have preceded them, and from their own experiences.

It follows that the people of the United States judge, and expect to be judged, by the standard of success, meaning something made of opportunity. There is the opportunity, in the sense of favorable conditions—the "opening," as it is sometimes called—and there is the seizing of the opportunity, the taking advantage of the opening. Success is thought of as the fruit of a marriage between circumstance and action.

American success must be recognized success—not by the God of Things as They Are, but by one's neighbors. Success must be not only measurable, but observed, recorded, applauded, and envied. Hence the close relation of success and publicity, attested by Mark Twain's famous description of the rival boy who went as an apprentice engineer on a Mississippi steamboat:

> That boy had been notoriously worldly, and I just the reverse; yet he was exalted to this eminence, and I left in obscurity and misery. . . . He would always manage to have a rusty bolt to scrub while his boat tarried at our town, and he would sit . . . and scrub it, where we could all see him and envy him and loathe him. . . . When his boat blew up at last, it diffused a tranquil contentment among us such as we had not known for months. But when he came home the next week, alive, renowned, and appeared in church all battered up and bandaged, a shining hero, stared at and wondered over by everybody, it seemed to us that the partiality of Providence for an undeserving reptile had reached a point where it was open to criticism.[3]

This was a local and juvenile social experience, but modern facilities of communication—moving pictures, illustrated magazines, radio, national newspapers, and political conventions—have only enlarged the scale. Applause must follow hard upon achievement; and the volume of applause tends to become the measure of achievement.

The American belief in success is not based on blind faith, or on trust, or on a mere elasticity of spirit, but on experience. Nature makes things big in America—mountains, rivers, deserts, plants and animals. It is no secret, least of all from the American people, that the little enterprise launched on the banks of the Delaware in 1776 turned out to be a big success. As these people look back over their history, or out upon the life of their times, they see (easily, with the naked eye) American success achieved and in the making; and their confidence seems to them to be justified. They feel themselves to be on the march; toward precisely what is not always clear, but anyway toward something bigger and better.

In America the moving of mountains is not a symbol of the impossible, but a familiar experience. Major Hutton, the assistant engineer of the Grand Coulee Dam, is reported to have said: "If a hard mountain gets in the way, move it. If it's just a soft mountain, freeze the darn thing, forget it, and keep on going."[4] *Keep on going!*

American pride of achievement is local as well as national. Each state and city and region is out to make records—in population, in volume of business, or in the height of its skyscrapers. If the press report is to be trusted, patriots of the State of Washington now propose to alter the geologic map in order to outstrip their rivals. To quote a certain Dr. C. A. Mittun of that State:

> Man will re-do Mother Nature's work and give Mount Rainier back its prominence in the world of mountains. . . . These two almost unknown sand dunes in Colorado, and that reverse gopher hole in California . . . are in for a bad time. . . . We're going to realize the dream of every Washington mountaineer who scraped the snow from the record-cairn at the top to pile something, anything—snow, rocks, ice—on the crater's rim so our mountain can regain the dignity it deserves.[5]

Here is movement, confidence, verified confidence, visible success, success on a large scale, efficiency, and, let it be confessed, a touch of boastfulness. For there is a belief in America, founded half on fiction and half on fact, that Americans owe their major blessings to themselves, rather than to history or inherited institutions—as though they had started from scratch with their bare hands.

It is largely because of a widespread belief in success that competition, while keen and intense, is, as a rule, not deadly or vindictive. No fight is taken to be the last fight. Defeat may not be accepted gracefully, but it is accepted cheerfully, because he who is defeated expects to fight again, with another opponent or on another field of battle. Sometime, somehow, somewhere, he expects to win.

Whether Americans are successful in their pursuit of happiness is another question; the contrary is often asserted. Nor is it clear that they pursue happiness methodically, or have, save for certain sects, such as Christian Science, developed any positive art of happiness. It would perhaps be more correct to say that they believe in the possibility of removing the causes of *un*happiness—pain, poverty, frustration, sickness, old age, and even death. They do not regard unhappiness as the necessary lot of man, to be accepted as a fatality and sublimated in tragic nobility. Even sin is regarded as curable; if not by divine grace, then by psychoanalysis.

American resourcefulness consists to no small extent in the fertility of its intellectual soil. America has become a universal seed bed and nursery for ideas from all the past and from all the world. The American public has become a sort of public at large—the great world-market for ideas. Its immense and voracious literacy creates the greatest aggregate demand for reading matter, for the visual arts, for music, for thoughts and fancies, for anything communicable, in human history. Now while this does convey, and rightly conveys, a suggestion of shallowness and lack of discrimination, it also gives the Americans the sense that they have everything. If they do not make it they can buy it. This does not offend their pride for they feel that they buy it with that which they *have* made.

American self-reliance is a plural, collective, self-reliance—not *"I can,"* but *"we can."* But it is still individualistic—a togetherness of several and not the isolation of one, or the absorption of all into a higher unity. The appropriate term is not "organism" but "organization"; *ad hoc* organization, extemporized to meet emergencies, and multiple organization in which the same individuals join many and surrender themselves to none. Americans do not take naturally to mechanized discipline. They remain an aggregate of spontaneities. Such organization develops and uses temporary leaders—"natural" leaders, and leaders for the business in hand, rather than established authorities.

This confidence in achievement through voluntary association and combined effort breeds among Americans a sense of invincible power, a tendency to centrifugal expansion, and a readiness to assume the role of a people chosen to head the march of human progress.

The idea of racial superiority did not begin with the political agitators of the South in the Reconstruction Era, nor has it been limited to the context of Negro slavery. It has been applied with equal arrogance to American Indians, to Mexicans, and to the "Mongolians" of the Orient. It was Thomas Hart Benton, voicing the spirit of the advancing westward frontier, and addressing the United States Senate in 1846, who said:

> For my part, I cannot murmur at what seems to be the effect of divine
> law. I cannot repine that this Capitol has replaced the wigwam—this

Christian people, replaced the savages—white matrons, the red squaws—and that such men as Washington, Franklin, and Jefferson, have taken the place of Powhattan, Opechonecanough, and other red men, howsoever respectable they may have been as savages. Civilization, or extinction, has been the fate of all people who have found themselves in the track of the advancing Whites, and civilization, always the preference of the Whites, has been pressed as an object, while extinction has followed as a consequence of its resistance. The Black and the Red races have often felt their ameliorating influence.[6]

The sense of collective power, demonstrated in the rapidity and extent of westward expansion, has led Americans to confuse bigger and better, and to identify value with velocity, area, altitude, and number. Jefferson was concerned to refute the thesis of Buffon that animal and plant life is smaller on the Western continent than in Europe; and he has been proved right. Even human stature has increased in America. The same cult of magnitude has led to that strain of half-believing, half-joking exaggeration which is a feature of American legend and folk-lore. Stories, like everything else, must be "big stories." The hyperbole of the imagination reflects the sense of vital exuberance. When all things are deemed possible, the line between the actual and the preposterous is hard to draw.

This same collective self-reliance, this urge to do something together, gives to the American mind a peculiar aptitude for industrialization and for the development of the technological arts. The American does not readily become a tool, but he is a born user of tools—especially of tools which are a symbol of organized rather than of single-handed action. The American's love of achievement, his impulse to make and to build, to make faster, to build bigger, to rebuild, to exceed others in making and building, leads to the multiplication and quick obsolescence of gadgets, and the deflection of thought from the wisdom of ends to the efficiency of means.

Publicity in America is valued above privacy. This is only one of the phenomena which attest the fact that American individualism is collected and not singular. Regimentation did not begin with the New Deal, and government regulation is one of the least of its causes. Americans are made alike by imitation, and by the overpowering pressures of mass opinion and sentiment. Agencies of publicity create and inculcate clichés; national advertising and mass production create uniformity of manners, clothing, and all the articles of daily life. Competition itself tends to uniformity among competitors, since they are matched against one another in like activities, calling for like talents. In order that a competitor may be exceeded he must be exceeded "at the same game."

This tendency to uniformity has been accentuated by modern developments of mass communication, but it is an old and persistent American trait. It was in 1837 that James Fenimore Cooper recorded the following impression of the difference between the English and the Americans:

> The English are to be distinguished from the Americans by greater independence of personal habits. Not only the institutions, but the physical condition of our own country has a tendency to reduce us all to the same level of usages. The steamboats, the overgrown taverns, the speculative character of the enterprises, and the consequent disposition to do all things in common aid the tendency of the system in bringing about such a result. In England a man dines by himself in a room filled with other hermits, he eats at his leisure, drinks his wine in silence, reads the paper by the hour; and, in all things, encourages his individuality and insists on his particular humours. The American is compelled to submit to a common rule; he eats when others eat, sleeps when others sleep, and he is lucky, indeed, if he can read a paper in a tavern without having a stranger looking over each shoulder.

At the same time Cooper reported the observation that "the American ever seems ready to resign his own opinion to that which is *made to seem* to be the opinion of the public."[7] In other words, the sanction of public opinion is invoked as an authority so coercive upon the individual that its name carries weight even in the absence of the fact.

———

The characteristic American blend of buoyancy, collective self-confidence, measuring of attainment by competitive success, hope of perpetual and limitless improvement, improvising of method and organization to meet exigencies as they arise, can be illustrated from various aspects of American life, some fundamental and some superficial: though which is fundamental and which superficial it would be difficult to say. This same blend of traits will at the same time serve to account for certain

American ways which seem to non-Americans paradoxical, if not objectionable.

Thus Americans are at one and the same time law-abiding and lawless. They live within a frame of law, and seem often to make a fetish of their written constitution. The law is the usual road to public office, and the lawyers are perhaps the most influential members of the community, with the businessmen running them a close second. The business lawyer is the higher synthesis of the two. At the same time Americans have a certain contempt for the law, as something which they have made, and which they sometimes take into their own hands. As in the case of the Prohibition Law, one of the accepted methods of changing the law is to break it. Americans employ lawyers to enable them to evade the law, or at any rate to mitigate its inconveniences.

Americans are highly litigious. Opposing lawyers engage in lively combat; prosecuting attorneys score their convictions and acquire thereby a prestige that may start them on the road to the Presidency; criminal lawyers score their acquittals. Appeal follows appeal from court to court; but while a negative verdict is not lightly accepted, it usually *is* accepted after every legal resort has been exhausted. Americans are more insistent in claiming legal rights than scrupulous in respecting them: in other words, they tend to assume that each will look after his own—which he usually does.

American politics are harshly competitive but rarely bloody or fatal. Candidates do not, as in England, "stand" for office—they "run" for office. Major campaigns are conducted as though the survival of the country were at stake; but nobody really means it. On the morrow the defeated candidate "concedes" his defeat and congratulates the victor whom the day before he has slain with invectives. As in sport, the punch is followed by the handshake. A government based on division of powers has become a struggle between powers—between the legislative and executive branches, or between the upper and lower houses of Congress. Even party solidarities tend to dissolve amidst the rivalries of persons, lobbies and pressure groups. And yet there is a saving grace, which somehow triumphs over dissension—a saving grace which is in part an incurable sense of humor, in part a common underlying faith, but in the main the belief that there is enough for everybody, and that what is lost today can be regained tomorrow. Disputes among optimists rarely become irreconcilable conflicts.

The world would be glad to discover the key to the foreign policy of the United States, which it views with mingled hope and distrust. There is no key; but the American mentality here described may throw some dim light on a question which is of no little importance for the future of mankind.

The traditional isolationism, which is still to be reckoned with, was originally based on fear of becoming embroiled in the affairs of a Europe whose yoke had been cast off; and this cautious isolationism was confirmed by the fact that later waves of immigration were composed of persons who, having for one reason or another turned their backs on Europe, desired to keep them turned. But these motives of distrust have gradually been superseded by a sense of self-sufficiency. While the surpluses of production have led to a growing recognition of the need of world markets, the average American businessman is still interested primarily in the domestic market; and while the experience of the present century has brought home the menace of world-war, the fact remains that American territory has not been invaded or seriously threatened with invasion for 130 years, so that those who reside in the interior of a wide continent bounded by two wide oceans still feel secure at home. The airplane and the atomic bomb have modified this attitude; but whereas Europeans know from *experience* that for better or worse they are dependent on the rest of the world, Americans still have to be *persuaded* that this is the case, and they do not always stay persuaded.

Opposed to this sense of continental self-sufficiency and disposition to isolationism there is a missionary spirit which inclines to adventure abroad: a belief, more or less justified, that what is good for the United States is good for everybody, and should be extended to other peoples, whether they like it or not and whether or not they are ready to receive it. Americans are disposed to "sell" their goods abroad, whether automobiles, typewriters, moving pictures, democracy, or various brands of Christianity. There is a readiness to embark on far-flung enterprises without a full recognition of their costs; or to talk about them without being prepared to follow through. Bold utterances are discounted at home, but when taken at their face value abroad they have often led to disappointment and resentment, by friends as well as enemies. It is not that Americans do not mean what they say, but that they do not always weigh their words and the implications of their words. Americans speak freely and lightly. Add to this the fact that our foreign policy reflects all the uncertainties arising from differences between Congress and the Executive, and from changing party majorities, and it is small wonder that other nations have learned to keep their fingers crossed.

The foreign policy of the United States must always be close to the electorate, and there is never a time when a nation-wide election is more than two years away. A large section of the press is commercially motivated, and caters to emotion and prejudice in order to compete for circulation. All publicity agencies—radio, cinema, and forum—tend similarly to quantity production and to mass appeal.

That, nevertheless, public policy should on the whole and in the long run have been judged sound by the verdict of history evidently requires explanation; whether it be by a Providence that watches over drunkards and democracies, or by a basic intelligence and good sense which makes the American people as a whole receptive to the enlightenment which spreads from their thoughtful minority by a sort of osmosis. Somehow, in the end, the sober second thought tends to prevail.

Once the people of the United States feel themselves fully committed to an enterprise their virtues come into play, and their very weaknesses become sources of strength. They discover natural leaders, invent techniques, improvise organizations, and are imbued with a confident determination to win. And in so far as they are impregnated with a sense of human solidarity, they can contribute to international organization their peculiar faculty for combining effort with the cheerful acceptance of temporary defeat, and their inexhaustible confidence that what needs to be done *can* be done, even on a world-wide scale, and whatever the odds against it. . . .

NOTES

1. Henry Pratt Fairchild, *The Melting-Pot Mistake* (Boston, 1926), pp. 201–02.

2. Gunnar Myrdal, *An American Dilemma: The Negro Problem and American Democracy,* vol. 1 (New York, 1944), p. xliv. Myrdal's own idea of Americanism is not essentially different from that which is proposed here, though he uses a variety of different expressions such as "practical idealism," "bright fatalism," "rationalism" (in the sense of organized efficiency), "humanistic liberalism," "moral optimism." Ibid., Introduction.

3. Mark Twain, *Life on the Mississippi* (Boston, 1883, rev. ed., 1901), pp. 32–34.

4. John Gunther, *Inside the U.S.A.* (New York, 1947), p. 124.

5. Quoted by the *New York Times,* Aug. 13, 1948, p. 17.

6. Thomas Hart Benton, "Superiority of the White Race," in *Speech of Mr. Benton of Missouri on the Oregon Question* (Washington, D.C., 1846), p. 30.

7. James Fenimore Cooper, *Gleanings in Europe,* vol. 2 (Philadelphia, 1837), pp. 248–49.

☆ • ☆ • ☆ • ☆ • ☆

As a philosopher for laymen, Ralph Barton Perry earned his pay. More than most writers on American character, he systematically discussed the problem of generalizing across regional differences, and he tried to define exactly what he meant in claiming that Americans were different from other people. What he did not quite say (but presumably took for granted) was that any American differentness could only be a *tendency,* a matter of varying degree, since all Americans were obviously not identical.

Mead and Perry's conceptions of national character represent two major approaches to the subject. Trained as a psychologist, Mead was concerned with *processes of personality,* involving basic feelings about oneself and others. Perry, as a philosopher, concentrated on *values and beliefs.* Of course these two approaches overlap: emotional feelings and relationships affect values, and vice versa. In the case of Mead and Perry, however, one can see the difference in the way they discussed the American wish to succeed and impress. In Mead's view, achievement drive begins in a domestic hothouse; brothers and sisters compete for their parents' approval. Perry, by contrast, is not interested in the psychological process that produces the success drive; he implies that Americans simply learn from the culture a value on success in the eyes of others, be they the neighbors or a media audience.

Compared with Mead's explanation of American character, Perry's gives a wider range of causes—mainly historical but economic and geographic too. Both writers stressed immigration, but Perry made much more of the early immigration of *ideas* and also the *kind* of people who came over. Although Perry stressed the formative influence of Anglo-Protestant culture, his suggestion that American immigrants included many entrepreneurial types has renewed relevance today amid the success of Asian-Americans and Cuban immigrants. It may indeed be more relevant today than in earliest New England. As the historian Roger Thompson has shown recently, whole communities and extended families of English puritans moved together to the New World in the seventeenth century. The decision to go was as much a group one as a matter of individual initiative; and religion was at least as important as economics.

Perry's essay did not in fact show how the six historical factors he discussed connected with his analysis of social character. One can more or less infer the connection between the historical factors and the individualist and dynamic elements of American character, as he described them, but it is not at all clear what produced the cooperative and conforming sides.

Perry's suggestion that American character has influenced U.S. foreign relations is very hypothetical, but this line of thinking has been followed by such distinguished political scientists as Gabriel Almond and Stanley Hoffman. Here as elsewhere, Perry's argument would have benefited from survey data on class differences in attitude. Even so, when applied to educated elites in and around government, his belief that Americans were often ready to "embark on far-flung enterprises without a full recognition of their costs" was prophetic of the Vietnam War. Other nations, too, have shown this tendency, and American leaders have perhaps learned caution since Vietnam, but Perry sounded a warning still useful today when he suggested that the idea of being "chosen to head the march of human progress" could become an attitude of racial superiority.

DAVID RIESMAN

From Inner-Direction to Other-Direction

Sociologist David Riesman was on the cover of *Time* magazine in 1954 largely because of his best-selling book, *The Lonely Crowd: A Study of the Changing American Character* (first published in 1950). Written with the help of two other sociologists, Nathan Glazer and Reuel Denney, *The Lonely Crowd* remains to this day the most influential modern book on American character. People have used its ideas and terminology often without realizing the source and even when they might not agree with the book's main thesis.

Unlike Perry and Mead, Riesman, Glazer, and Denney focused on what was changing in the American makeup. Intricately argued and elaborated (the book was not designed to be a bestseller), *The Lonely Crowd* portrayed a shift in American middle-class character between two phases of capitalism, each containing its own "mode of conformity." The nineteenth-century, "inner-directed" person, whose goals and values were internalized from parents, fitted an expanding, industrializing society concerned with making and acquiring *things*. The twentieth-century, "other-directed" person, shaped by "peer-group" and media, fitted a society of marketing, consumption, bureaucracy, and personal services, all concerned with relating to *people*.

Riesman connected these shifts to population changes (demographic ideas fascinated him) but retreated from this quite soon after writing the book. What he did hold onto was an ideal of "autonomy," introduced in the book's final part. Deeply concerned with personal freedom, the space to "be oneself," Riesman idealized an "autonomous" character, alive and self-aware, who could choose whether to conform or not.

Riesman, who was a law professor before he became a sociologist, thought about psychological stages of history while writing articles on historical and sociological aspects of law. The concept of a moralistic, "inner-directed" *type* came to him from reading Max Weber's *Protestant Ethic and the Spirit of Capitalism.* As for the newer, "other-directed" type, Riesman was not alone in identifying its essentials. Well before *The Lonely Crowd* was published, other writers led by Erich Fromm (who had been Riesman's analyst) had come up with almost every change in character and society described by Riesman. None of them, however, put it all together as completely as Riesman did in *The Lonely Crowd.*

He also added two important aspects: First, he moved the shaping of the new character type largely out of the home. Parents, he said, were losing power to the "peer-group"—the child's friends and contemporaries—and the media. For Margaret Mead, by contrast, parents were still the key agents in the making of young Americans. When she mentioned the media, and she did so much less, it was mainly for its influence on parents or on the small child at home. Riesman made more of the fact that young people played records and talked about radio and movie stars (television had barely arrived) in a network of friends and rivals outside the family.

Riesman's second major innovation was to connect the new character type to a political power structure. In the early 1940s Riesman's writing had put some stress on class and racial inequality and the power of big business to manipulate opinion. During the war, though, Riesman moved to what political scientists call a 'pluralistic' view of power. His experience as a lawyer for Sperry Gyroscope—a fairly chaotic defense contractor plagued by troubles with the government and unions—had helped persuade him that power in the United States was now fragmented into "veto groups" which had to bargain with each other. (His reaction was original, if not quirkish, since World War II generally fueled the *concentration* of economic power in the United States by favoring the biggest contractors and tying them more closely to government—a situation that Riesman believed to be truer of government-business relations at the turn of the century.) In Riesman's view, the negotiating and trade-offs demanded by a pluralistic power system suited the new "other-directed" character type which was geared to personal relations. Leadership styles had changed from desk-pounding and sermonizing to tact and compromise. People were generally more tolerant and sensitive; managers sought approval from subordinates (as parents did from children), but now they were also more manipulative.

Researched and written in 1948–49, *The Lonely Crowd* was very much a 1940s book. During World War II, Riesman had not been among those who thought that a protracted economic slump was likely after war spending ended; despite his political pluralism, he believed that government fiscal management and high defense budgets would keep the country out of depression. By the late 1940s prosperity seemed assured. *The Lonely Crowd* asserted that American culture was moving from a "scarcity psychology" to an "abundance psychology." Yet widespread abundance had not seemed to Riesman to make people happier or brighter-visioned: he saw about him a "poverty of wishes." The trouble in part was that group pressures to conform had invaded and drained people, leaving them with a vague feeling of apathy and malaise.

The Lonely Crowd research started right there, as a study of political and social apathy. Assisted by Nathan Glazer, then an editor at *Commentary* magazine, Riesman looked at the way different types of people—different in character and social class—responded to opinion-survey interviewers. At the very beginning of this research, Riesman had already evolved the categories that later became "inner-direction" and "other-direction"; he initially called them "the Protestant ethic" and the "marketing ethic." Riesman and Glazer elaborated the types as they read through opinion surveys and interview reports (including material that later went into C. Wright Mills's *White Collar*). At the time, Riesman was a sociology professor at the University of Chicago, but the research was done from Yale and New York and supplemented by interviews across the country.

In the summer of 1949, at Riesman's Vermont farmhouse, his Chicago colleague, Reuel Denney, helped him turn their pile of memos and reports into a book. Denney, who had been encouraged by Riesman to study jazz and sports among adolescents, contributed to the book sections on popular music and fiction, movies, and the relationship between work and play (the two, it seemed to the authors, were overlapping more and more).

The following excerpt is from *The Lonely Crowd*'s first chapter. We join it where the authors have just introduced another type of character, the *"tradition-directed"* type, a concept that historically came before the inner-directed type. Found mainly in highly stable, preindustrial cultures with nil population growth, "tradition-directed" people conformed by learning a detailed set of customs and practices. In the authors' view, even the United States still had some tradition-directed holdouts, especially in rural backwaters; and most people in modern America were a mix of all three types. The authors argued that Americans were becoming predominantly other-directed.

☆ • ☆ • ☆ • ☆ • ☆

. . . Inner-Directed Types

Except for the West, we know very little about the cumulation of small changes that can eventuate in a breakup of the tradition-directed type of society, leading it to realize its potential for high population growth.* As for the West, however, much has been learned about the slow decay of feudalism and the subsequent rise of a type of society in which inner-direction is the dominant mode of insuring conformity.

Critical historians, pushing the Renaissance ever back into the Middle Ages, seem sometimes to deny that any decisive change occurred at all. On the whole, however, it seems that the greatest social and characterological shift of recent centuries did indeed come when men were driven out of the primary ties that bound them to the western medieval version of tradition-directed society. All later shifts, including the shift from inner-direction to other-direction, seem unimportant by comparison, although of course this latter shift is still under way and we cannot tell what it will look like when—if ever—it is complete.

———

A change in the relatively stable ratio of births to deaths, which characterizes the period of high growth potential, is both the cause and

*"From Inner-Direction to Other-Direction," from *The Lonely Crowd* by David Riesman, with Nathan Glazer and Revel Denney. Copyright © 1950. Reprinted by permission of Yale University Press.

consequence of other profound social changes. In most of the cases known to us a decline takes place in mortality prior to a decline in fertility; hence there is some period in which the population expands rapidly. The drop in death rate occurs as the result of many interacting factors, among them sanitation, improved communications (which permit government to operate over a wider area and also permit easier transport of food to areas of shortage from areas of surplus), the decline, forced or otherwise, of infanticide, cannibalism, and other tribal kinds of violence. Because of improved methods of agriculture the land is able to support more people, and these in turn produce still more people.

Notestein's phrase, "transitional growth," is a mild way of putting it.[1] The "transition" is likely to be violent, disrupting the stabilized paths of existence in societies in which tradition-direction has been the principal mode of insuring conformity. The imbalance of births and deaths puts pressure on the society's customary ways. A new slate of character structures is called for or finds its opportunity in coping with the rapid changes—and the need for still more changes—in the social organization.

―――――

A definition of inner-direction. In western history the society that emerged with the Renaissance and Reformation and that is only now vanishing serves to illustrate the type of society in which inner-direction is the principal mode of securing conformity. Such a society is characterized by increased personal mobility, by a rapid accumulation of capital (teamed with devastating technological shifts), and by an almost constant *expansion:* intensive expansion in the production of goods and people, and extensive expansion in exploration, colonization, and imperialism. The greater choices this society gives—and the greater initiatives it demands in order to cope with its novel problems—are handled by character types who can manage to live socially without strict and self-evident tradition-direction. These are the inner-directed types.

The concept of inner-direction is intended to cover a very wide range of types. Thus, while it is essential for the study of certain problems to differentiate between Protestant and Catholic countries and their character types, between the effects of the Reformation and the effects of the Renaissance, between the puritan ethic of the European north and west

54

and the somewhat more hedonistic ethic of the European east and south, while all these are valid and, for certain purposes, important distinctions, the concentration of this study on the development of modes of conformity permits their neglect. It allows the grouping together of these otherwise distinct developments because they have one thing in common: *the source of direction for the individual is "inner" in the sense that it is implanted early in life by the elders and directed toward generalized but nonetheless inescapably destined goals.*

We can see what this means when we realize that, in societies in which tradition-direction is the dominant mode of insuring conformity, attention is focused on securing strict conformity in generally observable words and actions, that is to say, behavior. While behavior is minutely prescribed, individuality of character need not be highly developed to meet prescriptions that are objectified in ritual and etiquette—though to be sure, a social character *capable* of such behavioral attention and obedience is requisite. By contrast, societies in which inner-direction becomes important, though they also are concerned with behavioral conformity, cannot be satisfied with behavioral conformity alone. Too many novel situations are presented, situations which a code cannot encompass in advance. Consequently the problem of personal choice, solved in the earlier period of high growth potential by channeling choice through rigid social organization, in the period of transitional growth is solved by channeling choice through a rigid though highly individualized character.

This rigidity is a complex matter. While any society dependent on inner-direction seems to present people with a wide choice of aims—such as money, possessions, power, knowledge, fame, goodness—these aims are ideologically interrelated, and the selection made by any one individual remains relatively unalterable throughout his life. Moreover, the means to those ends, though not fitted into as tight a frame of social reference as in the society dependent on tradition-direction, are nevertheless limited by the new voluntary associations—for instance, the Quakers, the Masons, the Mechanics' Associations—to which people tie themselves. Indeed, the term "tradition-direction" could be misleading if the reader were to conclude that the force of tradition has no weight for the inner-directed character. On the contrary, he is very considerably bound by traditions: they limit his ends and inhibit his choice of means. The point is rather that a splintering of tradition takes place, connected in part with the increasing division of labor and stratification of society. Even if the individual's choice of tradition is largely determined for him by his family, as it is in most cases, he cannot help becoming aware of the existence of competing traditions—hence of tradition as such. As a result he possesses a somewhat greater degree of flexibility in adapting himself to ever changing requirements and in return requires more from his environment.

As the control of the primary group is loosened—the group that both socializes the young and controls the adult in the earlier era—a new psychological mechanism appropriate to the more open society is "invented": it is what I like to describe as a psychological gyroscope.[2] This instrument, once it is set by the parents and other authorities, keeps the inner-directed person, as we shall see, "on course" even when tradition, as responded to by his character, no longer dictates his moves. The inner-directed person becomes capable of maintaining a delicate balance between the demands upon him of his goal in life and the buffetings of his external environment.

This metaphor of the gyroscope, like any other, must not be taken literally. It would be a mistake to see the inner-directed man as incapable of learning from experience or as insensitive to public opinion in matters of external conformity. He can receive and utilize certain signals from outside, provided that they can be reconciled with the limited maneuverability that his gyroscope permits him. His pilot is not quite automatic.

Huizinga's *The Waning of the Middle Ages* gives a picture of the anguish and turmoil, the conflict of values, out of which the new forms slowly emerged. Already by the late Middle Ages people were forced to live under new conditions of awareness. As their self-consciousness and their individuality developed, they had to make themselves at home in the world in novel ways. They still have to.

. . . Other-Directed Types

The problem facing the societies in the stage of transitional growth is that of reaching a point at which resources become plentiful enough or are utilized effectively enough to permit a rapid accumulation of capital. This rapid accumulation has to be achieved even while the social product is being drawn on at an accelerated rate to maintain the rising population and satisfy the consumer demands that go with the way of life that has already been adopted. For most countries, unless capital and techniques can be imported from other countries in still later phases of the population curve, every effort to increase national resources at a rapid rate must actually be at the expense of current standards of living. We have seen this occur in the U.S.S.R., now in the stage of transitional growth. For western Europe this transition was long-drawn-out and painful. For America, Canada, and Australia—at once beneficiaries of European techniques and native resources—the transition was rapid and relatively easy.

The tradition-directed person, as has been said, hardly thinks of himself as an individual. Still less does it occur to him that he might shape his own destiny in terms of personal, lifelong goals or that the destiny of his children might be separate from that of the family group. He is not sufficiently separated psychologically from himself (or, therefore, sufficiently close to himself), his family, or group to think in these terms. In the phase of transitional growth, however, people of inner-directed character do gain a feeling of control over their own lives and see their children also as individuals with careers to make. At the same time, with the shift out of agriculture and, later, with the end of child labor, children no longer become an unequivocal economic asset. And with the growth of habits of scientific thought, religious and magical views of human fertility—views that in an earlier phase of the population curve made sense for the culture if it was to reproduce itself—give way to "rational," individualistic attitudes. Indeed, just as the rapid accumulation of productive capital requires that people be imbued with the "Protestant ethic" (as Max Weber characterized one manifestation of what is here termed inner-direction), so also the decreased number of progeny requires a profound change in values—a change so deep that, in all probability, it has to be rooted in character structure.

As the birth rate begins to follow the death rate downward, societies move toward the epoch of incipient decline of population. Fewer and fewer people work on the land or in the extractive industries or even in manufacturing. Hours are short. People may have material abundance and leisure besides. They pay for these changes however—here, as always, the solution of old problems gives rise to new ones—by finding themselves in a centralized and bureaucratized society and a world shrunken and agitated by the contact—accelerated by industrialization—of races, nations, and cultures.

The hard enduringness and enterprise of the inner-directed types are somewhat less necessary under these new conditions. Increasingly, *other people* are the problem, not the material environment. And as people mix more widely and become more sensitive to each other, the surviving traditions from the stage of high growth potential—much disrupted, in any case, during the violent spurt of industrialization—become still further attenuated. Gyroscopic control is no longer sufficiently flexible, and a new psychological mechanism is called for.

Furthermore, the "scarcity psychology" of many inner-directed people, which was socially adaptive during the period of heavy capital accumulation that accompanied transitional growth of population, needs to give way to an "abundance psychology" capable of "wasteful" luxury consumption of leisure and of the surplus product. Unless people want to destroy the surplus product in war, which still does require heavy capital equipment, they must learn to enjoy and engage in those services that are expensive in terms of man power but not of capital—poetry and philosophy, for instance.[3] Indeed, in the period of incipient decline, nonproductive consumers, both the increasing number of old people and the diminishing number of as yet untrained young, form a high proportion of the population, and these need both the economic opportunity to be prodigal and the character structure that allows it.

Has this need for still another slate of character types actually been acknowledged to any degree? My observations lead me to believe that in America it has.

A definition of other-direction. The type of character I shall describe as other-directed seems to be emerging in very recent years in the upper middle class of our larger cities: more prominently in New York than in Boston, in Los Angeles than in Spokane, in Cincinnati than in Chillicothe. Yet in some respects this type is strikingly similar to the American, whom Tocqueville and other curious and astonished visitors from Europe, even before the Revolution, thought to be a new kind of man. Indeed, travelers' reports on America impress us with their unanimity. The American is said to be shallower, freer with his money, friendlier, more uncertain of himself and his values, more demanding of approval than the European. It all adds up to a pattern which, without stretching matters too far, resembles the kind of character that a number of social scientists have seen as developing in contemporary, highly industrialized, and bureaucratic America: Fromm's "marketer," Mills's "fixer," Arnold Green's "middle class male child."[4]

It is my impression that the middle-class American of today is decisively different from those Americans of Tocqueville's writings who nevertheless strike us as so contemporary. . . . It is also my impression that the conditions I believe to be responsible for other-direction are affecting increasing numbers of people in the metropolitan centers of the advanced industrial countries. My analysis of the other-directed character is thus at once an analysis of the American and of contemporary man. Much of the time I find it hard or impossible to say where one ends and the other begins. Tentatively, I am inclined to think that the other-directed type does find itself most at home in America, due to certain unique elements in American society, such as its recruitment from Europe and its lack of any feudal past. As against this, I am also inclined to put more weight on capitalism, industrialism, and urbanization—these being international tendencies—than on any character-forming peculiarities of the American scene.

Bearing these qualifications in mind, it seems appropriate to treat contemporary metropolitan America as our illustration of a society—so far, perhaps, the only illustration—in which other-direction is the dominant mode of insuring conformity. It would be premature, however, to say that it is already the dominant mode in America as a whole. But since the other-directed types are to be found among the young, in the larger cities, and among the upper income groups, we may assume that, unless present trends are reversed, the hegemony of other-direction lies not far off.

If we wanted to cast our social character types into social class molds, we could say that inner-direction is the typical character of the "old" middle class—the banker, the tradesman, the small entrepreneur, the technically oriented engineer, etc.—while other-direction is becoming the typical character of the "new" middle class—the bureaucrat, the salaried employee in business, etc. Many of the economic factors associated with the recent growth of the "new" middle class are well known. They have been discussed by James Burnham, Colin Clark, Peter Drucker, and others. There is a decline in the numbers and in the proportion of the working population engaged in production and extraction—agriculture, heavy industry, heavy transport—and an increase in the numbers and the proportion engaged in white-collar work and the service trades. People who are literate, educated, and provided with the necessities of life by an ever more efficient machine industry and agriculture, turn increasingly to the "tertiary" economic realm. The service industries prosper among the people as a whole and no longer only in court circles.

Education, leisure, services, these go together with an increased consumption of words and images from the new mass media of communications. While societies in the phase of transitional growth step up the process of distributing words from urban centers, the flow becomes a torrent in the societies of incipient population decline. This process, while modulated by profound national and class differences, connected with differences in literacy and loquacity, takes place everywhere in the industrialized lands. Increasingly, relations with the outer world and with oneself are mediated by the flow of mass communication. For the other-directed types political events are likewise experienced through a screen of words by which the events are habitually atomized and personalized— or pseudo-personalized. For the inner-directed person who remains still extant in this period the tendency is rather to systematize and moralize this flow of words.

These developments lead, for large numbers of people, to changes in paths to success and to the requirement of more "socialized" behavior both for success and for marital and personal adaptation. Connected with such changes are changes in the family and in child-rearing practices. In the smaller families of urban life, and with the spread of "permissive" child care to ever wider strata of the population, there is a relaxation of older patterns of discipline. Under these newer patterns the peer-group (the group of one's associates of the same age and class) becomes much more important to the child, while the parents make him feel guilty not so much about violation of inner standards as about failure to be popular or otherwise to manage his relations with these other children. Moreover, the pressures of the school and the peer-group are reinforced and continued . . . by the mass media: movies, radio, comics, and popular culture media generally. Under these conditions types of character emerge that we shall here term other-directed. . . . *What is common to all the other-directed people is that their contemporaries are the source of direction for the individual—either those known to him or those with whom he is indirectly acquainted, through friends and through the mass media. This source is of course "internalized" in the sense that dependence on it for guidance in life is implanted early. The goals toward which the other-directed person strives shift with that guidance: it is only the process of striving itself and the process of paying close attention to the signals from others that remain unaltered throughout life.* This mode of keeping in touch with others permits a close behavioral conformity, not through drill in behavior itself, as in the tradition-directed character, but rather through an exceptional sensitivity to the actions and wishes of others.

Of course, it matters very much who these "others" are: whether they are the individual's immediate circle or a "higher" circle or the anonymous voices of the mass media; whether the individual fears the hostility of chance acquaintances or only of those who "count." But his need for approval and direction from others—and contemporary others rather than ancestors—goes beyond the reasons that lead most people in any era to care very much what others think of them. While all people want and need to be liked by some of the people some of the time, it is only the modern other-directed types who make this their chief source of direction and chief area of sensitivity.[5]

It is perhaps the insatiable force of this psychological need for approval that differentiates people of the metropolitan, American upper middle class, whom we regard as other-directed, from very similar types that have appeared in capital cities and among other classes in previous historical periods, whether in Imperial Canton, in eighteenth- and nineteenth-century Europe, or in ancient Athens, Alexandria, or Rome. In all these groups, fashion not only rules as a substitute for morals and customs, but it was a rapidly changing fashion that held sway. It could do so because, although the mass media were in their infancy, the group corresponding to the American upper middle class was comparably small and the elite structure was extremely reverberant. It can be argued, for example, that a copy of *The Spectator* covered its potential readership more thoroughly in the late eighteenth century than *The New Yorker* covers its readership today. In eighteenth- and nineteenth-century English, French, and Russian novels, we find portraits of the sort of people who operated in the upper reaches of bureaucracy and had to be prepared for rapid changes of signals. Stepan Arkadyevitch Oblonsky in *Anna Karenina* is one of the more likable and less opportunistic examples, especially striking because of the way Tolstoy contrasts him with Levin, a moralizing, inner-directed person. At any dinner party Stepan manifests exceptional social skills; his political skills as described in the following quotation are also highly social:

> *Stepan Arkadyevitch took in and read a liberal newspaper, not an extreme one, but one advocating the views held by the majority. And in spite of the fact that science, art, and politics had no special interest for him, he firmly held those views on all subjects which were held by the majority and by his paper, and he only changed them when the majority changed them—or, more strictly speaking, he did not change them, but they imperceptively changed of themselves within him.*
>
> *Stepan Arkadyevitch had not chosen his political opinions or his views; these political opinions and views had come to him of themselves, just as he did not choose the shapes of his hats or coats, but simply took those that were being worn. And for him, living in a certain society— owing to the need, ordinarily developed at years of discretion, for some degree of mental activity—to have views was just as indispensable as to have a hat. If there was a reason for his preferring liberal to conservative views, which were held also by many of his circle, it arose not from his considering liberalism more rational, but from its being in closer accord with his manner of life. . . . And so liberalism had become a habit of Stepan Arkadyevitch's, and he liked his newspaper, as he did his cigar after dinner, for the slight fog it diffused in his brain.*

Stepan, while his good-natured gregariousness makes him seem like a modern middle-class American, is not fully other-directed. This gregariousness alone, without a certain sensitivity to others as individuals and as a source of direction, is not the identifying trait. Just so, we must differentiate the nineteenth-century American—gregarious and subservient to public opinion though he was found to be by Tocqueville, Bryce, and others—from the other-directed American as he emerges today, an American who in his character is more capable of and more interested in maintaining responsive contact with others both at work and at play.[6]

This point needs to be emphasized, since the distinction is easily misunderstood. The inner-directed person, though he often sought and sometimes achieved a relative independence of public opinion and of what the neighbors thought of him, was in most cases very much concerned with his good repute and, at least in America, with "keeping up with the Joneses." These conformities, however, were primarily external, typified in such details as clothes, curtains, and bank credit. For, indeed, the conformities were to a standard, evidence of which was provided by the "best people" in one's milieu. In contrast with this pattern, the other-directed person, though he has his eye very much on the Joneses, aims to keep up with them not so much in external details as in the quality of his inner experience. That is, his great sensitivity keeps him in touch with others on many more levels than the externals of appearance and propriety. Nor does any ideal of independence or of reliance on God alone modify his desire to look to the others—and the "good guys" as well as the best people—for guidance in what experiences to seek and in how to interpret them.

———

The three types compared. One way to see the structural differences that mark the three types is to see the differences in the emotional sanction or control in each type.

The tradition-directed person feels the impact of his culture as a unit, but it is nevertheless mediated through the specific, small number of individuals with whom he is in daily contact. These expect of him not so much that he be a certain type of person but that he behave in the approved way. Consequently the sanction for behavior tends to be the fear of being *shamed.*

The inner-directed person has early incorporated a psychic gyroscope which is set going by his parents and can receive signals later on from other authorities who resemble his parents. He goes through life less independent than he seems, obeying this internal piloting. Getting off course, whether in response to inner impulses or to the fluctuating voices of contemporaries, may lead to the feeling of *guilt.*

Since the direction to be taken in life has been learned in the privacy of the home from a small number of guides and since principles, rather than details of behavior, are internalized, the inner-directed person is capable of great stability. Especially so when it turns out that his fellows have gyroscopes too, spinning at the same speed and set in the same direction. But many inner-directed individuals can remain stable even when the reinforcement of social approval is not available—as in the upright life of the stock Englishman isolated in the tropics.

Contrasted with such a type as this, the other-directed person learns to respond to signals from a far wider circle than is constituted by his parents. The family is no longer a closely knit unit to which he belongs but merely part of a wider social environment to which he early becomes attentive. In these respects the other-directed person resembles the tradition-directed person: both live in a group milieu and lack the inner-directed person's capacity to go it alone. The nature of this group milieu, however, differs radically in the two cases. The other-directed person is cosmopolitan. For him the border between the familiar and the strange—a border clearly marked in the societies depending on tradition-direction—has broken down. As the family continuously absorbs the strange and reshapes itself, so the strange becomes familiar. While the inner-directed person could be "at home abroad" by virtue of his relative insensitivity to others, the other-directed person is, in a sense, at home everywhere and nowhere, capable of a rapid if sometimes superficial intimacy with and response to everyone.

The tradition-directed person takes his signals from others, but they come in a cultural monotone; he needs no complex receiving equipment to pick them up. The other-directed person must be able to receive signals from far and near; the sources are many, the changes rapid. What can be internalized, then, is not a code of behavior but the elaborate equipment needed to attend to such messages and occasionally to participate in their circulation. As against guilt-and-shame controls, though of course these survive, one prime psychological lever of the other-directed person is a diffuse *anxiety*. This control equipment, instead of being like a gyroscope, is like a radar. . . .[7]

NOTES

1. Frank Notestein, "Population—the Long View," in *Food for the World*, ed. Theodore W. Schultz (Chicago, 1945).

2. Since writing the above I have discovered Gardner Murphy's use of the same metaphor in his volume *Personality* (New York, 1947). [The "gyroscope" metaphor came to Riesman from his war work with Sperry Gyroscope.]

3. These examples are given by Allan G. B. Fisher, *The Clash of Progress and Security* (London, 1935).

4. See Erich Fromm, *Man for Himself* (New York, 1947); C. Wright Mills, "The Competitive Personality," *Partisan Review* 13 (1946), p. 433; Arnold Green, "The Middle Class Male Child and Neurosis," *American Sociological Review* 11 (1946), p. 31. See also the work of Jurgen Ruesch, Martin B. Loeb, and co-workers on the "infantile personality."

5. This picture of the other-directed person has been stimulated by, and developed from, Erich Fromm's discussion of the "marketing orientation" in *Man for Himself*, pp. 67–82. I have also drawn on my portrait of "The Cash Customer," *Common Sense* 11 (1942), p. 183.

6. [Alexis de Tocqueville, *Democracy in America*, 2 vols. (Paris and London, 1835, 1840); James Bryce, *The American Commonwealth*, 2 vols. (New York and London, 1894, 1895)]

7. The "radar" metaphor was suggested by Karl Wittfogel.

☆ • ☆ • ☆ • ☆ • ☆

The Lonely Crowd based its argument on a new economic culture. Some of that culture was shorter-lived than the authors realized at the time. As Riesman said later, the belief that America had essentially solved the problems of production, freeing more and more people for leisure and consumption, looks dated and unrealistic today. It was the product of a postwar era when Americans did not feel they had to scramble to maintain living standards amid industrial problems and foreign competition. Yet even today, when the U.S. economy is far less dominant in the world, excessive consumption is part of its problem, manifested in high personal debt and low savings. Since modern mass consumption is bound up with advertising, media products, and leisure industries, *The Lonely Crowd*'s focus on leisure and the media is still relevant.

By the early 1960s *The Lonely Crowd* had put many scholars to work investigating the book's propositions—a whole volume of commentary, *Culture and Social Character: The Work of David Riesman Reviewed*, edited by S. M. Lipset and Leo Lowenthal, was devoted to the book. This did not, however, prevent misinterpretation. According to several scholars, distinguished enough to know better, *The Lonely Crowd* claimed that Americans had become *more* conformist. In fact Riesman said that inner-directed people were just as conformist as other-directeds; they conformed, though, in a different way (by internalizing the wishes of their elders) and their "mode of conformity" affected their values and goals.* One difference, says Riesman, is that inner-directed people wish to be *esteemed* whereas other-directed people want more deeply to be *liked* by others and (to use recent language) share their vibes.

This argument, that the psychological *timbre* of conformity had changed, has been criticized from two directions. In our own time, it has been suggested, what looks like other-directed behavior is less a matter of character needs than of role-playing. People smile and 'share the experience' to get by and get on in a culture of marketing and mass organization, but they do not do so because of new needs in their personalities. Toward the end of *The Lonely Crowd*, the authors in effect distinguish between conscious role-playing ("false personalization" is their term) and deeper needs to respond to others; but they do not discuss the difference.

The second criticism of *The Lonely Crowd* is historical. As the historian Carl Degler asked, "how does Riesman know" that the psychology of conformity was different in an era of inner-direction? European visitors often remarked on the way nineteenth-century Americans looked to the opinions of others. Despite his appetite for reading old diaries and letters, Riesman provided little evidence that these nineteenth-century attitudes did not reflect other-directed character needs.

Since *The Lonely Crowd* was published, several ingenious studies have tried to establish whether American values have shifted since the nineteenth century in the direction stated or implied by Riesman's theory of character change. To this end they have done 'content-analysis' of magazines, children's readers, and popular advice books. Sometimes they oversimplified what Riesman, Glazer, and Denney were saying, and they assumed (like Riesman himself) that one could

*The historian James Gilbert recalls to me that in a discussion of "conformity" at his high school near Chicago in 1959, parents accused the students of overconforming to their peer-group; students accused the parents of just wanting conformity to *them*.

get at a people's values through popular writing. In general their results were mixed. For example, a study of children's readers by Marshall Graney found a growing tendency to value leisure and peer-group popularity, but no trend in favor of consuming things rather than making them.

On the question of *when* the supposed changes took place, Riesman was ambiguous. *The Lonely Crowd* stated that other-direction "[seemed] to be emerging in very recent years." Riesman said the same in his article "The Saving Remnant," published in 1949, a year before *The Lonely Crowd;* but his article also claimed that "changes in the nature of work and leisure," involving new attitudes to consumption and the media, had appeared "in the last twenty-five years or so." This would seem to push the arrival of other-direction back to the 1920s rather than the "very recent years" of the 1940s. Riesman might have cleared up the contradiction by arguing that social change took time to work through into character needs via child-rearing and so on, but he never said this.

Several studies of advertising have shown that themes related to other-direction became more prominent between 1900 and 1930. During this time, advertising made more of appearances, prestige and popularity, group situations, and the authority of others. Does this mean that advertisers had found a new kind of American, or were they simply getting smarter at using social-psychological appeals? One reply can be found in novels of the late-nineteenth and early-twentieth centuries, ranging from Horatio Alger to Theodore Dreiser and Edith Wharton. Some of their characters indicate that elements of other-direction were already emerging in that period along with a new stress on mass merchandizing and the use of personable qualities in commercial life. (The bibliographical essay at the end of this book gives a wide survey of works bearing on *The Lonely Crowd;* see pp. 341–44.)

Another problem of *The Lonely Crowd* is that of age-groups. In the excerpt above, and elsewhere in the book, Riesman, Glazer, and Denney said that they expected other-direction to spread out and down from its beach-head among the well-to-do *young* in big cities. Young other-directeds, they assumed, would become older other-directeds and multiply. The authors did not consider that other-direction might inherently be strongest among adolescents, and not just in the United

States. Anyone who knows modern Western teenagers will also know how much they value peer-group fashions, media happenings, and the sharing of emotional experience. Because Riesman's case studies (sampled in a sequel book, *Faces in the Crowd,* 1952) largely concentrated on students and others under twenty-five, he did not ask whether other-direction might actually decline as a person matured.

Riesman did say that social and economic forces promoting other-direction were not confined to the United States. He qualified this by suggesting that other-direction "finds itself most at home in America" due to European immigration and "the lack of any feudal past." The meaning of this is unclear; one must presume he meant that immigrants and their offspring, set loose from a tight class identity, depended all the more on shifting messages from their contemporaries and the media. Be that as it may, the most distinctively American part of *The Lonely Crowd*'s story was the link it portrayed between *inner-direction* and an expanding, acquisitive frontier society.

Does other-direction (or inner-direction) hang together as a category? Might the term in fact cover a variety of sharply different characters? At the very beginning of *The Lonely Crowd* its authors warned that its psychological types did not cover all of a personality. At one point, too, Riesman played with the idea of using his interview material to identify further types, each a different combination of inner-direction, other-direction, and "autonomy." But he did not pursue this very far.

An important test study here is the complex, psychological research done on Brooklyn College freshmen by Elaine Sofer in 1954. As one might expect from *The Lonely Crowd,* Sofer found that those students who were "other-directed" in that they wanted to be popular and do things in a group (rather than working alone for distant goals) were more apt to be guided by outside influences, including articles in the press. They were *not*, however, more sensitively aware of other people (or of themselves). In this group at least, Riesman's metaphor of "radar" tuning did not fit.

Sofer's study suggests that Riesman was too quick to equate dependence on the media with sensitivity to acquaintances. Riesman acknowledged that the psychological difference between the two "mattered very much," but he never elaborated on the difference in *The Lonely Crowd*.

The Lonely Crowd showed nonetheless, and Riesman confirmed it in his interviews, that the media did not necessarily *atomize* people. For young people especially, listening to the radio or records could be a sociable experience, not a private and solitary one. Riesman's thinking about social character and the media bridged two important 'schools' of sociology, both of which were fascinated with mass communications. The first was the neo-Marxist 'Frankfurt School,' which believed that a monolithic capitalist power made ordinary people feel isolated and used the mass media to drug them into acquiescence ("narcotize" was the preferred word; see pp. 2–3). The second school investigated the way in which opinion was formed in small groups and communities. It challenged the Frankfurt School's picture of a one-way line of influence between powerful manipulators and powerless, atomized subjects. Local individuals, especially the 'opinion-leaders' of small communities, had some power to select and judge what the mass media put out.

The Lonely Crowd supported the second, group-opinion view, but it retained an overtone of the Frankfurt School. (Erich Fromm, Riesman's mentor, had been a Frankfurt member.) Riesman's research for the book had started with the proposition that America's new character type, responding passively to the mass media, had a sense of political helplessness. This was very 'Frankfurt.' As Riesman's thinking developed, however, his interest in political pluralism and the social psychology of local groups carried him toward the group-opinion school. In the end he combined both. The other-directed, he believed, adjusted swiftly to new groups, but at heart they were lonely: they were "at home everywhere and nowhere."

WILLIAM H. WHYTE

The Organization Man

By the late 1950s, orthodox liberal opinion had tagged President Eisenhower as a do-nothing, bureaucratic monarch, presiding over a lethargically fat society. Further down the heap, college students and new graduates earned bad grades from survey researchers for being politically passive and obsessed with economic security; some blamed this on the intimidating effects of McCarthyism and the Great Depression insecurity of their parents. For commentators and concerned citizens on all sides, 'conformity' was the new American middle-class problem, and the writer William Whyte, their prophet.

Published in 1956, Whyte's book, *The Organization Man,* focused largely on male business executives but was really about a wider shift in middle-class character and society; it had an intricate section on young mothers and fathers in the new suburbia (the subject of a spate of books in that period).

The basic cause of the change, said Whyte, was the rise of bureaucratic organizations at the turn of the century, coupled with Progressive-reform onslaughts on economic individualism. The collectivism of the early bureaucrats and reformers, necessary at the time, had nonetheless sparked off a shift in values that had become lopsided. America's "Protestant Ethic" of self-reliance—the "pursuit of individual salvation through hard work, thrift, and competitive struggle"—was giving way to a "Social Ethic [that] endorsed the pressures of society against the individual." (Whyte did not discuss whether Protestants had followed the "Protestant Ethic" more than Catholics, Jews, and others had—he used the term as a shorthand description.)

Much of the change, Whyte recognized, was not peculiar to the United States, but it caused a special tension there due to America's individualist traditions. According to the Social Ethic, a person's ultimate need was "belonging," and creativity came from the group, not the individual. The business corporation, archetype of the new collective, took care of the executive employee's welfare, encouraging him to consume hard as well as work hard. The result was some ambivalence about the claims of work versus leisure, office versus home. Competitiveness went into climbing the corporate ladder; few people thought big or bucked the collective standards. In the suburban neighborhood, too, people suppressed their own wishes to be private and different.

Whyte's thesis was quite similar to David Riesman's (see previous excerpt). Whyte's Protestant Ethic corresponded to Riesman's "inner-direction," the Social Ethic to "other-direction." Riesman said that the inner-directed type conformed too, but Whyte allowed that Americans had long been conformist in external matters; now, however, they depended more *deeply* and *directly* on the organized group. As the excerpt below demonstrates, Whyte also believed, like Riesman, that styles of leadership and authority had moved from tough demands to polite manipulation—and that was harder to rebel against.

The Organization Man came out of magazine articles and an earlier book by Whyte on corporate and suburban life. Following a distinguished war record in the marines, Whyte had gone to work at *Fortune* magazine. In 1949 he took charge of a *Fortune* research project on the way big business communicated its values—to others and to itself. Ironically, the project itself was a group effort, but that effort produced Whyte's first book, *Is Anybody Listening? How and Why U.S. Business Fumbles When It Talks with Human Beings* (1952).

Is Anybody Listening? contained phrases and themes that reappeared in *The Organization Man,* including the author's notion of "scientism." Corporate managers, said Whyte, were now using the language and claims of social science to promote the idea that individuals should conform to the group; that committees knew best. But the most *psychological* part of the book was its two chapters based on interviews with executive wives. Whyte picked up a cluster of attitudes that he returned to in *The Organization Man*—a mixture of anxious compliance, controlled ambition, and suppressed resentments against the system. The earlier book applied this to the women; *The Organization Man* made it a general portrait of the men as well.

The excerpt that follows is from a chapter in *The Organization*

Man in which the author becomes autobiographical. In 1939, fresh out of Princeton, where he had majored in English and won an undergraduate play-writing contest, "Holly" Whyte enrolled in a school of harder knocks—Vick Chemical's sales training program. The son of a railroad executive (railroads had produced America's first big corporate bureaucracy), Whyte was in a good position to compare Vick's old-style program with the 'human relations' approach of General Electric.

☆ • ☆ • ☆ • ☆ • ☆

On the surface the trainee programs of most big corporations would seem very much alike.* Beneath such new standardized trappings as testing, automatic rating, rotation, and the like, however, is a fundamental difference in policy.

One type of program sticks to what has been more or less the historic approach. The young man is hired to do a specific job; his orientation is usually brief in duration, and for many years what subsequent after hours training he will get will be directed at his particular job. If he proves himself executive material he may be enrolled in a management development course, but this is not likely to happen until he is in his mid-thirties.

The newer type of program is more than an intensification of the old. The company hires the young man as a potential manager and from the start he is given to thinking of himself as such. He and the other candidates are put together in a central pool, and they are not farmed out to regular jobs until they have been exposed, through a series of dry-run tasks, to the managerial view. The schooling may last as long as two years and occasionally as long as four or five.

At the risk of oversimplification, the difference can be described as that between the Protestant Ethic and the Social Ethic. In one type of program we will see that the primary emphasis is on work and on competition; in the other, on managing *others'* work and on co-operation. Needless to say, there are few pure examples of either approach; whichever way they incline, the majority of training programs have elements of both approaches, and some companies try to straddle directly over the fence.

But an inclination there is, and the new training program may prove the best of introductions to the "professional manager" of the future.

———

To sharpen the fundamental differences, I am going to contrast two outstanding trainee programs. For an example of the first type, I am going to take the training program of the Vick Chemical Company as it was in the late thirties. There are several reasons for the choice. First, it has been one of the best-known programs in the whole personnel field. Second, though it has often been cited as a pioneer example of modern practice, it was in its fundamentals the essence of the Protestant Ethic. . . . Third, I happen to have gone through it myself. If I grow unduly garrulous in these next pages, I bespeak the reader's indulgence; I have often pondered this odd experience, and since it furnishes so apt an illustration of certain principles of indoctrination, I would like to dwell on it at some length.

It was a school—the Vick School of Applied Merchandising, they called it. The idea, as it was presented to job-hunting seniors at the time, was that those who were chosen were not going off to a job, but to a postgraduate training institution set up by a farsighted management. In September, some thirty graduates would gather from different colleges to start a year's study in modern merchandising. There would be a spell of classroom work in New York, a continuing course in advertising, and, most important, eleven months of field study under the supervision of veteran students of merchandising and distribution. Theoretically, we should be charged a tuition, for though we understood we would do some work in connection with our studies, the company explained that its expenses far outweighed what incidental services we would perform. This notwithstanding, it was going to give us a salary of $75 a month and all traveling expenses. It would also, for reasons I was later to learn were substantial, give us an extra $25 a month to be held in escrow until the end of the course.

Let me now point out the first distinction between the Vick program and the more current type. It was not executive training or even junior-executive training. Vick's did argue that the program would help produce the leaders of tomorrow, and prominent on the walls of the office was a framed picture of a captain at the wheel, with a statement by the president that the greatest duty of management was to bring along younger men. This notwithstanding, the question of whether or not any of us would one day be executives was considered a matter that could very easily be deferred. The training was directed almost entirely to the immediate job. The only exception was an International Correspondence Schools course in advertising, one of the main virtues of which, I always felt, was to keep us so occupied during the week ends that we wouldn't have time to think about our situation.

The formal schooling we got was of the briefest character. During our four weeks in New York, we learned of Richardson's discovery of VapoRub, spent a day watching the VapoRub being mixed, and went through a battery of tests the company was fooling around with to find the Vick's type. Most of the time we spent in memorizing list prices, sales spiels, counters to objections, and the prices and techniques of Plough, Inc., whose Penetro line was one of Vick's most troublesome competitors. There was no talk about the social responsibilities of business or the broad view that I can remember, and I'm quite sure the phrase *human relations* never came up at all.

What management philosophy we did get was brief and to the point. Shortly before we were to set out from New York, the president, Mr. H. S. Richardson, took us up to the Cloud Club atop the Chrysler Building. The symbolism did not escape us. As we looked from this executive eyrie down on the skyscraper spires below, Golconda stretched out before us. One day, we gathered, some of us would be coming back up again—and not as temporary guests either. Some would not. The race would be to the swiftest.

Over coffee Mr. Richardson drove home to us the kind of philosophy that would get us back up. He posed a hypothetical problem. Suppose, he said, that you are a manufacturer and for years a small firm has been making paper cartons for your product. He has specialized so much to service you, as a matter of fact, that that's all he does make. He is utterly dependent on your business. For years the relationship has continued to be eminently satisfactory to both parties. But then one day another man walks in and says he will make the boxes for you cheaper. What do you do?

He bade each one of us in turn to answer.

But *how much* cheaper? we asked. How much time could we give the old supplier to match the new bid? Mr. Richardson became impatient. There was only one decision. Either you were a businessman or you were not a businessman. The new man, obviously, should get the contract. Mr. Richardson, who had strong views on the necessity of holding to the old American virtues, advised us emphatically against letting sentimentality obscure fundamentals. Business was survival of the fittest, he indicated, and we would soon learn the fact.

He was as good as his word. The Vick curriculum was just that—survival of the fittest. In the newer type of programs, companies will indeed fire incompetents, but a man joins with the idea that the company intends to keep him, and this is the company's wish also. The Vick School, however, was frankly based on the principle of elimination. It wouldn't make any difference how wonderful all of us might turn out to be; of the thirty-eight who sat there in the Cloud Club, the rules of the game dictated that only six or seven of us would be asked to stay with Vick. The rest would graduate to make way for the next batch of students.

————

Another difference between Vick's approach and that now more characteristic became very evident as soon as we arrived in the field. While the work, as the company said, was educational, it was in no sense make-work. Within a few days of our session at the Cloud Club, we were dispatched to the hinterland—in my case, the hill country of eastern Kentucky. Each of us was given a panel delivery truck, a full supply of signs, a ladder, a stock of samples, and an order pad. After several days under the eye of a senior salesman, we were each assigned a string of counties and left to shift for ourselves.

The merchandising was nothing if not applied. To take a typical day of any one of us, we would rise at 6:00 or 6:30 in some bleak boarding house or run-down hotel and after a greasy breakfast set off to squeeze in some advertising practice before the first call. This consisted of bostitching a quota of large fiber signs on barns and clamping smaller metal ones to telephone poles and trees by hog rings. By eight, we would have arrived at a general store for our exercise in merchandising. Our assignment was to persuade the dealer to take a year's supply all at once, or, preferably, more than a year's supply, so that he would have no money or shelf space left for other brands. After the sale, or no-sale, we would turn to market research and note down the amount sold him by "chiseling" competitors (i.e., competitors; there was no acknowledgment on our report blanks of any other kind).

Next we did some sampling work: "Tilt your head back, Mr. Jones," we would suddenly say to the dealer. For a brief second he would obey and we would quickly shoot a whopping dropperful of Vatronol up his nose. His eyes smarting from the sting, the dealer would smile with simple pleasure. Turning to the loungers by the stove, he would tell them to let the drummer fella give them some of that stuff. After the messy job was done, we plastered the place with cardboard signs, and left. Then, some more signposting in barnyards, and ten or twelve miles of mud road to the next call. So, on through the day, the routine was repeated until at length, long after dark, we would get back to our lodgings in time for dinner—and two hours' work on our report forms.

The acquisition of a proper frame of mind toward all this was a slow process. The faded yellow second sheets of our daily report book tell the story. At first, utter demoralization. Day after day, the number of calls would be a skimpy eight or nine, and the number of sales sometimes zero. But it was never our fault. In the large space left for explanations, we would affect a cheerful humor—the gay adventurer in the provinces—but this pathetic bravado could not mask a recurrent note of despair.*

To all these bids for sympathy, the home office was adamantine. The weekly letter written to each trainee would start with some perfunctory remarks that it was too bad about the clutch breaking down, the cut knee, and so on. But this spurious sympathy did not conceal a strong preoccupation with results, and lest we miss the point we were told of comrades who would no longer be with us. We too are sorry about those absent dealers, the office would say. Perhaps if you got up earlier in the morning?

As the office sensed quite correctly from my daily reports, I was

---

*I quote some entries from my own daily report forms: "They use 'dry' creek beds for roads in this country. 'Dry!' Ha! Ha! . . . Sorry about making only four calls today, but I had to go over to Ervine to pick up a drop shipment of 3/4 tins and my clutch broke down. . . . Everybody's on WPA in this county. Met only one dealer who sold more than a couple dozen VR a year. Ah, well, it's all in the game! . . . Bostitched my left thumb to a barn this morning and couldn't pick up my first call until after lunch. . . . The local brick plant here is shut down and nobody's buying anything. . . . Five, count 'em, *five* absent dealers in a row. . . . Sorry about the $20.85 but the clutch broke down again. . . ."

growing sorry for myself. I used to read timetables at night, and often in the evening I would somehow find myself by the C & O tracks when the George Washington swept by, its steamy windows a reminder of civilization left behind. I was also sorry for many of the storekeepers, most of whom existed on a precarious credit relationship with wholesalers, and as a consequence I sold them very little of anything.

The company sent its head training supervisor to see if anything could be salvaged. After several days with me, this old veteran of the road told me he knew what was the matter. It wasn't so much my routine, wretched as this was. It was my state of mind. "Fella," he told me, "you will never sell anybody anything until you learn one simple thing. The man on the other side of the counter is the *enemy*."

It was a gladiators' school we were in. Selling may be no less competitive now, but in the Vick program, strife was honored far more openly than today's climate would permit. Combat was the ideal—combat with the dealer, combat with the "chiseling competitors," and combat with each other. There was some talk about "the team," but it was highly abstract. Our success depended entirely on beating our fellow students, and while we got along when we met for occasional sales meetings the camaraderie was quite extracurricular.

Slowly, as our sales-to-calls ratios crept up, we gained in rapacity. Somewhere along the line, by accident or skill, each of us finally manipulated a person into doing what we wanted him to do. Innocence was lost, and by the end of six months, with the pack down to about twenty-three men, we were fairly ravening for the home stretch back to the Cloud Club. At this point, the company took us off general store and grocery work and turned us loose in the rich drugstore territory.

The advice of the old salesman now became invaluable. While he had a distaste for any kind of dealer, with druggists he was implacably combative. He was one of the most decent and kindly men I have ever met, but when he gave us pep talks about this enemy ahead of us, he spoke with great intensity. Some druggists were good enough fellows, he told us (i.e., successful ones who bought big deals), but the tough ones were a mean, servile crew; they would insult you, keep you waiting while they pretended to fill prescriptions, lie to you about their inventory, whine at anything less than a 300 per cent markup, and switch their customers to chiseling competitors.

The old salesman would bring us together in batches for several days of demonstration. It was a tremendous experience for us, for though he seemed outwardly a phlegmatic man, we knew him for the artist he was. Outside the store he was jumpy and sometimes perspired, but once inside, he was composed to the point of apparent boredom. He rarely smiled, almost never opened with a joke. His demeanor seemed to say, I am a busy man and you are damned lucky I have stopped by your miserable store. Sometimes, if the druggist was unusually insolent, he would blow cigar smoke at his face. "Can't sell it if you don't have it," he would say contemptuously, and then, rather pleased with himself, glance back at us, loitering in the wings, to see if we had marked that.

Only old pros like himself could get away with that, he told us in the post-mortem sessions, but there were lots of little tricks we could pick up. As we gathered around him, like Fagin's brood, he would demonstrate how to watch for the victim's shoulders to relax before throwing the clincher; how to pick up the one-size jar of a competitive line that had an especially thick glass bottom and chuckle knowingly; how to feign suppressed worry that maybe the deal was too big for "the smaller druggist like yourself" to take; how to disarm the nervous druggist by fumbling and dropping a pencil. No mercy, he would tell us; give the devils no mercy.

We couldn't either. As the acid test of our gall the company now challenged us to see how many drugstores we could desecrate with "flange" signs. By all the standards of the trade this signposting should have been an impossible task. Almost every "chiseling competitor" would give the druggist at least five dollars to let him put up a sign; we could not offer the druggist a nickel. Our signs, furthermore, were not the usual cardboard kind the druggist could throw away after we had left. They were of metal, they were hideous, and they were to be screwed to the druggists' cherished oak cabinets.

The trick was in the timing. When we were in peak form the procedure went like this: Just after the druggist had signed the order, his shoulders would subside, and this would signal a fleeting period of mutual bonhomie. "New fella, aren't you?" the druggist was likely to say, relaxing. This was his mistake. As soon as we judged the good will to be at full flood, we would ask him if he had a ladder. (There was a ladder out in the car, but the fuss of fetching it would have broken the mood.) The druggist's train of thought would not at that moment connect the request with what was to follow, and he would good-naturedly dispatch someone to bring out a ladder. After another moment of chatter, we would make way for the waiting customer who would engage the druggist's attention. Then, forthrightly, we would slap the ladder up against a spot we had previously reconnoitered. "Just going to get this sign up for you," we would say, as if doing him the greatest favor in the world. He would nod absent-mindedly. Then up the ladder we would go; a few quick turns of the awl, place the bracket in position, and then, the automatic screw driver. Bang! bang! Down went the sign. (If the druggist had been unusually mean, we could break the thread of the screw for good measure.) Then down with the ladder, shift it over to the second spot, and up again.

About this time the druggist would start looking up a little unhappily, but the good will, while ebbing, was still enough to inhibit him from action. *He* felt sorry for us. Imagine that young man thinking those signs are good looking! Just as he would be about to mumble something about one sign being enough, we would hold up the second one. It had a picture on it of a woman squirting nose drops up her nostrils. We would leer fatuously at it. "Just going to lay this blonde on the top of the cabinet for you, Mr. Jones," we would say, winking. We were giants in those days.

I suppose I should be ashamed, but I must confess I'm really not, and to this day when I enter a drugstore I sometimes fancy the sound of the awl biting irretrievably into the druggist's limed oak. I think the reader will understand, of course, that I am not holding up the Vick School of Applied Merchandising as an ideal model, yet I must add, in all fairness to Vick, that most of us were grateful for the experience. When we get together periodically (we have an informal alumni association), we wallow in talk about how they really separated the men from the boys then, etc. It was truly an experience, and if we shudder to recall the things we did, we must admit that as a cram course in reality it was extraordinarily efficient.

The General Electric program to which I now turn was in full force in the thirties and is actually an older one than the Vick's program. Where the latter was a late flowering of a philosophy already in the descendant, however, GE's was a harbinger of things to come. Even today, it is still somewhat ahead of its time; at this moment there are not many corporation training programs which come near General Electric's, either in the size or elaborateness of facilities or, more importantly, in consistency of principles. Yet I believe that as we take up these principal features of the General Electric program, we will be seeing what in a decade or so hence may be the middle of the road.[1]

The most immediately apparent thing about the General Electric program is the fact that it *is* a school. While the plants serve as part of the campus, the company maintains a full-time staff of 250 instructors and an educational plant complete to such details as company-published textbooks, examinations, classrooms, and alumni publications. In direct operating costs alone the company spends over five million dollars annually—a budget larger than many a medium-sized college.

The program is highly centralized. To keep this plant running, GE's corps of recruiters each year delivers between 1,000 and 1,500 college graduates, mostly engineers, to the company's Schenectady headquarters. There the trainees enter what is for them a continuation of college life. Like fraternity brothers, they live together in boarding houses and attend classes in groups. For afterhours recreation, they have the privileges of the Edison Club where, along with other GE employees with college degrees, they can meet after classes to play golf, bridge, and enjoy a planned series of parties and dances. (GE employees who haven't gone to college are eligible to join if they have achieved a supervisory rating.)

The curriculum is arranged in much the same manner as a university's. The trainee enters under one of several courses, such as engineering and accounting. All these courses will have much in common, however, for the trainee's first eighteen months are regarded as the basic part of his training. At the end of this time he will then go on to a "major." If he has been in the manufacturing training course, for example, he can elect as a major factory operations, manufacturing engineering, production and purchasing, or plant engineering.

The work the trainee does during this training is not, like Vick's applied merchandising, considered an end in itself. From time to time the trainee will work at specific jobs, but these jobs, while not mere makework, are outside the regular cost-accounted operations of the company.

The company considers them vehicles for training, and it rotates students from one to another on a regular schedule.

———

The most noteworthy feature of the General Electric approach is the emphasis on the "professional" manager. As in all training programs, the bulk of the instruction is on specifics. Unlike most, however, there is considerable study in subjects that cut across every kind of job. Trainees study personnel philosophy, labor relations, law, and, most important, the managerial viewpoint.[2]

Only a minority of the trainees will ever become managers; in ten years 1,500 to 2,000 executive slots will open up, and this means that most of the thousands of young men trained during this time will never get further than middle management. Nevertheless, it is those future executive slots that the company is thinking of, and it makes its concern plain to the trainee. On the report card form for trainees, there is a space for an evaluation as to whether the trainee is suited "for individual contribution" or whether, instead, he is suited "to manage the work of others." The company tells the trainees that it is perfectly all right for them to aim at "individual contribution," which is to say, a specialty. It would be a dull trainee, however, who did not pause before consigning himself to such a role. In one of GE's textbooks there is a picture of a man looking at two ladders. One leads up to a specialty, the other to general managing. The question before the young man, the textbook states, is: "Will I specialize in a particular field?"—or "Will I become broad-gauge, capable of effort in many fields?"

Who wants to be narrow-gauge? Trainees do not have to read too strenuously between the lines to see that one should aim to manage; as a matter of fact, they are predisposed to read a good bit more between the lines than many of their elders would like them to. Which brings us to an important point. In gauging the impact of the curriculum on the young man, his predispositions are as important as the weighting of the courses. Elders at General Electric can demonstrate that the actual amount of time devoted to the abstract arts of management is far less than the time devoted to specific skills. But the managerial part is what the trainees want to hear—and they want to hear it so much that one hour's exposure to the managerial view can be as four or five hours of something else in proportion to its effect on impressionable minds. Trainees are interested, to be sure, in how turbines are made, in the techniques of the accounting department and such, but they do not want to be *too* interested. It would make them unbalanced.

They regard specific work very much as many educators view "subject matter" courses: narrowing. As trainees play back the lesson, they see a distinction, sometimes a downright antithesis, between the qualities of the broad-gauge executive and the qualities that one must have to do a superlative piece of concrete work. Not work itself but the managing of other people's work is the skill that they aspire to. As they describe it, the manager is a man in charge of people getting along together, and his *expertise* is relatively independent of who or what is being managed. Or why.

Not surprisingly, the part of the curriculum for which they have the greatest affinity is the human-relations instruction. They are particularly enthusiastic about the "Effective Presentation" course worked up by the sales-training department. They can hardly be blamed. "YOU CAN ALWAYS GET ANYBODY TO DO WHAT YOU WISH," the textbook proclaims. To this end the students spend four months eagerly studying a battery of communication techniques and psychological principles which General Electric tells them will help them to be good managers. (Sample principle: "Never say anything controversial.")

There is nothing novel about teaching people how to manipulate other people, and GE's scientific psychological techniques bear a strong resemblance to the how-to-be-a-success precepts standard in the U.S. for decades. What is different about them is their justification. They are not presented on the grounds that they will help make people do what you want them to do so that you can make more money. GE trainees see it in much more eleemosynary terms. They do like the part about selling yourself to others so you can get ahead, for they think a lot about this. But they don't abide the thought of enemies on the other side of the counter; they see the manipulative skills as something that in the long run will make other people *happy*. When in years to come the trainees are charged with the destiny of subordinates—a possibility most take re-markably much for granted—they will be able to achieve a stable, well-adjusted work group. They won't drive subordinates, they explain. They will motivate them.

Trainees are also predisposed to emphasis on co-operation rather than competition, and this they get too. The emphasis is built into the structure of the school. For one thing, the student is given a high measure of security from the beginning, and while there may be promotion of the fittest there can be survival for all. There are exceptions, but one must be a very odd ball to be one. For the first two years the trainee is part of a system in which his salary raises will be automatic, and while later on he will be more on his own there will be no planned elimination as there was at Vick, nor an up-or-out policy such as the Navy's.

To get ahead, of course, one must compete—but not too much, and certainly not too obviously. While overt ambition is a bad posture for the ambitious anywhere, the GE system has especial sanctions for the rate-buster. The trainee is, first of all, a member of a group, and the group is entrusted to a surprising degree with the resolution of his future. How well, the company wants to know, does he fit in? His fellow trainees provide the answer, and in the "case study" group discussions the eager beaver or the deviant is quickly exposed. And brought to heel. Trainees speak frequently of the way close fraternity life atmosphere is valuable in ironing out some trainees' aberrant tendencies. It may be tough on him, they concede, but better now than later. In a few years the trainee will be released from this close association and the social character that he has perfected will be a fundamental necessity; he will be moving from one company branch to another, and he must be able to fit into the same kind of integrated social system.

The company officially recognizes the disciplining of the group. In its periodic rating of the man, the company frequently calls on his comrades to participate in the rating. If a man is liked especially well not only by his superiors but by his peers, he may be given the job of guiding about eight or ten of his fellow trainees. He is now a "sign-up," and if he keeps on maturing he may become a "head-of-tests," the seven "sign-ups" reporting to him. Since the opinions of one's peers are so integral to advancement, this system virtually insures that the overzealous or the "knocker" type of man will not get ahead—or, at the very least, that he will successfully remold himself to the managerial image.

The fact that the trainee must spend so much time thinking of what other people think of him does not oppress him. Quite the opposite, the constant surveillance is one of the things the average trainee talks about most enthusiastically. The rating system is highly standardized, he explains; it is the product of *many* people rather than one, and this denominator of judgments frees him from the harshness or caprice that might result from the traditional boss-employee relationship. He is also freed from being ignored; the system insures that other people must be thinking about him quite as much as he is thinking about them, and for this reason he won't get pigeonholed. At General Electric, as one trainee remarked, not only can't you get lost, you can't even hide.

Needless to say, ambition still pulses, and I am not trying to suggest that the General Electric man is any less set on the main chance than my Vick comrades. It is quite obvious, nevertheless, that he must pursue the main chance in a much more delicate fashion. To get ahead, he must co-operate with the others—but co-operate *better* than they do.

The rules of the game do permit a few lapses, but these lapses, characteristically, are the display of personality. Somewhere along the line the trainees must get themselves hired into a regular job, and to do this they must attract the attention of superiors. There is a tacit understanding among trainees that it is perfectly all right to make a bald play to get on a first-name basis with superiors that might do one some good. "As soon as you know your way around a new department you start telephoning," one trainee explains, tapping the intercommunication telephone directory. "Believe me, this little green book here is a man's best friend." The company encourages superiors to encourage this kind of contact. "I or anybody else," another trainee says, "can walk into a manager's office just as easily as we can each other's. By ten o'clock of the day I hit the New York office I was calling everybody by his first name."

NOTES

1. Even Vick has moved considerably in this direction. The heroic years are over; now it is "The Vick Executive Development Program," and though there has been no basic shift in underlying philosophy (Mr. Richardson is still at the helm), Vick now offers many of the material features of the GE program. Security is reasonably guaranteed; no longer are trainees "graduated"—of the roughly one hundred seniors taken in each year, all but a handful can remain as permanent employees. They are exposed to many more aspects of management and they don't have to do things like putting up flange signs.

2. Among other things, the trainees take HOBSO. This is the course in How Our Business System Operates, originally developed by Du Pont to inoculate blue-collar employees against creeping socialism. Though GE has no reason to fear its trainees are ideologically unsound, it explains that the course will help them "detect any bad guidance they receive from union and political leaders, and even from educational and spiritual leaders."

☆ · ☆ · ☆ · ☆ · ☆

There is good historical evidence, and not just in the United States, for Whyte's claim that managers have become more manipulative and less confrontational. The evidence, however, is mixed on Whyte's assertion (made in another part of his book) that conformity flowers most in large, bureaucratic organizations. Ironically, the most 'other-directed' behavior he describes in the excerpt is that of a small businessman, the druggist who can't even say 'stop!' when the awl bites into his woodwork.

This suggests that Whyte's historical explanation of character change was too narrowly based on the rise of bureaucracy. Whyte also underestimated the impulse to conform and to join tight-knit groups in earlier decades of American life, from New England puritanism to fraternal lodges in the nineteenth century. On the other hand, Whyte suggested more clearly than David Riesman that it took time for changes in institutions to work through into character change. He also recognized the flaw in assuming that because *younger* people seemed to hold the Social Ethic more deeply, it was bound to spread and predominate in the future. Nevertheless he made just this assumption.

Today the incentive to impress rivals and superiors with the style they respect can still produce a lot of conformity in executive suites. Nevertheless, business writers since Whyte have found a greater variety of executive types and tendencies than he did. In his study of high-tech firms spawned by aerospace in the 1960s and early 1970s, Michael Maccoby distinguished the "company man," corresponding to Whyte's organization man, from several other types, especially the "gamesman," an innovating, aggressive team-builder. Opinion seems divided as to whether the dull conformity described by White *did* apply to the 1950s or whether he exaggerated its extent even then.

The same questions apply to Whyte's discussion of suburbia (not in the excerpt). At the time he wrote, it was statistically valid to portray organization executives as overwhelmingly male and their spouses as suburban housewives, albeit civic joiners too. Large and growing minorities of middle-class wives had jobs outside the home but many of these were part-time. Since then, the rise of the two-career marriage and other changes have altered suburbia in many ways (as an article by Nicholas Lemann has shown). Among other things, there is much less of the bland but intrusive anti-intellectualism described by Whyte ("You're reading *Plato?*").

Yet even in his own time, Whyte was criticized for exaggerating the totalitarian quality of suburbia, and for concentrating his study on just one kind of executive-professional suburb exemplified by Park Forest near Chicago: a commercially created tract of *rented* garden apartments. Suburbs of house-owners might be expected to produce more puttering about one's own place at the beckon of DIY chores, and less communal and prying behavior. (Let us note, though, that as late as 1984 the neighbors of Stephen Kenney, a graduate student writing on Thoreau, got the Village Court of Kenmore, a Buffalo suburb, to arraign him for letting his grass grow wild!)

In recent years, left-wing writers have criticized Whyte for extolling an asocial individualism. Whyte did, it is true, argue that one could not have a close and democratic community without conformity. He wanted, however, not to destroy community but to restore a tension and balance between self-reliance and the claims of society—a condition that, he believed, had once flourished in the United States. Despite his years of investigating corporate America, Whyte had no proposals for changing its institutions and procedures. Mass organization, he had to assume, was here to stay. He left it up to the individual to fight its excesses from within.

GREGORY P. STONE

Halloween and the Mass Child

Gregory Stone's tale of Halloween in a midwestern town—Columbia, Missouri—is probably the most entertaining of the many test studies generated by *The Lonely Crowd* (p. 50). It illustrates and supports part of David Riesman's argument. At the time of writing, Stone was teaching sociology at the University of Missouri while finishing his Ph.D. thesis on "Clothing and Social Relations." A former graduate student at the University of Chicago, he upheld the belief of the 'Chicago school' of sociology that seemingly trivial bits of life contained a world of social meaning.

In 1957, two years before his essay on "Trick or Treat," Stone had published a study of a local clothing market in Michigan and the social psychology of shopping. This was a spin-off from Stone's work in the sociological field known as "symbolic interaction," which focused on the way people communicated and learned through symbols. Stone was particularly interested in what people signaled through their appearance and clothes, what these things said about their attitudes and status. Some of what he wrote was fairly obvious and descriptive, albeit wrapped in the language of sociological theory—the popular sociologist Vance Packard said it better in *The Status Seekers* (1959). Some of Stone's writing, however, anticipated later theories of 'body language,' for it dealt with the significance of body shape and facial expressions as well as clothes.

In thinking about the social meaning of clothes and costume—dressing up for different roles—Stone became fascinated with children's play. Halloween sparked a connection between all these interests and the more clear-cut, historical theory of *The Lonely Crowd*.

☆ · ☆ · ☆ · ☆ · ☆

I set these notes down with a sense of *déjà vu.** Certainly it has all been said before, and I may have read it all somewhere, but I cannot locate the sources. I have often thought about these things in the past. Then, too, as a sociologist, I like to think I am providing observations as well as impressions for my audience. I cannot recall any other counts and tabulations of the very few facts and happenings that I counted and tabulated this year in a small "near southern" town on the traditional hallowed evening.[1]

In brief, I found that Riesman's "other-directed man" may have exported his peculiar life style—tolerance and conformity organized by the prime activity of consumption—from his suburban northeastern habitat to areas westward and southward perilously close to the Mason-Dixon line.[2] The town I speak of is a university town. As such, it has undoubtedly recruited "other-directeds" from the universities of the northeast. For example, I have been there. Moreover, the part of town in which I carried on my quantitative survey (properly speaking, a "pilot study") is a kind of suburb—a sub-village, perhaps an "inner-urb"—the housing section maintained by most large universities where younger faculty are segregated from the rest of the community in World War II officers' quarters. "Other-directeds" are younger and better educated than "inner-directeds."

You will recall the main theme of *The Lonely Crowd:* the very *character* of American life has been revolutionized as the fundamental organizing activity of our waking hours has shifted from production to consumption. We used to work—at least ideally and Protestantly—because work was our life. By our works we were known. Max Weber, among others less careful and profound, has attempted to explain this in his *Protestant Ethic and the Spirit of Capitalism,* showing how a vocabulary of motive was required to consolidate the spread of capitalism in society and arguing that the sheer dialectic of class antagonism was not always sufficient to account for the institution of pervasive economic change. *Every social change requires a convincing rationale.* Protestant-

*"Halloween and the Mass Child" by Gregory P. Stone was first published in *American Quarterly*, Volume 11, No. 3 (Fall 1959). Copyright © 1959 and reprinted by permission of the American Studies Association.

ism supplied this in part, and its persistence may still be seen in the contrasting attitudes toward gambling *(gaming)*, for example, held by Protestant and Catholic churches. Only in the 1920s did the American Protestant churches relax their bans on such games, and then it was with the stipulation that they be played for amusement only. Risk and gain were cemented in the context of work; never in the context of play. The place of consumption in the "old" society—the industrial society—may be caricatured by referring to Marx's view that the cost of labor was the money and goods required for laborers to exist and reproduce themselves. Abbreviated: we consumed so that we might work. Today, for the most part, we work to live and live to consume. Abbreviated: we work to consume.

"Trick or Treat" is the contemporary quasi-ritual play and celebration of Halloween. Characteristically, the "trick-or-treater" is rewarded not for his work, but for his play. The practice is ostensibly a vast bribe exacted by the younger generation upon the older generation (by the "other-directeds" upon the "inner-directeds"?). The doorbell rings and is answered. The householder is greeted by a masked and costumed urchin with a bag—significantly, a *shopping* bag—and confronted with dire alternatives: the unknown peril of a devilishly conceived prank that will strike at the very core of his social self—his property; or the "payoff" in candy, cookies or coin for another year's respite from the antisocial incursions of the children. The householder pays.

In his *Psychology of Clothes*, J. C. Flügel has noted that the mask and costume free the individual from social obligation by concealing his identity and cloaking him in the absurd protective anonymity of a mythical or legendary creature—a clown, a ghost, a pirate or a witch. The householder must pay. For, by "dressing out," the urchin is symbolically immunized against those punishments that might ordinarily inhibit the promised violations of property and propriety. Punishment presupposes the identity of the offender.

Nonsense! This conception of "trick or treat" is clearly and grossly in error. In the mass society, the "protection racket" seems as archaic as the concepts of psychoanalysis. To revive either in the analysis of contemporary life betrays the nostalgia of the analyst. Both are but the dusty wreckage of long dead romances. Moreover, as we shall see, the mask invites the ready disclosure of the wearer's identity. Instead of protecting

89

the urchin, the costume is more akin to the Easter bonnet, designed to provoke the uncritical appreciations of the audience.

Even so, we can apprehend the "trick" as a production; the "treat" as a consumption. Just twenty-five years ago, when I was an urchin, Halloween was a time set aside for young tricksters—a time for creative productions. Creativity, I might remind the reader, is inevitably destructive, as it pushes the present into the past. Of course, it is never merely nor exclusively the destruction of established forms. Our destructive productions were immense (I wonder at my adolescence, as Marx wondered at the *bourgeoisie!*). I don't know now how we managed to silently detach the eave troughs from the house of the neighborhood "crab," remove his porch steps, then encourage him to give chase by hurling those eave troughs, with a terrifying clatter, upon his front porch. I do know it was long, hard and careful *work*. The devices of Halloween were also artfully and craftily produced, like the serrated spool used to rattle the windows of more congenial adults in the neighborhood. We had no conception of being treated by our victims, incidentally, to anything except silence which we hoped was studied, irate words, a chase (if we were lucky), or, most exciting of all, an investigation of the scene by the police whom we always managed to elude. Our masks, we believed, did confound our victims' attempts to identify us.

In sharp contrast to these nostalgic memories are the quantitative findings of my "pilot study." Being a sociologist, I must apologize for my sample first of all. An editorial in a local newspaper warned me that between seventy-five and one hundred children would visit my home on Halloween. Only eighteen urchins bedeviled me that evening, a fact that I attribute to two circumstances. First, I unwittingly left my dog at large early in the evening. A kind animal, a cross between a Weimeraner and some unknown, less nervous breed, she was upset by the curious costumes of the children, and, barking in fright, she frightened away some of the early celebrants. Second, I think that our segregated "inner-urb" was neglected in favor of more imposing, perhaps more lucrative, areas of town. My eighteen respondents ranged in age from about four years to about twelve. Half were girls and half were boys. Two of the six groups— one-third—were mixed. Twenty-five years ago the presence of girls in my own Halloween enterprises was unthinkable.

Was the choice proffered by these eighteen urchins, when they whined or muttered, "Trick or treat?" or stood mutely at my threshold, a choice between production and consumption? Was I being offered the opportunity to decide for these youngsters the ultimate direction they should take in later life by casting them in the role of producer or consumer? Was I located at some vortex of fate so that my very act could set the destiny of the future? Was there a choice at all? No. In each case, I asked, "Suppose I said, 'Trick.' What would you do?" Fifteen of the eighteen (83.3%) answered, "I don't know." The art of statistics, taken half-seriously, permits me to estimate with 95% confidence that the interval, .67–1.00, will include the proportion of children who don't know what a trick is in that "hypothetical universe" for which the eighteen constituted a random sample (this is a ruse employed by some sociologists who find out belatedly that the sample they have selected is inadequate).[3] . . . [Y]et it seems that at least two-thirds of the children like those who visited my house on Halloween probably have no conception of producing a trick! They aren't bribing anybody. They grace your and my doorsteps as consumers, pure and simple.

What of the three—the 16.7%—who did not respond, "I don't know"? One said nothing at all. I assume he really didn't know, but, being a careful quantitative researcher, I cannot include him with the others. Another did, in fact, say, "I don't know," but qualified his reply. Let me transcribe the dialogue.

> INTERVIEWER: Hello there.
> RESPONDENT: (Silence)
> INTERVIEWER: What do you want?
> RESPONDENT: Trick or treat?
> INTERVIEWER: Supposing I said, "Trick"?
> RESPONDENT: (Silence)
> INTERVIEWER: What would you do, if I said, "Trick"?
> RESPONDENT: *I don't know.* (Long pause.) I'd *probably* go home and get some sand *or something* and throw it on your porch. (Emphasis mine.)
> FIELD NOTES: The porches of the old officers' quarters are constructed from one-by-three slats so that about an inch of free space intervenes between each slat. In short, the porch simply would not hold sand, and the "trick" of the urchin could never be carried off!
> INTERVIEWER: O. K. I'll have to treat, I guess.

The third answered, without prompting, that he'd go home, get a water pistol and squirt my windows (which could have used a little squirting). The "tricks" did not seem so dire, after all! Moreover, the "means of production"—the sand and the water pistol—were left at home, a fact that reminds me of one of Riesman's acute observations to the effect that the home has become a workshop (work is consumed) and the factory, a ranch house (consumption is work).

Did the masks and costumes provide anonymity? To the contrary! I asked each child who he or she was. Happily and trustfully each revealed his or her identity, lifting the mask and disclosing the name. Had they ripped off *my* eave troughs, I would have had the police on them in short order! "Trick or Treat" is a highly personalized affair so that even its ritual quality is lost (for their persistence, rituals depend upon impersonal enactments, and my earlier use of the term, "quasi-ritual," is explained).

On the possibility that the costume might have been a production or a creation, I noted the incidence of ready-to-wear costumes. Two-thirds had been purchased in their entirety. Four of the others were mixed, consisting of homemade costumes and commercial masks. Two were completely homemade: one a ghost outfit, consisting of an old tattle-tale gray sheet with two eye holes; the other, a genuine creation. It was comprised by a mesh wastebasket inverted over an opening in a large cardboard box with armholes. On the front of the box, printed in a firm adult "hand," were the words: Take Me to Your Leader. Occasionally, adults produced, but only to ratify or validate the child in his masquerade as a consumer.

To ascertain the part played by adults in "Trick or Treat," I must, unfortunately, rely on recollections. In preparing my interview schedule and observational data sheets, I had not anticipated the adult, thinking that the celebrants of Halloween would be children. This impression was confirmed by my local newspaper which published the rules of Halloween, stipulating its age-graded character. "Trick or Treat" was set aside for the preadolescents of the town, while teen-agers were obliged to celebrate the event at parties. The rules were apparently enforced, as this news item on the November 1 front page shows:

> Police yesterday afternoon arrested, then released, a youth they said was dressed in a Halloween costume and asking for tricks [sic] or treats at downtown stores.
>
> They said the youth was about 17. He started the rounds of the stores early, he said, because he had to work last night.
>
> Police said they lectured the youth and explained the traditional [sic] trick-or-treat routine is normally reserved for children.

What adults were to do was not clarified by the local press. What many did do was to ease and expedite consumption by clothing their preadolescent children for the role, providing them with shopping bags and, in many instances, accompanying them on the rounds. At least three of the six groups of urchins that called at my house on Halloween were accompanied by adults (the father was always there, one alone!) who lurked uneasily and self-consciously in the darkness where night was mixed with the shadowed shafts cast by my porch light. In one case, a peer group of adults lurked in the shadows and exceeded in number the peer group of children begging on my porch. There they were: agents of socialization, teaching their children how to consume in the tolerant atmosphere of the mass society. The "anticipatory socialization" of the children—accomplished by an enactment of roles not normally played at the time, but roles that would be assumed in the future—was going on before my eyes. I wondered whether the parental preoccupation with the child's adjustment in the larger society could not have been put aside just for Halloween. Perhaps the hiding in the dark allegorically complemented my wish in the tacit expression of shame.

They were teaching a lesson in tolerance, not only a lesson in consumption, encouraging their children to savor the gracious and benign acceptance of their beggary by an obliging adult world. My questions made them nervous. The lone father was silent. He turned his face skywards, studying the stars. One couple spoke rapidly in hushed whispers, punctuating their remarks with nervous laughter. In another couple, the mother said sheepishly, "I wonder what they'll say? They've never been asked that." All the parents were relieved when I tactfully rescued the situation from deterioration by offering to treat the children with (purchased) goodies. Consider a typical protocol.

FIELD NOTES: The bell rings. I go to the door. On the porch are three children between five and nine years old, two boys—one in a clown suit, the other in a pirate suit—and a girl in a Japanese kimono, holding a fan. On the sidewalk are a mother and a father whose faces are hidden in darkness.

INTERVIEWER: Hi!

RESPONDENTS: (Silence.)

INTERVIEWER: What do you want?

RESPONDENTS: (Silence.)

THE CLOWN: Candy.

INTERVIEWER: Why?

FIELD NOTES: The married couple giggles. They shift their feet.

JAPANESE GIRL AND CLOWN: (Silence.)

PIRATE: I don't know.

FIELD NOTES: I look questioningly at the girl and the clown. Each is silent.

INTERVIEWER: What are you supposed to say?

JAPANESE GIRL: I don't know.

INTERVIEWER: Have you heard of "Trick or Treat"?

CLOWN: No.

FIELD NOTES: The married couple is silent. They lean forward expectantly, almost placing their faces in the circle of light arching out and around my porch and open front door, almost telling me who they are.

INTERVIEWER: Well, I guess I'll have to treat.

FIELD NOTES: I get a handful of corn candy from the living room, and divide it among the three outstretched open shopping bags. All the respondents laugh in an appreciative, relieved manner. My study is passed off as a joke. The world has been tolerant after all.

I am reminded of Ortega's remonstrances against the Mass Man, for whom *privileges had become rights*.[4] Standing there, existing, it was the clown's right to receive the treat, the candy. The treat or gift was at one time an act of deference in recognition of esteemed friendship. Herbert Spencer wrote of it in that way—the gift was a privilege. On Halloween, the gift has become the right of every child in the neighborhood, however he or his family is esteemed. Now, rights are not questioned. That such rights would be questioned was hardly anticipated by those who claimed them. It made them ill at ease and nervous, perhaps lest the questions betray an indignation—a state of mind more appropriate to an age when people were busy, or perhaps busier, more productive.

Yet, this is not a plea for a return to the "good old days"—ridiculous on the face of it. Certainly, the farther south the tolerance of the mass society creeps, the happier many of us will be. It seems to be unquestionably true that the younger people of the south are less opposed to segregated schools than the adults. There is nothing morally wrong with consumption, per se, as production was often the setting for ruthless destruction. The conformity of "other-direction" (no trick-or-treater came to my door by himself) need not disturb us. Each society must secure conformity from a substantial majority of its members if that society is to persist. Instead, I have tried to show only two things. First, Riesman's character type of "other-direction" may, indeed, be a *prototype* of American character and not some strange mutation in the northeast. Consumption, tolerance and conformity were recognizable in the Halloween masquerade of a near-southern town. Production, indignation and autonomy were not. Second, national holidays and observances may have been transformed into vast staging areas for the anticipatory socialization of mass men. By facilitating this change in life style, they can give impetus to the change in character conceived by Riesman (and many others). I am being very serious when I say that we need studies of what has happened to all these observances—the Fourth of July, Thanksgiving, Christmas and Easter—in all parts of America. After reading this report, you will agree that we need a study of Halloween.

It is not only as a sociologist, however, that I ask for these studies. Something does trouble me deeply about my observations—the "I don't know." Here is the source of our misgivings and dis-ease with respect to the mass man. It is not that he consumes, but, to the profit of the "hidden persuaders," that he consumes, not knowing why or just not knowing. It is not that he is tolerant, but that he is *unreasonably* tolerant. It is not that he conforms, but that he conforms for conformity's sake. *The mass society, like the industrial society, needs a vocabulary of motive—a rationale—to dignify the daily life.* That's what troubles me about my findings on Halloween. It was a rehearsal for consumership without a rationale. Beyond the stuffing of their pudgy stomachs, they didn't know why they were filling their shopping bags.

NOTES

1. This paper has had the benefit of criticism provided by Dr. Stuart Cuthbertson, retired chairman of the Department of Romance Languages at the University of Colorado, and Dr. David Bakan, professor of Psychology at the University of Missouri.

2. It may well be argued that "other-direction" is, like Babbitry, a midwestern phenomenon. Riesman has probably been unduly and misleadingly cautious in circumscribing his observations as he did. Thus, the notion of "other-direction" as an incipient character type originating in the Northeast is probably more a consequence of the locale in which his early investigations were conducted than a reflection of the actual spread of "other-direction" in the United States. I am grateful to David Bakan for the presentation of this point of view.

3. [The author, in other words, found a 95% probability that at least two-thirds (67%) of children in the larger population would not know 'Trick.']

4. [Jose Ortega y Gasset, *The Revolt of the Masses* (New York, 1932).]

☆ • ☆ • ☆ • ☆ • ☆

The charm of Stone's piece should not beguile us from noting that he misunderstood an important aspect of *The Lonely Crowd*. Riesman did not say that American other-direction originated in the suburban Northeast; he did not explicitly connect it with suburbia but saw it more generally as a product of the metropolis, including Los Angeles and even a place like Cincinnati, admittedly quite suburban but hardly northeastern. Stone, in fact, shifts from saying that the Northeast has "exported" other-direction "westward and southward" to suggesting (see note 2) that the Midwest itself produces other-direction.

Stone might also have said more about the social-character aspects of changes in Halloween, in line with his basic support of Riesman's theory. He could have argued, for example, that the new victory of "treat" over "trick" went with eagerness to please and fear of personal conflict.

Without denigrating Stone's thoughtful conclusion to his essay, let me end with a little story about one result of his study, told to me by the sociologist Howard Becker. A bandleader asked Becker (who played piano in his group) for an example of "good sociology." Becker put him onto Stone's piece, and the bandleader was impressed—until Halloween. Confident in his new knowledge, he said, "Trick!" to a little apparition and received a hard jet of ink from a water pistol. When he called Becker to deliver some unprintable comments on Stone, it did not help much to tell the victim that he had just learned another lesson about the social sciences: they are not very good at making predictions, especially about individual cases. Fortunately, most of us do not have to find this out the hard way.

A Changing American Character?

In 1963, the political sociologist Seymour Martin Lipset published *The First New Nation,* a book explaining America's political culture—a unique system, as the author saw it, of values and institutions. Taking a long historical view, Lipset identified a small cluster of traditional ideas that, he said, were still powerful after centuries of economic and social change. He explored their effects on a range of institutions—especially parties, churches, and labor unions—and he made many comparisons with other countries, Old World and New.

"A Changing American Character?"—the essay reprinted here— is an important chapter in Lipset's book. It takes issue with David Riesman and William Whyte (pp. 50–86) on several counts. Fundamentally, Lipset says, American character has *not* changed, and social character depends less on economic trends and institutions than Riesman and Whyte had supposed—cultural values and attitudes have a momentum of their own. Americans have always been other-directed, though admittedly the growth of a service economy and big cities and organizations have made them more so.

Lipset was more of an optimist than Riesman and Whyte. He believed that other-directed bureaucrats could be productive achievers while having a good inner life. He did not reject Riesman's basic distinction between other- and inner-directed types, but he thought it was more useful in distinguishing Americans of any period from other people than modern Americans from their predecessors. In a later section of the book on political styles, Lipset contrasted American other-direction with French inner-direction. Democracy, he said, needed degrees of both.

Lipset followed Louis Hartz and other political/social theorists in arguing that the Revolution and the lack of a "feudal past" were largely responsible for making Americans unique. Although Lipset was keenly aware of economic and racial inequality in America, he opposed the Marxist belief that an economic class system (e.g., capitalism) largely determined people's attitudes. His original introduction to *The First New Nation* adroitly quotes Friedrich Engels himself, a close associate of Marx, to the effect that one still needed to look at traditional values to explain differences of attitude and behavior between countries with the same economic system.

This is exactly what Lipset tried to do in his book. His route to it came out of a precocious background in the late 1930s and early 1940s when he had been active in student socialism, first at his New York high school and then at City College of New York. His father, a member of the Typographical Union, was often unemployed during the depression; Lipset's first book, *Agrarian Socialism* (1950), on Canadian farm radicals, was dedicated to his father, "who shared the same dreams as the farmers of Saskatchewan."

Lipset's socialist background produced two issues that propelled him toward his work on American character. One was the old question: Why had socialism been so weak in the United States compared with other industrial democracies? This took Lipset into his comparisons with Canada and elsewhere. One factor often cited as a cause of socialist weakness in the United States is the belief that America is a 'land of opportunity,' where a person can move up the ladder by his own efforts. In his book of 1959, *Social Mobility in Industrial Society* (written with Reinhard Bendix), Lipset showed that upward mobility in the United States was not much greater than in Britain, say, or Japan. One reason, he argued, for the American *belief* in opportunity lay in the realm of myth, ideology, and the egalitarian manners Americans used toward each other. This was very much a social-character explanation, though Lipset recognized other factors, including the spectacle of economic growth, the availability of college education, and ethnicity (poverty could be attributed to racial inferiority or the temporary handicap of being a new immigrant).

The second issue propelling Lipset was, as it seemed to him, the authoritarianism of many leaders of politial parties, especially on the Left. Amid factional disputes—sharpened by the Soviet invasion of Finland in 1940—Lipset had joined other anti-Stalin radicals in blaming communist and socialist failures on the leadership. As Lipset's socialism gave way to a more conservative concern with "democratic stability," he published studies of "extremist" politics and the appeal of demagogues, from Father Coughlin to Senator McCarthy. This involved Lipset in the *psychology* that underlay political attitudes—he was particularly interested in anxieties about status. This theme, too, entered his work on national character.

☆ • ☆ • ☆ • ☆ • ☆

Two themes, equality and achievement, emerged from the interplay between the Puritan tradition and the Revolutionary ethos in the early formation of America's institutions.* . . . The dynamic interaction of these two predominant values has been a constant element in determining American institutions and behavior. As we have seen, equalitarianism was an explicit part of the revolt against the traditions of the Old World, while an emphasis upon success and hard work had long been a part of the Protestant ethic. In addition, the need to maximize talent in the new nation's search to "overtake" the Old World placed an added premium on an individual's achievement, regardless of his social station. The relatively few changes that Andrew Jackson made in the civil service, despite his aggressive equalitarian ethos, and the fact that his appointments were well-trained, highly educated men, show that ability was valued along with equality in the young republic.

The relationship between these themes of equality and success has been complex. On the one hand, the ideal of equal opportunity institutionalized the notion that success should be the goal of *all*, without reference to accidents of birth or class or color. On the other hand, in actual operation these two dominant values resulted in considerable conflict. While everyone was supposed to succeed, obviously certain persons were able to achieve greater success than others. The wealth of the nation was never distributed as equally as the political franchise. The tendency for the ideal of achievement to undermine the fact of equality, and to bring about a society with a distinct class character, has been checked by the recurrent victories of the forces of equality in the political order. Much of our political history, as Tocqueville noted, can be interpreted in terms of a struggle between proponents of democratic equality and would-be aristocracies of birth or wealth.[1]

In recent years, many social analysts have sought to show how the increasing industrialization, urbanization, and bureaucratization of American society have modified the values of equality and achievement. In both the 1930s and the 1950s American social scientists were certain that the country was undergoing major structural changes. In the 1930s they were sure that these changes were making status lines more rigid, that there was a movement away from achieved status back to ascribed status, and that the equalitarian ethic was threatened as a consequence. Such typical writers of the 1950s as David Riesman and William H. Whyte contend that it is the achievement motive and the Protestant ethic of hard work that are dying: they think that the new society prefers security, emotional stability, and "getting along with others." Riesman posits a transformation of the American character structure from "inner direction" (i.e., responding to a fixed internal code of morality) to "other direction" (i.e., responding to demands of others in complex situations). Whyte believes that values themselves have changed. He argues that the old value system of the Protestant ethic, which he defines as the "pursuit of individual salvation through hard work, thrift, and competitive struggle," is being replaced by the "social ethic," whose basic tenets are a "belief in the group as the source of creativity; a belief in 'belongingness' as the ultimate need of the individual; and a belief in the application of science to achieve the belongingness."[2]

If the changes suggested by the critics of the 1930s or the 1950s were occurring in the drastic form indicated in their books, then America no longer could be said to possess the traits formed as a consequence of its origin as a new nation with a Protestant culture. As I read the historical record, however, it suggests that there is more continuity than change with respect to the main elements in the national value system. This does not mean that our society is basically static. Clearly, there have been great secular changes—industrialization, bureaucratization, and urbanization are real enough—and they have profoundly affected other aspects of the social structure. Many American sociologists have documented changes in work habits, leisure, personality, family patterns, and so forth. But this very concentration on the obvious social changes in a society that has spanned a continent in a century, that has moved from a predominantly rural culture as recently as 1870 to a metropolitan culture in the 1950s, has introduced a fundamental bias against looking at what has been relatively constant and unchanging.

Basic alterations of social character or values are rarely produced by change in the means of production, distribution, and exchange alone. Rather, as a society becomes more complex, its institutional arrangements make adjustments to new conditions within the framework of a dominant value system. In turn, the new institutional patterns may affect the socialization process which, from infancy upward, instills fundamental character traits. Through such a process, changes in the dominant value system develop slowly—or not at all. There are constant efforts to fit the "new" technological world into the social patterns of the old, familiar world.

. . . It is the basic value system, as solidified in the early days of the new nation, which can account for the kinds of changes that have taken place in the American character and in American institutions as these faced the need to adjust to the requirements of an urban, industrial, and bureaucratic society.

Marcus Cunliffe has remarked on the American tendency to assert that a wondrous opportunity has been ruined, "that a golden age has been tarnished, that the old ways have disappeared, or that they offer no useful guide to a newer generation."[3] He points out that, American belief to the contrary, there has been surprising continuity in American history as compared with the histories of European nations. This American propensity to feel that the country is going through a major change at any "present time" is related to an almost "inherent American tendency to believe that one has been cut off decisively from the past as if by a physical barrier." Cunliffe attributes this tendency to three main elements:

> First it is a consequence of the undeniable fact of continuous and rapid social change since the origins of settlement. This process has, understandably, revealed itself in regrets and neuroses as well as in pride and exuberance. Second, the tendency is rooted in the constant American determination to repudiate Europe—Europe equated with the Past, in contrast with America as the Future—and so to lose the Past altogether. Third, the tendency is a consequence of the American sense of a society which is

uniquely free to choose its own destiny. The sense of mission, of dedication and of infinite possibility, in part a fact and in part an article of faith, has led to acute if temporary despairs, to suspicions of betrayal and the like, as well as to more positive and flamboyant results.[4]

In a sense, Cunliffe's analysis shows how some of the values we have seen arising from America's revolutionary origins continue to be a part of its image of itself. And perhaps more important, his observation that there has been more continuity in American history than in European history suggests that the values around which American institutions are built have not changed abruptly. Others have pointed out that America is an example of a country where social change does not have to destroy the fabric of society, precisely because it is based upon an ideological commitment to change.

The thesis that the same basic values which arose in the American Revolution have shaped the society under changing geographical and economic conditions, has also been advanced by many historians. Thus Henry Nash Smith has sought to show how the rural frontier settlements established in the West on the Great Plains reflected not only the physical environment but also "the assumptions and aspirations of a whole society."[5] He has argued that revisions in the Homestead Act, which would have permitted large farms and a more economical use of arid land, were opposed by the new settlers because they believed in the ideal of the family farm. Walt Rostow suggests there is a "classic American style [which] . . . emerged distinctively toward the end of the seventeenth century as the imperatives and opportunities of a wild but ample land began to assert themselves over various transplanted autocratic attitudes and institutions which proved inappropriate to the colonial scene . . . [and] came fully to life . . . after the War of 1812." And he further contends that this style has not changed basically, since "the cast of American values and institutions and the tendency to adapt them by cumulative experiment rather than to change them radically has been progressively strengthened by the image of the gathering success of the American adventure."[6] Commager, writing of America in general, has said: "Circumstances change profoundly, but the character of the American people has not changed greatly or the nature of the principles of conduct, public and private, to which they subscribe." Three books dealing with American values, by Daniel Boorstin, Louis Hartz, and

Ralph Gabriel, have each, in a different way, argued the effective continuity of the fundamental ideals of the society.[7]

The conclusions of these historians are affirmed also in a "lexicographic analysis of alleged American characteristics, ideals, and principles" reported in a myriad of books and articles dealing with "the American way." American history was divided for the purposes of the study into four periods, "Pre–Civil War (to 1865), Civil War to World War (1866–1917), World War to Depression (1918–1929), and Depression to present (1930–1940)." For each period a list of traits alleged by observers was recorded, and "when the lists for each of the four time periods were compared, no important difference between the traits mentioned by modern observers and those writing in the earlier periods of American history was discovered." Among the traits mentioned in all four periods were "Belief in equality of all as a fact and as a right" and "uniformity and conformity."[8]

The Unchanging American Character

Foreign travelers' accounts of American life, manners, and character traits constitute a body of evidence with which to test the thesis that the American character has been transformed during the past century and a half. Their observations provide us with a kind of comparative mirror in which we can look at ourselves over time. It is important to note, therefore, that the type of behavior which Riesman and Whyte regard as distinctly modern, as reflecting the decline of the Protestant ethic, was repeatedly reported by many of the nineteenth-century travelers as a peculiarly American trait in their day. Thus the English writer Harriet Martineau at times might be paraphrasing *The Lonely Crowd* in her description of the American of the 1830s:

> [Americans] may travel over the world, and find no society but their own which will submit to the restraint of perpetual caution, and reference to the opinions of others. They may travel over the whole world, and find no country but their own where the very children beware of getting into scrapes, and talk of the effect of actions upon people's minds: where the youth of society determine in silence what opinions they shall bring forward, and what avow only in the family circle; where women write miserable letters, almost universally, because it is a settled matter that it is unsafe

to commit oneself on paper; and where elderly people seem to lack almost universally that faith in principles which inspires a free expression of them at any time, and under all circumstances . . .

There is fear of vulgarity, fear of responsibility; and above all, fear of singularity. . . . There is something little short of disgusting to the stranger who has been unused to witness such want of social confidence, in the caution which presents probably the strongest aspect of selfishness that he has ever seen. The Americans of the northern states are, from education and habit, as accustomed to the caution of which I speak, as to be unaware of its extent and singularity . . .

Few persons [Americans] really doubt this when the plain case is set down before them. They agree to it in church on Sundays, and in conversation by the fireside: and the reason why they are so backward as they are to act upon it in the world, is that habit and education are too strong for them. They have worn their chains so long that they feel them less than might be supposed.[9]

Harriet Martineau is only one observer of early American life, and not necessarily more reliable than others. But it is significant that her comments on American "other-directedness" and conformism do not flow, as do those of other nineteenth-century visitors who made comparable observations, from fear or dislike of democracy. Many upper-class visitors, such as Tocqueville or Ostrogorski, saw here a threat to genuine individuality and creativity in political and intellectual life, in that democracy and equalitarianism give the masses access to elites, so that the latter must be slaves to public opinion in order to survive. Harriet Martineau, as a left-wing English liberal, did not come to America with such fears or beliefs. She remained an ardent admirer of American democracy, even though she ultimately decided that "the worship of Opinion is, at this day, the established religion of the United States."[10]

The most celebrated post–Civil War nineteenth-century English visitor to America, James Bryce, saw inherent in American society "self-distruct, a despondency, a disposition to fall into line, to acquiesce in the dominant opinion. . . ." This "tendency to acquiescence and submission" is not to be "confounded with the tyranny of the majority. . . . [It] does not imply any compulsion exerted by the majority," in the sense discussed by Tocqueville. Rather Bryce, like Harriet Martineau fifty years earlier, described what he felt to be a basic psychological trait of Americans, their "fatalism," which involved a "loss of resisting power, a diminished sense of personal responsibility, and of the duty to battle for one's own opinions. . . ."[11]

Although Harriet Martineau and James Bryce stand out among nineteenth-century visitors in specifying that these other-directed traits were deeply rooted in the *personalities* of many Americans, the general *behaviors* that they and Tocqueville reported were mentioned by many other foreign travelers. For example, a summary of the writings of English travelers from 1785 to 1835 states that one important characteristic mentioned in a number of books "was the acute sensitiveness to opinion that the average American revealed."[12] A German aristocrat, who became a devotee of American democracy and a citizen of the country, stated in the 1830s that "nothing can excite the contempt of an educated European more than the continual fears and apprehensions in which even the 'most enlightened citizens' of the United States seem to live with regard to their next neighbors, lest their actions, principles, opinions, and beliefs should be condemned by their fellow creatures."[13] An interpreter of nineteenth-century foreign opinion, John Graham Brooks, mentions various other writers who noted the unwillingness of Americans to be critical of each other. He quotes James Muirhead, the English editor of the *Baedeker* guide to the United States, as saying: "Americans invented the slang word 'kicker,' but so far as I could see their vocabulary is here miles ahead of their practice; they dream noble deeds, but do not do them; Englishmen 'kick' much better without having a name for it." Brooks suggested that it was the American "hesitation to face unpleasant facts rather than be disagreeable and pugnacious about them, after the genius of our English cousins, that calls out the criticism."[14]

The observation that the early Americans were cautious and sensitive has been made not only by foreign visitors but also, at different times, by Americans—as in fact many of the foreign authors report. In 1898, the American writer John Jay Chapman echoed Tocqueville's dictum of seventy years before, that he knew "of no country in which there is so little independence of mind and real freedom of discussion as in America." Chapman saw the general caution and desire to please as the source of many of the ills of his day:

> "Live and let live," says our genial prudence. Well enough, but mark the event. No one ever lost his social standing merely because of his offenses,

but because of the talk about them. As free speech goes out the rascals come in.

Speech is a great part of social life, but not the whole of it. Dress, bearing, expression, betray a man, customs show character, all these various utterances mingle and merge into the general tone which is the voice of a national temperament; private motive is lost in it.

This tone penetrates and envelops everything in America. It is impossible to condemn it altogether. This desire to please, which has so much of the shopman's smile in it, graduates at one end of the scale into a general kindliness, into public benefactions, hospitals, and college foundations; at the other end it is seen melting into a desire to efface one's self rather than give offense, to hide rather than be noticed.

In Europe, the men in the pit at the theatre stand up between the acts, face the house, and examine the audience at leisure. The American dares not do this. He cannot stand the isolation, nor the publicity. The American in a horse car can give his seat to a lady, but dares not raise his voice while the conductor tramps over his toes.[15]

Although these accounts by travelers and American essayists cannot be taken as conclusive proof of an unchanging American character, they do suggest that the hypothesis which sees the American character changing with respect to the traits "inner-" and "other-directedness" may be incorrect.

The Unchanging American Values
and Their Connection with American Character

The foreign travelers were also impressed by the American insistence on equality in social relations, and on achievement in one's career. Indeed, many perceived an intimate connection between the other-directed behavior they witnessed and the prevalence of these values, such that the behavior could not be understood without reference to them. An analysis of the writings of hundreds of British travelers in America before the Civil War reports: "Most prominent of the many impressions that Britons took back with them [between 1836 and 1860] was the aggressive egalitarianism of the people."[16] If one studies the writings of such celebrated European visitors as Harriet Martineau, the Trollopes (both mother and son), Tocqueville, or James Bryce, it is easy to find many observations documenting this point.

Baedeker's advice to any European planning to visit the United States in the late nineteenth or early twentieth century was that he "should, from the outset, reconcile himself to the absence of deference, or servility, on the part of those he considers his social inferiors."[17] A detailed examination of the comments of European visitors from 1890 to 1910 reports general agreement concerning the depth and character of American equalitarianism:

> Whether they liked what they saw or not, most foreign observers did not doubt that America was a democratic society. . . . Different occupations of course, brought differences in prestige, but neither the occupation nor the prestige implied any fundamental difference in the value of individuals. . . . The similarity of conclusions based on diverse observations was simply another indication of the absence of sharp class differences. Even hostile visitors confirmed this judgment. . . . Some foreign observers found the arrogance of American workers intolerable.[18]

Even today this contrast between Europe and America with respect to patterns of equality in interpersonal relations among men of different social positions is striking. A comparison of writings of European visitors at the turn of this century with those made by British groups visiting here to study American industrial methods since World War II states that "the foreign descriptions of . . . America in 1890 and 1950 are remarkably similar. . . . The British teams [in the 1950s reported] . . . the same values . . . which impressed visitors a half century ago. Like them they found the American worker is more nearly the equal of other members of society than the European, with respect not only to his material prosperity, but also to . . . the attitudes of others toward him."[19] And this attitude is apparent at other levels of American society as well. As one commentator put it when describing the high-status Europeans who have come to America in recent years as political refugees from Nazism and Communism:

> With his deep sense of class and status, integration in American society is not easy for the émigré. The skilled engineer or physician who . . . finally establishes himself in his profession, discovers that he does not enjoy the same exalted status that he would have had in the old country. I met several young Croatian doctors in the Los Angeles area who were earning $25,000 to $35,000 a year, but still felt declassed.[20]

American emphasis on equalitarianism as a dominant value is significant in determining what to many of the Europeans were three closely related processes: competition, status uncertainty, and conformity. Tocqueville, for example, argued that equalitarianism maximizes competition among the members of a society. But if equalitarianism fosters competition for status, the combination of the two values of equality and achievement results, according to many of the travelers, in an amorphous social structure in which individuals are uncertain about their social position. In fact, those travelers who were so impressed with the pervasive equalitarianism of American society also suggested that, *precisely as a result of the emphasis on equality and opportunity,* Americans were *more* status-conscious than those who lived in the more aristocratic societies of Europe. They believed, for example, that it was easier for the *nouveaux riches* to be accepted in European high society than in American. British travelers before the Civil War noted that Americans seemed to love titles more than Englishmen. European observers, from Harriet Martineau and Frances Trollope in the 1830s to James Bryce in the 1880s and Denis Brogan in recent years, have pointed out that the actual strength of equality as a dominant American value—with the consequent lack of any well-defined deference structure linked to a legitimate aristocratic tradition where the propriety of social ranking is unquestioned—forces Americans to *emphasize* status background and symbolism. As Brogan has remarked, the American value system has formed "a society which, despite all efforts of school, advertising, clubs and the rest, makes the creation of effective social barriers difficult and their maintenance a perpetually repeated task. American social fences have to be continually repaired; in England they are like wild hedges, they grow if left alone."[21]

Status-striving and the resultant conformism have not been limited solely, or even primarily, to the more well-to-do classes in American society. Many of the early nineteenth-century travelers commented on the extent to which workers attempted to imitate middle-class styles of life. Smuts notes that visitors at the turn of this century were struck by "what they regarded as the spend-thrift pattern of the American worker's life"; Paul Bourget, a French observer, interpreted this behavior as reflecting "the profound feeling of equality [in America which] urges them to make a show." As Werner Sombart, the German sociologist and economist, put it, "since all are seeking success . . . everyone is forced into a struggle to beat every other individual; and a steeple-chase begins . . . that differs from all other races in that the goal is not fixed but constantly moves even further away from the runners." And in an equalitarian democracy "the universal striving for success [becomes a major cause of] . . . the worker's extravagance, for, as Münsterberg [a German psychologist] pointed out, the ability to spend was the only public sign of success at earning."[22] And lest it be thought that such concerns with conspicuous consumption emerged only in the Gilded Age of the 1890s as analyzed by Veblen, sixty years earlier a medical study of the "Influence of Trades, Professions, and Occupations, in the United States, in the Production of Disease," described and analyzed behavior in much the same terms:

> The population of the United States is beyond that of other countries an anxious one. All classes are either striving after wealth, or endeavoring to keep up its appearance. From the principle of imitation which is implanted in all of us, sharpened perhaps by the existing equality of conditions, the poor follow as closely as they are able the habits and manner of living of the rich. . . . From these causes, and perhaps from the nature of our political institutions, and the effects arising from them, we are an anxious, care-worn people.[23]

While some Europeans explained American behavior that they found strange—the sensitivity, kindliness, concern for others' feelings, and moral meekness—by reference to the nature of political democracy or the overbearing desire to make money, others saw these traits as consequences of the extreme emphasis on equality of opportunity, the basic American value which they properly regarded as unique. Many argued that this very emphasis on equality, and the constant challenging of any pretensions to permanent high status, has made Americans in all social positions extremely sensitive to the opinions of others, and causes status aspirants greater anxiety about the behavior and characteristics indicative of rank than is the case with their counterparts in more aristocratic societies. Discussing the writings of various travelers, John Graham Brooks states:

> One deeper reason why the English are blunt and abrupt about their rights . . . is because class lines are more sharply drawn there. Within these

limits, one is likely to develop the habit of demanding his dues. He insists on his prerogatives all the more because they are narrowly defined. When an English writer (Jowett) says, "We are not nearly so much afraid of one another as you are in the States," he expressed this truth. In a democracy every one at least hopes to get on and up. This ascent depends not upon the favor of a class, but upon the good-will of the whole. This social whole has to be conciliated. It must be conciliated in both directions—at the top and at the bottom. To make one's self conspicuous and disagreeable, is to arouse enmities that block one's way.[24]

One may find an elaboration of this causal analysis among many writers at different periods. Thus Max Weber, after a visit to America in the early 1900s, noted the high degree of "submission to fashion in America, to a degree unknown in Germany" and explained it in terms of the lack of inherited class status.[25] Seven decades earlier another German, Francis Grund, who saw in American equality and democracy the hope of the world, nevertheless also believed that the ambiguous class structure made status-striving tantamount to conformity. He presents both sides of the picture in the following items:

> Society in America . . . is characterized by a spirit of exclusiveness and persecution unknown in any other country. Its gradations not being regulated according to rank and title, selfishness and conceit are its principal elements . . . What man is there in this city [New York] that dares to be independent, at the risk of being considered bad company? And who can venture to infringe upon a single rule of society?
>
> This habit of conforming to each other's opinions, and the penalty set upon every transgression of that kind, are sufficient to prevent a man from wearing a coat cut in a different fashion, or a shirt collar no longer *à la mode*, or, in fact, to do, say, or appear anything which could render him unpopular among a certain set. In no other place, I believe, is there such a stress laid upon "saving appearances."[26]

James Bryce, a half-century later, also linked conformity to the ambiguity of the status system, particularly as it affected the wealthy classes. He pointed out that it was precisely the emphasis on equality, and the absence of well-defined rules of deference, which made Americans so concerned with the behavior of others and seemingly more, rather than less, snobbish toward each other than were comparably placed Englishmen.

It may seem a paradox to observe that a millionaire has a better and easier social career open to him in England, than in America . . . In America, if his private character be bad, if he be mean or openly immoral, or personally vulgar, or dishonest, the best society may keep its doors closed against him. In England great wealth, skillfully employed, will more readily force these doors to open. . . . The existence of a system of artificial rank enables a stamp to be given to base metal in Europe which cannot be given in a thoroughly republican country.[27]

In comparing the reactions of Englishmen and Americans to criticism, James Muirhead (the editor of the American *Baedeker*) stated that "the Briton's indifference to criticism is linked to the fact of caste, that it frankly and even brutally asserts the essential inequality of man. . . . Social adaptability is not his [the Briton's] foible. He accepts the conventionality of his class and wears it as an impenetrable armor."[28]

A number of the foreign travelers, particularly those who visited America after the 1880s, were startled to find overt signs of anti-Semitism, such as placards barring Jews from upper-class resorts and social clubs which denied them membership. But this, too, could be perceived as a consequence of the fact that "the very absence of titular distinction often causes the lines to be more clearly drawn; as Mr. Charles Dudley Warner says: 'Popular commingling in pleasure resorts is safe enough in aristocratic countries, but it will not answer in a republic.' "[29] The most recent effort by a sociologist, Howard Brotz, to account for the greater concern about close contact with Jews in America than in England, also suggests that "in a democracy snobbishness can be far more vicious than in an aristocracy."

Lacking that natural confirmation of superiority which political authority alone can give, the rich and particularly the new rich, feel threatened by mere contact with their inferiors. . . . Nothing could be more fantastic than this to an English lord living in the country in the midst, not of other peers, but of his tenants. His position is such that he is at ease in the presence of members of the lower classes and in associating with them in recreation. . . . It is this "democratic" attitude which, in the first instance, makes for an openness to social relations with Jews. One cannot be declassed, so to speak, by play activities.[30]

The intimate connection between other-directedness and equalitarian values perceived by these observers recalls the same connection noted by Plato in his theoretical analysis of democracy. In *The Republic* we find these words:

> [In a democracy, the father] accustoms himself to become like his child and to fear his sons. . . . Metic [resident alien] is like citizen and citizen like metic, and stranger like both. . . . The schoolmaster fears and flatters his pupils. . . . The young act like their seniors, and compete with them in speech and action, while the old men condescend to the young and become triumphs of versatility and wit, imitating their juniors in order to avoid the appearance of being sour or despotic. . . . And the wonderful equality of law and . . . liberty prevails in the mutual relations of men and women . . . the main result of all these things, taken together, is that it makes the souls of the citizens so sensitive that they take offense and will not put up with the faintest suspicion of slavery [strong authority] that anyone may introduce.[31]

Plato's analysis points up the main question to which this chapter is addressed: Are the conformity and the sensitivity to others—"other directedness"—observed in the contemporary American character solely a function of the technology and social structure of a bureaucratic, industrialized, urban society, as Riesman and Whyte imply, or are they also to some considerable degree an expected consequence of a social system founded upon the values of equality and achievement? It seems that sociological theory, especially as expounded by Max Weber and Talcott Parsons, and much historical and comparative evidence, lend credence to the belief that the basic value system is at least a major, if not the preeminent, source of these traits.

As Plato noted, and as the foreign travelers testify, democratic man is deeply imbued with the desire to accommodate to others, which results in kindness and generosity in personal relations, and in a reluctance to offend. All books that are published are "exalted to the skies," teachers "admire their pupils," and flattery is general.[32] The travelers also bear out Plato's remarks about the socialization of children in a democracy. It appears that equalitarian principles were applied to child-rearing early in the history of the republic. Early British opinions of American children have a modern flavor:

> The independence and maturity of American children furnished another surprise for the British visitor. Children ripened early. . . . But such precosity, some visitors feared, was too often achieved at the loss of paren-

tal control. Combe claimed that discipline was lacking in the home, and children did what they pleased. Marryat corroborated this. . . . Children were not whipped here [as in England], but treated like rational beings.[33]

Harriet Martineau's description of child-rearing in the America of Andrew Jackson sounds like a commentary on the progressive other-directed parent of the mid-twentieth century:

> My [parent] friend observed that the only thing to be done [in child-rearing] is to avoid to the utmost the exercise of authority, and to make children friends from the very beginning. . . . They [the parents] do not lay aside their democratic principles in this relation, more than in others. . . . They watch and guard: they remove stumbling blocks: they manifest approbation and disapprobation: they express wishes, but, at the same time, study the wishes of their little people: they leave as much as possible to natural retribution: they impose no opinions, and quarrel with none: in short, they exercise the tenderest friendship without presuming upon it. . . . The children of Americans have the advantage of the best possible early discipline; that of activity and self-dependence.[34]

What struck the democratic Miss Martineau as progressive was interpreted quite differently by Anthony Trollope, who visited this country in 1860: "I must protest that American babies are an unhappy race. They eat and drink as they please; they are never punished; they are never banished, snubbed, and kept in the background as children are kept with us."[35] And forty years later, another English visitor, typical of the many who described American child-parent relations during a century and a half, tells us that nowhere else, as in America, "is the child so constantly in evidence; nowhere are his wishes so carefully consulted; nowhere is he allowed to make his mark so strongly on society. . . . The theory of the equality of man is rampant in the nursery. . . . You will actually hear an American mother say of a child of two or three years of age: 'I can't *induce* him to do this. . . .' "[36]

If these reports from the middle and late nineteenth century are reminiscent of contemporary views, it is still more amazing to find, in a systematic summary of English travelers' opinion *in the last part of the eighteenth and early years of the nineteenth centuries*, that the emphasis on equality and democracy had *already* created the distinctive American child-oriented family which astonished the later visitors:

A close connection was made by the stranger between the republican form of government and the unlimited liberty which was allowed the younger generation. . . . They were rarely punished at home, and strict discipline was not tolerated in the schools. . . . It was feared that respect for elders or for any other form of authority would soon be eliminated from American life. . . . As he could not be punished in the school, he learned to regard his teacher as an inferior and to disregard all law and order.[37]

Equality was thus perceived by many of the foreign travelers as affecting the socialization of the child not only within the family but in the school as well. The German psychologist Hugo Münsterberg joins the late–eighteenth-century visitors in complaining, over a century later in 1900, that "the feeling of equality will crop up where nature designed none, as for instance between youth and mature years. . . . Parents even make it a principle to implore and persuade their children, holding it to be a mistake to compel or punish them; and they believe that the schools should be conducted in the same spirit."[38] Various visitors were struck by the extent to which the schools did carry out this objective. The following description by an Englishman of schools in the New York area in 1833 sounds particularly modern:

The pupils are entirely independent of their teacher. No correction, no coercion, no manner of restraint is permitted to be used. . . . Parents also have as little control over their offspring at home, as the master has at school. . . . Corporal punishment has almost disappeared from American day-schools; and a teacher, who should now give recourse at such means of enforcing instruction, would meet with reprehension from the parents and perhaps retaliation from his scholars.[39]

Tocqueville also found examples of the American's mistrust of authority "even in the schools," where he marveled that "the children in their games are wont to submit to rules which they have themselves established."[40]

The educational policies which have become linked with the name of John Dewey and labeled "progressive education" actually began in a number of school systems around the country long before Dewey wrote on the subject: "To name but one example, the lower schools of St. Louis had adopted a system intended to develop spontaneously the inventive and intellectual faculties of the children by the use of games and with no formal teaching of ideas, no matter how practical."[41]

The Inadequacy of a Materialistic
Interpretation of Change

Many of the foreign observers referred to above explained the other-directedness and status-seeking of Americans by the prevalence of the twin values of equality and achievement. Character and behavior were thus explained by values. They pointed out that the ethic of equality not only pervaded status relations but that it influenced the principal spheres of socialization, the family, and the school, as well.

Both Whyte's and Riesman's arguments, in contrast, explain character and values by reference to the supposed demands of a certain type of economy and its unique organization. The economy, in order to be productive, requires certain types of individuals, and requires that they hold certain values. In the final analysis, theirs is a purely materialistic interpretation of social phenomena and is open to the criticisms to which such interpretations are susceptible.

The inadequacy of such an explanation of change in values and social character is best demonstrated by comparative analysis. British and Swedish societies, for example, have for many decades possessed occupational structures similar to that of America. Britain, in fact, reached the stage of an advanced industrial society, thoroughly urbanized, where the majority of the population worked for big business or government, long before any other nation. The occupational profiles of Sweden, Germany, and the United States have been similar for decades. If the casual connection between technology and social character were direct, then the patterns described as typical of "other-direction" or "the organization man" should have occurred in Great Britain prior to their occurrence in the United States, and should now be found to predominate in other European nations. Yet "other-direction" and the "social ethic" appear to be pre-eminently American traits. In Europe, one sees the continued, even though declining, strength of deferential norms, enjoining conformity to class standards of behavior.

Thus, comparative analysis strikingly suggests that the derivation of social character almost exclusively from the traits associated with occupational or population profiles is invalid. So important an element in a social system as social character must be deeply affected by the dominant value system. For the value system is perhaps the most enduring part of what we think of as society, or a social system. Comparative history shows that nations may still present striking differences, even when their technological, demographic, or political patterns are similar. Thus it is necessary to work out the implications of the value system within a given material setting—while always observing, of course, the gradual, cumulative effect that technological change has upon values.

In attempting to determine how American values have been intertwined with the profound changes that have taken place in American society, it is not sufficient to point out that American values are peculiarly congenial to change. Although equality and achievement have reinforced each other over the course of American history, they have never been entirely compatible either. Many of the changes that have taken place in family structure, education, religion, and "culture," as America has become a "modern" society, have manifested themselves in a constant conflict between the democratic equalitarianism, proclaimed as a national ideal in the basic documents of the American Revolution, and the strong emphasis on competition, success, and the acquisition of status—the achievement orientation—which is also deeply embedded in our national value system.

Richard Hofstadter has urged the recurring pattern of value *conflict* and *continuity* in commenting on papers presented at a conference on changes in American society:

> Culturally and anthropologically, human societies are cast in a great variety of molds, but once a society has been cast in its mold—Mr. Rostow is right that our mold as a nation was established by the early nineteenth century—the number of ways in which, short of dire calamity, it will alter its pattern are rather limited. I find it helpful also to point to another principle upon which Mr. Rostow has remarked—the frequency with which commentators find societies having certain paradox polarities in them. . . . We may find in this something functional; that is, *Societies have a need to find ways of checking their own tendencies. In these polarities there may be something of a clue to social systems. . . .*
>
> Mr. Kluckhohn's report contains some evidence that we have already passed the peak of this shift about which I have been speaking. I find some additional evidence myself in the growing revolt of middle-class parents

against those practices in our education that seem to sacrifice individualism and creativity for adjustment and group values. Granted the initial polarities of the success ethic, which is one of the molds in which our society is cast, this ethic must in some way give rise, sooner or later, to a reaction. . . . I do not think that we must be persuaded that our system of values has ceased to operate.[42]

The analyses of American history and culture in the nineteenth and twentieth centuries, by both foreign and native interpreters, often differ according to whether they stress democracy and equality, or capitalism and achievement. Generally, conservatives have found fault with the decline of individuality and the pampering of children, and have seen both as manifestations of democracy and equality; while liberals have noted, with dismay, tendencies toward inequality and aristocracy, and have blamed them upon the growth of big business. These contrary political philosophies have also characterized the interpretation of American culture that predominates at any given period. Arthur Schlesinger, Sr., has even tried to measure the systematic characteristic duration of the "epochs of radicalism and conservatism [that] have followed each other in alternating order" in American history.[43]

A cursory examination of the numerous differences between the conclusions of American social scientists in the 1930s and in the 1950s shows the way in which interpretation of American culture vary with social conditions. Writers of the 1930s amassed evidence of the decline of equalitarianism and the effect of this on a variety of institutions. Karen Horney in *The Neurotic Personality of Our Time,* for example, named anxiety over chances of economic success as the curse of what she, with many of her contemporaries, regarded as a completely pecuniary, achievement-oriented culture dominated by the giant corporations. Such analysts as Robert S. Lynd and W. L. Warner all agreed that the egalitarian emphasis in American democracy was declining sharply under the growth of the large-scale corporation, monopoly capitalism, and economic competition. They asserted categorically that mobility had decreased, and Warner predicted the development of rigid status lines based on family background.

Twenty years later, these interpretations are almost unanimously rejected. Warner himself in one of his most recent works shows that chances of rising into the top echelons of the largest corporations are *greater* than they were in the 1920s. As indicated earlier in this chapter, typical writers of the 1950s are concerned that the emphasis on achievement in American society may be dying out.

In large measure, the difference between writers of the two decades reflects the contrast between the economic circumstances of the times. The depression of the 1930s inclined intellectuals toward an equalitarian radicalism, which condemned capitalism and achievement orientation as the source of evils. Even a conservative like Warner was led to emphasize the growth of inequality and the restriction of opportunity. The prosperity of the 1950s, however, renewed the legitimacy of many conservative institutions and values, and discredited some of the innovations of the previous decades. The social analyses of the 1950s, even those written by men who still considered themselves liberals or socialists, involved at least a critique of the radical excesses of the former period, if not a critique of equalitarian values themselves. Perhaps the similarity in attitudes between the analysts of the 1950s and many of the foreign travelers of the last century is due to the fact that most of the European visitors have been conservatives, or members of the elite of much more aristocratic societies, and the modern Americans reflect the post-war revival of conservative values.

While Riesman and Whyte would deny that their works contain conservative value preferences, and insist that they are simply analyzing changes, it seems fairly evident that like the more elitist travelers of the nineteenth century, they deplore many of the dominant trends. They point to the spread of progressive education, with its disbelief in rewards for hard work, as illustrating the decay of the Protestant ethic, and they assume, as a result of this, a decline in the opportunity for developing creativity. Whyte points to the shift in scientific research from individual to group projects, which in his opinion are less creative. Neither Riesman nor Whyte explicitly asserts that there is more conformity now than in the past, for the reason that men have always conformed to the values of the day; but both argue that contemporary values and personality traits emphasize accommodation to others, while the declining Protestant ethic and the inner-directed character structure stressed conformity to a fixed rule of conduct rather than to the fluctuating actions and moods of others.

This reaction against the apparent decline of the Protestant ethic of achievement and hard work, which has become a dominant theme among

119

the intellectual middle class of the 1950s and early 1960s, should be viewed as the counterpart of the concern with the seeming breakdown of equality which moved comparable groups in the 1930s. The differences in the concerns of the two periods illustrate the important point that although the equalitarian ethos of the American Revolution and the achievement orientation of the Protestant ethic are mutually supporting, they also involve normative conflict. Complete commitment to equality involves rejecting some of the implications of valuing achievement; and the opposite is also true. Thus, when the equalitarianism of left or liberal politics is dominant, there is a reaction against achievement, and when the values of achievement prevail in a conservative political and economic atmosphere, men tend to depreciate some of the consequences of equality, such as the influence of popular taste on culture.

The supremacy of equalitarian values and liberal politics in the 1930s was reflected in the school system in the triumph of progressive education, a cause always associated with left-of-center leaders and ideologies; in industry, by the introduction of the human relations approach as an attempt to "keep the worker happy"; and in the society at large by efforts toward a general redistribution of goods and services. Social scientists and others interested in family structure criticized the supposedly typical middle-class family as too authoritarian and rigid in its treatment of children, suggesting that, in contrast to the more democratic and affectionate working-class family, it bred "authoritarian" and "neurotic" personalities. Popular psychology saw the "competitive personality" of our time as the source of many personal and social evils. Historians pictured the creators of American industry as "robber barons" and as irresponsible exploiters of American resources.

This equalitarian liberalism was perhaps strongest in the school system, where educators carried the ideal of equal treatment to a point where even intellectual differences were ignored. Special encouragement of the gifted child was regarded as an unfair privilege that inflicted psychic punishment on the less gifted: personality adjustment for *all* became the objective. In New York City, Fiorello La Guardia, the militant progressive mayor, abolished Townsend Harris High School—a special school for gifted boys in which four years of work was completed in three—on the grounds that the very existence of such a school was undemocratic, because it conferred special privileges on a minority.*

In the prosperous 1950s and 1960s, these tendencies have been almost completely reversed. Big business and business careers once more have become legitimate. The Republicans held office in the 1950s, and centrists rather than liberals dominate the revived Democratic Party of the 1960s. Although Keynesian economics has remained official government policy, and is still supported by most economists, some leading members of that profession have emerged who oppose almost all government intervention. Studies of the social structure of the family have reversed the findings of the 1930s, suggesting that it is the working-class family that is more likely to be a source of "authoritarian" personality traits. Vulgarizations of the theses of Riesman and Whyte have been published in many magazines and are cited at P.T.A. meetings all over the country, where outraged middle-class parents demand a return to "old-fashioned" methods of teaching, in which hard work is rewarded and the gifted receive special attention. Many middle-class parents have placed their children in private schools. While the rapid growth of private schools in large part stems from the increasing prosperity of the country, it also reflects the desire of middle-class parents that their children receive an elite education.

The political battle between the reactions stemming from the prewar depression and those reflecting the postwar prosperity, between equality and achievement, has been most conspicuously joined today in the debate over schools. As the "progressive educationalists" begin to counterattack, they appeal specifically to the values of equality and democracy. A speech by Professor A. Harry Passow of Columbia University Teachers' College attacked a proposal to create twenty-five elite high schools for gifted children in the following terms: "It is a perversion of democracy to set aside certain youngsters and give them privileges which automatically set them apart as an elite group of society. It goes against the basic idea of American education, which is to give all children an equal opportunity for the best possible education."[44]

A leading expert, who has testified before congressional committees for the past twenty years or more concerning the need for educational research, once reported that when a committee was discussing research on

*This was Lipset's high school.

121

underprivileged or mentally deficient children, the Democrats on the committee would exhibit great interest; but when the committee turned to the question of the gifted child, the Republicans perked up and the Democrats sat back. The two parties did not, of course, oppose each other formally on these questions, since both favored research on all questions; but Republicans were simply more interested in *achievement,* or the problem of the gifted child, while Democrats were more interested in *equality,* or the problem of the underprivileged.

To stress the coincidence of these differing interpretations of American social trends with the political and economic cycle is not to suggest that they are simply ideological reflections of material conditions or of the climate of opinion. Most of them have pointed out genuine aspects of the culture, and in so doing have improved our understanding of the functions of different institutions and values. Both strands, the equalitarian and the achievement-oriented, remain strong, but changing conditions sometimes fortify one at the expense of the other, or alter the internal content of each. Thus opportunity, as measured by the chances of success in building up a major enterprise of one's own, has given way to opportunity measured by advancement in the bureaucratic elites. The politics of liberalism and equality have fostered institutional changes, such as the constant spread of public education and of training facilities within corporations, which have increased opportunities for advancement.

Conclusion

This chapter essentially has urged that a materialistic interpretation of American society sharply underestimates the extent to which basic national values, once institutionalized, give shape to the consequences of technological and economic change. Clearly, many nations may be described as urbanized, industrialized, and capitalist, but they vary considerably in their status systems, their political institutions, parent-child relations, and so forth. The absence of a feudal past, with a concomitant emphasis on equality of manners and of opportunity, has played a major role in differentiating American behavior from that of other nations.

On the other hand, it may be argued that the entire Western world has been moving in the American direction in their patterns of class relationships, family structure, and "other-directedness," and that America, which was democratic and equalitarian before industrialization, has merely led the way in these patterns. Thus, at any given time, the differences between America and much of Europe may have remained constant, but this difference might have represented little more than a time lag.

If one compares the America of the 1960s with the America of the 1880s or the 1830s, one would undoubtedly note changes in the direction suggested by Riesman. The vast majority of early– and mid–nineteenth-century Americans were self-employed and lived on farms or in small towns, while today most people are employees and live in cities. This change alone has many consequences along the lines suggested by *The Lonely Crowd:*

> We can contrast the small grocer who must please his individual patrons, perhaps by a "counter-side manner," with the chain-store employee who must please both the patrons and his co-workers. . . . The colleague, like the peer-grouper, is the very person with whom one engages in competition for the *scarce commodity of approval* and the very person to whom one looks for guidance as to what is desirable.[45]

The entrepreneur becomes an "other-directed person [who] gives up the one-face policy of the inner-directed man for a multiface policy that he sets in secrecy and varies with each set of encounters."[46] An employee has less freedom and motivation to be individualistic than does the self-employed. Farm and small-town dwellers know each other as total human beings rather than as actors in specific relations, and are presumably less motivated to exhibit status-seeking or to seek the good opinion of those whom they have known all their lives and who are "significant others" in a variety of limited contexts. Residents of small communities are judged by their total background and personal history and by any specific set of acts. As many sociological studies of such communities have revealed, they tend to have a relatively static status system, permitting much less social mobility than that occurring in large cities. Consequently, the resident of the small town tends to be somewhat like the citizens of more rigidly stratified European states. The awareness of the relative permanence of status position reduces the anxiety to win the good opinion of others that exists where status is less stable.

There can be little question that Riesman and Whyte are right also in showing how bureaucratization and urbanization *reinforce* those social mechanisms which breed other-directedness. Success in a bureaucracy, and in the proliferating service occupations of modern society, depends primarily on the ability to get along well with others.

But it cannot be stressed too often that these mechanisms operate within the context of an historic American value-system and status structure that had also generated such traits in a non-bureaucratic and non-urban society. Other-direction, or, to put it less dramatically, sensitivity to the judgments of others, is an epiphenomenon of the American equalitarian ethos, of the opportunities for rapid status mobility, *and* of the general growth of an urban, bureaucratic society. The increasing complexity introduced by industrialization and urbanization makes adherence to a rigid normative code obsolete, because such a code cannot be used as a guide to the great variety of situations confronting modern, bureaucratic man. This Riesman and Whyte have well noted. However, the greater flexibility and need to adapt to others that are demanded by urban and bureaucratic life add to an already existing disposition to be concerned with the opinions of others, a disposition caused by equalitarianism and by the emphasis placed on social mobility.

Even despite the changes brought about by urbanization and bureaucratization, Americans still appear to be quite achievement oriented when compared to persons from more status-bound nations. Foreign travelers are still struck by the individual American's striving to get ahead. Indeed, there is some evidence that the higher valuation placed on social skills in present American socialization practices is precisely oriented toward upward social mobility in contemporary society. A study comparing British and American beliefs about socialization points out that while it places "getting along with others" as the most important aim of socialization, the American pattern differs from the British in that it aims "at a smoothly functioning individual, equipped for getting ahead with a varied armament of social skills."[47]

Some evidence that achievement still ranks high in the United States as compared to other nations may be seen in the data from a comparative study of the attitudes of school youth in five countries—the United States, Norway, West Germany, England, and France. Surprisingly, at least so far as concerns the expectations of the researchers,

American children were less "other-directed" than those in the European countries, except Norway, as judged by their responses to the question: "Would you rather be the most popular person in your class or the one who gets the highest grades?" Among both ten-year-olds and fourteen-year-olds, Americans were more likely to prefer high grades to popularity than were German, English, and French youth.

Another indicator of the relatively high level of concern for academic achievement may be seen in the response to a question concerning anxiety over school examinations. American and French youth led in the proportion who reported worrying about exams (63 per cent); Norwegians were slightly less anxious as a group (60 per cent), while English and German students showed considerably less concern (48 and 28 per cent).

Comparative evidence that achievement orientation and other-directedness may, in fact, be mutually reinforcing has been presented by David McClelland as a conclusion of his extensive comparative studies of the psychological processes which are related to economic development. He suggests that " 'other-directedness' is an essential feature of rapid economic development even in its early stages, rather than a special feature of advanced urban culture in the United States as Riesman suggests."[48] As he puts it:

> [W]hat a modern society needs for successful development is flexibility in a man's role relationships. His entire network of relations to others should not be traditionally determined by his caste or even his occupational sta-

Preference for Highest Grades Rather Than Popularity
Among Students in Five Nations

Nation	Percent Preferring Highest Grades		
	10 Year Olds	14 Year Olds	Combined Ages
Norway	86%	83%	85%
United States	82	63	73
West Germany	62	50	56
England	63	45	54
France	53	30	42

Source: George Gallup and Evan Hill, "Is European Education Better than Ours?" *Saturday Evening Post* 233 (Dec. 24, 1960), p. 70.

tus. . . . The transition to the new order is certainly likely to be helped if people can learn to listen to what "other people" say is the right thing to do.[49]

An increase in other-directedness helps facilitate economic development by making individuals more receptive to "the opinion of the 'generalized other.'" It creates greater willingness to accept new norms or techniques, and it helps reduce particularistic ties, thus facilitating the operation of pure market criteria.

To test the hypothesis of the interrelationship of other-directedness and achievement orientation, McClelland analyzed children's readers from over thirty countries in 1925 and 1950 by coding the themes of the stories in terms of measures of other-directedness and achievement motivation. Countries were then classified as above or below the median score for other-directedness and achievement motivation in each period. Nations could be categorized as high on both dimensions, low on both, or high on one and low on the other. Looking then at the various countries and the extent to which they grew economically during the succeeding years (as indicated by growth in electric power), McClelland found that nations which were high on both factors greatly outperformed countries which were low on both, "whereas those that were high on one and low on the other showed an average gain somewhere in between."[50]

It may come as something of a shock to realize that more could have been learned about the rate of future economic growth of a number of these countries in 1925 or 1950 by reading elementary school books than by studying such presumably more relevant matters as power politics, wars and depressions, economic statistics, or government policies governing international trade, taxation, or public finance. The reason apparently lies in the fact that the readers reflect sufficiently accurately the motives and values of key groups of men in a country which *in the long run* determine the general drift of economic and political decisions and their effect on productivity. Economic and political policies are of course the means by which economic change is brought about, but whether policies will be implemented, or even decided on in the first place, appears to depend ultimately on the motives and values of men as we have succeeded in detecting them in the stories which they think it is right for their children to read.[51]

The two orientations of other-directedness and achievement motivation, therefore, may be viewed as mutually supportive, rather than, as Riesman and Whyte suggest, mutually contradictory.

The concern with specifying how various structural changes have weakened the Protestant ethic or inner-directed traits in American life has led Riesman and others sometimes to ignore the beneficial consequences of these changes. Thus, I have pointed out elsewhere that while bureaucratization results in a heightened need to make personality adjustments to win the esteem of colleagues and supervisors, it also sets bounds to arbitrary power. By establishing rules of fair treatment, and by reducing the area of personal discretion in personnel policy, bureaucracy can reduce the fear of the employer or of the supervisor. Trade unions, found most commonly under conditions of large industry, accurately reflect their members' desires when their policies involve more, rather than less, bureaucratization of factory life. (As an example of this, unions have sought seniority rules in hiring, firing, and promoting, which increase bureaucratization and reduce arbitrary power.)

Similarly, it may be urged that some of the consequences of bureaucratization reinforce, rather than weaken, strong work and achievement orientations, particularly—but not exclusively—in the upper echelons of white-collar and executive life. The shift from the family-owned company to the management-run corporation, as Whyte pointed out, has made group activities and adjustment to group norms seem more important than before. But whatever else group dynamics in industry may be concerned with, it certainly provides an excellent way of getting men to work hard for the company. Traditionally, it has been a postulate of business management, and an empirical finding of industrial sociology, that men do not work as hard as they are able when the rewards of their work seem to be going to others. Holding other factors constant, no one works so hard as the head of an organization, or the self-employed or the creative professional who is directly rewarded for his labors. By extending the control of work to committees at different levels in the corporation, contemporary American business has found a means of inculcating into a large number of people a sense of responsibility for the whole organization. "Non-owners" now feel individually responsible, and the number of hard-working executives who never watch the clock, and who take work home with them, has been enormously enlarged. Thus, while other-direction may have increased, the motivation for competition and hard work remains, because the best are chosen to move up the bureaucratic hierarchy.

It is a peculiar paradox that the same structural processes may account for diverse and even sharply conflicting tendencies. Many analyses of American society have stressed the fact that individualism *and* conformism, creative innovation *and* dominance by low-level mass taste, are outgrowths of identical forces. For example, the pronounced spread of higher education and a high standard of living have caused an unprecedented increase in both the proportion of the population involved in genuinely creative, intellectual activities, and the influence by the populace on the major expressions of art, literature, and drama. Alexis de Tocqueville was fully aware of these dual tendencies when he pointed out that "the same equality that renders him [the American] independent of each of his fellow citizens, taken severally, exposes him alone and unprotected to the influence of the greater number. . . . I very clearly discern two tendencies; one leading the mind of every man to untried thoughts, the other prohibiting him from thinking at all."[52]

Today, too, there are many trends making for an increase in autonomous behavior, in free choice. Various social scientists have recently begun to document these countervailing tendencies, a phenomenon that may reflect the ever-present cyclical pattern of social analysis. Rowland Berthoff points to the seeming "gradual decline since 1920 of those make-shift communities, the fraternal lodges," which were part of the associational pattern that impressed Tocqueville, and suggests that "the psychic energy that Americans formerly expended on maintaining the jerry-built framework of such 'institutions' as these has in our more assured institutional structure of recent years been freed, at least potentially, for the creation of more valuable kinds of 'culture.' " He also infers that "the recent popular success of books deploring the unworthiness of status striving indicates that Americans are throwing off this obsession and making it, as in other societies, including pre-industrial America, merely one concern among many."[53] Robert Wood suggests, in the same vein, that "the pattern of inconspicuous consumption, the web of friendship, and the outgoing life that Whyte describes also have something of the flavor of a renaissance. Although 'keeping down with the Joneses' may indicate group tyranny, it is still better than keeping up with them. At least it displays disapproval of overt snobbishness. . . . While Whyte finds pressures for benevolent conformity, he also discovers brotherhood."[54] Daniel Bell has argued that the growth in education, among other factors, has reduced conformity. He comments that "one would be hard put to find today the 'conformity' *Main Street* exacted of Carol Kennicott thirty years ago. With rising educational levels, more individuals are able to indulge a wider variety of interests," such as serious music, good books, high-level FM radio, and the like.[55]

It may be fitting to conclude this chapter with the paradox formulated by Clyde Kluckhohn, who has suggested:

> Today's kind of "conformity" may actually be a step toward more genuine individuality in the United States. "Conformity" is less of a personal and psychological problem—less tinged with anxiety and guilt. . . . If someone accepts outwardly the conventions of one's group, one may have greater psychic energy to develop and fulfill one's private potentialities as a unique person. I have encountered no substantial evidence that this "conformity" is thoroughgoingly "inward."[56]

As status-seeking is the by-product of strong equalitarianism, so conformity and other-directedness may permit, or even demand, inner autonomy. . . .

NOTES

[These notes are reduced to basic references, largely as abridged in *The Character of Americans*, ed., Michael McGiffert (Homewood, Il, 1970). The original publication has more complete notes: see Lipset, *First New Nation* (1963, 1979), chap. 3.]

1. Alexis de Tocqueville, *Democracy in America*, 2 vols. (Paris and London, 1835, 1840).

2. David Riesman, *The Lonely Crowd* (New Haven, Conn., 1950). William H. Whyte, *The Organization Man* (New York, 1956).

3. Marcus Cunliffe, "American Watersheds," *American Quarterly* 13 (1961), pp. 479–94.

4. Ibid., pp. 489–90.

5. Henry Nash Smith, *Virgin Land: The American West as Symbol and Myth* (Cambridge, Mass., 1950), p. 12.

6. W. W. Rostow, "The National Style," in *The American Style: Essays in Value and Performance*, ed. Elting E. Morison (New York, 1958), pp. 247, 259.

7. Henry Steele Commager, *Living Ideas in America* (New York, 1951), p. xviii; Daniel Boorstin, *The Genius of American Politics* (Chicago, 1953); Boorstin, *The Lost World of Thomas Jefferson* (New York, 1948); Louis M. Hartz, *The Liberal Tradition in America: An Interpretation of American Thought since the Revolution* (New York, 1955); Ralph H. Gabriel, *The Course of American Democratic Thought* (New York, 1956).

8. Lee Coleman, "What Is American? A Study of Alleged American Traits," *Social Forces* 19 (1941), pp. 492–99.

9. Harriet Martineau, *Society in America*, vol. 3 (New York, 1837), pp. 14–15, 17.

10. Ibid., p. 7.

11. James Bryce, *The American Commonwealth*, Macmillan ed., vol. 2 (New York, 1912), pp. 351–52.

12. Jane L. Mesick, *The English Traveller in America 1785–1835* (New York, 1922), p. 301.

13. Francis J. Grund, *Aristocracy in America: From the Sketch-book of a German Nobleman*, Harper ed. (New York, 1959), p. 162.

14. J. G. Brooks, *As Others See Us* (New York, 1908), p. 95.

15. *The Selected Writings of John Jay Chapman*, ed. Jacques Barzun (New York, 1959), p. 278.

16. Max Berger, *The British Traveller in America, 1836–1860* (New York, 1943), pp. 54–55.

17. Quoted by Philip Burne-Jones, *Dollars and Democracy* (London, 1904), p. 69.

18. Robert W. Smuts, *European Impressions of the American Worker* (New York, 1953), pp. 3–7.

19. Ibid., p. 54.

20. Bogden Raditsa, "Clash of Two Immigrant Generations," *Commentary* 25 (1958), p. 12.

21. Denis W. Brogan, *The English People* (London, 1943), p. 99.

22. Smuts, *European Impressions of the American Worker*, p. 13.

23. Benjamin McCready, "On the Influence of Trades, Professions, and Occupations in the United States, in the Production of Disease," *Transactions of the Medical Society of the State of New York* (1836–1837), vol. 3, pp. 146–47.

24. Brooks, *As Others See Us*, p. 97.

25. H. H. Gerth and C. Wright Mills, eds., *From Max Weber: Essays in Sociology* (New York, 1946), p. 188.

26. Grund, *Aristocracy in America*, pp. 52, 157.

27. Bryce, *The American Commonwealth*, vol. 2, p. 815.

28. James Fullerton Muirhead, *America, the Land of Contrasts: A Briton's View of His American Kin* (London, 1898), p. 91.

29. Ibid., p. 27.

30. Howard Brotz, "The Position of the Jews in English Society," *Jewish Journal of Sociology* 1 (1959), p. 97.

31. Plato, *The Republic*, ed. Ernest Rhys (London, 1935), pp. 200–26.

32. Martineau, *Society in America*, vol. 3, pp. 63–64.

33. Berger, *The British Traveller in America*, pp. 83–84.

34. Martineau, *Society in America*, pp. 168, 177.

35. Anthony Trollope, *North America* (New York, 1951), p. 142.

36. Muirhead, *America, The Land of Contrasts*, pp. 67–68. (Emphasis in original.)

37. Mesick, *The English Traveller in America*, pp. 83–84.

38. Hugo Münsterberg, *The Americans* (New York, 1904), p. 28.

39. Isaac Fidler, *Observations in Professions, Literature, Manners and Emigration, in the United States and Canada, Made During a Residence There in 1832* (New York, 1833), pp. 40–41.

40. Tocqueville, *Democracy in America*, Vintage ed., vol. 1 (New York, 1954), p. 198.

41. Andrew J. Torrielli, *Italian Opinion on America as Revealed by Italian Travelers, 1850–1900* (Cambridge, Mass., 1941), p. 115.

42. Richard Hofstadter, "Commentary: Have There Been Discernible Shifts in Values During the Past Generation?" in *The American Style: Essays in Value and Performance*, ed. Elting E. Morison (New York, 1958), p. 357. (Emphasis mine.)

43. Arthur M. Schlesinger, Sr., *New Viewpoints in American History* (New York, 1922), p. 123.

44. See "Plan of Schools for 'Elite' Scored," *New York Times* (Mar. 25, 1958), p. 25.

45. Riesman, *The Lonely Crowd*, p. 140. (Emphasis mine.)

46. Ibid., p. 147.

47. Maurice L. Farber, "English and American Values in the Socialization Process," *Journal of Psychology* 36 (1953), pp. 243–50.

48. David C. McClelland, *The Achieving Society* (Princeton, N.J., 1961), p. 192.

49. Ibid., p. 194.

50. Ibid., pp. 201–202.

51. Ibid., p. 202.

52. Tocqueville, *Democracy in America*, vol. 1, p. 12.

53. Rowland Berthoff, "The American Social Order: A Conservative Hypothesis," *American Historical Review* 65 (1960), p. 512.

54. Robert Wood, *Suburbia: Its People and Their Politics* (Boston, 1959), p. 15.

55. Daniel Bell, "The Theory of Mass Society," *Commentary* 22 (1956), p. 82.

56. Clyde Kluckhohn, "Have There Been Discernible Shifts in American Values during the Past Generation?" in *The American Style*, ed. Morison, p. 187.

Although Lipset centered American character and culture on very few basic values, he discussed these with range and sophistication. As I noted in the general introduction to this volume, Lipset was rare among writers on American character in making systematic comparisons between the United States and other countries. He used attitude surveys as well as foreign visitors' narratives, though, curiously, his comparisons with Canada and Australia near the end of the book did not employ survey data.

Using an excellent array of quotations, Lipset makes a good case that other-direction, in Riesman's sense of that term, goes back into the nineteenth century. (See especially his quotation on p. 107 from John Jay Chapman: "the shopman's smile . . .") Ironically, Lipset may concede too much to Riesman when he acknowledges that the modern chain-store employee may have to be more other-directed than the old-style grocer. My own observation of a very traditional village in Exmoor, England, is that keepers of the village shop, who have to live with their customers, day in and day out, must be the soul of tact and human relations.

Like Tocqueville, Lipset was interested in the way Americans combined individualist striving with sociable conformity, and a spirit of equality with status-seeking snobbery. His own discussion of this puts together two lines of thinking. The first, pursued by H. L. Mencken and George Jean Nathan in the 1920s and James Truslow Adams and Francis Hsu in the 1940s and 1950s, held that the drive to achieve and climb socially led Americans to identify with superior status-groups and distance themselves from those below. In the opinion of Hsu, a Chinese-American anthropologist, this explained a lot of American racism.

The second line of thought, represented in the late 1940s by Ralph Barton Perry (p. 33) and the British political scientist Harold Laski, took note of conformity too but also stressed that Americans teamed up to get things done: they got together to realize their opportunities.

In his essay here, and elsewhere, Lipset essentially recognizes three kinds of equality—equal *opportunity* to seek society's rewards; equal economic and social *condition* (little difference between people in wealth and status); and equality of *manners* (in which people act as equals toward each other, without social deference or a superior manner). Lipset implies that American traditional values endorse equality of opportunity and manners rather than condition; Americans have often supported equal opportunity to win *unequal* rewards. But he does not discuss these distinctions until the book's last chapter (not excerpted here).

Nor does Lipset say much about gender. Written on the eve of the 1960s women's movement, his book did not observe that American men had seldom extended their ideas of equality to women. The book as a whole said more about blacks and immigrants; at the time of writing, the civil rights movement was well under way.

Historically, Lipset's essay jumped too fast from the Revolutionary era to the 'common man' 1830s (when in fact economic inequality was growing), and despite his reference to David McClelland on the character needs of rapid economic growth, he made little real concession to the formative effect of American history after the Revolution. His idea of what made Americans unique restricts itself too much to a founding ideology.

DAVID M. POTTER

American Women and the American Character

O n the last page of Lipset's *The First New Nation* (excerpted previously), he acknowledged that a more *economic* explanation of "American values and behavior" was still possible. He noted in this regard David Potter's book of 1954, *People of Plenty: Economic Abundance and the American Character.*

Of all modern writing on American character, *People of Plenty* seems to draw the most praise from American historians. A respected historian himself, Potter discussed the history of different approaches to national character before giving his own ideas about the manifold effects of American-style abundance. Potter's explanation was not totally materialist: he believed that an aptitude for organizing technology was needed to bring forth the country's natural wealth and give it the power to affect lives. He was vague, however, about the sources of that aptitude.

On several counts, in fact, *People of Plenty* is equivocal, even muddled. In a chapter on advertising, Potter says Americans have long enjoyed abundance, but he also agrees with David Riesman that Americans have moved from a culture of scarcity and production to one of abundance and consumption. Elsewhere in the book he declares that widespread abundance excites competition; he then hopes that even greater abundance will moderate it. *People of Plenty* was not Potter's masterpiece; it was, rather, his first step in a series of studies of American character that became more rigorous.

From the start of his career in the 1930s to his death in 1971, David Potter was a historian of the South and the national conflicts that led to civil war. Born and educated in Georgia, he spent most of his working life in the North, at Yale until 1961 and then at Stanford. His first wife, also a southerner, was a psychologist, but David Potter was always skeptical about assigning great influence to psychological motives and ideologies. Yet his background also encouraged an interest in social character.

Race, status, violence, sex—the historic entwining of these in southern white attitudes had given a strong psychological slant to some studies of southern society. In the early 1940s, Potter showed interest in this writing: the classic, *Caste and Class in a Southern Town* (1937) was written by Potter's Yale colleague, the psychologist John Dollard. Potter was also fascinated by another classic, W. J. Cash's *The Mind of the South* (1941). In thinking about the South, its history, and its fraught relations with the North, Potter wrote about sectionalism, nationalism, and problems of generalizing about regions and countries. By the mid-1950s, though, he believed that the different regions of the United States were growing more alike.

In short, Potter's background and temperament made him aware of the attractions as well as the problems of studying social character; it also impelled him to transcend the South and interpret the nation as a whole. By most southern standards in the 1930s he was an out-of-place liberal; but he never felt himself to be a northerner.

Throughout his career Potter was interested in how historians could use the social sciences. This soon led him into economic history as well as sociology and psychology—hence the economic theme in *People of Plenty*. That book, Potter hoped, would succeed Frederick Jackson Turner's famous 'frontier' explanation of American history and character. In Potter's view, the most important aspect of the frontier mentioned by Turner was the plenteousness of land. Potter's "abundance" corresponded to this but was not restricted to land or the frontier.

Like *People of Plenty*, the essay reprinted here on "American Women and the American Character" made much of economic forces. Both studies discussed the effects of technology and of advertising. In the 1950s the power of advertising became a popular concern, as shown by the impact of Vance Packard's book, *The Hidden Persuaders* (1957).

But Potter's essay broke newer ground than this. Originating as a lecture at Stetson University in 1959, it anticipated many of the things feminists would say in the 1960s and 1970s about women's work and status. On first impressions Potter looked an unlikely prophet of

135

feminists. He remained in many ways a southern gentleman, and *People of Plenty* only discussed women in the context of child-rearing. He did, though, give a Delphic explanation of how he came to do the essay on American women. When a faculty wife at Stanford asked him just this question, Potter replied, "Well, you see, I have a daughter."

☆ · ☆ · ☆ · ☆ · ☆

There is an old riddle which children used to ask one another concerning two Indians.* One was a big Indian, the other was a little Indian, and they were sitting on a fence. The little Indian, the riddle tells us, was the big Indian's son, but the big Indian, was not the little Indian's father. How, asks the riddle, can this be?

Boys and girls for a long time have found that this riddle succeeds very well in mystifying many people. And the fact that it does presents another puzzle as to why the riddle is hard to answer. If we were to state the question in more general terms: there are two human beings, one adult and one child; the child is the son of the adult, but the adult is not the father of the child, probably no one would have much difficulty in recognizing that the adult is the mother. Why then do the Indians on a fence perplex us? If we examine the structure of the riddle, I think we will find that it contains two devices which inhibit our recognition that the big Indian is a female. First, the two Indians are described as being in a very specific situation—they are sitting on a fence. But women, at least in our culture, do not usually sit on fences; if the two Indians had been roasting some ears of corn, or mending their teepee, how much easier the riddle would have been. Second, we are perhaps especially prone to think of Indians as masculine. If the riddle had said two South Sea Islanders, or perhaps, two Circassians, the possibility of their being female might occur to us much more easily.

But most of all, the riddle owes its baffling effect to the fact that our social generalization is mostly in masculine terms. If we said that the little Indian is the big Indian's daughter, but that the big Indian is not the little

*"American Women and American Character" by David M. Potter, *Stetson University Bulletin*, July 1962, pp. 1–22, reprinted in John A. Hague, ed., *American Character and Culture: Some Twentieth Century Perspectives* (DeLand, FL: Everett Edwards Press, 1964), pp. 65–84. Reprinted by permission of Stetson University.

Indian's mother, the possibility that the big Indian is the father would come to mind readily enough. For in our culture, men are still in a general category, while women are in a special category. When we speak of mankind, we mean men and women collectively, but when we speak of womenkind, we mean the ladies, God bless them. The word humanity is itself derived from *homo,* that is man, and the species is *Homo sapiens.* Neuter nouns or general nouns which are ambiguous as to sex—nouns like infant, baby, child, sibling, adolescent, adult, spouse, parent, citizen, person, individual, etc.—all take masculine pronouns. In our culture, a woman, at marriage takes her husband's name. Though born a Cabot, if she marries Joe Doaks, Mrs. Joe Doaks she becomes and Mrs. Doaks she remains, usually for the rest of her life.

This masculine orientation is to be expected, of course, in a society which is traditionally and culturally male-dominated—in what we call a patriarchal rather than a matriarchal society. Even women themselves have connived at maintaining the notion of masculine ascendancy, and in the rather numerous concrete situations in which they actually dominate their men, they often dissimulate their control by pretending to be weak, dependent, or "flighty." In such a situation one must expect that men will be regarded as the normative figures in the society, and that, in popular thought at least, the qualities of the masculine component in the society will pass for the qualities of the society as a whole.

If this habit were confined to popular thought, it would hardly be worth examining. But it also sometimes creeps into academic and scholarly thought, which ought to have more rigor, and when it does so, it can sometimes distort our picture of society. Thus a writer may sometimes make observations on the traits or values of American men, and then may generalize these as the traits or values of the American people. If he did this deliberately, on the theory that since male values dominate the society, they must therefore be American values, we would have to concede that he is aware of what he is doing, even though we might question his results. But when he does so unconsciously, his method may easily lead him to assume first that since American men are dominant, the characteristics of American men are the characteristics of the American people, and that since women are people, the characteristics of the American people are the characteristics of American women, or in short, that the characteristics of American men are the characteristics of American women.

To avoid this trap, when one meets with a social generalization it is frequently worthwhile to ask concretely: Does it apply to women, or only to the masculine component in the population? Does the statement that Prussians are domineering mean that Prussian women are domineering, or only Prussian men? Does the statement that Americans are individualistic mean American women as well as American men? The question seems worth asking, for it appears more than possible that many of our social generalizations which are stated sweepingly to cover the entire society are in fact based on the masculine population, and that if we took the feminine population into account, the generalization might have to be qualified, or might even run in an entirely different direction.

A notable example of this can perhaps be found in Frederick Jackson Turner's famous frontier hypothesis, stated so brilliantly at Chicago almost seventy years ago. The gist of Turner's argument was, of course, that the frontier had been a basic influence in shaping the character of the American people. Primarily, as he saw it, the frontier provided economic opportunity in the form of free land. When this free land was suddenly conferred upon a people who had previously been held in dependence by the land monopolies of the Old World, it made the American economically independent and this independence made him more individualistic and more egalitarian in his attitudes. Also, the necessity for subduing the wilderness by his own personal exertions, in a situation where he could not call upon doctors, dentists, policemen, lawyers, contractors, well-drillers, repairmen, soil analysts, and other specialists to aid him, made him more self-reliant.

Not even Turner's harshest critics deny that there was much truth in his observations, but many of them have pointed to his lack of precision, and it is fair to question to what extent Turner's generalizations applied to all frontier people, or to what extent they applied restrictively to frontier men. Sometimes it becomes clear that the life-process which he identifies with the frontier was primarily though not wholly an experience shared by men rather than by women. There is one famous passage, for instance, which begins, "The wilderness masters the colonist." Now *colonist* is a neuter noun, and could apply to a female colonist. But the passage continues to say that the wilderness, finding the colonist "European in dress, industry, modes of travel, and thought, . . . takes him from the railroad car and puts him in a birch canoe [This sounds progressively less as if it could be a woman.]. It strips off the garments of civilization and arrays him in the hunting shirt and the moccasin." Soon, this colonist hears the call of the wild almost as clearly as Jack London's dog, and when he does, "he shouts the war cry and takes the scalp in orthodox Indian fashion."[1] Here, at least, the pioneer in question is hardly a woman.

Certainly it is true that the frontier offered economic opportunity, and certainly, also, frontier women shared in some of the social consequences which flowed from the fact that this opportunity was available to their men. But is it not true, in cold fact, that the opportunities offered by the West were opportunities for men and not, in any direct sense, opportunities for women? The free acres of the West were valuable to those who could clear, and break, and plow and harvest them. But clearing and breaking, plowing and harvesting were men's work, in which women rarely participated. The nuggets of gold in the streambeds of California in 1849 represented opportunity to those who could prospect for them. But the life of the prospector and the sourdough was not a woman's life, and the opportunities were not women's opportunities. Similarly, the grass-covered plateau of the Great Plains represented economic opportunity for those who could use it as an open range for the holding and grazing of Longhorn cattle. But the individuals who could do this were men; the Cattle Kingdom was a man's world. Thus, when Turner says that "so long as free land exists, the opportunity for a competency exists," he means, in effect, an opportunity for males.

Again, it may bear repeating, there is no question here that the frontier influenced women as well as men. It had its Molly Pitcher and its Jemima Boone, as well as its Davy Crockett, and its Kit Carson. It left its stamp upon the pioneer women as well as the pioneer men. But when Turner states that it furnished "a new field of opportunity, a gate of escape from the bondage of the past," one must ask, exactly what was the nature of women's participation in this opportunity? Before this question can be analyzed, it is perhaps necessary to recognize that women's place in our society is invariably complicated by the fact that they have, as men do not, a dual status. Almost every woman shares the status of the men in her family—her father or her husband—and if this is a privileged position, she is a recipient of some of the privilege. This is an affiliated status, but if her men gain, she gains with them. Thus, if her family became landowners on the frontier, she participated in their advancement, and no one can deny that free land was, in this indirect sense, opportunity for her also. But woman also has a personal status, which is a sex status, as a female. As a female, on the frontier, women were especially dependent upon having a man in the family, for there was no division of labor there, as there was in settled communities, and most of the tasks of the frontier—the hunting, the wood-chopping, the plowing— could hardly be performed by women, though many of them, of course, rose to these tasks in time of emergency. In fact, the frontier was brutally harsh for females, and it furnished its own verdict on its differential impact upon the sexes. "This country," said the frontier aphorism, "is all right for men and dogs, but it's hell on women and horses."

If we accept Turner's own assumption that economic opportunity is what matters, and that the frontier was significant as the context within which economic opportunity occurred, then we must observe that for American women, as individuals, opportunity began pretty much where the frontier left off. For opportunity lay in access to independent employment, and the employments of the frontier were not primarily accessible to women. But in the growing cities, opportunities for female employment began to proliferate. Where the work of the frontier called for the strong back and the powerful muscles of a primeval man, the work of the city—clerical work, secretarial work, the tending of machines—has called for the supple fingers and the ready adaptability of a young woman, and it was in this environment, for the first time in America, that women found on any scale worth mentioning, access to independent earning power. Once a woman possessed access to such earning power, whether she used it or not, the historic basis for her traditional subordination had been swept away. The male monopoly upon jobs was broken, and the breaking of this monopoly was no less significant for American women than the breaking of the landlord's monopoly upon fertile soil had been for American pioneer men. As a symbol, the typewriter evokes fewer emotions than the plow, but like the plow, it played a vital part in the fulfillment of the American promise of opportunity and independence. The wilderness may have been the frontier for American men, and the cabin in the clearing the symbol of their independence, but the city was the frontier for American women and the business office was what gave them economic independence and the opportunity to follow a course of their own.

———

Another social generalization which is often stated as if it applied to all Americans, men and women alike, is that our society has experienced a vast transformation in the occupational activities of its people, and that we have passed from the independent, self-directed work, of the kind done by a landowning farmer, to the regimented, externally-directed activity of the employee who labors for pay. In 1850, 63% of the gainfully employed workers in the United States were engaged in agriculture, and a high proportion of these were landowning farmers—perhaps as nearly independent as people can be. In the past the farmer, more than most of his fellows, was in position to plan, decide, and act for himself—to maintain his own values without regard for the approval or disapproval of his fellow man, to work at his own pace, to set his own routine. But today, as the census figures show, the American who labors is no longer self-employed. In 1958, it was estimated that 50,000,000 people gainfully employed in the United States received salaries or wages, while only 8,000,000 were self-employed, which means that in general the American worker does not work for himself. He works under direction in an office or a factory. He does not decide what to do, when to do it, or for what purpose, but he waits for instructions which come to him through channels. Even the junior executive, despite his prestige, is no more a self-employed man than the factory worker, and if we may believe *The Organization Man* [see pp. 70], he is in fact considerably less independent after hours. With these ideas in mind, we speak in broad terms about the disappearance of the old forms of autonomous, self-directed activity.

Yet none of this applies in any sense to women, except for women who are employees, and although female employment has increased steadily to a point where nearly one-third of all women are employed it is still true that two out of three American women are not employees, but find their occupation chiefly in the maintaining of homes and the rearing of children. Millions of housewives continue to exercise personal choice and decision not only in arranging their own time-table and routine but also in deciding what food the family shall have and how it shall be

141

prepared, what articles of purchase shall have the highest priority on the family budget, and, in short, how the home shall be operated. Despite strong tendencies toward conformity in American life, it is clear that American women exercise a very wide latitude of decision in these matters, and everyone knows that there are great variations between the regimes in various American homes. Indeed it seems fairly evident that the housewife of today, with the wide range of consumer goods available for her purchase and the wide variety of mechanical devices to free her from drudgery, has a far broader set of alternatives for her household procedure than the farm wife of two or three generations ago.[2] Moreover there are now great numbers of women working independently in their own homes, who a generation ago would have been working very much under direction as domestic servants in the homes of other women. If we based our social generalizations upon the experience of women rather than that of men, we might drop the familiar observation about the decreasing independence of Americans in their occupational pursuits. Instead we might emphasize that in the largest single occupational group in the country—the group which cooks and keeps house and rears children—there is a far greater measure of independent and self-directed work than there was in the past.

Closely connected to this question of the disappearance of the independent worker is another commonplace generalization, namely that the American people have become the victims of extreme specialization. Everyone is familiar with the burden of this lament: American industry has forced the craftsman to abandon his craft, and with it the satisfaction of creative labor, and has reduced him to operating a machine or to performing a single operation on the assembly-line as if he were a machine himself. Further, the complaint continues, modern conditions provide fewer and fewer opportunities for a worker to be an all-round person of varied skills and resources, as the American farmer used to be, and instead conditions make of him a diminished person, a narrow specialist hardly fit for anything save his narrow specialty.

Despite the exaggerated and somewhat hackneyed character of this outcry, it contains an important element of truth as regards the work of American male workers. But this generalization, too, is in fact applicable largely to the male component in the population rather than to the American people as a whole. For the American housewife is not a specialist, and in fact her modern role requires that she be far more versatile than her grandmother was, despite the greater skill of the grandmother in cooking, sewing, and other household crafts. A good housewife today must not only serve food to please the family palate, but must also know about calories, vitamins, and the principles of a balanced diet. She must also be an economist, both in her knowledge of the quality of the products offered to her and in her ability to do the impossible with a budget. She must not only maintain a comfortable home, but must also possess enough skill in interior decoration to assure that her own ménage will not seem dowdy or unappealing by comparison with the latest interiors shown in Hollywood films. She must not only rear children, but must also have mastered enough child psychology to be able to spare the rod and still not spoil the child. She must not only get the children ready for school, but must also, in many cases, act as a kind of transportation manager, participating in an elaborate car pool to convey them to and fro. In addition to all this, society now enjoins her not to rely upon the marriage vows to hold her husband, but to keep her personality and her appearance so attractive that he will have no incentive to stray. Whatever else she may be, she is certainly not a specialist, and even if she fails to meet all these varied demands upon her, her mere effort to do so would remove her from the category of specialists. If we based our social generalizations upon women rather than upon men, we might quite justifiably affirm that the modern age is an age of diversified activity rather than an age of specialization.

The profound differences between the patterns of men's work and women's work are seldom understood by most men, and perhaps even by most women. In terms of the time-tables of life, however, the contrasts are almost startling. For instance, man usually begins work in the early twenties, labors at precisely timed intervals for eight hours a day and five days a week, until he is sixty-five, when his life as a worker may be cut off with brutal abruptness and he is left idle. Woman, also usually begins work in the early twenties, perhaps in an office on the same time-table as a man, but after a very few years she becomes a wife, whose work is keeping house, and a mother whose work is rearing children. As such she labors often for from fifty-one to fifty-six hours a week, and she does not have the alternation of work and leisure which helps to lend variety and pace to the life of her husband. Her work load will continue to be heavier than her husband's until the children are older, after which it will gradually diminish, and she may ultimately re-enter employment. But most women do not; they continue to keep house.[3] And as long as a woman does keep house, either as a wife or as a widow, she never experiences the traumatic, sudden transition from daily work as the focus of life to enforced idleness—the transition which we call retirement.

———

Another far-reaching consequence of the difference between man's work and woman's work is forcibly expressed in a public interest advertisement in *Harper's Magazine* by Frank R. Neu, entitled "We May Be Sitting Ourselves to Death." Neu presents some very impressive data about the poor physical fitness of a large percentage of American men, and about the deleterious effects of the sedentary life of Mr. Joe Citizen as an office worker whose principal exercise is to go around a golf course on an electric cart on the week-end. Then Mr. Neu says, "Let's consider Jill, Joe's wife, for a moment. Chances are, on the basis of current statistics, Jill will outlive Joe by anywhere from five to twenty-five years. Medical science is not sure yet whether this is because Jill has different hormones from Joe or whether it is a result of the different roles which Joe and Jill fulfill in our society.

"The average suburban Jill is likely to be a homemaker responsible for rearing two or more children. It is safe to assume that any woman with this responsibility is going to get a lot of daily exercise no matter how many gadgets she has to help her do the housework. A homemaker does a lot of walking each day merely to push the buttons and start the machines that wash the clothes, cook the meals, and remove the dust. And she also does a good deal of bending each day to pick up after Joe and the junior members of the family. All in all, Jill is likely to get much more exercise than Joe. This may have a significant relationship to Jill's outliving Joe, who no longer hikes the dusty trail to bring home the buffalo meat and hides to feed and clothe his family."[4]

In the light of differences so great that they may radically alter the duration of life, it is again evident that a serious fallacy results when generalizations derived from the experience of American men are applied indiscriminately to the American people in such a way as to exclude the experience of American women.

As a further illustration of the readiness with which one can fall into a fallacy in this way, let me suggest one more generalization about Americans which has been widely popular in recent years. This is the proposition, formulated by David Riesman in *The Lonely Crowd*, that the American has been transformed, in the past century, from an inner-directed individual to an other-directed individual. A century or so ago, the argument runs, the American learned certain values from his elders, in his youth. He internalized these values, as matters of principle, so that, in Riesman's phrase, they served as a kind of gyroscope to hold him on his course, and he stood by them throughout his life whether they were popular or unpopular. When these values were involved, he did not hesitate to go against the crowd. Thus he was inner-directed. But today, says Riesman, in a universe of rapidly changing circumstances, where the good will of our associates is more important to our success than it ever was to the nineteenth-century farmer, the American no longer internalizes his values in the old way. Instead, he responds very perceptively, very sensitively, to the values of others, and adjusts his course to meet their expectations. Indeed their expectations are a kind of radar-screen for his guidance. Thus he is other-directed, or to use an older and less precise term, he is much more a conformist.

Riesman does not discuss whether his thesis about "the changing American character" is applicable to American women, as well as to American men.[5] But we are entitled to ask, does he really believe that American women were so inner-directed as his analysis would suggest? Perhaps yes, if you believe that women have been more steadfast than men in defending the values on which the security of the home is based. But on the other hand, woman, historically, was a dependent person, and as a dependent person, she developed a most perceptive sensitivity to the expectations of others and a responsiveness in adapting herself to the moods and interests of others. She has always had a radar screen. If women are quicker to conform to the expectations of a group of other women than men are to a group of other men, and if we should say that this has been true in the past, what it would mean is that women have been other-directed all along, and that when Riesman says Americans are

145

becoming other-directed, what he means is that American men are becoming other-directed. As women gain more economic and social independence, it might be supposed in terms of Riesman's own analysis, that more than half of the American people are becoming less other-directed rather than more so. With the gradual disappearance of the so-called "clinging vine" type, who dared not call her soul her own, this is, in fact, apparently just what is happening.

If many of the generalizations which apply to American men, and which purport to apply to Americans generally, do not actually apply to American women, anyone who attempts to study the American character is forced to ask: to what extent has the impact of American historical experience been the same for both sexes, and to what extent has it been dissimilar? Viewed in these terms, the answer would probably have to be a balanced one. Certainly the main values that have prevailed in American society—the belief in individualism, the belief in equality, the belief in progress, have shaped the thought of American women as well as of American men, and American women are no doubt more committed to individualism, and to equality, and to progress, than women in many other societies. But on the other hand, some of the major forces that have been at work in American history have impinged upon men and upon women in differential ways. For instance, as I have already suggested, the frontier placed a premium upon qualities of brute strength and of habituation to physical danger which women did not possess in the same degree as men, either for biological or for cultural reasons. The result has been a differential historical experience for American men and American women which must be analyzed if there is any basis to be found for asserting that there are differences in the character types of the two sexes.

What then, we might ask, have been the principal transformations that history has brought in the lives of American women? Surprisingly enough, this is largely an unexplored field, but there are certain answers which appear more or less self-evident.

One of these is that our society has, during the last century and a half, found ways to do most of its heavy work without the use of human brawn and muscle. Water power, steam power, electric power, jet power, and the power of internal combustion have largely eliminated the need for brute strength and great physical stamina in most forms of work. This transformation has emancipated men in a revolutionary degree, but it has even more strikingly emancipated women, for women are physiologically smaller than men, and they lack the muscular strength and physical endurance of men. As the factor of hard labor in human work is reduced and the factor of skill is enhanced, therefore, women have found that inequality in ability to meet the requirements of work is greatly diminished. This basic fact, by itself, has probably done more than anything else to promote the equality of women.

But if this is the most fundamental effect of the mechanization of work, mechanization has also had a number of other sweeping consequences. One of these is that it has destroyed the subsistence farm as a unit of American life, and the disappearance of the subsistence farm, in turn, has had the most far-reaching implications.

To appreciate this, we must remember what life was like on the subsistence farm. The only division of labor that existed in this unit was the primitive division between men and women. The men constructed the dwelling, planted and cultivated the crops, raised the cattle and hogs and poultry, sheared the sheep, and chopped wood for the stoves and the fireplaces. In short the man was the producer—the producer of food, of fuel, of the raw materials for clothing. The farm wife, in turn, not only cooked, kept house, and cared for the children, as modern wives still do, but she also performed certain other tasks. She used ashes to make her own soap, she put up vast quantities of preserved food, she spun fibers into cloth, and made cloth into clothing. In economic terms, she and her daughters were processors. Together, they worked in a small, close-knit community, in which all lived very much together.

It hardly needs saying what happened to this typical unit of life in an earlier America. The use of machinery, the increased specialization of labor, and the development of an economy of exchange superseded it, and rendered it almost obsolete. Today a limited number of farmers with machines raise enough food for the entire population. Men go out to work instead of working on their own place, with their own sons, and their reward is not a harvest but a weekly wage or a monthly salary. Instead of "making a living" they make an income. All this is obvious, and oft-repeated. But what are the implications for the American woman?

Some embittered critics have retorted that modern woman, no longer a processor of goods, has lost her economic function, and that she retains only a biological function as mate and mother and a social function in the family. This loss of function, they would say, accounts for the frustration and sense of futility which seems to plague modern woman even more than it does modern man. But if we take a hard look at this argument, clearly it will not stand up. What has happened is that women have acquired a new role, in a new division of labor. With her husband away from the home, held by the compulsions of the clock, it falls to her, first of all, to use the family's income to take care of the family's needs. In short, while her husband has changed from a producer to an earner, she has changed from a processor to a consumer in a society where consumption is an increasingly important economic function.

The responsibilities of the consumer are no mean task. To handle them successfully, a person must be something of a dietitian, a judge of the quality of many goods, a successful planner, a skillful decorator, and a budget manager. The business of converting a monthly sum of money into a physical basis for a pleasant life involves a real art, and it might be counted as a major activity even if there were not children to rear and meals to prepare. But the increased specialization of the work of men at offices and factories away—frequently far away—from the home has also shifted certain cultural duties and certain community tasks in ever-greater measure to women.

In the Old World, upper-class men, claiming leisure as the principal advantage of their status, have made themselves the custodians of culture and the leaders in the cultural life of their communities. In America, upper-class men, primarily businessmen, working more compulsively and for longer hours than any other class, have resigned their cultural responsibilities to women and then have gone on to disparage literature and the arts because these pursuits, in the hands of females, began to seem feminine. Women have shouldered the responsibility, have borne the condescension with which their cultural activities were often treated, have provided the entire teaching force for the elementary schools, and most of the force for the secondary schools, and have done far more than their share to keep community life alive. This is another of the results, impinging in a differential way upon women, of the great social transformation of the last two centuries.

So far as we have examined them, all of these changes would seem to operate somewhat to the advantage of women, to have an emancipating effect, and to diminish her traditional subordination. No longer handicapped by a labor system in which biceps are at a premium, she has moved into the realms of employment, and has even preempted the typewriter and the teacher's desk as her own. If she has exercised a choice, which she never had before, and has decided to remain in her home, she has encountered a new economic role as a consumer rather than as a processor, with a broad range of activities, and with a new social role in keeping up the vigor of the community activities. In either case, the orbit of her activities is far wider than what used to be regarded as women's sphere, and it has been wide enough in fact to lead some optimistic observers to speak of the equality of women as if it were something which had reached some kind of absolute fulfillment and completeness about the time of the ratification of the woman's suffrage amendment in 1920.

Yet before we conclude our story with the ending that they all lived happily ever after, it is necessary to face up to the fact that women have not found all these changes quite as emancipating as they were expected to be. Indeed, much of the serious literature about American women is pessimistic in tone, and makes the dissatisfactions and the sexual frustration of modern American women its principal theme. Great stress is laid upon the fundamental dilemma that sexual fulfillment seems to depend upon one set of psychological attitudes—attitudes of submissiveness and passivity—while the fulfillment of equality seems to depend upon an opposite set—attitudes of competitiveness and self-assertion. At its grimmest level, this literature stresses the contention of Sigmund Freud that women instinctively envy the maleness of a man and reject their own sex. There is no doubt that these psychoanalytic views are important and that attention to questions of the sex life of an individual is basic, but a very respectable argument can be and has been made that what women envy about men is not their maleness in purely sexual terms but their dominance in the society and their immunity from the dilemmas which the needs of sexual and biological fulfillment on one hand and of personal fulfillment on the other pose for women.[6] The inescapable fact that males can have offspring without either bearing them or rearing them means that the values of family life and of personal achievement can be complementary for men, where they are conflicting values for women.

This one immutable and timeless fact, more than anything else, seems to stand forever in the way of the complete and absolute equality of men and women. Political and legal emancipation and even the complete equality of women in social relations and in occupational opportunities could not remove this handicap. So long as it remains, therefore, no one who finds a measure of inequality still remaining will have to look for an explanation in social terms. But it is legitimate to ask whether this is the only remaining barrier to emancipation, or whether other factors also serve to maintain adverse differentials against woman, even in modern America, where she seems to be more nearly equal than she has been in any other time or place, except perhaps in certain matriarchal tribes.

There are, perhaps, two aspects of woman's role as housekeeper and as consumer which also contribute, in a new way historically, to work against the prevailing tendencies toward a fuller equality. These aspects have, in a subtle way, caused society to devalue the modern activities of women as compared with those of men, and thus may even have contributed to bring about a new sort of subordination.

One of these is the advent of the money economy, in which income is the index of achievement, and the housewife is the only worker who does not get paid. On the farm home, in the days of the subsistence economy, neither she nor her husband got paid, at least not very much, and they were economic partners in the enterprise of making a living. But today, the lowliest and most trivial job which pays a wage counts as employment, while the most demanding and vital tasks which lack the sanction of pecuniary remuneration do not so count. A recent, and in fact very able book entitled *Women Who Work* deals, just as you would expect, not with women who work, but with women who get paid for their work. Sociologists regard it as an axiom that the amount of income is as important as any other criterion in measuring social status today, and in one sense, a woman's status may reflect the income of her husband, but in another sense it should be a corollary of the axiom that if income is esteemed, lack of income is followed by lack of esteem, and even by lack of self-esteem. If it needed proving, Komarovsky has shown that the American housewife tends to disparage herself as well as her work, as both being unworthy because they do not receive recognition in terms of cash income.[7]

If woman does not command respect as an earner, she is also likely to incur a certain subtle lack of respect for herself in her role as a consumer. For there is a strong tendency in some phases of American advertising to regard the consumer as someone who may be flattered or may be bullied, but who need not be treated as a mature person. Insofar as the consumer is an object of condescension, someone to be managed rather than someone to be consulted, someone on whom the will of the advertiser is to be imposed by psychological manipulation, and insofar as consumers are primarily women, it means that women become the objects of more than their share of the low esteem in which the consumer is held, and more than their share of the stultifying efforts to play upon human yearnings for prestige and popularity or upon human psychological in-securities. Anyone who recalls the recent publications about the rate at which the blinking of women's eyes increases when they view the display of goods in a supermarket, and the extent to which this display causes them to spend impulsively, rather than according to need, will recognize that the role of the consumer has not enhanced the dignity of women.[8] This aspect was very clearly and wittily recognized by Sylvia Wright in an article in *Harper's* in 1955, in which she dealt ironically with the assertion which we sometimes hear, that America has become a woman's world.

"Whatever it is," she wrote, "I'll thank you to stop saying it's mine. If it were a woman's world, people wouldn't yammer at me so much. They're always telling me to do, be, or make something. . . .

"The one thing they don't want me to be is me. 'A few drops of Abano Bath Oil' they say, 'and you're not you . . . you're Somebody New lolling in perfumed luxury.' But I'm not allowed to loll long. The next minute I have to spring out in order to be Fire and Ice, swathed in satin, not a thing to do but look stark, and wait for a man to pounce. Turn the page, I've got to make sure it's Johnson's cotton buds with which I swab the baby. A few pages later, the baby gets into the act yelling for full-weight diapers. . . .

"I'm supposed to use a lot of make-up to keep my husband's love, but I must avoid make-up clog. I'm supposed to be gay, spontaneous and outgoing, but I mustn't get 'expression lines' [Expression lines are to wrinkles as morticians are to undertakers]. . . .

"In the old days, I only had to have a natural aptitude for cooking, cleaning, bringing up children, entertaining, teaching Sunday School and tatting. . . .

"Now I also have to reconstitute knocked-down furniture and build on porches."[9]

If woman's status is somewhat confused today, therefore, it is partly because, at the very time when efforts to exploit her as a female began to abate, the efforts to exploit her as a consumer began to increase. And at the time when the intrinsic value of her work was gaining in dignity as compared with that of the male, the superficial value as measured in terms of money income was diminishing. The essential strength of her position has increased, but the combined effect of the manipulation by the media and the emphasis upon monetary earning as a standard for the valuation of work has threatened her with a new kind of subordination, imposed by the system of values which she herself accepts, rather than by masculine values imposed upon her against her will.

If a woman as a consumer in a world of producers and as an unpaid worker in a world of salaried employees has lost some of the ground she had gained by emancipation as a female in a world of males, even the emancipation itself has created some new problems for her. For instance, it has confronted her with a dilemma she never faced in the days when she was confined to her own feminine sphere. This is the dilemma that she is now expected to attain a competence in the realm of men's affairs, but that she must never succeed in this realm too much. It is well for her to be intelligent, but not intelligent enough to make a young man feel inferior; well for her to find employment and enjoy it, but not enjoy it enough to be unwilling to give it up for the cradle and the sink; well for her to be able to look after herself, but never to be so visibly able that it will inhibit the impulse of the right man to want to look after her; well for her to be ambitious, but never ambitious enough to actually put her personal objectives first. When a man marries, no one expects him to cease being a commuter and to become a farmer because it would be good for the children—though in fact it might. But when a woman marries, her occupation becomes an auxiliary activity.

Here we come back to the presence of a fundamental dualism which has made the so-called "emancipation" of women different from the emancipation of any other group in society. Other emancipated groups have sought to substitute a new condition in place of an old one and to obliterate the old, but except for a few of the most militant women in a generation of crusading suffragettes, now almost extinct, women have never renounced the roles of wife and mother. The result has been that their objective was to reconcile a new condition with an old one, to hold in balance the principle of equality, which denies a difference, and the practice of wifehood and motherhood which recognizes a difference in the roles of men and women. The eternal presence of this dualism has not only caused a distressing amount of confusion and tension among women themselves; it has also caused confusion among their many volunteer critics. The result is that we encounter more wildly inconsistent generalizations about modern American women than about almost any other subject.

For example, modern woman, we are told, is gloriously free from the inferiority of the past, but she is miserable and insecure in her new freedom. She holds the purse strings of the nation and has become dominant over a world of increasingly less-masculine men who no longer trust themselves to buy a suit of clothes without their wife's approval. But also she does the routine work at typewriter and sink while the men still run the universe. Similarly, we are assured that the modern woman is an idle, parasitic, bridge-playing victim of technological unemployment in her own mechanized home, and also that she is the busy manager of a family and household and budget whose demands make the domestic chores of the past look easy by comparison. She escapes from reality into the wretched, petty little world of soap opera and neighborhood gossip, but she excels in her knowledge of public affairs and she became an effective guardian of literary and artistic values when her money-grubbing husband defaulted on this responsibility. She is rearing the best crop of children ever produced on this planet, by the most improved methods ever devised, while her over-protectiveness has bred "momism" and her unwillingness to stay at home has bred delinquency.

Clearly, we are still a long way from having arrived at any monotonous unanimity of opinion about the character of American women. Yet if we will focus carefully upon what we really know with some degree of assurance, we can perhaps begin the process of striking a balance. We certainly know, for instance, that many of the trends of American history have been operative for both men and women in somewhat the same way. The emphasis upon the right of the individual has operated to remove legal disabilities upon women, to open many avenues to gainful employment, to confer the suffrage, and so on. Even our divorce rate is an ironic tribute to the fact that the interests of the individual, and perhaps in a majority of cases the individual woman, are placed ahead of the protection of a social institution—namely the family. The rejection of authority in American life, which has made our child-rearing permissive and has weakened the quality of leadership in our politics, has also meant that the relation of husband and wife is more of a partnership and less of an autocracy in this age and in this country than at any other time or place in Western civilization. The competitive strain in American life has impelled American women as well as American men to strive hard for their goals, and to assert themselves in the strife—indeed European critics complain that they assert themselves far more strenuously than European women and entirely too much for the tranquility of society.

On the other hand, we also know that the experience of women remains in many ways a distinctive experience. Biologically, there are still the age-old facts that women are not as big as men and not as strong; that the sex act involves consequences for them which it does not involve for the male; that the awareness of these consequences conditions the psychological attitudes of women very deeply; and that motherhood is a biological function while fatherhood is, in a sense, a cultural phenomenon. Historically, there is the formidable truth that the transformations of modern life have impinged upon men and women in different ways. The avenues of employment opened to men are not the same as the avenues of employment opened to women. The revolution in our economy has deepened the division between work in the home and work outside the home by according the sanction of monetary reward to the one and denying it to the other—thus devaluing in a new way work which is distinctively woman's. The economic revolution, while converting most men from producers to earners, has converted most women from processors to consumers, and the exploitation of the consumer has, again, added a new devaluation to women's role. Society has given her the opportunity to fulfill her personal ambitions through the same career activities as a man, but it cannot make her career aspirations and her family aspirations fit together as they do for a man. The result of all this is a certain tension between her old role and her new one. More of an individualist than women in traditional societies, she is by no means as whole-heartedly individualistic as the American male, and as a study at Berkeley recently showed, she still hesitates to claim individualism as a quality of her own.[10] If she enters the competitive race, she does so with an awareness that the top posts are still pretty much the monopoly of men, and with a certain limitation upon her competitive commitment. In short, she is constantly holding in balance her general opportunities as a person and her distinctive needs as a woman, and when we consider how badly these two go together in principle can we not say that she is maintaining the operative equilibrium between them with a remarkable degree of skill and of success?

The answer to my childish riddle was that the big Indian is the little Indian's mother. To say that she is a squaw is not to deny that she is an Indian—but it is to say that she is an Indian for whom the expectations of the masculine world of Indians, or of Americans, do not apply. It is to say that her qualities and traits, whether she is an Indian, or an American, will reflect the influence of the same sweeping forces which influence the world of men, but that it will reflect them with a difference. In this sense, what we say about the character of the American people should be said not in terms of half of the American population—even if it is the male half—but in terms of the character of the totality of the people. In this sense, also, attention to the historic character of American women is important not only as a specialty for female scholars or for men who happen to take an interest in feminism, but as a coordinate major part of the overall, comprehensive study of the American character as a whole. For the character of any nation is the composite of the character of its men and of its women and though these may be deeply similar in many ways, they are almost never entirely the same.

NOTES

1. Frederick Jackson Turner, *The Frontier in American History* (New York, 1920), p. 4.

2. Robert Lynd, "The People as Consumers," writes that there is "probably today a greater variation from house to house in the actual inventory list of family possessions . . . than at any previous era in man's history." U.S. President's Commission on Social Trends, *Recent Social Trends in the United States,* vol. 2. (New York, 1933), pp. 857–911.

3. In 1957, of the 21,000,000 women in the work force, 11,000,000 were wives. Female employment was highest (45%) in the age brackets 20 to 24, declined to 39% in bracket 25 to 44, rose to 40% in the bracket 45 to 64, and declined to 10% in the bracket 65 and over.

4. *Harper's Magazine* 223 (Nov. 1961), p. 23.

5. David Riesman, *"The Lonely Crowd:* A Reconsideration in 1960" in *Culture and Social Character: The Work of David Riesman Reviewed,* eds. Seymour Martin Lipset and Leo Lowenthal (Glencoe, Ill., 1961), p. 428, discusses an investigation by Michael S. Olmsted which showed that Smith College girls regarded themselves as more other-directed than men and regarded other girls as more other-directed than their group, but Riesman does not state what his own belief is in this matter.

6. Probably the best of the literature which emphasizes the sex frustration of the modern American woman is found in professional publications in the fields of psychology and psychoanalysis which do not reach a popular audience. In the literature for the layman, probably the best presentation of this point of view is Simone de Beauvoir's excellent *The Second Sex* (New York, 1953), but other items have enjoyed a circulation which they hardly deserve. Two cases in point are Ferdinand Lundberg and Marynia F. Farnham, *Modern Woman: The Lost Sex* (New York, 1947), and Eric John Dingwall, *The American Woman: An Historical Study* (New York, 1958). Denis W. Brogan's judicious and yet precise evaluation that Dingwall's book is "strictly for the birds" would be equally applicable to Lundberg. For an able argument that the condition of modern woman must be understood partly in social terms, and that the concept of "genital trauma" has been overdone, see Mirra Komarovsky, *Women in the Modern World: Their Education and Their Dilemmas* (Boston, 1953), pp. 31–52.

7. Komarovsky, *Women in the Modern World,* pp. 127–53.

8. Experiments on the rate of eye blink, as conducted by James M. Vicary, a leading exponent of motivation research, were reported in Vance Packard, *The Hidden Persuaders* (New York, 1957), pp. 106–108.

9. Sylvia Wright, "Whose World? and Welcome to It," *Harper's Magazine* 210 (May 1955), pp. 35–38.

10. John P. McKee and A. C. Sheriffs, "Men's and Women's Beliefs, Ideals, and Self-Concepts," *American Journal of Sociology* 64 (1959), pp. 356–63.

☆ • ☆ • ☆ • ☆ • ☆

This is not the only study of American character that discusses women: David Potter was wrong to assert that David Riesman left them out (he also oversimplified what Riesman said about conformity). What *is* true is that Riesman's *Lonely Crowd,* like some later writing by others, found parallels rather than contrasts in the forces shaping male and female character. With the exception of a few studies involving 'Momism,' Potter's article is, I believe, the only modern study of American character that sharply distinguishes American women from American men *as well as* from foreign women.

To appreciate Potter's vision, one must remember that in 1959, when he gave the lecture on which the article was based, the modern women's movement had not really begun. Yet his essay compares very well with Betty Friedan's book of 1963, *The Feminine Mystique,* usually considered a founding document of modern feminism. Unlike Potter's study, Friedan's book is almost entirely about domesticity; it has nothing on women at work outside the home. It was Potter in 1959, not Friedan in 1963, who wrote about women at the typewriter as well as at the sink, though even he did not write about the pressures of going out to work *and* being a perfect homemaker at the same time.

Potter's piece, however, has not escaped feminist criticism. In the late 1970s the historian Alice Kessler-Harris took him to task for giving women too "passive" a role. He did not observe, she said, that female values of humane care and cooperation were challenging the competitive, individualist, male realm of capitalism and had sometimes done so in the past. Kessler-Harris omitted to say that some American men, too, had challenged this realm, and she tended to blame Potter for not seeing perfectly in 1959 (or 1962, the publication date of his article) what would seem more evident in the late 1970s. In the 'post-Vietnam' period when Kessler-Harris wrote, there was positive talk of 'androgeny,' a coming-together of male and female character against the excesses of tough-guy masculinity. And as the women's movement reached into politics, it was easier to visualize a new female influence on male attitudes.

Kessler-Harris's criticism of Potter was also part of a pendulum pattern in left-wing writing—European as well as American. If you stress too much that an underdog group lacked power and was victimized, you are accused of denying 'agency' to that group—of demeaning it by neglecting its ability to forge a life and influence of its own. If, however, you stress the group's 'agency,' you will be charged with cruelly underestimating its miserable situation. Had Potter declared

157

that women had the power to shape male attitudes and character, you can be sure he would have been just as much criticized—hit by the pendulum going the other way.

Since Potter wrote, the women's movement has generated a wealth of historical studies, showing how women lived and worked, on farm and frontier as well as in the city, and exploring the ideas that revolved around their roles. What Potter said about them holds up remarkably well in the light of this new knowledge.

DAVID M. POTTER

American Individualism in the Twentieth Century

The second essay by Potter reprinted here represents a change of emphasis from *People of Plenty* (see p. 134). It pays some attention to economic and geographic factors but gives a new weight to ideas themselves. Potter analyzes the way in which different American values connect and conflict.

In the 1950s and 1960s, Potter was writing his greatest book, *The Impending Crisis, 1848–1861*, on the political developments that led to the Civil War. Again and again he interrupted it to produce a stream of essays on American character and culture and problems related to Southern history. The book was not published until after he died in 1971, but an early section of it, probably written in the late 1950s, made a link with his analysis of American values. In five brilliant pages he explored the way in which a Northerner could hold contradictory attitudes about slavery, freedom, and national union.

Potter's thinking about American character and values was also informed by comparative history. As a young instructor at the University of Mississippi he taught a huge grab-bag of Western history from the ancient Greeks on. This may have encouraged his fondness for comparing different countries, their myths as well as their economies. Unlike Seymour Martin Lipset (pp. 98–133), Potter did not use survey data to compare national attitudes, but in the 1960s he moved toward Lipset's belief that a nation's distinctive political past was at least as important as its economy in determining its values—actually, his own writing about the Civil War had implicitly supported this view. In an essay of 1967, comparing Canadian and U.S. identities, he approvingly cited Lipset, and the two men spoke of writing a book together not long before Potter died.

Another influence on Potter was the American Studies movement.

Yale, where Potter taught between 1942 and 1961, was at the forefront of this movement and Potter was part of it. American Studies at the time was largely in the business of combining American literature with history, and it tended to stress the uniqueness of American culture.

In his essay "The Quest for the National Character" (1962), Potter tried to explain the American interest in finding a national identity; he then gave his own thoughts as to what that identity was. After discussing Frederick Jackson Turner's 'frontier thesis,' he centered his discussion on the views of Alexis de Tocqueville (see pp. 10–11). Elaborating on Tocqueville, Potter distinguished two egalitarian traditions in America: the belief in equal opportunity for unequal success, and the insistence that all people shared a common humanity and basic rights to individual dignity. The first tradition, best suited to a "new, undeveloped frontier country," stressed a competitive self-reliance. The second tradition corresponded to Lipset's equality of manners (p. 132): it was antiauthoritarian, tabooed snobbish airs and overbearing behavior, and encouraged leadership by signals and persuasion rather than command. If it produced independence of mind, it also produced the opposite, a submissiveness to majority opinion.

"American Individualism in the Twentieth Century," the essay reprinted below, cut the cake of national values a different way. Instead of comparing two coexisting traditions, it presented a shift from one kind of individualism, strongest in the twentieth century, to another, twentieth-century version. The shift, however, was not simple: there were overlaps and parallels between them.

Potter's essay has a political undertone. It was written in the Kennedy years when big-government liberalism seemed again, as in the 1930s, to be a rising force against the private power of big business; and academic brains and artistic talent commanded a new respect. It was also a time of political activism among youth; 'Freedom Rides' and civil-rights marches in the South; and the birth of a hippie 'counterculture,' succeeding the smaller 'beat' movement of the 1950s. Stationed at Stanford, an elite campus where student and faculty attitudes seemed to be getting more liberal by the hour, David Potter felt some unease. By the standards of the time and place, he was a humane conservative—a southerner who loathed racism and knew it a lot better than most northern white liberals; who believed the South was too easily scapegoated for the nation's racial sins; who perceived that academic liberalism had its own conformities and shibboleths; and who disliked government regulation, especially when it banned *some* obnoxious behaviors and tolerated others. Directly or indirectly, all these feelings find a place in what follows.

☆ • ☆ • ☆ • ☆ • ☆

At the beginning of his essay, "Individualism Reconsidered," David Riesman remarks, "Such terms as 'society' and 'individual' tend to pose a false as well as a shifting dichotomy."* We might take Riesman's remark and extend it by observing that, in general, we tend to discuss questions too much in terms of antitheses, and frequently in terms of antitheses which are deceptive.[1] Thus, we speak in polarities about liberty versus authority, dissent versus conformity, and, of course, individualism versus collectivism. But in fact we know all the while that no one intends to choose starkly between these alternatives. Liberty would be intolerable to the most independent-minded person without some measure of authority, or dissent without some conformity. In fact, human life presents us with a whole series of situations in which diverse and, to some extent, conflicting values must be kept in some kind of working relationship with one another. Two junior officers both bucking for promotion will presumably work together for the improvement of their unit while they work in rivalry with one another for advancement. Indeed, the principle of "antagonistic cooperation" probably goes much deeper than this, for even nature seems to abound in situations where two elements are linked in a relationship of tension and at the same time of interdependence. The basic case is the relationship of men and women, eternally needing one another and eternally engaged in a "battle of the sexes"; but there is also the case of youth and age, with youth forever restive under its dependence upon the elders, and the elders forever vexed by the brashness of a youth which they have lost, and with each unwillingly drawing upon the other for qualities which it, itself, lacks. Along with these classic dualisms, there is also the relationship between man alone, and man in society—

"American Individualism in the Twentieth Century," by David M. Potter was first published in the *Texas Quarterly*, Volume VI, No. 2 (Summer 1963), pp. 140–51. Reprinted by permission of the University of Texas Press.

man constantly straining against the compulsion imposed by the group, and man continuously driven by need for identity with the group. These conflicting needs must forever be mediated and accommodated, and the ultimate choice of either one to the complete exclusion of the other would be equally unthinkable. In our literature, any story of the complete isolation, either physical or psychological, of a man from his fellow man, such as the story of Robinson Crusoe before he found a human footprint on the beach, is regarded as essentially a horror story. But the tale of any man having his identity completely swallowed up by total absorption into the group, as happened for the members of the Party in Oceania in George Orwell's *1984*, is also regarded as a kind of nightmare.

If this principle of balance or beneficent tension between conflicting values has any validity in the cases which I have mentioned, it might be argued that it has even more in the case of individualism, especially in the United States. For is it not notoriously true that historically American individualism has always been sanctioned only within very sharply de-fined limits? The word "individualism," of course, has been included in our litany of sacred terms, and in many respects, America has placed an immense premium upon the individualistic values of independence, self-reliance, and rejection of authority. But American society has never, I believe, sanctioned the attempt of a person to practice the kind of individ-ualism which one would find in a society with a recognized elite. An elite or aristocratic individualist is likely to regard the principles of individual-ism as conferring a franchise for self-indulgence as well as for self-expres-sion. This was the kind of individualism which Lord Byron practiced— the kind which he defended in his epic of Don Juan. It lends itself to the idea that the talented man may become a superman and that he is quite justified in sacrificing less talented men and in riding roughshod over them. Nietzsche is unfavorably remembered for exalting this superman version of individualism, and of course one finds the ideal set forth also in Shaw's *Man and Superman.*

Individualism in this form seems profoundly alien to the American tradition—so alien that we who are in the American tradition do not usually even recognize it as a form of individualism. Yet occasionally we will find a traveler from overseas who regards individualism as involving the right of the individualist to indulge his own impulses at the expense of others, to attain self-expression regardless of its effect on other people.

Such a person is astonished that American individualism carries no such franchise. The writings of Tocqueville abound in observations on the lack of real variety in American life, despite all its claims to individualism. But the most vivid statement of the point that I think I have ever seen was made by Tocqueville's compatriot, Michael de Chevalier, also in the 1830s:

> As for us [the French], who resemble each other in nothing except in differing from everybody else, for us, to whom variety is as necessary as the air, to whom a life of rules would be a subject of horror, the Yankee system would be torture. Their liberty is not the liberty to outrage all that is sacred on earth, to set religion at defiance, to laugh morals to scorn, to undermine the foundations of social order, to mock at all traditions and received opinions. It is neither the liberty of being a monarchist in a republican country, nor that of sacrificing the honor of the poor man's wife or daughter to one's base passions; it is not even the liberty to enjoy one's wealth by a public display, for public opinion has its sumptuary laws, to which all must conform under pain of moral outlawry; nor even that of living in private differently from the rest of the world.[2]

Just how serious Chevalier was in asserting the right to seduce a poor man's wife as one of the prerequisites of individualism in its Gallic form, I do not know. But his mere voicing of this assertion gives us, I believe, a kind of benchmark which may help to define the limits of individualism in its Yankee form. This assertion of individualism would not do at all for Americans; and why, we may ask, would it not? Why are Chevalier's suggestions more or less offensive to us, and why, particularly, does the suggestion about the poor man's wife grate on us more than the proposal to "outrage all that is sacred"? I would suggest that it is because Chevalier is implicitly denying the American proposition that men are intrinsically equal, even though their physical circumstances may vary immensely. For a rich man to seduce the wife of another rich man might be accepted in a spirit of joviality, under the axiom that all is fair in love and war, but for him to seduce the wife of a poor man is to treat a fellow man as less than an equal simply because he is poor. In the American creed this is, perhaps, the sin against the Holy Ghost.

It may seem that I am dwelling too much here upon what may have been a random phrase in the writing of one Frenchman now dead for more than a century, but I have lingered over it because I believe it may illustrate, in a particularly vivid way, the fact that American individualism has always been limited and held in balance by other cherished principles which were not entirely consistent with it. It could never be asserted in a way which would violate the principle of equality, and we will do well to look twice before we even assume that it placed the values of man in isolation ahead of the values of man in a group, or man in society.

At this point it may be necessary for me to pause and declare myself as to what I understand individualism to have meant in American life. If so, I must venture an assertion that American individualism in the nineteenth century and American individualism in the twentieth century have had two fundamentally different emphases, but that both of them have placed great weight upon the belief that individualism should serve as a means to group welfare rather than as a way of exalting man in isolation. This assertion may be difficult to prove, but let us examine it. To specify more fully, let me suggest that the individualism of the nineteenth century stressed the element of self-reliance while that of the twentieth century has stressed the element of nonconformity or dissent, but that in each case there was a strong emphasis upon the value of the quality in question for society as a whole and not simply for the individual apart from society.

Theoretically, perhaps, it might be supposed that these two emphases are not very different: that self-reliance and nonconformity would go together and would tend to converge. It is logical to argue that a man who does not depend on other people for his physical welfare will certainly not be very quick to borrow his ideas from them. If he has the habit of fending for himself, will he not also have the habit of thinking for himself? If he shows initiative in his endeavors to attain success, will he not also show initiative in forming his social ideas? If individualism equals independence and independence equals freedom and freedom equals dissent, then doesn't it follow that individualism equals dissent? Perhaps the plausibility of this kind of equation has led us to the fallacy of using one term, "individualism," to express the ideas of both self-reliance and nonconformity.

But history often mocks logic, and in our historical experience, the believers in self-reliance, in the sense of taking care of oneself, and the believers in nonconformity, in the sense of encouraging dissent, have often been far, far apart. In fact, these two types of individualists seem to be almost natural antagonists, for the "rugged individualist" of laissez-faire economics is likely to be what we call a conservative, as orthodox in his ideas of success as he is enterprising in his efforts to succeed, while the nonconforming individualist is likely to treasure unconventional forms of self-expression and to regard the orthodoxy of the laissez-faire individualist as a threat to such self-expression and to novel ideas in general.

As these two types of individualist feud with one another, it is ironical that the ultimate accusation which each makes is that the other is betraying the community. Thus, while each in his own way places the individual before the group, each at the same time pays inverted tribute to the importance of the group by making the betrayal of the group the basis of his rejection of the other. To the nonconforming individualist the sin of the laissez-faire individualist is that he sacrifices the weak to the strong and that he values the opportunity for private advantage more than he values the general welfare. To the self-reliant individualist, the sin of the nonconforming individualist is that he denies the community the means of protecting its values and the morale of its members against injury by hostile or irresponsible persons or groups. His concept of the right of dissent is so absolute that he extends it not only to responsible critics who want to improve the society, but also to enemies who want to destroy it and to exploiters who are alert to every chance for arousing and playing upon the anxieties, the lusts, and the sadistic impulses which society, from the beginning of time, has struggled to control.

But before looking further at the relationship of these two modes of individualism to one another, let us first look at the historical context of the two. The individualism of self-reliance was essentially the response or adaptation of a people who had an undeveloped continent in front of them and who lacked institutional or technological devices for conquering it. Society needed persons who were what we call self-starters, persons who would go ahead and tackle the wilderness without waiting for signals to be given or for arrangements that would make it easy. It needed qualities of initiative and of ruggedness. It needed the attitude of Stonewall Jackson when he said that he would care for his own wounded and bury his own dead. In the conditions of pioneer America, where the services of the police and the church and the school and the hospital and the specialized economic occupations were often not available, it needed a man who could tote his own gun, pray his own prayers, and learn to read, write, and cipher by the light of a pine-knot fire. Andrew Jackson's mother is said to have admonished him at the parental knee, "Andy, never sue nobody. Always settle them matters yourself."

America needed a breed of men who would swarm over a wilderness which was a continent wide, and it produced the adaptation that was needed—the frontier American, famous in song and story as well as in the classic formulations of Frederick Jackson Turner. He was, it appears, rugged; he was self-reliant; he seems to have been magnificently successful; and he did tame the continent in record time—with the important aid, it must be added, of a tremendously effective new technology of power and machines. But was his self-reliance individualism? And, insofar as it was individualism, what were the social costs of developing this kind of individualism to such a pronounced degree? These questions are somewhat harder to answer.

Turner himself suggested that the frontier experience stimulated innovation, which of course means a break with conformity, a break with the past. He offered the hypothesis, which research has failed to vindicate, that the frontiersmen showed great fertility in working out new and untraditional political devices for the governments of their new states. But in fact, the tendency to imitate and copy the older political models was high. Professor Walter P. Webb has made a considerably more tenable argument that the men of the Great Plains seized upon certain technological innovations: the six-shooter, barbed wire, and the windmill. But this seems more a matter of physical adaptation than of a capacity for independent or deviant thought. The status of the frontiersman as an independent thinker is questionable indeed. Perhaps, one might add, it is unfair even to expect of him that he should have been an independent thinker. The physical demands upon him were very rigid, and rigid demands necessarily require one specific response, thus limiting the range or spectrum or variety of response. Nonconformity and diversity in attitude will flourish where the demands of the physical environment are not so harshly rigorous, and where they leave more latitude for variation from man to man. Nonconformity implies the possibility of varied reactions to the same situation; but the frontier, with its rigorous conditions of life, was too exacting in its demands to allow much choice for the frontiersman in the mode of his reaction.

In the past generation we have come to see, with increasing clarity, that the individualism of the American frontier was an individualism of personal self-reliance and of hardihood and stamina rather than an individualism of intellectual independence and personal self-expression. Arthur Schlesinger, Jr., for instance, has argued, I think convincingly, that the frontier was slow to perceive the problems arising in connection with the application of democracy to an industrial society and slow to develop social ideas of reform, so that these ideas, in fact, developed predominantly in the cities. At the same time when we were recognizing this, we were also beginning to count the social costs of the individualism of self-reliance, so that there has grown up a tendency to doubt whether the frontier influence was altogether a beneficial one in American life. As far back as Alexis de Tocqueville, we were warned in the clearest possible terms that American equality, which is peculiarly identified with the frontier, was conducive to conformity rather than to freedom, since it places the stigma of arrogance upon any man who ventures to set his personal judgment against the judgment of a majority of his equals. Arthur K. Moore, in his study of the frontier mind as exemplified in the backwoodsmen of Kentucky, has shown how readily the practicality of the frontier took the form of a blighting anti-intellectualism.[3] Many writers have begun to say that the frontiersman was spiritually and culturally impoverished by his isolation and by his predilection for a society in which the ties of community life were so weakened that he ceased to be, in any adequate sense, a social being. One who has stated this most strikingly, and perhaps in the most controversial way, is Leslie Fiedler with his famous (or, as some citizens of Montana would say, infamous) comments on his earliest impressions of the people of that frontier state. Upon his arrival in Montana, says Fiedler:

> I was met unexpectedly by the Montana Face. What I had been expecting, I do not clearly know; zest, I suppose, naiveté, a ruddy and straightforward kind of vigor—perhaps even honest brutality. What I found seemed, at first glance, reticent, sullen, weary—full of self-sufficient stupidity; a little later it appeared simply inarticulate, with all the dumb pathos of what cannot declare itself; a face developed not for sociability or feeling, but for facing into the weather. It said friendly things to be sure, and meant them;

167

but it had no adequate physical expressions even for friendliness, and the muscles around the mouth and eyes were obviously unprepared to cope with the demands of any more complicated emotion. I felt a kind of innocence behind it, but an innocence difficult to distinguish from simple ignorance. In a way there was something heartening in dealing with people who had never seen, for instance, a Negro or a Jew or a servant, and were immune to all their bitter meanings; but the same people, I knew, had never seen an art museum or a ballet or even a movie in any language but their own, and the poverty of experience had left the possibilities of the human face in them completely unrealized.[4]

Here, in effect, is the assertion that society had to pay too high a price for frontier individualism—that men as a group were penalized for the freedom of men as separate beings, and, in short, that individualism is not justified if it serves only individuals. It must serve society. Our conviction that it must is why we have never had any elite individualism that amounted to anything, and is also a striking commentary upon the paradoxical elements in the fact that we are committed to individualism at all.

Along with frontier individualism, the nineteenth century also sub-scribed to the economic individualism of *laissez-faire*. The two had a great deal in common. Both exalted strength and stamina and scorned weakness or lack of practicality. Both enjoined the individual to fight for his own aspirations first and to subordinate consideration for the group to consideration for the enterpriser acting alone. Both made a virtue of independence, but their independence meant a self-propelled drive to-ward the goals which society had prescribed rather than any real indepen-dence of mind in setting the goals for which to strive. Both were individu-alistic in a sense—certainly in the sense of "rugged individualism"—but it was an individualism that was more conservative than liberal, more hostile to dissent than favorable toward it.

It is a notable fact about *laissez-faire* individualism, however, that while it exalted the virtues of unregimented, uncontrolled, independent action by man acting alone, it never for a moment contended that the success of the unusual individual was more important than the welfare of the community. Instead, it constantly stressed the idea that the bold enterpriser served the community by daring to undertake projects which the community needed but which the rank and file were too unimaginative to initiate. The argument was much like that of the modern noncon-forming individualist who defends dissenters not on the ground that the dissenter matters and that the conventional thinkers from whom he dissents do not, but that the community needs ideas which the conventional or orthodox thinkers cannot supply.

There is no need for me to recite here the elaborate arguments which Adam Smith stated so ingeniously, and which nineteenth-century publicists so dearly loved to repeat, that a providentially designed economic system (the unseen hand of God at work) took the selfish impulses and selfish actions of individuals and translated them into results which served the welfare of the community. This concept that the antagonistic rivalries of selfish and competing producers would create an optimum relationship between the social need for goods and the economic supply of goods is not only a subtle but by no means a preposterous economic theory. It is also a renewed testimony that even the ardent individualists of the nineteenth century were not willing to base their faith in individualism upon any concept of the primacy of the interests of the individual over the interests of the group. Instead they made the interests of the group—that is, the society—the ground for their insistence that society must not be deprived of the contribution which the independent-minded individual can make.

During the Great Depression, a great many Americans grew to doubt that *laissez-faire* individualism really did serve the interests of the whole society. Our government under the New Deal abandoned it, and though we have had a span of a quarter of a century since that time, with two Republican administrations in the interim, there is no indication that we will return to the old faith in self-reliance and private action. Richard Hofstadter has subtitled his essay on Herbert Hoover "The Last Stand of Rugged Individualism," and there are probably not many, even among the conservatives, who would quarrel very much with this verdict.

In saying that the individualism of self-reliance has passed its high tide, I don't mean to suggest by any means that it has disappeared, or even that it does not remain, in some forms, a very dominant American attitude. Anyone who thinks that it is becoming extinct might well ponder over an analysis which Martha Wolfenstein and Nathan Leites made only a few years ago of the plots of a year's crop of American motion pictures of the A grade.

The major plot configuration in American films [they wrote] contrasts with both the British and the French. Winning is terrifically important and always possible though it may be a tough fight. The conflict is not an internal one [as in Hamlet]; it is not our own impulses which endanger us nor our own scruples that stand in our way. The hazards are all external, but they are not rooted in the nature of life itself. They are the hazards of a particular situation with which we find ourselves confronted. The hero is typically in a strange town where there are apt to be dangerous men and women of ambiguous character and where the forces of law and order are not to be relied on. If he sizes up the situation correctly, if he does not go off half-cocked but is still able to beat the other fellow to the punch once he is sure who the enemy is, if he relies on no one but himself, if he demands sufficient evidence of virtue from the girl, he will emerge triumphant. He will defeat the dangerous men, get the right girl, and show the authorities what's what.[5]

We all know that American boys, from the early years of childhood, are taught to stand up and fight back. Margaret Mead, incidentally, has commented cogently on this point.[6] So long as this is true, and so long as the self-reliant protagonist in the movie gets the desirable girl, it would be premature indeed to suggest that all the bark has been rubbed off the tradition of individualism in its rugged form. But certainly the tradition has come under attack and certainly it is, as we might say, selling at a discount.

Now what is the basis of our discontent with the tradition of self-reliance? This is certainly a complex and difficult question, to which it may be brash to venture a simple answer, but in many respects it appears that the point of the criticism is that stress on self-reliance was carried to a point where it emphasized private goals and private values too much at the cost of community goals and community values. The coherence of the community was impaired, the vitality of the community was lowered. Leslie Fiedler's men with the Montana face are essentially men who have been starved of the psychological nourishment which community life could offer.

This criticism can be detected, I think, in quite a number of different forms. For instance, Stanley Elkins, in his comparison of slavery in North America and in South America, comments on the fact that in South America certain community institutions such as the church and the government were strong enough to assert a concern for the slave, and to stand, as it were, in certain respects, between the slave and his master.[7] But in North America, the naked authority of the master was tempered in hardly any way by the institutional force of the community. This amounts to saying that private values had eclipsed public values in the United States. Many other writers have expressed concern about the lack of corporate *esprit* among Americans, and some of the concern about the lack of reciprocal support for one another among American prisoners of war in Korea, as contrasted, for instance, with that among Turkish prisoners of war, was also addressed to the fear that we have emphasized private values, or what may be called privatism, too much and community values not enough. The old Yankee prayer

> God save me and my wife,
> My son John and his wife,
> Us four and no more

may have expressed an attitude that was rooted too deep for comfort.

Many of the comments that we have had on privatism as an unfortunate dimension of American individualism have been expressed in strong and somewhat controversial terms, but Gabriel Almond, in his *The American People and Foreign Policy*, gave us what might be regarded as a sober and measured statement of this point.

> The American, [said Almond] is primarily concerned with "private values," as distinguished from social-group, political, or religious-moral values. His concern with private, worldly success is his most absorbing aim. In this regard it may be suggested by way of hypothesis that in other cultures there is a greater stress on corporate loyalties and values and a greater personal involvement with political issues or with other worldly religious values.[8]

With the twentieth century, as I have already tried to suggest, American individualism took on a new emphasis. The frontier was disappearing, and *laissez-faire* was having its wings clipped. According to a well-known phrase which is perhaps a trifle too pat, human rights were replacing property rights. The new expounders of the American tradition reexamined the sacred documents and concluded that the priceless feature of our heritage was the principle of nonconformity, or dissent. Of course, they had perfectly sound historical grounds for tracing the principle of dissent far back in American history. Puritanism itself was a fairly radical form of dissent, as well as a harsh system for enforcing conformity. Ralph W. Emerson, that great apostle of individualism, had not only exalted self-reliance; he had exalted dissent also. "Who so would be a man," Emerson said, "must be a non-conformist." In our own day, the sanction which we give to dissent is suggested quite clearly in the antithesis which we constantly set up of liberty versus authority and of self-expression versus conformity.

The exponents of this new kind of individualism went forward rejoicing, for quite some time, that individualism was now purged of the taints of privatism and of conformity. For the spokesmen of the individualism of nonconformity were very often men who could in no sense be accused of indifference to the interests of the group, of society. Most of them are what we call liberals—using the term with a fairly clear understanding of what kind of people we mean, even if we cannot quite define their exact quality—and the liberals were so concerned with the welfare of the group that they often gave it a priority over the rights of the individual. Their opponents offered an implicit recognition of this fact by angrily denouncing them as "collectivists." How could a man whose fault, if he has one, is that he is too collectivist—too group-minded—legitimately be accused of privatism? How could a man who supports the American Civil Liberties Union and consistently disparages the bourgeoisie be suspected of conformity? The new individualism, then, was an emancipated individualism, cleansed of its old, middle-class sins of privatism and of conformity.

Yet before we accept the conclusion that the nineteenth-century doctrine of progress has been vindicated again, and that individualism has reached a new and perfected condition, it may be worthwhile to apply one of the weapons of dissent, the weapon of skepticism, and to ask in a truly searching way whether conformity and privatism are really dead, whether true self-expression has come into its own at last, or whether, to some extent, conformity and privatism have merely found new modes of expression.

To pursue this question, as it relates to conformity, one would have to ask whether we have ceased to follow the crowd, or whether we have to some extent merely changed the crowd which we follow? Have we ceased to be cultists, or have we primarily changed our cults? Does the liberal who makes a fetish of his nonconformity actually show much more readiness to get out of step with his fellow liberals than does the avowedly conformist conservative with his fellow conservatives?

Stated a little differently and a little more abstractly, conformity is the faithful, unquestioning compliance with the standards imposed by a group. But to say this is to say that whether you call a man a conformist or a dissenter is very often not a question of his intrinsic independence, but a question of what group you measure him by. A Communist, for instance, measured by the reference group of the American public, is a dissenter and a nonconformist, but measured by the reference group of his own adoption, the Communist group, he is the supreme conformist— more so than a Baptist or a Rotarian, for he has completely abdicated his capacity to judge questions on their own merits and has embraced, *verbatim et literatim,* a whole body of doctrine which, like medieval theology, has answered all questions before they arise.

David Riesman has dealt with this point with sharp perception in his essay "The Saving Remnant," where he says, "The Bohemians and rebels are not usually autonomous; on the contrary, they are zealously tuned in to the signals of a defiant group that finds the meaning of life in a compulsive nonconformity to the majority group."[9] In an extraordinarily acute article called "The Bored and the Violent," Arthur Miller has discussed this point in connection with extreme manifestations of sadistic violence among juvenile delinquents. Miller makes the striking point that, among these youths, who are responding to society by defiance in its most extreme form, the real pattern is not one of deviation but of conformity—a blind, abject conformity to the expectations of their peers. As Miller says, "The delinquent, far from being the rebel, is the conformist par excellence. He is actually incapable of doing anything alone."[10] His reliance upon his gang is, of course, the measure of this lack of capability. Here, one is reminded of a cartoon in the *New Yorker* some time ago showing a young woman, attractive and appearing very much an average American girl, speaking somewhat crossly to her husband, who was dressed in the prescribed uniform of a beatnik. Her question to him was, "Why do you have to be a nonconformist like everyone else?"

If there is any group in our society which makes a truly earnest effort to cultivate real intellectual freedom and fearless inquiry, it is no doubt the academic and intellectual community. Yet even here, do we not have a certain incidence of what might be called academic conformity? Would not an academic who in 1960 spoke out loud and clear for Richard Nixon have shocked the sense of propriety of a gathering of academics as much as an overt glorification of the New Frontier would shock a group of investment bankers? Do not even the academics have their orthodoxies and their conventions? Do not these conventions require that in the case of a novelist, for example, he make a conforming obeisance to nonconformity by following the practice of employing as frequently as possible the monosyllabic words for the functions of sex and bodily elimination which have now become almost trite but which still have a gratifying capacity to startle a good many readers and to attract a good many buyers who hope to be startled? And do not the conventions also require that the book reviewer also conform and prove that he too is an emancipated spirit by dutifully praising the fearless realism of the author without reference to whether his work has merit?

One more illustration may be in order here—the case of an academic of irreproachable standing. When Hannah Arendt published an article questioning whether the integration of public schools ought to be attempted by the exercise of public authority, the result was not, as one might have hoped, a rough-and-tumble scrimmage between her and persons who disagreed with her. It was rather a shocked silence, a polite looking in the other direction as if no one had noticed. It was, indeed, the same reaction as if she had belched in church. Miss Arendt had questioned a point on which liberals have established a dogma to which they require conformity, and they were shocked in a prudish way to hear this dogma questioned.

If there is some question about the completeness of the triumph of nonconformity, there is perhaps also a question concerning the finality of the victory over privatism. Surely the old nineteenth-century brand of rugged individualism is gone for good, and we will no longer sacrifice the interests of society to the individualism of *laissez-faire.* But can any generation, even our own, completely reconcile the social needs of the group with other personal needs of the individual? And must we not expect that even the new style of defense of individual right will sometimes be conducted at the expense of what might best serve society as a whole? The new individualism firmly repudiates all the nineteenth-century freebooters who used to exploit the public economically, but it still thinks, and perhaps ought to think, in terms of man as separate rather than of man in the group. Thus, when it is confronted with what we call crime—the large-scale incidence of violence in our society—it seems more concerned with the rehabilitation of the deviant individual who has committed the violence than with safeguarding those anonymous persons upon whom the violence is committed. When confronted with the sale in every drugstore of magazines which exploit sex, it does not really ask whether it would be better for society if the drugstores did not purvey this material. It does not ask whether the publisher who makes a fast buck by this shoddy commercial enterprise is different from a patent-medicine manufacturer who also makes a fast buck by selling nostrums but is regulated, hopefully, by the Pure Food and Drug Act. It asks instead who will dare to violate freedom of the press in maintaining an informed public opinion.

Perhaps this is the right question to ask. I would hesitate to say that it is clearly wrong. But what I do venture to suggest is that the freedom of the individual, in relation to his society, cannot be absolute, basically because the individual and the society are not really separate. The individual acquires his full identity only as a member of society, and society itself is, in the last analysis, a multiplicity of individuals. The American tradition, which rejected elite individualism from the beginning, has always shown enough concern for the social values to seek to justify its individualism—whether self-reliant or nonconformist—in social terms. Thus the competitive system in economics was defended not on the ground of the great profits which it would bring to some individuals, but with the claim that it would assure economic vigor for the society. Similarly, the sanctions which have surrounded dissent were based less upon approval of the dissenter than upon the need of society for an unrestricted "free trade in ideas." Moreover, each school of individualism cared enough for social values to attack the other for betraying them. Thus the dissentients accused the self-reliants of sacrificing the weak to the strong and the community to its predatory members, while the self-reliants accused the dissentients of sacrificing the strong to the weak and the community to its aberrant members. Perhaps both accusations have been justified, for both groups have remained primarily committed to a strong individualistic emphasis, and in the long struggle between two schools of individualism, the values of the community have often lacked effective defenders on either side. Neither form of individualism has had enough genuine concern for real group values, shared community values, to hold a proper balance between the centrifugal and the centripetal forces.

Neither one has been willing to recognize that the tension between the individual and the group can never be treated as a simple antithesis, involving a simple choice. For each, in its logically pure form, contains implications which are unacceptable to most of us. The emphasis on the individual essentially implies a component of privatism which would sacrifice the interests of the group to the interests of a limited number of its members, and this implication is not acceptable in the long run to a democratic society; the emphasis on the group implies the subordination of the qualities of the mind and spirit of man, standing by himself, to the pressures of men in a herd, and this implication, too, is unacceptable to a people who believe that society exists for man and not man for society. Therefore, we can never make a clear-cut, exclusive choice in favor of either individualism, as it is called, or collectivism, as it is called. While philosophers are engaged in pursuing one or the other of these two to their logical extremes and even their logical absurdities, people in everyday life will go on, trying in the future, as they have tried in the past, to accommodate these two and imperfectly to reconcile the indispensable values which are inherent in them both. As Riesman stated it, "Such terms as 'society' and 'individual' tend to pose a false, as well as a shifting dichotomy."

NOTES

1. David Riesman, *Individualism Reconsidered, and Other Essays* (Glencoe, Ill., 1954), p. 26. [The phrase "antagonistic cooperation," used below, is from Riesman, Glazer, and Denney, *The Lonely Crowd* (New Haven, Conn., 1950).]

2. John William Ward, ed., *Society, Manners, and Politics in the United States: Letters on North America by Michael Chevalier* (Garden City, N.Y., 1961), pp. 327–28.

3. Arthur K. Moore, *The Frontier Mind* (Lexington, Ky., 1957).

4. Leslie A. Fiedler, *An End of Innocence* (Boston, 1955), pp. 134–35. Courtesy also of the *Kenyon Review*.

5. Martha Wolfenstein and Nathan Leites, *Movies: A Psychological Study* (Glencoe, Ill., 1950), p. 298.

6. Margaret Mead, *And Keep Your Powder Dry: An Anthropologist Looks at America* (New York, 1942), p. 141.

7. Stanley M. Elkins, *Slavery: A Problem in American Institutional and Intellectual Life* (Chicago, 1959), pp. 27–80.

8. Gabriel A. Almond, *The American People and Foreign Policy* (New York, 1950), p. 48.

9. Riesman, *Individualism Reconsidered*, p. 117.

10. Arthur Miller, "The Bored and the Violent," *Harper's Magazine* (Nov. 1962), pp. 51–52.

Potter's essay is one of the few studies of American character to divide individualism into sharply different types. His distinction between the conservative's individualism of economic self-reliance and the liberal's individualism of self-expression helps to explain why each type can accuse the other of betraying freedom, for each side cherishes a different kind of liberty. This mutual misunderstanding is not confined to the United States.

Potter makes two basic arguments: One, Americans have always believed that their individualism should be within society and serve it. Two, despite cross-currents, the tide of time has changed American individualism's predominant form.

Despite his reference to the Yankee prayer, "God save . . . us four and no more," Potter's first argument says too little about the predator who only pays lip service, if that, to the notion that self-serving behavior should also serve society. Potter does not observe that winning and getting are often goals in themselves, whether or not they are rationalized as socially desirable.

Potter also oversimplifies American distrust of authority and elite power. That distrust is enshrined in the U.S. Constitution and in much of the decentralizing of American society. But Americans also have a tradition of respect for big, dominating leaders, from Teddy Roosevelt to General George Patton. The cult of efficiency and winning still rewards the tough boss and the hard-driving coach; Americans have also been pushovers for the charismatic hero who 'speaks for the people' and embodies the 'self-made man' (an Eisenhower, a Reagan).*

Like many Americans, Potter associated elitism with the Old

*Just recently a senior British manager who has worked for the same multinational firm in Britain, the United States, Australia, and the Netherlands told me that in his experience the operating structure of American corporations—unlike American politics—was particularly undemocratic.

177

World and overlooked American forms of it. (Seymour Martin Lipset was less fooled: see pp. 109–12.) Since Potter wrote, it has become more obvious that the old displays of success, the mansions and carriages of Gilded Age tycoons, have been succeeded by the perquisites of bureaucratic elites. Limousines, private planes and yachts, elegant dining and tailoring—anything that may impress the client or ease the path of the 'key executive'—can be justified on the grounds of generating yet more success.

Potter also underestimated American techniques for disguising snobbery—you can laugh, for example, at an uneducated accent by describing it not in class terms but geographically: 'Brooklyn,' 'hillbilly,' and so on. In Potter's defense, though, it could be said that the very need to disguise and rationalize shows an underlying value on equality.

Potter's second argument, that American individualism had moved unevenly from conformist self-reliance toward dissent and self-expression, compares interestingly with William Whyte's view (p. 70). Both Potter and Whyte asserted that Americans had shifted away from economic individualism, but Whyte associated the shift with a deepening conformity, whereas Potter on the whole linked it with less conformity.

Potter explains the economic and social conditions that gave rise to his nineteenth-century type of individualism, but he does not really do this for the twentieth-century type. Even in the nineteenth century, his picture of nineteenth-century rural and frontier life is too one-sided: he simply leaves out the socialistic elements. No mention of farmers' 'grange' clubs, economic cooperatives, and populist political movements in the late nineteenth century, or the many local offices held by western socialists in the early twentieth.

Ironically, one of Potter's finest pieces of writing was his long introduction to *Trail to California* (1945), the edited diary of two 1849 gold rushers traveling in an overland company of wagons. Like many other such companies, the members traveled as a team under semimilitary discipline. Their goals were individualistic—to make their fortunes in California—but their style of cooperation, well appreciated by Potter in his introduction, gets no recognition in his essay on American individualism.

Finally, what of the word "American" in his essay title? More needs to be said here than Potter's brief comparison with French *hauteur* (he said nothing, incidently, about the constraints of French etiquette and formalism). Through the first half of this century, observers of British character noted its individualism too. They connected it with a dislike of compulsory restriction and a deep habit of privacy, in spite of being quick to form crowds and teams. The implicit comparison was usually with other Europeans, but in the early 1920s the English writer Henry Stuart contrasted a British tolerance of diversity, as he saw it, with an American "melting pot" pressure to conform. In the early 1950s a survey of child-rearing attitudes by the American psychologist Maurice Farber came to somewhat different conclusions. The British, he found, stressed self-reliance and self-control, whereas Americans were keener on originality as well as getting along with others. As Potter himself implied, individualism per se is not specially American. It is the *kind* of individualism that counts, and this varies according to time and place as well as the observer's standpoint.

GEORGE W. PIERSON

The M-Factor

"Why, hello! Thought you were abroad. Aren't you on sabbatical?"

Professor P————— nodded a bit sheepishly. It was the fourth time within the week that some colleague had demanded to know what on earth he was "doing in town." Without much conviction, he repeated something about trying to get ahead on his book by doing some quiet work in the library. But it seemed to help much more when he added that he and his wife would be taking off for Greece in the spring. Travel? That made sense. His friend's face lighted up. Perhaps, after all, P————— wasn't such a hopeless stick-in-the-mud.

This is how the historian George Pierson, whom we may take to be Professor P—————, started one of his essays on the American yen for moving and its effects on the culture.* His story was apposite, for Pierson, who spent a large slice of his career writing about the American "M-Factor"—movement, migration, mobility—was himself successfully *immobile*. After graduating in 1922 from Groton School, Massachusetts, Pierson followed in his father's footsteps to Yale, and there he stayed, as undergraduate, graduate student, professor, and official historian of the university—a Yale Institution. Just as Pierson's Yale colleague, David Potter, derived a sharp sense of American values by coming from the South, a region historically at odds with American mainstreams, so Pierson may have found his perspective on American movement by standing just outside it.

Like Potter, Pierson was fascinated with Frederick Jackson Turner's frontier thesis but sought to revise it (see p. 11). Both historians picked out an element of Turner's frontier and expanded it beyond

*"Under a Wandering Star," *Virginia Quarterly Review,* 39 (Autumn 1963), pp. 621–38.

the frontier context. For Potter, the key element was "free land," which became his more general concept of abundance. For Pierson, the key was a moving population. Yes, said Pierson, frontier opportunity had invited Americans to move, but they had been movers before they reached America, and they went on moving long after the frontier closed.

Pierson published several essays on Turner in the early 1940s, but he reached the subject from his 1933 Yale Ph.D. dissertation, which became a book: a study of the American travels of Alexis de Tocqueville and his companion, Gustave de Beaumont, and the writing of Tocqueville's classic, *Democracy in America* (pp. 10–11). Pierson traveled vicariously with the pair; he enjoyed piecing together where they went and who they talked with. He was struck, too, by Tocqueville's repeated observation that Americans were so *restless*. This encouraged his own thinking about the subjective side of American movement—it was a matter of mind as well as behavior.

Pierson was also interested in the way ideas migrated, and how different regions and nations influenced each other. From the 1930s until his retirement in 1973, he taught a course on the "Foreign Relations of American Culture, from Province to World Power." Pierson, indeed, was one of the first interpreters of American culture to be influenced by the modern, big-power status of the United States. It sharpened his interest in the nature of Americans as seen by the growing number of peoples with whom they had to deal. Two of Pierson's major articles on American mobility, one published in 1954, the other ten years later, starts with foreign impressions—largely unfavorable— of American culture and character.

"The M-Factor in American History," Pierson's essay reprinted here, originated as a conference paper at the University of Munich in 1961. It was a sequel to his article of 1954, "The Moving American."

☆ • ☆ • ☆ • ☆ • ☆

Is there any such thing as "national character"?* In particular, is there, or has there ever been, an American Character? Many critics question, or even deny the idea. Students of American civilization generally seem to start out by thinking there must be an American Character. But then they encounter great difficulties in defining this character—that is, they find too many different or contradictory types, none of the types unique, all of them appearing also in other cultures, a few of them perhaps unstable across the years. The result? Conscientious scholars are driven to despair, and decide that American society is neither consistent nor original nor completely different; therefore we have no distinctive character.

Now this, I submit, may be just a little foolish. For theoretically it isn't scientific, and practically it doesn't make sense. Theoretically, is it not a poor kind of science which says that, because you and I cannot wholly know a thing or exactly define it, it doesn't exist? Just because we cannot scientifically define Americanism would seem a quite insufficient reason for ignoring its existence. What has not existed, rather, may be that intuition of causes, that exact grasp of detail, that art of proportion, that science of social structure, which will enable us to say: this is, in a sum total way, different, *sui generis*, peculiar. After all, a combination does not have to be unique in all its elements, or even in a single one of these elements, to be different in sum total. I will assert that theoretically there may be an American Character, even though that character may have been composed of familiar elements, even though it is only the proportions which have been different, even though the resulting society may be mixed, contradictory, pluralistic, unjelled. The very indeterminism of a society may be a distinguishing mark. Theoretically, I see no barrier to believing that an American Character may exist.

On the contrary, on the grounds of common sense, I see many reasons to believe that there is and has been an American Character, for one thing because the most intelligent thinkers and observers have thought so, and have kept on thinking so, across the years. These observers may have differed in the labels they attached to us, they may have

*"The M-Factor," by George W. Pierson was first published as "The M-Factor in American History," *American Quarterly*, Volume 14, No. 2, Part 2 (Summer 1962). Copyright © 1962 and reprinted by permission of the American Studies Association.

argued about the causes of our American peculiarities, but every one of them has thought that the Americans are a little odd in their psychology, and a little different in their social institutions. Crèvecoeur went so far as to call the American a "New Man." And he defined this new man as the Progressive: "He is an American who leaves behind his ancient prejudices and manners." But whatever the definition, from Crèvecoeur to Tocqueville to André Siegfried, from Dickens to Bryce to Denis Brogan, from Lieber to Keyserling or Robert Jungk, the most thoughtful commentators have asserted that there is and has been (and, alas, will continue to be) an American Character.[1]

What caused this Americanism to emerge? Many things, no doubt; far too many even to list in this paper. So I shall confine my attention to a single prevailing characteristic of our people: the migration factor in our history, our excessive mobility. Yet before I take up the Moving American, allow me to recall some classic interpretations which have exercised a strong influence on the writing of American history, and on thinking about America generally.

How are Americans different? In the beginning was the Word, and the Word had it that we were a Chosen People, a seed sifted out of the populations of Europe, a community of saints destined to create a better society on this earth. Like the Israelites of old, we were a people under divine command. As we sang in the old hymn: "O God, beneath thy guiding hand our exiled fathers crossed the sea!"

After about one hundred and fifty years, there succeeded to this Biblical interpretation the thought that, if we were not always more holy, we were at least more free. As an independent nation, our destiny was to bring liberty, self-government, republicanism, the art of federal decentralization to the succor of oppressed mankind. So to the religious mission there succeeded a political mission—which was what Alexis de Tocqueville came to study.

From the beginning, also, there had always been an economic mission. America was El Dorado: the golden opportunity, the country of get-rich-quick, the land of the second chance, the asylum for the poverty-stricken. So, as foreign and native observers alike commented, America was (1) the land of goodness, (2) the land of liberty, and (3) the land of plenty.

For a long while these three national myths satisfied. Toward the

183

end of the nineteenth century, however, there emerged a series of more sophisticated, or "scientific," explanations, and, in particular, one which has exercised enormous influence. What was it changed Europeans into Americans?

For historians of the past generation, the Frontier Hypothesis of Frederick Jackson Turner supplied the classic answer. It was the *frontier* experience which made us different. That is, it was our struggle with the wilderness—it was exploiting the vast free lands of the interior—it was freeing ourselves from the past, "breaking the cake of custom," leaving behind the fetters of settled society and the refinements of civilization to start over again in the woods—it was the lonely pioneers chopping out clearings on the road westward—it was getting together with other pioneers to rebuild a simpler, freer society—it was pulling up stakes and repeating the process—it was moving and moving again until in 1890 the free land and the West were all used up. On the frontier, said Turner, society became atomic, individualism flourished, democracy was generated, national legislation was encouraged. The opportunities of the West also opened a gate of escape for the oppressed of the East, and so contributed to the democratization and Americanization of the seaboard. The frontier also transformed personal character. As Turner phrased it:

> That coarseness and strength combined with acuteness and inquisitiveness; that practical, inventive turn of mind, quick to find expedients; that masterful grasp of material things, lacking in the artistic but powerful to effect great ends; that restless, nervous energy; that dominant individualism, working for good and evil, and withal that buoyancy and exuberance which comes with freedom—these are traits of the frontier, or traits called out elsewhere because of the existence of the frontier.[2]

In effect, said Turner, it was primarily the molding influence of the Frontier which had transformed so many European materials into a new American amalgam. In his oft-quoted phrase, the frontier was "the line of most rapid and effective Americanization."

For a long while this satisfied. But about thirty years ago, when Turner died, and his imaginative idea was making its way into popular speech, and Franklin Delano Roosevelt was using the disappearance of the frontier to justify a welfare state, a number of people discovered political reasons for questioning the doctrine. Historians themselves grew uneasy. For one thing, the hypothesis seemed too nationalistic, too provincial. For another, the Frontier concept embraced too many overlapping or discordant influences. Again, the frontier cause seemed to be credited with inconsistent results: it made Americans both sectional and nationalistic, cooperative and individualistic, repetitive yet original. Once again, one wondered how many Americans could have been affected. And how were we to stay American after 1890, when the frontier disappeared? In the upshot, the frontier theory seemed to explain far too much by far too little.

Yet, for all this, it was a difficult theory to discard. For if the frontier did not produce the effects ascribed to it, what did?

I believe we now have at least a small part of the answer. It has been hinted by many perceptive observers, not least by Tocqueville or by Francis Lieber or by Sarmiento.[3] I call it the M-Factor in American history.

What made and kept us different was not just the wildness of the North American continent, nor its vast empty spaces, nor even its wealth of resources, powerful as must have been those influences. No. It was, first of all, the M-Factor: the factor of movement, migration, mobility. Colonization was one part of it; immigration, another; the westward movement itself was a fraction, but only a fraction, of the whole. This whole began with many old-world uprootings. It gathered force with the transatlantic passage. It flooded on to the farmlands of the mid-continent. But increasingly it meant movement also *away* from the frontier, from farm to town, from region to region, from city to city. Individuals, families, churches, villages, on occasion whole countrysides have participated—and continue to participate. Francis Lieber said that in America he felt as if tied to the arms of a windmill. To him, movement had become our "historical task." And Sarmiento was so staggered by our propensity for traveling around that he predicted that, if the trump of doom were suddenly to sound, it would surprise two-thirds of the Americans, out on the roads like ants.

In all this, I repeat, the frontier played an important but limited part. For if people moved to the frontier, they moved also before there was a frontier, moved behind and away from the frontier, and kept on moving even more enthusiastically when the frontier closed.

Let us put it this way: Frederick Jackson Turner was a great poet-historian, who more than half-sensed the power that was in migration, but then imprisoned this giant in the rough homespun of the vanishing pioneers. So we of a later generation must once again return to the great question: What has made and still makes Europeans into restless Americans? I venture herewith some tentative speculations, in the hope that we will find in them ideas worth working out.

My basic proposition is obvious: Movement means change. To transfer is in some part to transform. *"Wanderung meint wandlung,"* as the Germans put it. And all forms of movement, from mass exodus to simple milling around, have shared in this subtle process of alteration.

Why should motion cause change? First, because *institutions* do not move easily. A few will be destroyed; many more are damaged; nearly all are shaken, and have to be pruned, simplified, or otherwise adjusted to survive the transplanting. To a degree *displacement* means *replacement* of institutions.

Why again should migration cause modification? Because the migrants are not average people. As a group they do not represent a fair cross-section of the society they are leaving; as individuals they tend toward exaggerations of one sort or another; as settlers they won't wish to reproduce the society they have left, or succeed in reproducing it even should they so desire.

This brings us to the third great reason for change, the new circumstances: that is, the hardships and accidents of the crossing, the strangers encountered on the road, the unaccustomed climate and geography of their new environment. Movement means exposure, and successive exposures compel unexpected changes.

It may be urged that more credit should go to the strangers and the new countries. Or it may be observed that migrations are often the result or the symptom of changes that have already taken place in the parent society. And with both these ideas I agree. On the one hand, many immigrants were Americanized only long after they got over. On the other, not a few American types, like the puritan and the businessman, had already appeared in sixteenth-century Europe. So migration served both as prologue and as epilogue; it has been the means of change and the effect of change (as well as the cause). Yet no movement of people or institutions, however started or motivated, can take place without further alterations. For migration selects special types for moving; it subjects them to exceptional strains on the journey; and it then compels them to rebuild, with liberty to choose or refuse from the mail-order catalogue of Western experience. On top of all that, repeated movements, such as we in our country have known, seem to have a cumulative, or progressive, effect.

What parts of a civilization, what elements in a society, does the M-Factor attack? Apparently, all parts. Before his death Ellsworth Huntington, who was one of the earliest American scientists to become curious about this phenomenon, came to see in migration a selective force so strong that it affected the stock and temperament of a people as well as its culture. After some hesitations, I believe we will concur. For I believe it can be demonstrated that movement changes the physical population, the institutions and group structures, the social habits and traditions, the personal character and attitudes of the migrants.

Allow me to offer some random, familiar illustrations at this point.

The American population? It was formed and re-formed by migration. To begin with we were all immigrants. Moreover, because the Atlantic was open, people from many lands and nations came to these shores, until we were the leading conglomerate of the West, a Rainbow Division of Europe. Political scientists call us a pluralistic society. Sociologists find culture conflicts endemic.

Again because the migrants did not all come at once, but in intermittent surges, and because in free movements the later comers, as strangers, are handicapped and must enter the lower levels of their class and occupation, the natives or earlier-comers have repeatedly found themselves pushed upstairs, to the more skilled jobs, to the managerial posts, to the position of employers and capitalists. At the same time, moving upstairs was difficult, so difficult that the older stock felt it had to cut down on the number of its own children, if it was to graduate them into the higher levels of living—so difficult that the next-to-last comers tended to resent the labor competition of the newcomers and tried to exclude them. Thus the Yankees industrialized with the aid of other people's children. Meanwhile these laboring generations, as they matured, tried to keep the jobs for themselves and, whether as skilled artisans or later trade union bosses, as Know-Nothings in the 1850s or McCarthyites a century later, became the strongest champions of immigration restriction, the most suspicious of new foreigners, the uncompromising 100 percenters. So from 1820 to 1920 what ought to have been for the Anglo-American population a series

187

of European additions became instead a progressive physical substitution. And after 1920 the freedom to immigrate was shut off by the votes of the very groups which had benefited from it earlier. But why did not and has not this stepladder movement of infiltration produced a stratified, hierarchical, skyscraper society? The answer is again the M-Factor, but this time internal migration. Inside, the freedom to move remained, and a man could get out of his cellar in town by building a one-story cabin up-country, or he could come off his eroded acres into Chicago, where the rising buildings and professions had elevators in them.

If we now turn from questions of nationality and occupation to the age and sex characteristics of our population, we find that here, too, the M-Factor has left deep marks. For three hundred years, or at least until the Great Depression, we were a young country. We boasted of it. Foreigners rarely failed to mention the childlike innocence, the boyish enthusiasm, the youthful drive and bustle and activity-for-activity's sake of these strange Americans. The youth of America, quipped Oscar Wilde, is its oldest tradition. And perhaps we were guilty of a certain "shortage of adults." At least the demographers have proved that our Constitution was made for adolescents—as late as 1820 the median age of the population was only 16 years, and it was not until well into the twentieth century that that median soared above 25. That is, it was only after preventive medicine had started to prolong the lives of the infirm, and immigration restriction had cut down on the annual influx of bachelors and young marrieds, that we first really began to feel middle-aged. How does the M-Factor figure in this? Well, students of migration have rediscovered the fact that it is overwhelmingly the young, between the ages of 15 and 25, who move—and in the first waves or pioneer phases, it is primarily the young men. The frontiers, whether of farm or factory, start emphatically male *(Oh Susannah, don't you cry for me!)*.

Yet the men were not to have it all their own way, for the M-Factor can give things a sardonic twist. Migration has perennially represented rebellion against past tyrannies or authorities, against the father no less than against the lord or priest, against the husband no less than against the father. Thus, after the first settlements had been established, the open spaces and open opportunities of this country just invited the younger generation to leave home and strike out on their own, and the able young men accepted the invitation. Even today it is the rare son of ability, who does not insist on leaving the town where he was born to try to make his way in a larger world. Meanwhile the pioneer women, being scarce as well as weak, found that they had inadvertently acquired a scarcity value. For them, as well as for the children, migration meant progressive emancipation—an emancipation eventually crowned by woman suffrage, Mother's Day and much symbolic statuary. Thus, as our lonely forefathers pushed relentlessly westward, and the idea of equality came galloping up behind, the Pioneer Mother replaced the Pilgrim Father on the sculptor's pedestal in the town square. (Whether the statuesque Miss America has now replaced her bronzed mother in the popular imagination I leave to braver men to say—we may note only the querulous complaints of our English and Continental friends that we are today a woman-run and child-dominated subcivilization.)

If we next pursue the M-Factor from our population to our economy, what will we find? An economy in which transportation has loomed extraordinarily large—witness the railroads, the automobile age and the airplane industry of today—witness also in our myths how prairie schooners and pony express, paddle wheelers and the long whistle of the trains, Ford cars and the Spirit of St. Louis have entered into the folklore of our people.

> The wheels are singing on the railroad track
> If you go, you can't come back.
> Hear the whistle blow[4]

For Americans, it has been said, the automobile restates a national principle, since, after all, the settler was the first auto-mobile. In the U.S. a mile is something to put behind you. Where else would you find a place named Stillwater Junction?

More soberly, if our interest runs rather to our religious peculiarities, it might be observed that the need for settlers, and the ease of exit and entrance from one colony to the other, made toleration and disestablishment of churches almost inevitable from the start. The same ease of escape then long made it difficult for the states to impose adequate taxation, or any other really burdensome regulation, on their footloose citizens. A Virginian did not have to stay in Virginia. A Yorker could go to Michigan. If a business failed, or a marriage, the simplest thing was to decamp. Other states would welcome you. So, by and by, Reno became a monument to our vagrant fancies in matters matrimonial.

Again, politically our moving habits not only made possible but reinforced a decentralizing, federal tendency. Legally, the absence of customary law in the new settlements must have fostered the excessive American dependence on statute law. Migration also splintered our first establishments of higher education, in the sense that it led to the founding of many colleges instead of concentration on a few national universities. Thus my own institution, through the efforts of its migrating graduates, became a mother of colleges a full century before it could accumulate enough substance in New Haven to rival the great foundations of Europe. Finally, our peculiar instability of family homesite, and the lack of a national capital or home, shifted emotional loyalties to things that could be carried with us, such as declarations of principle and constitutional theories. And eventually, to bind ourselves together, we were forced to insist with an unusual, almost tyrannical, emphasis on such assimilative codes and social practices as are commonly summed up in that telltale phrase: "The American *Way* of Life."

But enough of such random illustrations.

Let us now proceed to ask, on a more systematic basis, how, just how, have migration and movement acted to convert Europeans into something rich and strange?

Considering the matter first on a broad social scale, I would propose that the M-Factor has been (turn by turn or even all at once): (1) the great Eliminator; (2) the persistent Distorter; (3) an arch-Conservator; (4) an almost irresistible Disintegrator or Atomizer; (5) a heart Stimulant or Energizer and (6) the prime source of Optimism in the American atmosphere, a never-failing ozone of hope. Also, (7) the Secularizer and Externalizer of our beliefs, and (8) the Equalizer and Democratizer of social classes. Indeed a little reflection will suggest still other ways in which migration has shaken its European ingredients into new patterns. But on this occasion let us consider merely some of these eight, with just a hint or two of historic events by way of illumination.

Migration was the great Eliminator? Nothing could be plainer. In theory you can't take everything with you when you move. Some goods are too bulky or delicate to be put on ship; some household possessions will fall out of the covered wagon. Again, in a free migration, not all elements in a society will wish to move; the dregs will be too spiritless and

impoverished to emigrate unaided; the ruling classes entirely too successful and satisfied. Check this theory against history and what do we find?
In the early colonization there came out of England the rising middle
classes, with some admixture of the lowest elements, but with only a few
aristocratic leaders. Ours started, therefore, as a decapitated society,
virtually without nobles or bishops, judges or learned lawyers, artists,
playwrights or great poets. Taking a hopeful view, a student of mine once
maintained that settlement transferred the accent from *nobility* to *ability*. Considering the transfer culturally, however, one must recognize a
tragic impoverishment. Despite all our gains of goodness or plenty or
freedom, the men of the highest attainments and greatest skills had
stayed home—and with them their arts and refinements, their leisure-
class culture. The same process of abandonment, of flight from the elite
and their standards, would be discernible later in the settlement of the
West. Axiomatically, the fine arts, the theoretical sciences, the most
advanced tools and machinery, are not found or produced on moving
frontiers. Like war or fire or inflation, migration has been a great destroyer of inherited treasure.

At first glance such destruction may seem only temporary, to be
replaced "when we have time." Yet meanwhile some elements are missing, the balance is changed, the old society has been distorted—and
before long one may get reconciled to doing without. On top of this, the
M-Factor has promoted distortion in an even more drastic way. For
moving forces the reclassification of values. Why? Because the land of
destination attracts more strongly for one or two presumed goods than for
the others (as for economic opportunity perhaps, or political freedom, or
the right to worship in one's own way). So if a family is to go, they have
to believe, or persuade themselves, that the particular goods to be realized
are more important to them than all the other social goods, which may be
diminished, or even be left behind altogether. If similar movements are
made by later generations for like reasons, then these cherished values
may rise almost to the status of holy commandments or natural rights,
and in the nineteenth century become the polar magnets in a new value
system. By elimination and wilful distortion a moving people becomes a
narrower society: thinner and shallower, yet in some things much more
intense.

This calls attention to a third and almost paradoxical characteristic of migration: its conservatism. People moved to save as well as to improve. But when they found they couldn't take everything with them, then a curious thing often happened. They came to value even more highly what they had succeeded in preserving. Having suffered such privations, having sacrificed so many other possessions, they clung to what was saved with a fiercer passion. Witness the Puritans with their Wilderness Zion, the Mormons under Brigham Young, or even Turner's leapfrogging pioneers. For these last, as for so many others, it had become easier to move than to change their vocation, their habits, their antiquated methods. To put this bluntly, for them the cheap lands of the West made it easier to keep on with their soil-mining and strip-farming, and possible to avoid such painful changes as learning a proper care of the land, or the new crop rotation of the advanced parts of Europe and the East. So for the American farmer—or agriculturally speaking—the westward movement became the great postponement of American history. They profited personally, but it was a postponement nonetheless—just as in the flight of the New England textile industry to the South in our times. In France, before De Gaulle, the peasant and small shopkeeper clung stubbornly to his land or shop, but politically moved constantly to the left. That is, economically, he might be a selfish reactionary, and even vote for Poujade, but by changing the name of his party leftward he was sure he was making "progress." Did not some of our American pioneers give themselves the same feeling of progress by moving westward? Migration, I would suggest, could be a way of promoting change—and of avoiding it, too. Flight can be an escape from the future as well as from the past.

The M-Factor, we must next realize, was an almost irresistible Disintegrator or Atomizer. Few authoritarian institutions from Europe could stand the strain of Atlantic distances or the explosion of American space. So either they decentralized or died. Witness the early church. In Virginia the episcopal organization proved so little suited to the far-flung tobacco plantations that the Church of England almost withered away, whereas in New England the Puritan branch of the same church developed a localized or Congregational organization, and flourished. Then, later, when the Irish immigration poured life and vigor into American Catholicism, the hierarchy, intuitively recognizing that moving out on the lands might cripple the Church as well as weaken the individual's faith, did their best to hold the new arrivals in the seaport towns, at least until some interior communities could be effectively churched. Ultimately, I believe it will be found that our Catholics have moved less often, less widely and less soon than their Protestant neighbors, hence have missed certain corrosive acids and opportunities in the M-Factor.

One of these opportunities, of course, was to stand on your own feet, to make your own way, and if need be to move again. In our expanding settlements the arm of the State (like the authority of the bishops) shriveled, and a kind of physical individualism sprouted. On the trail, society tended to break down into chance parties of moving families or individuals. And at the destination everything was to be reconstructed. It took energy and courage to move, and more energy to make the move succeed. Hence migration was a great stimulant to action—and when such action repeatedly succeeded (or, as we may say, "worked"), then perhaps the beginnings of a habit of action had been established, both for oneself and for one's neighbor. The American reputation for activism, as for self-help and neighborly helpfulness, surely needs no underlining.

Migration was not only the Destroyer, Distorter, Conservator, Atomizer, and Energizer of western society, but its most effective "Optimizer." First of all, out of the welter of old-world classes and temperaments it selected the up-and-coming and the hopeful. Pessimists didn't bother; you had to be an optimist to move. Next it required sacrifice and waiting, and so captured many believers, the men of faith. Finally, it rewarded the successful—and those who weren't lucky were given a second try. America the Golden was the land of the second chance. And from failure it offered a full timetable of escapes.

I realize that it is customary at this point to do a ritualistic dance around the statue of the golden calf—and credit our optimism or success primarily to the sheer wealth of the continent. But if we did become a "people of plenty," and if that plenty left its mark even on the size of our automobiles, let us not forget that the beginnings were almost invariably hard, and what the land long offered most of was tough places and violent weather. What kind of plenty was it converted the gravel patch of New England into smiling farms? Lots of hard work, I should say, and plenty of faith. Again, who but a lunkheaded optimist would grow wheat in western Kansas? Or who in his right mind would go settle in Dakota? No. The Black Hills gold and the U.S. farm bounties, these bonanzas were later and almost accidental discoveries. In my book, optimism made more states than vice versa. Many a town existed first, or only, in the imagination. "Boost, don't knock" has been the slogan of new communities just abuilding, and the booster is Mr. Johnny-come-lately. We began as migrants, that is, wishful thinkers, and each wave of immigration, each boatload from abroad, brought us fresh injections of this heart stimulant. For Europe's poor, the freedom to come changed "tomorrow" from a threat into a promise. For its men of faith, the act of moving and moving again substituted "the future" for "the heavenly hereafter." And with time the mission of American idealists came to be in and for this world. From infant damnation to the social gospel is but a long tramp.

I hope I may be forgiven if I now pass over the secularizing and externalizing influences of mobility (which Sorokin has explored) in favor of its equalitarian and leveling effects.[5] For these democratic tendencies seem to me particularly important, and I have stumbled on some odd illustrations.

Here the theoretical argument would be that the M-Factors are often democratic in their consequences, first because for the lower classes emigration means *"getting out from under,"* the first step on the road up; secondly because the hardships of the journey are no respecters of birth (witness the miserable failure of the early "Gentlemen" of the Jamestown Colony in Virginia). In the third place, and most significantly, the process of resettlement is a process of making new mixtures, out of a gathering of strangers, each without authority, credentials, reputation or other priority than that of arrival. In a new community (frontier or town) family and past performance hardly count. Everyone has to make his own mark, and stands equal with his fellow-strangers. The social competition, as it were, starts over, with all the camaraderie and "gamesmanship" of a new catch-as-catch-can. Migration has been a great Mixmaster. And mixtures of anonymous elements are necessarily more democratic, at least at first. So much for doctrine. Now for my illustrations.

My first illustration, if you will allow the personal reference, comes out of an effort to understand my own university. How explain Yale College of the 1890s, a college that prided itself on its democracy? It is true there were a few Whitneys, Vanderbilts or Harknesses, with social pretensions and inordinate allowances. Yet evidently the game was wide open, and any self-help student from no matter how humble a background or obscure a school had a chance to show what he could do and rise to the top and be the honor man in the Senior Society elections, if he had what it took. Now how was it possible that a college like Yale, with almost two hundred years of tradition and family attachments, could still offer so fair and square an opportunity to all comers? Because Yale was, in a sense, an annually renewed community, and because its constituents came, not just from around New Haven or New England but from all over the country, without prior knowledge of each other or claims to authority. It was a skeptical Harvard professor, European born, who first taught me this truth. Listen to George Santayana:

> The relations of one Yale student to another are completely simple and direct. They are like passengers in a ship. . . . They live in a sort of primitive brotherhood with a ready enthusiasm for every good or bad project, and a contagious good humor.
> . . . Nothing could be more American. . . . Here is sound, healthy principle, but no scrupulousness, love of life, trust in success, a ready jocoseness, a democratic amiability, and a radiant conviction that there is nothing better than oneself. It is a boyish type of character, earnest and quick in things practical, hasty and frivolous in things intellectual, but the boyishness is a healthy one, and in a young man, as in a young nation, it is perfection to have only the faults of youth.[6]

What Yale College and the Frontier, and indeed much of the rest of America, had in common, Santayana suggests, was young Americans in a new mixture.

If this first illustration comes with a strange sound, let me hasten to propose my second. It concerns dogs. In France, on sabbatical a few years ago, I seemed to run into only two kinds of dogs. One was the pampered, pedigreed poodle, sitting with his mistress in the restaurants, even eating from her plate: the fine flower of canine aristocracy, and most grandly indifferent to strangers. The second type was nondescript and fierce, the savage watchdog at peasant doorway or château gate, guarding the family domain and inherited possessions, *"les situations acquises."* This character disliked strangers on sight, and promptly tried to chew them up. After one or two close calls with such receptionists, I came back to the States— and found dogs of all sorts of ancestry, chiefly mixed. But what they showed mostly was curiosity, and a sort of friendly expectancy. Their tails said: "Howdy, stranger." For they were not guarding any particular place. They belonged to traveling men, and had been around.

My third illumination, if we can call it that, concerns money. Foreigners still accuse us of being excessively money-minded, of measuring
everything by the almighty dollar. Our defenders answer: it's not the
money, it's the power and the achievement. You make a million to prove
you're a man; then, like as not, you give it away. After all, you can't take
it with you.

Yet can't you? As I was once thinking about the M-Factor, it suddenly came to me that on a journey, or in a new community, money was
one of the few things that you could take along. Cash took the place of
your pedigree or family letter of credit. It spoke with a certain authority,
East or West. Money was power? Yes. But especially it was currency: the
power that you could take with you. So on the moving frontier, in the new
towns, it was differentiation by dollars that first disturbed the democracy
of new mixtures.

Having got diverted by some of the social consequences of the
M-Factor, I cannot do justice to some of the most interesting effects of all:
the influence of migration on personal character and attitudes. In the
moment remaining let me merely suggest possibilities.

Was it not the psychological imperatives of migration, even more
than frontier land, that helped make and keep us a nation of optimists?
Was it not the physical demands of colonization and resettlement, as well
as Calvinism and middle-class origins, that made us into such a nation of
workers, activists, materialists, instrumentalists? The difference between
what André Siegfried calls "homo faber" or the American, and homo
sapiens or the European, is it not perhaps that one of these characters has
been sitting still? Whereas we, poor pilgrims, have itching feet. Restless
to start with, we have become more so with repeated displacement. *Here
today and gone tomorrow.* The wandering mania has got into our blood,
our houses, our attention, our very ways of speech. *Come on! Get going!
Don't be a stick-in-the-mud! You don't want to get left, do you? It's a
good year to make the move. So long! I don't know where I'm going, but
I'm on my way. Anywhere I hang my hat is home, sweet home, to me.*

In the revealing American vernacular it is impressive to observe how
many things are defined in terms of movement. A man *on the road* to
success is a *comer*, a *go-getter. That's going some*, we say—and by and
by we listen for the magic words that we also have *arrived*. So also with

failure. *He missed the bus.* Or, *he missed the boat. He is not getting anywhere. She got left in the lurch. He got bogged down with administration.* A man who is growing old is *slowing up,* and then by and by he reaches *the end of the trail.* Death itself used to be spoken of as *crossing the divide.*

Reinforcing the testimony of our vernacular are our social habits. Unable to stay put, thrown among fellow transients, having newcomers flood in about us, we have perforce become hospitable, and genial with strangers. Not knowing their ancestry, and caring less, first names have been all we needed. There is a fellowship in our country, known to some of you perhaps, where last names are absolutely prohibited. And, incidentally, this illustrates another American trait: our propensity for "joining." Lonely from disassociation, we will make ten lodges grow where but one *bierstube* stood before. Frightened and not quite able to bear our independence, we oscillate between assertiveness and timidity, between an almost violent aggression and an almost cowardly conformity. Imaginative and suggestible, we are notorious for our fads and our instability. Insecure in our values, we have become adept at inventing dogmas to comfort ourselves. Not quite sure that our abandonment of the old world and of the past was justified, we have long been haunted by ambivalent feelings: a mixture of scorn and guilt complex about the older civilizations of Europe.

"It is a complex fate, being an American," said Henry James, "and one of the responsibilities it entails is fighting against a superstitious valuation of Europe." Ralph Waldo Emerson felt the same way: "Can we never extract the tapeworm of Europe from the brain of our countrymen?"

Finally, because migration appealed for diverse reasons especially to extremists—to saints and real sinners, to fundamentalist and free thinkers, to dreamers and "tough bastards," to groupists and individualists side by side—our society has never received its fair share of balanced, equable, middle-of-the-road temperaments, but has been shot through with violent contradictions. Hence so many of our seeming inconsistencies, to this very day.

To me the migrant seems not a single or a simple character, but is he not recognizably different—and American?

Paradoxically, if we turn up the other side of the coin, there are the

197

Europeans, fearful of becoming Americanized. Is this entirely out of weakness, or envy, or admiration? Hardly. Let us rather take note of a curious and unappreciated development. In the last generation mobility has swept the continent. With their *vacances payés*, their *campings*, their folkwagons, our cousins have found a new freedom. So, if today there is Americanization in Europe, and if our ways of life seem to be coming closer together, may it not be in part because the Old World societies are as never before in movement, and because Siegfried's "homo sapiens," too, is taking to the roads?

NOTES

1. [J. Hector St. John Crèvecoeur, *Letters from an American Farmer* (London, 1782); Alexis de Tocqueville, *Democracy in America*, 2 vols. (Paris and London, 1835, 1840); André Siegfried, *America Comes of Age: A French Analysis* (London, 1927); Siegfried, *America at Mid-Century* (New York, 1955); Charles Dickens, *American Notes* (London, 1842); Dickens, *Martin Chuzzlewit* (London, 1843); D. W. Brogan, *The American Character* (New York, 1944); Francis Lieber, *The Stranger in America* (London, 1835); (Count) Hermann Keyserling, *Travel Diary of a Philosopher*, vol. 2 (London, 1925); Keyserling, *America Set Free* (New York, 1929); Robert Jungk, *Tomorrow Is Already Here: Scenes from a Man-Made World* (New York, 1954).]

2. [Frederick Jackson Turner, "The Significance of the Frontier in American History" (1893) in *The Frontier in American History*, ed. Turner (New York, 1920), p. 37.]

3. [Cf. Domingo F. Sarmiento, "Travels in the United States in 1947," in *A Sarmiento Anthology*, trans. S. E. Rummon, ed. A. W. Bunkley (Princeton, 1948).]

4. From "Fast Freight" as rendered by the Kingston Trio in the late 1950s.

5. [Cf. Pitirim A. Sorokin, *Social Mobility* (New York, 1927).]

6. [George Santayana, "A Glimpse of Yale," *Harvard Monthly* 15 (Dec. 1892), pp. 89–97.]

☆ • ☆ • ☆ • ☆ • ☆

Along with Ralph Barton Perry (pp. 33–49), George Pierson is one of the few modern theorists of American character to stress what visitors to the country have always recognized, the sheer dynamic bustle of Americans—'git-up-and-git,' as it was called in the last century. Like Perry, Pierson stressed continuity rather than change in American character, and the importance of immigration in shaping that character.

Migration was both cause and effect. It recruited people who were dynamic, moving types to begin with; in this sense, character produced movement rather than vice versa; but the act of moving in turn affected attitudes and behavior. Pierson perceived better than David Potter (pp. 165–66) that Americans throughout their history had offset their loneliness by getting together in groups.

Yet the groups did not make for a 'thick' society. Pierson's passing comment that a "moving people" created a "thinner and shallower society" became a more sustained criticism in subsequent articles. In 1963 he said it made him "shiver a little" to be told that a quarter of his neighbors would be living in a different state in ten years' time. In 1964 he alleged that the "spectacular refusal" of young marrieds to live with parents or in-laws had "produced not only skyscraper suburbs but endless villages of ranch-type or split-level houses, plastered in dreary monotony across mile on mile of once smiling countryside." American moving about had turned "home" into a mere "domicile"; it had fostered a superficial sociability and eroded civilization itself. At one point, in his 1963 piece, Pierson even asserted that for most Americans their "wandering star [was] baleful and ultimately destructive."

He applied this to minorities too. Responding in 1963 to a new national focus on poverty and on black Americans, Pierson wrote presciently of the blighting effect on ghettos when their "substantial citizens" moved out and gangs took over. He also wrote, with some truth but a little insensitively, of the way those left behind lavished more care on the appearance of their cars—symbols of movement and escape—than on their homes.

Mobility also meant destruction of the environment. In 1962 the science writer Rachel Carson published *The Silent Spring*, her bestseller on the poisoning of the earth by insecticides and other chemicals. Pierson's essay of 1964, "A Restless Temper . . ." noted the chemical onslaught of fertilizers and "sprayed poisons" and attributed it to a basic conception of nature. Nature was there to be taken—depleted, controlled, pseudo-prettified—before one moved on.

Despite this swelling undercurrent of criticism, it remained just that—an undercurrent. Pierson's tone was predominantly upbeat. In all his writing about the M-factor, he assumed too easily that moving was always felt to be an act of choice, of optimistic self-betterment rather than desperate survival. Paying little heed to class differences,

199

he ignored the great population of impoverished people who, from colonial times into the twentieth century, had moved from town to town, sometimes *forced* to move by local communities concerned about order and their welfare rolls.

Even here the *idea* of moving may have been a factor, but Pierson overlooked the element of economic desperation. The rural 'Okies' of the Great Depression who drove out of the dustbowl in their jalopies dreamed of prosperity in California (a dream promoted by Californian fruit farmers seeking cheap labor), but they also *had* to move: the bankers had foreclosed on their ruined land.

Pierson did not believe, in fact, that economic conditions themselves did much to shape character and behavior. If he overstated the case, he administered a sharp corrective to the "people of plenty" thesis of his Yale colleague David Potter: his paragraph on that subject (pp. 193–94) is one of his liveliest. Pierson respected Potter's work, but for him the *idea* of *finding* plenty was more significant than plenty itself. Nor was it the only source of American immigration and movement; as Pierson suggested near the beginning of his "M-Factor" piece, immigrants also came to America in search of "goodness" and "liberty."

In a letter of 1989, Pierson elaborated on these three conceptions; his words are a coda to all his writing on the M-factor.

> I have come to think of America as settled (originally and sometimes repeatedly) by three different kinds of people: those who wanted goodness, those who wanted freedom, and those who wanted a richer, better life: the people of Plenty. There were some zealots or monomaniacs; but most of us were mixed: the saints didn't want to starve, the freedom riders hoped for a better world, the economic-minded didn't want to be controlled. But when push came to shove, there were Puritans who would sacrifice to create a City on a Hill, more refugees and freedom lovers who could go into the wilderness to get loose, and a vast tide of immigrants who chose prosperity over godliness and independence. And these three dispositions (in my judgment) have been fighting for control of our destiny ever since.

PHILIP E. SLATER

The Pursuit of Loneliness

Written at the end of the 1960s, Philip Slater's *The Pursuit of Loneliness,* excerpted below, is an all-out attack on American individualism. Like George Pierson in the previous selection, Slater stresses the impact of migration on American character, but his tone is completely different: Pierson's critical undercurrent becomes, in Slater's book, an angry torrent. Where Pierson said in passing that Americans had used mobility to escape from problems, Slater makes "the avoiding tendency" a central theme. Where Pierson observed that migration thinned out social ties but also impelled people all the more to join together, Slater sees mainly an isolating effect, made worse by technical gadgets which encourage Americans to hide away in their homes and watch 'society' on television.

Slater's career started conventionally enough. As a young Harvard sociologist in the 1950s, he worked with Talcott Parsons and Robert Bales on the social dynamics of small groups and families. He was particularly interested in the way that people in a small group regarded different roles and role-players. Moving to Brandeis in the early 1960s, he joined this interest to a concern with everyday democracy: how one learned it, how one practiced it. The result was a book, *The Temporary Society* (1968), coauthored with Warren Bennis, a specialist in organization and leadership.

At this stage Slater accepted without much complaint that America was a "nation of itinerants"—he cited George Pierson on the diverse effects of movement. The question for Slater and Bennis was how to produce effective and democratic organizations that brought different talents together to cope with changing demands. The answer lay in *temporary* organizations: "task forces organized around temporary problems."

The detail was not spelled out, but Slater seemed to envisage a social character like David Riesman's "other-directed" type, a person who could relate easily, if superficially, to others before moving on. Such people would mitigate the harsher, isolating effects of mobility. In the right organizational setting, Slater believed, people could share some uniformity while being varied and whole individuals. The complex relationship between group ties and individual variety was something that Slater would return to in *The Pursuit of Loneliness*.

Unlike *The Pursuit of Loneliness*, however, *The Temporary Society* was an optimistic book. It tapped a playful belief of the early to mid-sixties that one could devise new and supple outfits to solve problems and live better—from Kennedy-style policy groups to hippie communes.

The Pursuit of Loneliness, in contrast, has a tone of bitter disillusion. By the time of its writing, the Vietnam War had escalated. In the 1968 election, Richard Nixon and George Wallace both capitalized on a 'Middle American' backlash against student radicals and antiwar protests. Inflation, fueled by the war, had checked government spending on Lyndon Johnson's poverty programs and made them more unpopular.

Slater's book reflected all these developments. A chapter on the psychology of technological violence (not reprinted here) has a large section on the bombing and shelling of Vietnam. In the excerpt below, Slater's picture of self-repressed conservatives is clearly aimed at the backlash against the ghetto riots and campus rebellions of the late 1960s. And in claiming that Americans ducked social problems, he had in mind the conservative reactions against welfare programs and social planning.

Slater's use of depth-psychology to attack what he disliked in America made him a member of what has been called 'the Freudian left.' In 1968, publication year of *The Temporary Society*, Slater also published *The Glory of Hera*. This book took a psychoanalytic view of ancient Greek myths. Essentially, Slater argued, they were a projection of Greek family relationships.

Shaped thus by psychoanalysis and by the hopes and traumas of the 1960s, Slater's interest in family and social relations produced a scorching critique of American character.

☆ • ☆ • ☆ • ☆ • ☆

I would like to suggest three human desires that are deeply and uniquely frustrated by American culture:*

(1) The desire for *community*—the wish to live in trust and fraternal cooperation with one's fellows in a total and visible collective entity.

(2) The desire for *engagement*—the wish to come directly to grips with social and interpersonal problems and to confront on equal terms an environment which is not composed of ego-extensions.

(3) The desire for *dependence*—the wish to share responsibility for the control of one's impulses and the direction of one's life.

When I say that these three desires are frustrated by American culture, this need not conjure up romantic images of the individual struggling against society. In every case it is fair to say that we participate eagerly in producing the frustration we endure—it is not something merely done to us. For these desires are in each case subordinate to their opposites in that vague entity called the American Character. . . . Americans have voluntarily created and voluntarily maintain a society which increasingly frustrates and aggravates these secondary yearnings, to the point where they threaten to become primary. Groups that in any way personify this threat are therefore feared in an exaggerated way, and will be until Americans as a group are able to recognize and accept those needs within themselves.

Community and Competition

We are so accustomed to living in a society that stresses individualism that we need to be reminded that 'collectivism' in a broad sense has always been the more usual lot of mankind, as well as of most other species. Most people in most societies have been born into and died in stable communities in which the subordination of the individual to the welfare of the group was taken for granted while the aggrandizement of the individual at the expense of his fellows was simply a crime.

This is not to say that competition is an American invention—all societies involve some sort of admixture of cooperative and competitive

*"The Pursuit of Loneliness," from *The Pursuit of Loneliness* by Philip Slater. Copyright © 1970, 1976 by Philip E. Slater. Reprinted by permission of Beacon Press.

institutions. But our society lies near or on the competitive extreme, and although it contains cooperative institutions I think it is fair to say that Americans suffer from their relative weakness and peripherality. Studies of business executives have revealed, for example, a deep hunger for an atmosphere of trust and fraternity with their colleagues (with whom they must, in the short run, engage in what [David] Riesman calls "antagonistic cooperation"). The competitive life is a lonely one, and its satisfactions are very short-lived indeed, for each race leads only to a new one.

In the past, as so many have pointed out, there were in our society many oases in which one could take refuge from the frenzied invidiousness of our economic system—institutions such as the extended family and the stable local neighborhood in which one could take pleasure from something other than winning a symbolic victory over one of his fellows. But these have disappeared one by one, leaving the individual more and more in a situation in which he must try to satisfy his affiliative and invidious needs in the same place. This has made the balance a more precarious one—the appeal of cooperative living more seductive, and the need to suppress our longing for it more acute.

In recent decades the principal vehicle for the tolerated expression of this longing has been the mass media. Popular songs and film comedies have continually engaged in a sentimental rejection of the dominant mores, maintaining that the best things in life are free, that love is more important than success, that keeping up with the Joneses is absurd, that personal integrity should take precedence over winning, and so on. But these protestations must be understood for what they are: a safety valve for the dissatisfactions that the modal American experiences when he behaves as he thinks he should. The same man who chuckles and sentimentalizes over a happy-go-lucky hero in a film would view his real-life counterpart as frivolous and irresponsible, and suburbanites who philosophize over their back fence with complete sincerity about their 'dog-eat-dog world,' and what-is-it-all-for, and you-can't-take-it-with-you, and success-doesn't-make-you-happy-it-just-gives-you-ulcers-and-a-heart-condition—would be enraged should their children pay serious attention to such a viewpoint. Indeed, the degree of rage is, up to a point, a function of the degree of sincerity: if the individual did not feel these things, he would not have to fight them so vigorously. The peculiarly exaggerated hostility that hippies tend to arouse suggests that the life they strive for is highly seductive to middle-aged Americans.

The intensity of this reaction can in part be attributed to a kind of circularity that characterizes American individualism. When a value is as strongly held as is individualism in America, the illnesses it produces tend to be treated by increasing the dosage, in the same way an alcoholic treats a hangover or a drug addict his withdrawal symptoms. Technological change, mobility, and the individualistic ethos combine to rupture the bonds that tie each individual to a family, a community, a kinship network, a geographical location—bonds that give him a comfortable sense of himself. As this sense of himself erodes, he seeks ways of affirming it. But his efforts at self-enhancement automatically accelerate the very erosion he seeks to halt.

It is easy to produce examples of the many ways in which Americans attempt to minimize, circumvent, or deny the interdependence upon which all human societies are based. We seek a private house, a private means of transportation, a private garden, a private laundry, self-service stores, and do-it-yourself skills of every kind. An enormous technology seems to have set itself the task of making it unnecessary for one human being ever to ask anything of another in the course of going about his daily business. Even within the family Americans are unique in their feeling that each member should have a separate room, and even a separate telephone, television, and car, when economically possible. We seek more and more privacy, and feel more and more alienated and lonely when we get it. What accidental contacts we do have, furthermore, seem more intrusive, not only because they are unsought but because they are unconnected with any familiar pattern of interdependence.

Most important, our encounters with others tend increasingly to be competitive as a result of the search for privacy. We less and less often meet our fellow man to share and exchange, and more and more often encounter him as an impediment or a nuisance: making the highway crowded when we are rushing somewhere, cluttering and littering the beach or park or wood, pushing in front of us at the supermarket, taking the last parking place, polluting our air and water, building a highway through our house, blocking our view, and so on. Because we have cut off so much communication with each other we keep bumping into each other, and thus a higher and higher percentage of our interpersonal contacts are abrasive. . . .

Since our contacts with others are increasingly competitive, unanticipated and abrasive, we seek still more apartness and accelerate the trend. The desire to be somehow special inaugurates an even more competitive quest for progressively more rare and expensive symbols—a quest that is ultimately futile since it is individualism itself that produces uniformity.

This is poorly understood by Americans, who tend to confuse uniformity with 'conformity,' in the sense of compliance with or submission to group demands. Many societies exert far more pressure on the individual to mold himself to fit a particularized segment of a total group pattern, but there is variation among these circumscribed roles. Our society gives far more leeway to the individual to pursue his own ends, but, since *it* defines what is worthy and desirable, everyone tends, independently but monotonously, to pursue the same things in the same way. The first pattern combines cooperation, conformity and variety; the second, competition, individualism and uniformity.

These relationships are exemplified by two familiar processes in contemporary America: the flight to the suburb and the do-it-yourself movement. Both attempt to deny human interdependence and pursue unrealistic fantasies of self-sufficiency. The first tries to overlook our dependence upon the city for the maintenance of the level of culture we demand. 'Civilized' means, literally, 'citified,' and the state of the city is an accurate index of the condition of the culture as a whole. We behave toward our cities like an irascible farmer who never feeds his cow and then kicks her when she fails to give enough milk. But the flight to the suburb is in any case self-defeating, its goals subverted by the mass quality of the exodus. The suburban dweller seeks peace, privacy, nature, community, and a child-rearing environment which is healthy and culturally optimal. Instead he finds neither the beauty and serenity of the countryside, the stimulation of the city, nor the stability and sense of community of the small town, and his children are exposed to a cultural deprivation equaling that of any slum child with a television set. Living in a narrow age-graded and class-segregated society, it is little wonder that suburban families have contributed so little to the national talent pool in proportion to their numbers, wealth and other social advantages.* And this transplantation, which has caused the transplants to atrophy, has blighted the countryside and impoverished the city. A final irony of the suburban dream is that, for many Americans, reaching the pinnacle of one's social ambitions (owning a house in the suburbs) requires one to perform all kinds of menial tasks (carrying garbage cans, mowing lawns, shoveling snow, and so on) that were performed for him when he occupied a less exalted status.

Some of this manual labor, however, is voluntary—an attempt to deny the elaborate division of labor required in a complex society. Many Americans seem quite willing to pay this price for their reluctance to engage in interpersonal encounters with servants and artisans—a price which is rather high unless the householder particularly relishes the work (some find in it a tangible relief from the intangibles they manipulate in their own jobs) or is especially good at it, or cannot command a higher rate of pay in the job market than the servant or artisan.

The do-it-yourself movement has accompanied, paradoxically, increasing specialization in the occupational sphere. As one's job narrows, perhaps, one seeks the challenge of new skill-acquisition in the home. But specialization also means that one's interpersonal encounters with artisans in the home proliferate and become more impersonal. It is not a matter of a familiar encounter with the local smith or grocer—a few well-known individuals performing a relatively large number of functions, and with whom one's casual interpersonal contacts may be a source of satisfaction, and are in any case a testimony to the stability and meaningful interrelatedness of human affairs. One finds instead a multiplicity of narrow specialists—each perhaps a stranger (the same type of repair may be performed by a different person each time). Every relationship, such as it is, must start from scratch, and it is small wonder that the householder turns away from such an unrewarding prospect in apathy and despair. . . .

*Using cities, small towns and rural areas for comparison. The small Midwestern town achieves its legendary dullness by a process akin to evaporation—all the warm and energetic particles depart for coastal cities, leaving their place of origin colder and flatter than they found it. But the restless spirit in a small town knows he lives in the sticks and has a limited range of experience, while his suburban counterpart can sustain an illusion of cosmopolitanism in an environment which is far more constricted (a small town is a microcosm, a suburb merely a layer).

Engagement and Uninvolvement

Many of the phenomena we have discussed can also be linked to a compulsive American tendency to avoid confrontation of chronic social problems. . . . The avoiding tendency lies at the very root of American character. This nation was settled and continuously repopulated by people who were not personally successful in confronting the social conditions obtaining in their mother country, but fled these conditions in the hope of a better life. This series of choices (reproduced in the westward movement) provided a complex selection process—populating America disproportionately with a certain kind of person.

In the past we have always, explicitly or implicitly, stressed the positive side of this selection, implying that America thereby found itself blessed with an unusual number of energetic, mobile, ambitious, daring and optimistic persons. Now there is no reason to deny that a number of traits must have helped to differentiate those who chose to come from those who chose to stay, nor that these differences must have generated social institutions and habits of mind that tended to preserve and reproduce these characteristics. But very little attention has been paid to the more negative aspects of the selection. If we gained the energetic and daring we also gained the lion's share of the rootless, the unscrupulous, those who value money over relationships, and those who put self-aggrandizement ahead of love and loyalty. And most of all, we gained a critically undue proportion of persons who, when faced with a difficult situation, tended to chuck the whole thing and flee to a new environment. Escaping, evading and avoiding are responses which lie at the base of much that is peculiarly American—the suburb, the automobile, the self-service store, and so on.

These responses also contribute to the appalling discrepancy between our material resources and our treatment of those who cannot adequately care for themselves. This is not an argument against institutionalization: American society is not geared to handle these problems in any other way, and this is in fact the point I wish to make. One cannot successfully alter one facet of a social system if everything else is left the same, for the patterns are interdependent and reinforce one another. In a cooperative, stable society the aged, infirm, or psychotic person can be absorbed by the local community, which knows and understands him. He presents a difficulty which is familiar and which can be confronted daily and directly. This condition cannot be reproduced in our society today—the burden must be carried by a small, isolated, mobile family unit that is not really equipped for it.

But understanding the forces that require us to incarcerate those who cannot function independently in our society does not give us license to ignore the significance of doing so. The institutions we provide for those who cannot care for themselves are human garbage heaps—they result from and reinforce our tendency to avoid confronting social and interpersonal problems. They make life 'easier' for the rest of society, just as does the automobile. And just as we find ourselves having to devise ridiculous exercises to counteract the harmful effects of our dependence upon the automobile, so the 'ease' of our nonconfronting social technology makes us bored, flabby and interpersonally insensitive, and our lives empty and mechanical.

Our ideas about institutionalizing the aged, psychotic, retarded and infirm are based on a pattern of thought that we might call the toilet assumption—the notion that unwanted matter, unwanted difficulties, unwanted complexities and obstacles will disappear if they are removed from our immediate field of vision. We do not connect the trash we throw from the car window with the trash in our streets, and we assume that replacing old buildings with new expensive ones will alleviate poverty in the slums. We throw the aged and psychotic into institutional holes where they cannot be seen. Our approach to social problems is to decrease their visibility: out of sight, out of mind. This is the real foundation of racial segregation, especially its most extreme case, the Indian 'reservation.' The result of our social efforts has been to remove the underlying problems of our society farther and farther from daily experience and daily consciousness, and hence to decrease, in the mass of the population, the knowledge, skill, resources and motivation necessary to deal with them.

When these discarded problems rise to the surface again—a riot, a protest, an *exposé* in the mass media—we react as if a sewer had backed up. We are shocked, disgusted and angered, and immediately call for the emergency plumber (the special commission, the crash program) to ensure that the problem is once again removed from consciousness.

The toilet assumption is not merely a facetious metaphor. Prior to the widespread use of the flush toilet all of humanity was daily confronted with the immediate reality of human waste and its disposal. They knew where it was and how it got there. Nothing miraculously vanished. Excrement was conspicuously present in the outhouse or chamber pot, and the slops that went out the window went visibly and noticeably into the street. The most aristocratic Victorian ladies strolling in fashionable city parks thought nothing of retiring to the bushes to relieve themselves. Similarly, garbage did not disappear down a disposal unit—it remained nearby.

As with physical waste, so with social problems. The biblical adage, 'the poor are always with us' had a more literal meaning before World War I. The poor were visible and all around. Psychosis was not a strange phenomenon in a textbook but a familiar neighbor or village character. The aged were in every house. Everyone had seen animals slaughtered and knew what they were eating when they ate them; illness and death were a part of everyone's immediate experience.

In contemporary life the book of experience is filled with blank and mysterious pages. Occupational specialization and plumbing have exerted a kind of censorship over our understanding of the world we live in and how it operates. And when we come into immediate contact with anything that does not seem to fit into the ordinary pattern of our somewhat bowdlerized existence our spontaneous reaction is to try somehow to flush it away, bomb it away, throw it down the jail.

But in some small degree we also feel bored and uneasy with the orderly chrome and porcelain vacuum of our lives, from which so much of life has been removed. Evasion creates self-distaste as well as comfort, and radical confrontations are exciting as well as disruptive. The answering chord that they produce within us terrifies us, and although we cannot entirely contain our fascination, it is relatively easy to project our self-disgust onto the perpetrators of the confrontations.

This ambivalence is reflected in the mass media. The hunger for confrontation and experience attracts a lot of attention to social problems, but these are usually dealt with in such a way as to reinforce the avoidance process. The T.V. documentary presents a tidy package with opposing views and an implication of progress. Reports in popular magazines attempt to provide a substitute for actual experience. Important book and film reviews, for example, give just the blend of titillation and condescension to make the reader imagine that he is already 'in' and need not undergo the experience itself—that he has not only participated in the

210

novel adventure but already outgrown it. Thus the ultimate effect of the media is to reinforce the avoiding response by providing an effigy of confrontation and experience. . . .

We interact largely with extensions of our own egos. We stumble over the consequences of our past acts. We are drowning in our own excreta (another consequence of the toilet assumption). We rarely come into contact with a force which is clearly and cleanly Not Us. Every struggle is a struggle with ourselves, because there is a little piece of ourselves in everything we encounter—houses, clothes, cars, cities, machines, even our foods. There is an uneasy, anesthetized feeling about this kind of life—like being trapped forever inside an air-conditioned car with power steering and power brakes and only a telephone to talk to. Our world is only a mirror, and our efforts mere shadowboxing—yet shadowboxing in which we frequently manage to hurt ourselves.

Even that part of the world which is not man-made impinges upon us through a symbolic network we have created. We encounter primarily our own fantasies: we have a concept and image of a mountain, a lake or a forest almost before we ever see one. Travel posters tell us what it means to be in a strange land, the events of life become news items before they actually happen—all experience receives preliminary structure and interpretation. Public relations, television drama and life become indistinguishable. . . .

Dependence and Independence

Independence training in American society begins almost at birth— babies are held and carried less than in most societies and spend more time in complete isolation—and continues, despite occasional parental ambivalence, throughout childhood and adolescence. When a child is admonished to be a 'big boy' or 'big girl' this usually means doing something alone or without help (the rest of the time it involves strangling feelings, but this norm seems to be on the wane). Signs of independence are usually rewarded, and a child who in too obvious a manner calls attention to the fact that human intelligence is based almost entirely on the process of imitation is ridiculed by calling him a copycat or a monkey (after the paradoxical habit humans have of projecting their most uniquely human attributes onto animals).

There have been many complaints in recent years that independence training is less rigorous than it once was, but again, as in the case of competitiveness, this is hard to assess. To be on one's own in a simple, stable and familiar environment requires a good deal less internal 'independence' than to be on one's own in a complex, shifting and strange one. Certainly a child could run about more freely a century ago without coming to harm, and his errors and misdeeds had far more trivial consequences than today; but this decline in the child's freedom of movement says nothing about the degree to which the child is asked to forgo the pleasures of depending upon his parents for nurturance and support. If the objective need is greater, it may offset a small increase in parental tolerance for dependent behavior, and cause the child to experience the independence training as more severe rather than less. . . .

Many of the mechanisms through which dependency is counteracted in our society have already been discussed in the preceding sections, but a word should be said about the complex problem of internalized controls. In stable societies, as many authors have pointed out, the control of human impulses is usually a collective responsibility. The individual is viewed as not having within himself the controls required to guarantee that his impulses will not break out in ways disapproved by the community. But this matters very little, since the group is always near at hand to stop him or shame him or punish him should he forget himself.

In more fluid, changing societies we are more apt to find controls that are internalized—that do not depend to so great an extent on control and enforcement by external agents. This has long been characteristic of American society—de Tocqueville observed in 1830 that American women were much more independent than European women, freer from chaperonage, and able to appear in what a European would consider 'compromising' situations without any sign of sexual involvement.

Chaperonage is in fact the simplest way to illustrate the difference between external and internalized controls. In chaperon cultures—such as traditional Middle Eastern and Latin societies—it simply did not occur to anyone that a man and woman could be alone together and not have sexual intercourse. In America, which represents the opposite extreme, there is almost no situation in which a man and woman could find themselves in which sexual intercourse could not at least be considered problematic (Hollywood comedies have exploited this phenomenon—

well past the point of exhaustion and nausea—over the past thirty-five years). Americans are virtuosi of internalized control of sexual expression (the current relaxation of sexual norms in no way changes this), and this has caused difficulties whenever the two systems have come into contact. An unchaperoned girl in a bikini or mini-skirt means one thing in America, another in Baghdad. It is a mistake to consider a chaperon society more prudish—the compliment is likely to be returned when the difference is understood. Even Americans consider some situations inherently sexual: if a girl from some mythical culture came to an American's house, stripped and climbed into bed with him, he would assume she was making a sexual overture and would be rather indignant if he found that she was merely expressing casual friendship according to her native customs. He would also be puzzled if *he* were called prudish, and we need not speculate as to what he would call *her*.

But how are internalized controls created? We know that they are closely tied to what are usually called 'love-oriented' techniques of discipline in childhood. These techniques avoid physical punishment and deprivation of privileges and stress reasoning and the withdrawal of parental affection. The basic difference between 'love-oriented' and 'fear-oriented' techniques (such as physical punishment) is that in the latter case the child simply learns to avoid punishment while in the former he tends to incorporate parental values as his own in order to avoid losing parental love and approval. When fear-oriented techniques prevail, the child is in the position of inhabitants of an occupied country, who obey to avoid getting hurt but disobey whenever they think they can get away with it. Like them, the child does not have any emotional commitment to his rulers—he does not fear losing their love.

Love-oriented techniques require by definition that love and discipline emanate from the same source. When this happens it is not merely a question of avoiding the punisher: the child wishes to anticipate the displeasure of the loved and loving parent, wants to be like the parent, and takes into himself as a part of himself the values and attitudes of the parent. He wants to please, not placate, and because he has taken the parent's attitudes as his own, pleasing the parent comes to mean making him feel good about himself. Thus while individuals raised with fear-oriented techniques tend to direct anger outward under stress, those raised with love-oriented techniques tend to direct it inward in the form of guilt—a distinction that has important physiological correlates.[1]

Under stable conditions external controls work perfectly well. Everyone knows his own place and his neighbor's, and deviations from expected behavior will be quickly met from all sides. When social conditions fluctuate, social norms change, and people move frequently from one social setting to another and are often among strangers, this will no longer do. An individual cannot take his whole community with him wherever he goes, and in any case the rules differ from place to place. The mobile individual must travel light, and internalized controls are portable and transistorized, as it were.

Anger directed inward is also made for mobile conditions. In a stable community two youths who start to get into a fight will be held back by their friends—they depend upon this restraint and can abandon themselves to their passion, knowing that it will not produce harmful consequences. But where one moves among strangers it becomes increasingly important to have other mechanisms for handling aggression. In situations of high mobility and flux the individual must have a built-in readiness to feel himself responsible when things go wrong.

Most modern societies are a confused mixture of both systems, a fact that enables conservative spokesmen to attribute rising crime rates to permissive child-rearing techniques. The overwhelming majority of ordinary crimes, however, are committed by individuals who have *not* been reared with love-oriented techniques, but, insofar as the parent or parents have been able to rear them at all, by the haphazard use of fear-oriented discipline. Love-oriented child-rearing techniques are a luxury that slum parents, for example, can seldom afford.

Furthermore, it is rather misleading to refer to the heavily guilt-inducing socialization techniques of middle-class parents as 'permissive.' Misbehavior in a lower-class child is more often greeted with a cuff, possibly accompanied by some noninformative response such as: 'Stop that!' But it may not be at all clear to the child which of the many motions he is now performing 'that' is; and, indeed, 'that' may be punished only when the parent is feeling irritable. A child would have to have achieved an enormously high intelligence level (which, of course, it has not, for this very reason) to be able to form a moral concept out of a hundred irritable 'stop-thats.' What he usually forms is merely a crude sense of when the 'old man' or the 'old lady' is to be avoided. The self-conscious, highly verbal, middle-class parent is at the opposite extreme. He or she feels that discipline should relate to the child's act, not the parent's own emotional state, and is very careful to emphasize verbally the principle involved in the misbehavior ('it's bad to hit people' or 'we have to share with guests'). Concept-formation is made very easy for the middle-class child, and he tends to think of moral questions in terms of principles.

As he grows older this tendency is reinforced by his encounter with different groups with different norms. In a mobile society, one cannot simply accept the absolute validity of any rule because one experiences competing moral codes. As a result the middle-class child tends to evolve a system of meta-rules, that is, rules for assessing the relative validity of these codes. The meta-rules tend to be based upon the earliest and most general principles expressed by the parents, such as prohibitions on violence against others, egalitarianism, mutuality, and so on. This ability to treat rules in a highly secular fashion while maintaining a strong moral position is baffling to those whose control mechanisms are more primitive, but it presupposes a powerful and articulate conscience. Such an individual can expose himself to physical harm and to violence-arousing situations without losing control and while maintaining a moral position. This may seem inconceivable to an uneducated working-class policeman whose own impulses are barely held in line by a jerry-built structure of poorly articulated and mutually contradictory moral absolutes. Hence he tends to misinterpret radical middle-class behavior as a hypocritical mask for mere delinquency.

The point of this long digression, however, is that internalization is a mixed blessing. It may enable one to get his head smashed in a good cause, but the capacity to give oneself up completely to an emotion is almost altogether lost in the process. Where internalization is high there is often a feeling that the controls themselves are out of control—that emotion cannot be expressed when the individual would like to express it. Life is muted, experience filtered, emotion anesthetized, affective discharge incomplete. Efforts to shake free from this hypertrophied control system include not only drugs, and sensation-retrieval techniques such as those developed at the Esalen Institute in California, but also confused attempts to reestablish external systems of direction and control—the vogue currently enjoyed by astrology is an expression of this. The simplest technique, of course, would be the establishment of a more authoritarian social structure, which would relieve the individual of the great burden of examining and moderating his own responses. He could become as a child, light-hearted, spontaneous, and passionate, secure in the knowledge that others would prevent his impulses from causing harm.

Realization of this goal is prevented by democratic values and the social conditions that foster them (complexity, fluidity, change). But the desire plays a significant part in conventional reactions to radical minorities, who are all felt to be seeking the abandonment of self-restraints of one kind or another and at the same time demanding *more* responsible behavior from the establishment. This is both infuriating and contagious to white middle-class adults, who would like very much to do the same, and their call for law and order (that is, more *external* control) is an expression of that desire as well as an attempt to smother it. This conflict over dependency and internalization also helps explain why official American anti-Communism always lays so much stress on the authoritarian (rather than the socialistic) aspects of Communist states.

NOTE

1. S. H. King and A. F. Henry, "Aggression and Cardiovascular Reactions Related to Parental Control over Behavior," *Journal of Abnormal and Social Psychology* 53 (1955), pp. 206–10.

☆ • ☆ • ☆ • ☆ • ☆

From early in his career Philip Slater had been interested in attitudes to the aged. This surfaced in *The Pursuit of Loneliness* when he claimed that Americans displayed a "toilet assumption," flushing away unwanted people as well as problems. Here as elsewhere, he did not always make it clear whether he was indicting modern Western society in general or specific American traditions and attitudes.

Though Slater's analysis is a radical attack on the U.S. social system, it is not Marxist: it does not target capitalism per se, or even class inequality. Slater refers to class differences in child-rearing, but his view of the mental makeup of an "uneducated working-class policeman" borders on contempt. "A jerry-built structure of poorly articulated and mutually contradictory moral absolutes"—one wonders how many policemen Slater really knew. He implied too that education made it harder to hold contradictory attitudes—a dubious proposition.

There is also a trace of snobbery in his dismissal of suburbia. As an urban intellectual, he finds it ridiculous that the peak of "social ambition" should entail a life of "menial tasks (carrying garbage cans, mowing lawns, shoveling snow . . .)." Did it not occur to Slater that mowing and shoveling might give a bit of physical balance to executives and professionals who spent most of the week in an office? His comment here was male-biased too. "Menial tasks" might be new to the *man* recently arrived in suburbia; they were not new to the woman, of almost any class.

This is not to say that Slater's picture of suburban deprivation is entirely unsupported. One-sided and oversimplified it certainly is. More recently, however, a leading historian of suburbia, Kenneth Jackson, has depicted a "loss of community" in somewhat the same way that Slater did. As Jackson put it, front-porch society, where everyone met everyone, had given way to a collection of "overequipped" houses and yards, "small, private islands." Unlike Slater, though, Jackson conceded that suburbia still showed signs of community life, from teenagers' hangouts in shopping malls to the work of their elders for PTA, Community Chest, hospital boards, and so on.

What may irritate readers of the above excerpt is Slater's use of psychiatry to *pathologize* his political opponents: to tell them they are sick, not just wrong. Slater implies that conservative Americans attack rebels not on principled or rational grounds, but because they have unhealthily repressed their own expressive, rebellious urges and need to attack those urges in others. Slater's assertion here is a kind of psychological imperialism. As a rebel himself, he is saying to conservatives, 'you are denying the *me* in *you*.'

To be fair to Slater (fairer than he is to others), one must credit him with a gritty psychological imagination. He is one of the very few modern writers to see a deep and direct link between conformity and individualistic self-reliance. In Slater's view an excessive use of *self-control* (the anxious cop inside one) to keep social order meant a self-enforced censorship of 'wild' and varied behavior. This picture implied that David Riesman's "inner-directed" puritan was still very

much around. The paradox for Slater was that if Americans let themselves depend more on the community and its external controls, they
would be more tolerant of individual expressiveness since they would
not need to take a personal, policing attitude toward it.

Unfortunately, Slater used this kind of thinking to explain away
political values and beliefs. Hence his claim (at the end of the excerpt)
that when Americans called for "law and order" while denouncing
communist authoritarianism, they were simultaneously expressing and
denying their desires for authority. The "law and order" side of this
argument has some truth, but to write off anti-communism as a form
of psychological self-repression is farfetched, to say the least.

Slater's basic theory of conformity and self-censorship can be read
as a call for more tolerance of the 1960s 'youth culture' as well as
Afro-American movements. (He himself liked the communal, egalitarian side of the hippie scene but believed it was contradicted by a selfish
individualism.) When one thinks about America's kaleidoscope of self-
expression in the 1960s and 1970s, it is clear that Slater exaggerated the
reach of repressive puritanism. Political backlash did not generally
become a *cultural* backlash.

What Slater did do was to describe one kind of conservative
malaise, the discomfort of "a puritan in Babylon" as President Coo-
lidge was described by the journalist William Allen White. Slater also
highlighted the need for more *interdependence* between people. As the
'me decade' of the 1970s unfolded, other writers would take up this
point and attach it to a different critique, not of puritanism but of
hedonism.

CHARLES REICH

The Greening of America

Ⅰn 1970, the year Philip Slater published *The Pursuit of Loneli-ness* (excerpted above), Charles Reich published *The Greening of America*. A runaway bestseller, it could be fairly called a hippie critique of American society and character, but its author was a Yale law profes-sor, and a long preview article by him in the *New Yorker* produced one of the biggest mail responses in that august magazine's history. Unlike Slater's book, which came out of an optimism turned bitter, Reich's was conceived in a pessimism that turned to joyous discovery as the author became involved in the youthful 'counterculture.' Although both authors were writing during the Vietnam War and disliked much of what they saw around them, the mood of Reich's book was centered on the hippie optimism of 1967; Slater's, on the conservative backlash of 1968.

In the excerpt that follows, Reich identifies three American char-acter types: "Consciousness I," "Consciousness II," and (hailed by Reich) "Consciousness III." As he saw it, all three were very much around at the time he wrote, but they corresponded to three historical eras. Consciousness I people were frontier and small-business individu-alists and a mass of ordinary people. Consciousness II were agents of the modern "corporate state"—'New Deal' reformers; managers and professionals; practitioners of rational order and hierarchy. Conscious-ness III were the new wave, heirs to Thoreau and Whitman but reborn in the hippie dream of *openness*—open to experience, feelings, nature, oneself, others. As Reich acknowledged, the very notion of classifying people in such a way was alien to Consciousness III; mental pigeonhol-ing was the practice of Consciousness II.

It is easy to associate Reich with the 1960s because of his writing about Consciousness III, but his picture of Consciousness II was just as

much a product of the time. Its epitome was the Kennedy-type professional celebrated in some of Eugene Burdick's stories: liberal, analytical, proud of his 'tough-minded' realism. In Reich's view the political
and economic structure behind Consciousness II was a fusion of big
business and government shaped by planners and regulators. Reich
said little about capitalism per se, but he and other radicals and liberals
of the time were sharply aware that big business had profitably en-
twined itself with big government, securing fat contracts and favorable
regulations. (In the Reagan years, the publicity given to 'deregulation'
and the president's rhetoric of free enterprise somewhat obscured the
government-business link.)

Reich's book cites Karl Marx among the sources of his ideas, but
he was more directly influenced by Herbert Marcuse, the neo-Marxist
philosophy professor who became a beacon to young radicals in the
1960s. Like Marcuse, Reich stressed the economic system's *psychological* effects on everyone rather than its relation to class power. In his
critique of Consciousness II, Reich borrowed heavily from Marcuse's
notion of a "technological rationality" which stunted the emotional
and spiritual life of its subjects. This provided another way of attacking
what young radicals in the Vietnam War often called "technocracy"
and many others (starting with President Eisenhower's farewell address) had called the "military-industrial complex." Reich did not,
however, attack all technology; he believed it could be used in a way
that expanded everyday life and respected nature.

How would a law professor come to write all this? A hint of it
appeared in "The New Property," an important article by Reich in the
Yale Law Journal (1964). Reich saw dangerous power in the "largesse"
of modern government. The state awarded benefits, contracts, licenses,
and franchises, often in return for demands that infringed civil liberties.
In 1950, for instance, a candidate in the Illinois bar exam was told he
would be denied a license if he refused to answer questions about his
political past on First Amendment grounds that political expression
should not be penalized. The Supreme Court upheld the denial.

Reich's article has a libertarian flavor; it poses the dead hand of
bureaucratic power against a flowering of the human spirit. Reich also
believed that bureaucratic power was biased; its rules tended to favor
the more powerful interests. He did not, he said, wish to turn the clock

back to minimal government and laissez-faire. He accepted the expansion of an administrative state, but he wished to secure more individual rights within that state—including the right to livelihood. In a subsequent article, Reich called for a more openly and democratically "Planned Society," against the current system of largely hidden planning by administrative experts serving big private interests. Reich's thinking here was close to that of the widely read economist J. K. Galbraith, and indeed Reich later claimed that Galbraith's book *The New Industrial State* (1967), spurred many of the ideas that went into *The Greening of America*. *The Greening of America* took off from Reich's ideas about administrative power, saying more about the kinds of people it produced.

The Greening of America also came out of Reich's own experience in law firms, first in New York and then in Washington. In his autobiography, *The Sorcerer of Bolinas Reef*, Reich tells of his loneliness among law-firm colleagues—he liked them but felt oppressed by the masks and competitive roles they had to adopt. By the time he moved to Yale Law School in 1960, he was writing a book provisionally titled "The Coming of the Closed Society." It became *The Greening of America*, but only after a change of mood. The youth movement inspired him: he saw its members not as a bunch of airheads but as people whose heightened consciousness cut through the restrictions and pretenses of conventional society. In 1967 a summer in Berkeley gave him a religious awakening; he now believed that society could change through the "affirmative flow of new values." Mingling with his students, he taught an immensely popular undergraduate course, "The Individual in America." It too became *The Greening of America*.

☆ · ☆ · ☆ · ☆ · ☆

Consciousness I: Loss of Reality

. . . To the people who came here, America represented a new beginning.* They had been granted freedom from the past—a second chance. They

*From Charles Reich, *The Greening of America* (New York, 1970), chap. 2 ("Consciousness I: Loss of Reality"), chap. 4 ("Consciousness II"), chap. 9 ("Consciousness III: The New Generation"), copyright © 1970 by Charles Reich.

believed that the earth belongs to the living, and that they need not be bound by traditions, customs or authority from other lands. America would be, for them, a new community. R. W. B. Lewis, in *The American Adam* (1955), described them thus, emphasizing, above all, the admired quality of innocence. They had an idealistic view of what man could be in the new community. The American dream was not, at least at the beginning, a rags-to-riches type of narrow materialism. At its most exalted, in Whitman's words, it was a spiritual and humanistic vision of man's possibilities:

> Each of us inevitable,
> Each of us limitless—each of us with
>   his or her right upon the earth,
> Each of us allow'd the eternal purports
>   of the earth.
>   "SALUT AU MONDE!"

> Divine am I inside and out, and I
>   make holy whatever I touch or
>   am touch'd from . . .

> I dote on myself, there is a lot of
>   me and all so luscious,
> Each moment and whatever happens
>   thrills me with joy . . .
>   "SONG OF MYSELF"

Whitman could be speaking for today's youth. But he was also summing up one side of the original American dream—the dream shared by the colonists and the immigrants, by Jefferson, Emerson, the Puritan preachers and the western cowboy—a dream premised on human dignity, a dignity that made each man an equal being in a spiritual sense, and envisioned a community based upon individual dignity.

This broad humanism, as distinct from materialism, is revealed in the literature of the western frontier. Here was a search for adventure and challenge, for man-in-nature, for the non-specialized individual able to do many different kinds of work. It was a search for a kind of human companionship built out of sharing. It had a strong spiritual element, as the Mormon quest shows. As Pierre Berton unforgettably relates in *The Klondike Fever* (1958), even where the object seemed to be material— gold—the real finding was an expansion of man's nature which was remembered long after gold had become a dim memory. . . .

There was another side to the American character—the harsh side of self-interest, competitiveness, suspicion of others. Each individual would go it alone, refusing to trust his neighbors, seeing another man's advantage as his loss, seeing the world as a rat race with no rewards to losers. Underlying this attitude was the assumption that human nature is fundamentally bad, and that a struggle against his fellow men is man's natural condition. 'There'll always be aggression and a struggle for power, and there'll always be a pecking order,' says Consciousness I. There is a deep isolation and suspicion of others in Consciousness I and more faith in winning than in love. The belief in self-interest led to the corruption of American life and government by venality, dishonesty, the sale of offices, favors and votes, all under the theory that each man has a right to pursue his opportunities wherever he finds them, that 'the game' is winning and getting rich and powerful, and nothing else, and that no higher community exists beyond each individual's selfish appraisal of his interests.

But it was not merely corruption that undermined the America of Consciousness I. Consciousness I proved unable to change with the changing realities of America. Today it still sees America as if it were a world of small towns and simple virtues. Invention and machinery and production are the equivalent of progress; material success is the road to happiness; nature is beautiful but must be conquered and put to use. Competition is the law of nature and man; life is a harsh pursuit of individual self-interest. Consciousness I believes that the American dream is still possible, and that success is determined by character, morality, hard work and self-denial. It does not accept the fact that organizations predominate over individuals in American life, or that social problems are due to something other than bad character, or that the possibility of individual success, based on ability and enterprise, is largely out of date. Consciousness I still thinks that the least government governs best. It votes for a candidate who seems to possess personal moral virtues and who promises a return to earlier conditions of life, law and order, rectitude and lower taxes. It believes that the present American crisis requires reducing government programs and expenditures, greater reliance on private business, forcing people now on welfare to go to work, taking stern measures to put down subversion at home and threats from abroad, and, above all, a general moral reawakening in the people. Today Consciousness I includes a great variety of Americans: farmers, owners of small businesses, immigrants who retain their sense of nationality, AMA-type doctors, many members of Congress, gangsters, Republicans and 'just plain folks.' In the second half of the twentieth century the beliefs of Consciousness I are drastically at variance with reality. But they are held in a stubborn, belligerent, opinionated way against all contrary evidence. . . .

Consciousness II

. . . Consciousness II came into existence as a consequence of the disastrous failure of Consciousness I. In the twentieth century Consciousness I had led to monstrous consequences: robber barons, business piracy, ruinous competition, unreliable products and false advertising, grotesque inequality and the chaos of excessive individualism and lack of coordination and planning, leading to a gangster world.

For many people this chaos meant a profound insecurity and sense of powerlessness. In a mass industrial society ungoverned by any law except self-interest, the individual became the plaything of circumstances and forces beyond his control. A lifetime of hard work could be wiped out by a business failure. The Great Depression brought the whole nation to the brink of disaster. In Germany and Italy similar insecurity led to fascism. In America it led to a breach in the existing consciousness, a turn away from individualism. A large number of people continued as Consciousness I, but another group began to develop a new consciousness.

To the newer consciousness, what the realities of the times seemed to demand was the organization and coordination of activity, the arrangement of things in a rational hierarchy of authority and responsibility, the dedication of each individual to training, work and goals beyond himself. This seemed a matter of the utmost biological necessity; this way of life was what 'had to be' if the society was to keep on functioning. Consciousness I sacrificed for individual good; now it seemed necessary to sacrifice for a common good. Discipline and hierarchy were seen as necessary because the society was not yet prepared to offer each person the kind of work he wanted or the chance to perform his work with a measure of independence. . . .

The categories of people in the general area of Consciousness II are very diverse, including businessmen (new type), liberal intellectuals, the educated professionals and technicians, middle-class suburbanites, labor-union leaders, Gene McCarthy supporters, blue-collar workers with newly purchased homes, old-line leftists and members of the Communist Party, U.S.A. Classic examples of Consciousness II are the Kennedys and the editorial page of the *New York Times*. It is the consciousness of 'liberalism,' the consciousness largely appealed to by the Democratic Party, the consciousness of 'reform.' Most political battles in America are still fought between Consciousness I and Consciousness II. Consciousness II believes that the present American crisis can be solved by greater commitment of individuals to the public interest, more social responsibility by private business, and, above all, by more affirmative government action—regulation, planning, more of a welfare state, better and more rational administration and management.

Behind a facade of optimism Consciousness II has a profoundly pessimistic view of man. It sees man in Hobbesian terms; human beings are by nature aggressive, competitive, power-seeking; uncivilized man is a jungle beast. Freud took a somewhat similar view in *Civilization and Its Discontents*. Hence the vital need for law: without law we would all be at one anothers' throats; 'only the law makes us free.' Consciousness II is deeply cynical about human motives and good intentions, and it doubts that man can be much improved. It is this philosophy that helps to explain the great emphasis on society and institutions: these are designed to do the best possible job of administering the doubtful and deficient raw material that is 'human nature.' Believing that the best and most hopeful part of man is his gift of reason, Consciousness II seeks to design a world in which reason will prevail.

At the heart of Consciousness II is the insistence that what man produces by means of reason—the state, laws, technology, manufactured goods—constitutes the true reality. Just as Consciousness I centers on the fiction of the American Adam, the competitive struggle and the triumph of the virtuous and strong individual, so Consciousness II rests on the fiction of logic and machinery; what it considers unreal is nature and subjective man. Consciousness II believes more in the automobile than in walking, more in the decision of an institution than in the feelings of an

225

individual, more in a distant but rational goal than in the immediate present. . . .

Consciousness II is deeply committed to reform. We can thank its reformist tendencies for changes in the criminal law, for social security, the movement against racial discrimination, regulation of business, government economic planning, internationalism, an end of corruption in government, public projects like the TVA, collective bargaining and improvement of work conditions, and so on down a long, honorable and admirable list. These reforms help to define Consciousness II because they may be seen as part of a battle with the past. Much of the energy of Consciousness II has gone into battling the evils that resulted from Consciousness I—prejudice, discrimination, irrationality, self-seeking, isolationism, localism, outworn traditions and superstitions; Consciousness II has worn itself out fighting the know-nothingism of an earlier America. Consciousness II believes optimistically in the possibility of social progress (as distinguished from individual progress, which it doubts). Confront men of Consciousness II with any list of evils and the response is cheerfulness: they know what measures can be taken, they see signs of improvement, and they compare the present favorably with the evils of the past which have been overcome. Even today they still believe America's problems can be solved by pushing ahead with material progress, equality, a greater public commitment to social welfare, to rebuilding cities and to revised domestic priorities.

Consciousness II believes in the central ideology of technology, the domination of man and environment by technique. Accordingly, science, technology, organization and planning are prime values. Different groups within Consciousness II might disagree—aircraft executives might think the nation should be dominated by machine and computer technology, while professors of English, horrified by this, would think the world should be dominated by rationally critical thought—but the idea of domination is common to both, although neither would necessarily acknowledge that similarity. Throughout all of Consciousness II runs the theme that society will function best if it is planned, organized, rationalized, administered. . . .

Between the values of his working life and those of his home life Consciousness II draws a strict line. His home life is characterized by many values which are contrary to those of his job; here he may be gentle, human, playful; here he may deplore what the organized part of society is doing. He is made sick by pollution of water and air, denounces dehumanization in organizations, scorns those who are motivated solely by institutional goals; but these values appear within a closely guarded shelter of privateness. Consciousness II puts all his earnings into an individual burrow for himself and his family; he prefers owning a private home at a ski resort to living at a ski lodge; he wants a private summer house at the beach. This privateness and the 'good' values that go with it seem to be related. What Consciousness II does is to 'buy out' of the system. Taking no personal responsibility for the evils of society, he shelters himself from them in a private enclave, and from that sanctuary allows his 'real' values a carefully limited expression. He does not risk himself or his family by this process. His children get 'all the advantages' that he can give them in life's struggle. He does not have to live with his own work-values.

Thus a crucial aspect of Consciousness II is a profound schizophrenia, a split between his working and his private self. It is this split that sometimes infuriates his children when they become of college age, for they see it as hypocrisy or selling out. But it is schizophrenia, not hypocrisy. The individual has two roles, two lives, two masks, two sets of values. It cannot be said, as is true of the hypocrite, that one self is real and the other false. These two values simply co-exist; they are part of the basic definition of 'reality'; the 'reality' of Consciousness II is that there is a 'public' and a 'private' man. Neither the man at work nor the man at home is the whole man; it is impossible to know, talk to, or confront the whole man, for the wholeness is precisely what does not exist. The only thing that is real is two separate men. . . .

Because of his lack of wholeness, because of his enforced playing of roles and subjection to outside standards, the consciousness of a Consciousness II person becomes vulnerable to outside manipulation. The individual has no inner reality against which to test what the outside world tells him is real. And the Corporate State does not ignore this vulnerability. As we have already shown, the Corporate State needs to administer, to the maximum degree possible, the working and consuming (home) lives of its people. It can do this by rule and organization, but it is far more effective to administer consciousness; no force is needed, no police, and no resistance is encountered. The optimum administrative state is one that administers consciousness, and as Herbert Marcuse shows us in *One-Dimensional Man,* the American Corporate State has gone a long way in this direction.

The apparatus for consciousness creation and manipulation is vast and formidable. We start with the entire advertising industry, which deliberately sets out to influence the values and wants of the people it reaches. The mass media are perhaps an even more important factor; by showing us a way of life, they insist on a particular picture of reality, and by creating that picture of outside events known as 'news' they further affect reality. Government makes other direct efforts to influence consciousness, the most important of which is compulsory education. Perhaps the greatest influence of all is the culture and environment that society creates. In the aggregate, the forces working to create consciousness are overwhelming. And it should not be supposed that these forces are undirected. They are directed in at least two ways. First, by what is deliberately excluded. For example, many attitudes, points of view and pictures of reality cannot get shown on television; this includes not only political ideas, but also the strictly non-political, such as a real view of middle-class life in place of the cheerful comedies one usually sees. Secondly, some views of reality are heavily subsidized while others are not. A much-publicized example of this was the CIA subsidy of certain student organizations: this was explained as aberrational when in fact subsidy of existing consciousness-creating forces is the rule and not the exception. The state does not wish to leave consciousness to chance, and nothing is more subsidized in our society than commercial advertising itself. Given a people who are vulnerable and a machinery with this power, the consequence is that much of Consciousness II is 'false consciousness,' a consciousness imposed by the state for its own purposes.

False consciousness is most readily described in terms of a lower-middle-class family, one which is just beginning to enjoy the material benefits of society. This is the family whose wants are most vulnerable to manipulation by television: the expensive home appliances, the new car, the boat, the vicarious world of sports. And this is the family where the 'falsity' is most apparent; they 'see' the countryside in a speeding car, tear up a fragile lake with a power boat, stand in long lines for 'pleasures.' It is also the family with the most easily manipulated political consciousness. They have been convinced that communism is trying to destroy

America, that the Cold War is necessary, that the nation's arms–space–highway priorities are right, that welfare recipients are freeloaders.

Let us imagine a young attractive couple, both college-educated, with a home and several children, he with a profession or executive position in some organization. Their house is furnished in good taste; there are antiques and simple, fine modern things; the art includes some striking original prints and drawings; there are plenty of books. They have small dinner parties with exceptionally good food, wine and conversation. They love the out-of-doors, ski in the winter, play tennis and enjoy a small sailboat in the summer (they do all of these things very well), and manage to travel to some offbeat place each year. They read a lot, are interested in politics, are strongly modern in their views, enjoy good movies, music and plays, spend time with their children, have many friends. What is wrong with this picture?

What is 'wrong' is clearly not in the interests and activities themselves; any of these things could be part of a true culture or true consciousness. How then have we the right to suggest that with our young couple all of their living is false? Marx and Marcuse distinguish between those needs which are a product of a person's authentic self, and those which are imposed from the outside by society. Why does an individual ski? Is it based on self-knowledge, or on a lack of self-knowledge, on advertising, and other pressures from society? If the latter, then the activity will not really satisfy the self or enable the self to grow. The activity will have an essential emptiness, even though the person doing it may 'think' he enjoys it. We can see many obvious examples of this type of false consciousness in America today, from the unathletic secretary who risks life and limb to ski on an occasional weekend, to the man in the Nehru jacket, turtleneck or sideburns, to 'That Cosmopolitan Girl' whose 'favorite magazine' tells her what to cook, wear and think. Some of what our young couple does may thus be simply a consequence of these imposed standards; they may be just another television couple trying to live the life pictured by the tube. Although much of our culture is indeed that and no more, there is more involved; the falseness of the picture goes deeper.

Our young couple are role-players. They have an image of what is fitting to their roles. And in choosing the activities and interests that make up their life, they are choosing from sources outside themselves;

they are choosing from a pre-existing assortment of activities which complement, harmonize with, or add to the role-picture. Their choices need not come out of a popular magazine. They can come out of a sense that a young lawyer (a) has political interests, (b) has cultural interests, (c) likes sports, (d) does things that are offbeat and in good taste. The selection of particular interests and activities does not matter so much. There is a curious interchangeability among them. There is the suspicion that our young couple would like Acapulco just as much as Aspen, camping just as much as sailing, playing the violin just as much as playing the recorder. And each activity also has a similarity of limits—in a sense, they are all blind alleys. Whether it is cooking or tennis or reading, it must be kept within bounds, not permitted to keep on expanding until it takes up more than a just proportion. There is a limit to the commitment. Will the young lawyer become a ski bum? Will he sail around the world? That is not part of the picture. And the activities are not integrated into a whole life; like the dichotomy between working life and home life, they have separate existences. All of the young couple's activities have the quality of separateness from self, of fitting some pattern—a pattern already known and only waiting to be fulfilled.

But we are not yet at the heart of the matter. Any experience, no matter why it is entered into, or with what lack of self-knowledge, still has some potential for self-discovery; a person can try Mozart or skiing for all the wrong reasons and yet have something happen to him in consequence. No—there is a deeper falsity in all of the different interests and activities that comprise the life of Consciousness II. It is that not enough happens to our young couple as a result of any experience they have.

If there is one characteristic that is shared by all the different groups we have called Consciousness II—aircraft employees, old leftists, young doctors, Kennedy men, suburban housewives—it is the insistence on being competent and knowledgeable, on having 'already been there.' The aircraft worker, if he is a weekend camper, knows all about boots, camping equipment, maps, trails and weather. The young lawyer's sophisticated wife converses about Camus, the *New York Review of Books* and Mozart at a dinner party, and she speaks with the same knowledge and assurance that the aircraft worker has in his own area of interest. Her husband is an *excellent* tennis player or skier. The professor of law *knows all about* the latest theory of pluralism and the latest development in mergers; he seems to listen at a cocktail party but really does not; there is nothing for him to learn. Mention sex, restaurants, travel, everybody knows all about them. One can't tell them anything; they adamantly resist and belittle any new information or experience. . . .

Consciousness III: The New Generation

Beginning with a few individuals in the mid-1960s, and gathering numbers ever more rapidly thereafter, Consciousness III has sprouted up, astonishingly and miraculously, out of the stony soil of the American Corporate State. So spontaneous was its appearance that no one, not the most astute or the most radical, foresaw what was coming or recognized it when it began. It is not surprising that many people think it a conspiracy, for it was spread, here and abroad, by means invisible. Hardly anybody of the older generation, even the FBI or the sociologists, know much about it, for its language and thought are so different from Consciousness II as to make it virtually an undecipherable secret code. Consciousness III is, as of this writing, the greatest secret in America, although its members have shouted as loudly as they could to be heard.

We must pause over the origins of Consciousness III, lest it seem too improbable and too transitory to be deemed as fundamental as Consciousness I and Consciousness II. . . . The new consciousness is the product of two interacting forces: the promise of life that is made to young Americans by all of our affluence, technology, liberation and ideals, and the threat to that promise posed by everything from neon ugliness and boring jobs to the Vietnam War and the shadow of nuclear holocaust. Neither the promise nor the threat is the cause by itself; but the two together have done it. . . .

If a history of Consciousness III were to be written, it would show a fascinating progression. The earliest sources were among those exceptional individuals who are found at any time in any society: the artistic, the highly sensitive, the tormented. Thoreau, James Joyce and Wallace Stevens all speak directly to Consciousness III. Salinger's Holden Caulfield was a fictional version of the first young precursors of Consciousness III. Perhaps there was always a bit of Consciousness III in every teenager, but normally it quickly vanished. Holden sees through the established world: they are phonies and he is merciless in his honesty. But what was someone like Holden to do? A subculture of 'beats' grew up, and a beatnik world flourished briefly, but for most people it represented only another dead end. Other Holdens might reject the legal profession and try teaching literature or writing instead, letting their hair grow a bit longer as well. But they remained separated individuals, usually ones from affluent but unhappy, tortured family backgrounds, and their differences with society were paid for by isolation.

Unquestionably the blacks made a substantial contribution to the origins of the new consciousness. They were left out of the Corporate State, and thus they had to have a culture and life-style in opposition to the State. Their music, with its 'guts,' contrasted with the insipid white music. This way of life seemed more earthy, more sensual than that of whites. They were the first to openly scorn the Establishment and its values; as Eldridge Cleaver shows in *Soul on Ice,* and Malcolm X shows in his autobiography, they were radicalized by the realities of their situation. When their music began to be heard by white teenagers through the medium of rock 'n' roll, and when their view of America became visible through the civil rights movement, it gave new impetus to the subterranean awareness of the beat generation and the Holden Caulfields.

The great change took place when Consciousness III began to appear among young people who had endured no special emotional conditions, but were simply bright, sensitive children of the affluent middle class. It is hard to be precise about the time when this happened. One chronology is based on the college class of 1969, which entered as freshmen in the fall of 1965. Another important date is the summer of 1967, when the full force of the cultural revolution was first visible. But even in the fall of 1967 the numbers involved were still very small. The new group drew heavily from those who had been exposed to the very best of liberal arts education—poetry, art, theatre, literature, philosophy, good conversation. Later, the group began to include 'ordinary' middle-class students. In time there were college athletes as well as college intellectuals, and lovers of motorcycles and skiing as well as lovers of art and literature. But the core group was always white, well-educated and middle-class. . . .

The foundation of Consciousness III is liberation. It comes into being the moment the individual frees himself from automatic acceptance of the imperatives of society and the false consciousness which society imposes. For example, the individual no longer accepts unthinkingly the personal goals proposed by society; a change of personal goals is one of the first and most basic elements of Consciousness III. The meaning of liberation is that the individual is free to build his own philosophy and values, his own life-style, and his own culture from a new beginning.

Consciousness III starts with self. In contrast to Consciousness II, which accepts society, the public interest, and institutions as the primary reality, III declares that the individual self is the only true reality. Thus it returns to the earlier America: 'Myself I sing.' The first commandment is: 'Thou shalt not do violence to thyself.' It is a crime to allow oneself to become an instrumental being, a projectile designed to accomplish some extrinsic end, a part of an organization or a machine. It is a crime to be alienated from oneself, to be a divided or schizophrenic being, to defer meaning to the future. One must live completely at each moment, not with the frenzied 'nowness' of advertising, but with the utter *wholeness* that Heidegger expresses. The commandment is: 'Be true to oneself.'

To start from self does not mean to be selfish. It means to start from premises based on human life and the rest of nature, rather than premises that are the artificial products of the Corporate State, such as power or status. It is not an 'ego trip' but a radical subjectivity designed to find genuine values in a world whose official values are false and distorted. It is not egocentricity, but honesty, wholeness, genuineness in all things. It starts from self because human life is found as individual units, not as corporations and institutions; its intent is to start from life.

Consciousness III postulates the absolute worth of every human being—every self. Consciousness III does not believe in the antagonistic or competitive doctrine of life. Competition, within the limits of a sport like tennis or swimming, is accepted for its own pleasure, although even as athletes IIIs are far less competitive (and sometimes, but not always, poorer athletes as a result). But IIIs do not compete in 'real life.' They do not measure others, they do not see others as something to struggle against. People are brothers, the world is ample for all. In consequence, one never hears the disparagements, the snickers, the judgments that are so common among Is and IIs. A boy who was odd in some way used to suffer derision all through his school days. Today there would be no persecution; one might even hear one boy speak, with affection, of 'my freaky friend.' Instead of insisting that everyone be measured by given standards, the new generation values what is unique and different in each self; there is no pressure that anyone be an athlete unless he wants to; a harpsichord player is accepted on equal terms. No one judges anyone else. This is a second commandment.

Consciousness III rejects the whole concept of excellence and comparative merit that is so central to Consciousness II. III refuses to evaluate people by general standards, it refuses to classify people or analyze them. Each person has his own individuality, not to be compared to that of anyone else. Someone may be a brilliant thinker, but he is not 'better' at thinking than anyone else, he simply possesses his own excellence. A person who thinks very poorly is still excellent in his own way. Therefore people are in no hurry to find out another person's background, schools, achievements, as a means of knowing him; they regard all of that as secondary, preferring to know him unadorned. Because there are no governing standards, no one is rejected. Everyone is entitled to pride in himself, and no one should act in a way that is servile, or feel inferior, or allow himself to be treated as if he were inferior.

It is upon these premises that the Consciousness III idea of community and of personal relationships rests. In place of the world seen as a jungle, with every man for himself (Consciousness I) or the world seen as a meritocracy leading to a great corporate hierarchy of rigidly-drawn relations and maneuvers for position (Consciousness I), the world is a community. People all belong to the same family, whether they have met each other or not. It is as simple as that. There are no 'tough guys' among the youth of Consciousness III. Hitch-hikers smile at approaching cars, people smile at each other on the street, the human race rediscovers its need for each other. . . .

All of the various efforts of the new generation to increase awareness combine to produce a remarkable phenomenon: the Consciousness III person, no matter how young and inexperienced he may be, seems to possess an extraordinary 'new knowledge.' Governor Rockefeller goes on an official trip to Latin America and returns 'heartened' by his reception; the ordinary citizen, if he is not particularly sophisticated, may actually believe that the Governor was well received; the person with 'new knowledge' sees right through the pretense and knows, without reading the newspapers carefully, that the Governor was practically run out of each country and survived only by virtue of forceful repression of protest by each régime. He does not 'know' the facts, but he still 'knows' the truth that seems hidden from others. The explanation for this political sophistication is primarily the repeal of pretense and absurdities. It is absurd to think that someone named Rockefeller, representing the United States from a limousine, will be 'warmly' welcomed by a populace, just as it is absurd to think that high-school students revere their principal or believe what is patriotically said at school assemblies. In a country as burdened as ours with hypocrisy and myth, the mere repeal of untruth becomes a profound insight.

One of the ways to describe this 'new knowledge' is to say that it is capable of ignoring categories. We are all limited in our thinking by artificially drawn lines; we cannot get beyond the idea that a university is 'private property' or that prose is different from poetry. When the category-barriers are removed, 'new' relationships are seen. But the 'new knowledge' is more than this; it is as if everything, from political affairs to aesthetics, were seen with new eyes; the young people of Consciousness III see effortlessly what is phony or dishonest in politics, or what is ugly and meretricious in architecture and city planning, whereas an older person has to go through years of education to make himself equally aware. It might take a Consciousness II person twenty years of reading radical literature to know that law is a tool of oppression; the young drug-user just plain knows it. Nothing is more difficult for an older person to believe in than this 'new knowledge,' but it is such a striking phenomenon, extending even to long-haired California teen-agers hitch-hiking their way to the beach, whose experience with political thinking or newspaper reading is limited, that it must be taken seriously.

Much of what we have said is summed up by the phrase 'where his head is at.' The implication of the phrase is that we are dealing with some dimension utterly outside of the way most people in America have become accustomed to the world. One has only to look at *Head Comix* of R. Crumb to realize what it means to have a head that is in some extraordinary place; the world of R. Crumb is not merely brilliant or satiric or grotesque, it is *in another place* than most people have been. It is a common observation among today's college students that freshmen and, even more so, high-school students, have heads that are amazing even to the college students.

Perhaps the deepest source of consciousness is nature. Members of the new generation seek out the beach, the woods and the mountains. They do not litter these places with beer cans, they do not shatter the silences with power boats or motorcycle noises. They do not go to nature as a holiday from what is real. They go to nature as a source. The salt water of the sea is the salt in their blood; the freedom of the sea is their freedom. The forest is where they came from, it is the place where they feel closest to themselves, it is renewal. They do not pay much attention to hiking equipment, or picnic gear for the beach, or swimming attire; they are likely to wade into the salt water with blue jeans still on. Nature is not some foreign element that requires equipment. Nature is them.

All of this search for increased consciousness culminates in an attitude that is the very antithesis of Consciousness II: a desire for innocence, for the ability to be in a state of wonder or awe. It is of the essence of the thinking of the new generation that man should be constantly open to new experience, constantly ready to have his old ways of thinking changed, constantly hoping that he will be sensitive enough and receptive enough to let the wonders of nature and mankind come to him. . . .

☆ • ☆ • ☆ • ☆ • ☆

The reputation of *The Greening of America* has not held up well. At the time of its publication (late 1970) it sold far more copies than did the other American-character book published the same year—Philip Slater's *Pursuit of Loneliness*—but it has long been out of print, whereas Slater's book went on to a 1976, revised edition and stayed in print through a Twentieth Anniversary edition published in 1990.

Because of its hippie persuasion, intellectuals have found it easy—too easy—to dismiss *The Greening of America* as a period piece and a work of naive fancy. Even at its publication, most leading reviews of it were unfavorable. This is certainly true of the reviews and comments collected by Philip Nobile and published in 1971 as *The Con III Controversy: The Critics Look at "The Greening of America."* Reich's critics charged him with ignoring the down side of Consciousness III. Having beautiful thoughts too often meant a sloppy thinking incapable of building the world Reich wanted. The demand for freedom to experiment and experience was more likely to become a withdrawal into private self-indulgence, freeing men more than women (who would literally be left holding the baby) and playing into the hands of consumer capitalism. It is significant that one of the more favorable pieces in Nobile's book was a *Fortune* editorial that claimed that the growth of the existing economic system was already creating the social and spiritual freedoms that Reich called for.

Nobile's writers said little about Reich's view of American history and his notion of Consciousness I and II. They might have noted that his portrait of "Consciousness I" workers was contemptuous and snobbish: "minds closed to new ideas and feelings [how did he know?], their bodies slumped in front of television to watch the ballgame Sunday." On Consciousness III, however, the critics made telling points. Reich *did* wear rosy spectacles (he said almost nothing about drugs and his Consciousness III characters never seem to be dirty or smelly!). Even so, I believe that *The Greening of America* has been seriously underestimated.

In the first place, Reich delivers some of the best prose in these pages. (Look, for example, at the two paragraphs following the ellipses at the bottom of p. 226.) This applies equally to his law journal articles and his autobiography. Reich is a master of the specific case or portrait that makes a general point.

Secondly, Consciousness III is not just a dream of the past. A national survey by Joseph Veroff and others comparing Americans in 1976 with an earlier sample in 1957 found that the second generation were more apt to say they valued emotional fulfillment and sensitive relationships; and they were less likely to classify people according to their official roles—vice-president, teacher, wife. All this was in the spirit of Consciousness III. And of all modern writers on American character, Reich is virtually the only one to consider the importance of Afro-Americans in making the whole culture more expressive.

Reich's ideas have a philosophical significance too. His picture of Consciousness III heralded the modern interest in transcendent states of mind and being: the sense that our rationalist, workaday selves are only a small part of us; the belief (sharpened by ecological threat) that we must find a new (or very old) harmony between humans and nature and that this cannot be separated from our spiritual condition. This outlook is far from the bustling, competitive intelligence of Consciousness II (what some Buddhists have called 'monkey mind'); nor is it reached by Consciousness II's urge—in Reich's words—to "dominate experience" as it dominates nature and society. Influenced by Eastern philosophies, the modern hunger for alternative consciousness is not to be written off as a 'New Age' fashion. Though it is strongest in California, it is of course not confined to the United States; but American cultural pluralism gives it space and it chimes with some American beliefs: that people can remake themselves; that the spirit can be a frontier too; that technology can and must be harmonized with nature.

Like Philip Slater (p. 201), Charles Reich believed that Americans impoverished themselves by hiding away from society in private enclaves. His remedy, though, reversed Slater's. Slater believed that if people depended more on their communities, they would paradoxically feel freer to express themselves as individuals. Reich believed that if people first developed themselves as individuals, they would naturally be open to others and find community. In *The Lonely Crowd*, David Riesman had briefly said much the same thing. Its essence lay in the old Catholic teaching that to love others, you must love yourself.

As other writers have pointed out, Reich's historical types— Consciousness I, II, and III—are roughly similar (not identical) to David Riesman's "inner-direction," "other-direction," and "autonomy," and the first two correspond to William Whyte's "Protestant Ethic" entrepreneurs and "Social Ethic" organization men. Reich did recognize that early American, Consciousness I individualists were also cooperators, but he romanticized too much their ideas of community. He did not appreciate enough that when early American farmers and frontier people got together, they often did so for practical reasons—to raise a roof or dig a ditch.

Reich was more at home in the present. One of his most striking passages in the excerpt above comes when he moves from the lower-middle–class, power-boating family to the tasteful, college-educated couple and suggests that their experiences too are prefabricated, unspontaneous, essentially *false*. Contentious as it is, his argument echoes David Riesman's portrait of "The Cash Customer" (1942), which in turn owes much to Riesman's mentor, Erich Fromm. *The Greening of America* makes no mention of Riesman or Fromm, but its conception of "false consciousness" goes back through Fromm to Karl Marx.

The term "false consciousness" was coined by Marx's associate, Friedrich Engels, in 1893, but Marx and Engels had the idea much earlier. For them it meant the way in which one's class position distorted one's view of society. It involved working-class misperceptions of class interest, and the ability of a bourgeois ruling class to control ideas.

By the time the notion of "false consciousness" had reached Charles Reich, it had become more personal and psychological, and less confined to political and economic attitudes. Having no integrated self (see p. 228), Reich's Consciousness II character had a weak sense of reality and was therefore open to manipulation in all kinds of ways. Reich's view here was quite like that of the radical anthropologist, Jules Henry. Writing in the late 1950s and early 1960s, Henry claimed that the economic system, especially advertising, had superimposed a consumer "pseudo self" over the individual's truer, deeper values.

The basic distinction here between a "pseudo" self of imposed roles and a spontaneous "real" self was formulated by Erich Fromm in the 1930s and 1940s. Like Herbert Marcuse, Erich Fromm was among the left-wing intellectuals who left Germany for America in the 1930s. In different ways both of them combined the Freudian idea that society repressed emotional life with the Marxian idea that powerful economic systems controlled people's attitudes. In *The Greening of America*, as in other works on American character, Fromm's view converged with an old American fear: the specter of a virtuous people of nature captured and contaminated by insidious social forces.

Reich's notion of "false consciousness" was also a breakaway from theories of roles and role-playing that sociologists (including Philip Slater) had developed in the 1950s and early 1960s. These scholars, even the irreverent Erving Goffman—author of *The Presentation of Self in Everyday Life* (1959)—accepted role-playing as inevitable. Reich did not. Instead he joined the youthful 'New Left,' who frequently attacked mainstream sociologists for supporting a 'repressive status quo' under the mantle of 'value-free' science.

Such attacks, however, did not clear up a central problem with Reich's "false consciousness" and the "pseudo self" of Fromm and Jules Henry—how to decide what was false or pseudo. Is manipulation by advertising, say, more artificial, false, imposed, than manipulation by parents—or teachers? Fromm recognized that all character was socially conditioned, but he never fully explained the difference between this and the imposition of "pseudo" roles and behavior. (Still less did Jules Henry. David Riesman's position was more complicated. He rejected Fromm's clear-cut distinction between a "pseudo" and "real" self, and he placed the media on a par with parents as an instrument of character-forming; but he never wholly abandoned the idea that media messages and peer-group pressures had an external, *imposed* quality that created a passive malaise in many people.)

Charles Reich for his part ran wild and free of such conundrums. Believing that humans were naturally good, he did not recognize that they needed much training or conditioning to be nice to each other and practice community. Although his Consciousness III people had imbibed liberal values from their parents, the essence of Consciousness III came from listening to a pure and natural self. Reich did not therefore bother about distinctions between "false" and necessary conditioning. The important thing for Reich was to achieve a full and open relationship with nature: everything would then come right. In this he was truly a romantic optimist.

CHRISTOPHER LASCH

The Culture of Narcissism

Encounter groups, rolfing, ESP, yoga . . . by the mid-1970s the world of Charles Reich's Consciousness III (discussed in the previous selection) had become a marketplace of middle-class groups, each following its own route to psychological health and awareness. In a series of sparkling essays on their culture, Tom Wolfe used his term "the Me Decade" to describe what he thought was happening. While successful working-class Americans had run off to the suburbs to express themselves in houses stuffed with knickknacks, many middle-class Americans were showing off in more psychic ways. Their motto 'let's talk about ME' meant 'let's *look* at me' as well as 'help me be free to grow.' In spite of his debunking style, Wolfe showed some respect for the religious element in all this, but he also noted its narcissism.

At the end of the decade, there appeared a harsher analysis of these trends. The big-selling *Culture of Narcissism* by the intellectual historian Christopher Lasch started off with an indictment of the "awareness movement" for betraying the New Left counterculture from which it sprang. For a "brief period" in the mid-1960s, said Lasch, the New Left had put together a political critique that made "the quality of personal life" inseparable from the nature of the social system. Soon, however, the politics fell away, and the counterculture degenerated into a shallow search for experience and therapy.

This decline, according to Lasch, was part of a much longer-term process: the growth of mass consumption and hierarchical organization. In subtle, devastating ways, this had caused American individualism to turn in on itself.

Like Reich, Lasch indicted government bureaucracy and the professions as well as corporations and advertisers; unlike Reich and Philip Slater (pp. 201–40), he explicitly attacked "capitalism," in which he included all the institutions of the modern state. Capitalism, in Lasch's view, had "severed the ties of personal dependence only to revive dependence under cover of bureaucratic rationality"; by surrounding the individual with a net of public relations and pseudosmiles, it had undermined "patriarchy"—the tough, moral leadership of fathers and father figures. Modern organization had taken away people's sense of personal, moral responsibility without providing a clear authority of its own. It encouraged people to manipulate each other aggressively while it massaged them with consumer goods and packaged experiences.

Without giving people a sense of place, mass organization had taken over and distorted their sense of reality by barraging them with media power, from advertising and managed news to television shows and videos. Information was increasingly secondhand and prerecorded. Society had become a "hall of mirrors" in which fictions mocked other fictions ('soaps' spoofing other 'soaps'). Overpowered by these smoke-screens and degraded by the impersonal routines of modern work, people escaped into fantasy or into cynical detachment. Along the way they became unable to tell truth from untruth and to distinguish themselves clearly from others (this last was a clinical feature of narcissism).

Just as the synthetic reality of the media had invaded the self, so the professional propaganda of child-rearing—put out by counselors, progressive teachers, and advice-book writers—had invaded the family. Even when the current fad told parents to 'act out' their feelings, parents followed the advice too anxiously to behave naturally to their children. Eager to be loving and encouraging, but really wrapped up in themselves, parents conveyed an underlying coolness to their children. They in turn became insecure narcissists: self-aggrandizing, hungry for immediate gratifications, and eager to be admired, yet emotionally passive and distant. The result of all this was a personality that felt isolated, empty, and vaguely vengeful.

Throughout his complex arguments, Lasch stressed the effect of existential terror. The fear of annihilation, sharpened by the Jewish Holocaust and nuclear weapons, was magnified by the media's swiftness to report violence and disasters across the world. On top of this there were economic and ecological worries. These fears made people live all the more for themselves in the present. They had lost a sense of community, not just with each other but with past and future generations.

Lasch was at pains to deny he was just one popular pundit on what's-wrong-with-America, but the sense of national decline was very much an intellectual mood by the late 1970s. Watergate and the Vietnam defeat, OPEC* and 'the energy crisis,' 'stagflation' and a fall in most people's real incomes, the collapse of old industrial areas and the rise of foreign competition—all fed the mood.

When the slowing growth in U.S. industrial productivity (amount produced per worker) became outright decline in 1979 and 1980, some commentators were quick to blame it on a failure of national 'will.' Through the 1970s and early 1980s, opinion polls found low confidence in the nation's institutions and leaders and a growing economic pessimism. The subtitle of Lasch's book, *American Life in an Age of Diminishing Expectations,* seemed apt indeed—all the more so when President Carter extolled the book and then gave his famous 'malaise speech,' declaring that the country had splintered into uncompromising interest groups and consumer self-indulgence.

This is not to say that Lasch's book was just a passing response to the 1970s. Taking a long-term view of history, Lasch outflanked business conservatism by declaring that capitalism was not conservative at all; instead it was destabilizing, divisive, and destructive. In the 1980s this line of attack became popular among left-wing intellectuals, and not just in the United States; it was used with special vehemence against Thatcherism while still being a critique of capitalism in general.

Lasch's support for this argument had its own psychological twist, but like Charles Reich, he owed much to mixtures of Marx and Freud produced by such writers as Erich Fromm and Herbert Marcuse (see pp. 239–40). Lasch, Marcuse, Fromm, and others were all concerned, as Lasch himself put it, with the "cultural and psychological devastation brought about by industrial capitalism." Lasch recognized that concentrating on psychological issues did not *have to* mean a neglect of social class relations; but in fact it did so in a very American

---

*The Organization of Petroleum Exporting Countries in the Middle East hiked oil prices by several hundred percent in 1973.

way. (Marxism Freudianized and Americanized is Marxism without Class.) Lasch waits almost to the end of the book to give a class comparison—between the family cohesion and confidence of an "old propertied upper class" and the anxieties of a new "managerial elite."

In stressing narcissism, Lasch built on two streams of thought: social-character studies, from Fromm through Riesman to Slater, which referred to narcissism without making much of it; and more technical writing by psychologists in the 1970s that declared that narcissistic personality disorders and related problems had increased.

Lasch also drew on themes in his own previous writing. As a historian of American liberalism and the Left, Lasch charged that American social critics and reformers had too often gone on false trails. As a result, they did not liberate people; they diminished them or at best simply failed them.

Lasch made a lot of this in the book that immediately preceded *The Culture of Narcissism*. *Haven in a Heartless World: The Family Besieged* (1977) is largely about the way in which social scientists and therapists through the twentieth century invaded the family and undermined its authority. Here, in a restricted sense, Lasch did use a notion of class, for he saw the family experts as a "new class," guiding the capitalist control of families. *The Culture of Narcissism* more or less repeated what the earlier book said about family experts in the 1960s and 1970s. Promoting the freedom of "alternative life-styles" and "nonbinding commitments," they had unraveled the family until its members felt rejected, vulnerable, and distrustful of the future.

In the excerpt that follows—a chapter from *The Culture of Narcissism*—Lasch moves out from the family to the world of middle-class work. Looking back to the eighteenth century, he sees a massive and ominous change since then in the nature of American individualism.

☆ • ☆ • ☆ • ☆ • ☆

American society is marked by a central stress upon personal achievement, especially secular occupational achievement. The "success story" and the respect accorded to the self-made man are distinctly American if anything is. . . . [American Society] has endorsed Horatio Alger and has glorified the rail splitter who became president.   —ROBIN WILLIAMS[1]

_____

The man of ambition is still with us, as in all times, but now he needs a more subtle initiative, a deeper capacity to manipulate the democracy of emotions, if he is to maintain his separate identity and significantly augment it with success. . . . The sexual problems of the neurotic competing for some ephemeral kudos in mid-century Manhattan are very different from the problems of the neurotic in turn-of-the-century Vienna. History changes the expression of neurosis even if it does not change the underlying mechanisms. —PHILIP RIEFF[2]

The Original Meaning of the Work Ethic

Until recently, the Protestant work ethic stood as one of the most important underpinnings of American culture.* According to the myth of capitalist enterprise, thrift and industry held the key to material success and spiritual fulfillment. America's reputation as a land of opportunity rested on its claim that the destruction of hereditary obstacles to advancement had created conditions in which social mobility depended on individual initiative alone. The self-made man, archetypical embodiment of the American dream, owed his advancement to habits of industry, sobriety, moderation, self-discipline, and avoidance of debt. He lived for the future, shunning self-indulgence in favor of patient, painstaking accumulation; and as long as the collective prospect looked on the whole so bright, he found in the deferral of gratification not only his principal gratification but an abundant source of profits. In an expanding economy, the value of investments could be expected to multiply with time, as the spokesmen for self-help, for all their celebration of work as its own reward, seldom neglected to point out.

In an age of diminishing expectations, the Protestant virtues no longer excite enthusiasm. Inflation erodes investments and savings. Advertising undermines the horror of indebtedness, exhorting the consumer to buy now and pay later. As the future becomes menacing and uncertain, only fools put off until tomorrow the fun they can have today. A profound

*"Changing Modes of Making It: From Horatio Alger to the Happy Hooker," from _The Culture of Narcissism: American Life in an Age of Diminishing Expectations_ by Christopher Lasch. Copyright © 1979 by Christopher Lasch. Reprinted by permission of W. W. Norton & Company, Inc.

shift in our sense of time has transformed work habits, values, and the definition of success. Self-preservation has replaced self-improvement as the goal of earthly existence. In a lawless, violent, and unpredictable society, in which the normal conditions of everyday life come to resemble those formerly confined to the underworld, men live by their wits. They hope not so much to prosper as simply to survive, although survival itself increasingly demands a large income. In earlier times, the self-made man took pride in his judgment of character and probity; today he anxiously scans the faces of his fellows not so as to evaluate their credit but in order to gauge their susceptibility to his own blandishments. He practices the classic arts of seduction and with the same indifference to moral niceties, hoping to win your heart while picking your pocket. The happy hooker stands in place of Horatio Alger as the prototype of personal success. If Robinson Crusoe embodied the ideal type of economic man, the hero of bourgeois society in its ascendancy, the spirit of Moll Flanders presides over its dotage.

The new ethic of self-preservation has been a long time taking shape; it did not emerge overnight. In the first three centuries of our history, the work ethic constantly changed its meaning; these vicissitudes, often imperceptible at the time, foreshadowed its eventual transformation into an ethic of personal survival. For the Puritans, a godly man worked diligently at his calling not so much in order to accumulate personal wealth as to add to the comfort and convenience of the community. Every Christian had a "general calling" to serve God and a "personal calling," in the words of Cotton Mather, "by which his Usefulness, in his Neighborhood, is distinguished." This personal calling arose from the circumstance that "God hath made man a Sociable Creature." The Puritans recognized that a man might get rich at his calling, but they saw personal aggrandizement as incidental to social labor—the collective transformation of nature and the progress of useful arts and useful knowledge. They instructed men who prospered not to lord it over their neighbors. The true Christian, according to Calvinist conceptions of an honorable and godly existence, bore both good fortune and bad with equanimity, contenting himself with what came to his lot. "This he had learned to doe," said John Cotton, "if God prosper him, he had learned not to be puffed up, and if he should be exposed to want, he could do it without murmuring. It is the same act of unbeleefe, that makes a man murmure in crosses, which puffes him up in prosperity."³

Whatever the moral reservations with which Calvinism surrounded the pursuit of wealth, many of its practitioners, especially in New England, waxed fat and prosperous on the trade in rum and slaves. As the Puritan gave way to the Yankee, a secularized version of the Protestant ethic emerged. Whereas Cotton Mather advised against going into debt on the grounds that it injured the creditor ("Let it be uneasy unto you, at any time to think, *I have so much of another mans Estate in my Hands, and I to his damage detain it from him*"), Benjamin Franklin argued that indebtedness injured the debtor himself, putting him into his creditors' hands. Puritan sermons on the calling quoted copiously from the Bible; Franklin codified popular common sense in the sayings of Poor Richard. *God helps them that help themselves. Lost time is never found again. Never leave that till to-morrow which you can do today. If you would know the value of money, go and try to borrow some; for he that goes a borrowing goes a sorrowing.*

The Puritans urged the importance of socially useful work; the Yankee stressed self-improvement. Yet he understood self-improvement to consist of more than money-making. This important concept also implied self-discipline, the training and cultivation of God-given talents, above all the cultivation of reason. The eighteenth-century ideal of prosperity included not only material comfort but good health, good temper, wisdom, usefulness, and the satisfaction of knowing that you had earned the good opinion of others. In the section of his *Autobiography* devoted to "The Art of Virtue," Franklin summed up the results of a lifelong program of moral self-improvement:

> To Temperance he ascribes his long-continu'd Health, and what is still left to him of a good Constitution. To Industry and Frugality, the early Easiness of his Circumstances, and Acquisition of his Fortune, with all that Knowledge which enabled him to be an useful Citizen, and obtain'd for him some Degree of Reputation among the Learned. To Sincerity and Justice the Confidence of his Country, and the honourable Employs it conferr'd upon him. And to the joint influence of the whole Mass of the Virtues, evenness of Temper, and that Cheerfulness in Conversation which makes his Company still sought for, and agreeable even to his younger Acquaintance.

Virtue pays, in the eighteenth-century version of the work ethic; but what it pays cannot be measured simply in money. The real reward of virtue is to have little to apologize for or to repent of at the end of your life. Wealth is to be valued, but chiefly because it serves as one of the necessary preconditions of moral and intellectual cultivation.*

From "Self-Culture" to Self-Promotion Through "Winning Images"

In the nineteenth century, the ideal of self-improvement degenerated into a cult of compulsive industry. P. T. Barnum, who made a fortune in a calling the very nature of which the Puritans would have condemned ("Every calling, whereby God will be Dishonored; every Calling whereby none but the Lusts of men are Nourished: . . . every such Calling is to be Rejected"), delivered many times a lecture frankly entitled "The Art of Money-Getting," which epitomized the nineteenth-century conception of worldly success.[5] Barnum quoted freely from Franklin but without Franklin's concern for the attainment of wisdom or the promotion of useful knowledge. "Information" interested Barnum merely as a means of mastering the market. Thus he condemned the "false economy" of the farm wife who douses her candle at dusk rather than lighting another for reading, not realizing that the "information" gained through reading is worth far more than the price of the candles. "Always take a trustworthy newspaper," Barnum advised young men on the make, "and thus keep thoroughly posted in regard to the transactions of the world. He who is without a newspaper is cut off from his species."

Barnum valued the good opinion of others not as a sign of one's usefulness but as a means of getting credit. "Uncompromising integrity of character is invaluable." The nineteenth century attempted to express all values in monetary terms. Everything had its price. Charity was a

---

*Efforts to reduce Franklin's "art of virtue" to a purely prudential ethic of money-getting and self-advancement miss its finer shadings. "All Franklin's moral attitudes," wrote Max Weber in *The Protestant Ethic and the Spirit of Capitalism*, "are coloured with utilitarianism. . . . Virtues . . . are only in so far virtues as they are actually useful to the individual. . . . Man is dominated by the making of money, by acquisition as the ultimate purpose of his life."[4] D. H. Lawrence expressed a somewhat similar opinion in *Studies in Classic American Literature*. These interpretations ignore the connections, so important in the bourgeois outlook of the eighteenth century, between money-making, sociability, and the progress of the useful arts; between the spirit of capitalism and the spirit of invention and workmanship. Self-improvement is not the same thing as self-advancement, in Franklin's eyes; indeed, ambition, in the eighteenth century, was a Hamiltonian much more than a Franklinian or Jeffersonian virtue.

moral duty because "the liberal man will command patronage, while the sordid, uncharitable miser will be avoided." The sin of pride was not that it offended God but that it led to extravagant expenditures. "A spirit of pride and vanity, when permitted to have full sway, is the undying cankerworm which gnaws the very vitals of a man's worldly possessions."

The eighteenth century made a virtue of temperance but did not condemn moderate indulgence in the service of sociability. "Rational conversation," on the contrary, appeared to Franklin and his contemporaries to represent an important value in its own right. The nineteenth century condemned sociability itself, on the grounds that it might interfere with business. "How many good opportunities have passed, never to return, while a man was sipping a 'social glass' with his friend!" Preachments on self-help now breathed the spirit of compulsive enterprise. Henry Ward Beecher defined "the *beau ideal* of happiness" as a state of mind in which "a man [is] so busy that he does not know whether he is or is not happy."[6] Russell Sage remarked that "work has been the chief, and, you might say, the only source of pleasure in my life."[7]

Even at the height of the Gilded Age, however, the Protestant ethic did not completely lose its original meaning. In the success manuals, the McGuffey readers, the Peter Parley Books, and the hortatory writings of the great capitalists themselves, the Protestant virtues—industry, thrift, temperance—still appeared not merely as stepping-stones to success but as their own reward.

The spirit of self-improvement lived on, in debased form, in the cult of "self-culture"—proper care and training of mind and body, nurture of the mind through "great books," development of "character." The social contribution of individual accumulation still survived as an undercurrent in the celebration of success, and the social conditions of early industrial capitalism, in which the pursuit of wealth undeniably increased the supply of useful objects, gave some substance to the claim that "accumulated capital means progress." In condemning speculation and extravagance, in upholding the importance of patient industry, in urging young men to start at the bottom and submit to "the discipline of daily life," even the most unabashed exponents of self-enrichment clung to the notion that wealth derives its value from its contribution to the general good and to the happiness of future generations.[8]

The nineteenth-century cult of success placed surprisingly little emphasis on competition. It measured achievement not against the achievements of others but against an abstract ideal of discipline and self-denial. At the turn of the century, however, preachments on success began to stress the will to win. The bureaucratization of the corporate career changed the conditions of self-advancement; ambitious young men now had to compete with their peers for the attention and approval of their superiors. The struggle to surpass the previous generation and to provide for the next gave way to a form of sibling rivalry, in which men of approximately equal abilities jostled against each other in competition for a limited number of places. Advancement now depended on "will-power, self-confidence, energy, and initiative"—the qualities celebrated in such exemplary writings as George Lorimer's *Letters from a Self-Made Merchant to His Son*. "By the end of the nineteenth century," writes John Cawelti in his study of the success myth, "self-help books were dominated by the ethos of salesmanship and boosterism. Personal magnetism, a quality which supposedly enabled a man to influence and dominate others, became one of the major keys to success."[9] In 1907, both Lorimer's *Saturday Evening Post* and Orison Swett Marden's *Success* magazine inaugurated departments of instruction in the "art of conversation," fashion, and "culture." The management of interpersonal relations came to be seen as the essence of self-advancement. The captain of industry gave way to the confidence man, the master of impressions. Young men were told that they had to sell themselves in order to succeed.

At first, self-testing through competition remained almost indistinguishable from moral self-discipline and self-culture, but the difference became unmistakable when Dale Carnegie and then Norman Vincent Peale restated and transformed the tradition of Mather, Franklin, Barnum, and Lorimer. As a formula for success, winning friends and influencing people had little in common with industry and thrift. The prophets of positive thinking disparaged "the old adage that hard work alone is the magic key that will unlock the door to our desires."[10] They praised the love of money, officially condemned even by the crudest of Gilded Age materialists, as a useful incentive. "You can never have riches in great quantities," wrote Napoleon Hill in his *Think and Grow Rich*, "unless you can work yourself into a white heat of *desire* for money."[11] The pursuit of wealth lost the few shreds of moral meaning that still clung to it. Formerly the Protestant virtues appeared to have an independent value of their own. Even when they became purely instrumental, in the second half of the nineteenth century, success itself retained moral and social overtones, by virtue of its contribution to the sum of human comfort and progress. Now success appeared as an end in its own right, the victory over your competitors that alone retained the capacity to instill a sense of self-approval. The latest success manuals differ from earlier ones—even surpassing the cynicism of Dale Carnegie and Peale—in their frank acceptance of the need to exploit and intimidate others, in their lack of interest in the substance of success, and in the candor with which they insist that appearances—"winning images"—count for more than performance, ascription for more than achievement. One author seems to imply that the self consists of little more than its "image" reflected in others' eyes. "Although I'm not being original when I say it, I'm sure you'll agree that the way you see yourself will reflect the image you portray to others."[12] Nothing succeeds like the appearance of success.

The Eclipse of Achievement

In a society in which the dream of success has been drained of any meaning beyond itself, men have nothing against which to measure their achievements except the achievements of others. Self-approval depends on public recognition and acclaim, and the quality of this approval has undergone important changes in its own right. The good opinion of friends and neighbors, which formerly informed a man that he had lived a useful life, rested on appreciation of his accomplishments. Today men seek the kind of approval that applauds not their actions but their personal attributes. They wish to be not so much esteemed as admired. They crave not fame but the glamour and excitement of celebrity. They want to be envied rather than respected. Pride and acquisitiveness, the sins of an ascendant capitalism, have given way to vanity. Most Americans would still define success as riches, fame, and power, but their actions show that they have little interest in the substance of these attainments. What a man does matters less than the fact that he has "made it." Whereas fame depends on the performance of notable deeds acclaimed in biography and works of history, celebrity—the reward of those who project a vivid or pleasing exterior or have otherwise attracted attention to themselves—is

251

acclaimed in the news media, in gossip columns, on talk shows, in magazines devoted to "personalities." Accordingly it is evanescent, like news itself, which loses its interest when it loses its novelty. Worldly success has always carried with it a certain poignancy, an awareness that "you can't take it with you"; but in our time, when success is so largely a function of youth, glamour, and novelty, glory is more fleeting than ever, and those who win the attention of the public worry incessantly about losing it.

Success in our society has to be ratified by publicity. The tycoon who lives in personal obscurity, the empire builder who controls the destinies of nations from behind the scenes, are vanishing types. Even nonelective officials, ostensibly preoccupied with questions of high policy, have to keep themselves constantly on view; all politics becomes a form of spectacle. It is well known that Madison Avenue packages politicians and markets them as if they were cereals or deodorants; but the art of public relations penetrates even more deeply into political life, transforming policy making itself. The modern prince does not much care that "there's a job to be done"—the slogan of American capitalism at an earlier and more enterprising stage of its development; what interests him is that "relevant audiences," in the language of the Pentagon Papers, have to be cajoled, won over, seduced. He confuses successful completion of the task at hand with the impression he makes or hopes to make on others. Thus American officials blundered into the war in Vietnam because they could not distinguish the country's military and strategic interests from "our reputation as a guarantor," as one of them put it. More concerned with the trappings than with the reality of power, they convinced themselves that failure to intervene would damage American "credibility." They borrowed the rhetoric of games theory to dignify their obsession with appearances, arguing that American policy in Vietnam had to address itself to "the relevant 'audiences' of U.S. actions"—the communists, the South Vietnamese, "our allies (who must trust us as 'underwriters')," and the American public.[13]

When policy making, the search for power, and the pursuit of wealth have no other objects than to excite admiration or envy, men lose the sense of objectivity, always precarious under the best of circumstances. Impressions overshadow achievements. Public men fret about their ability to rise to crisis, to project an image of decisiveness, to give a convincing performance of executive power. Their critics resort to the same standards: when doubts began to be raised about the leadership of the Johnson administration, they focused on the "credibility gap." Public relations and propaganda have exalted the image and the pseudo-event. People "talk constantly," Daniel Boorstin has written, "not of things themselves, but of their images."[14]

In the corporate structure as in government, the rhetoric of achievement, of single-minded devotion to the task at hand—the rhetoric of performance, efficiency, and productivity—no longer provides an accurate description of the struggle for personal survival. "Hard work," according to Eugene Emerson Jennings, ". . . constitutes a necessary but not sufficient cause of upward mobility. It is not a route to the top."[15] A newspaper man with experience both in journalism and in the Southern Regional Council has reported that "in neither, I realized, did it matter to the people in charge how well or how badly I performed. . . . Not the goals, but keeping the organization going, became the important thing."[16] Even the welfare of the organization, however, no longer excites the enthusiasm it generated in the fifties. The "self-sacrificing company man," writes Jennings, has become "an obvious anachronism."* The upwardly mobile corporate executive "does not view himself as an organization man." His "anti-organizational posture," in fact, has emerged as his "chief characteristic."[17] He advances through the corporate ranks not by serving the organization but by convincing his associates that he possesses the attributes of a "winner."

As the object of the corporate career shifts "from task-orientation and task-mastery to the control of the other player's moves," in the words of Thomas Szasz, success depends on "information about the personality of the other players."[19] The better the corporate executive or bureaucrat understands the personal characteristics of his subordinates, the better he can exploit their mistakes in order to control them and to reassert his own supremacy. If he knows that his subordinates lie to him, the lie communi-

---

*In the 1950s, the organization man thought of an attractive, socially gifted wife as an important asset to his career. Today executives are warned of the "apparent serious conflict between marriage and a management career." A recent report compares the "elite corps of professional managers" to the Janissaries, elite soldiers of the Ottoman empire who were taken from their parents as children, raised by the state, and never allowed to marry. "A young man considering [a managerial] career might well think of himself as a modern-day Janissary—and consider very, very carefully whether marriage in any way conforms to his chosen life."[18]

cates the important information that they fear and wish to please him. "By accepting the bribe, as it were, of flattery, cajolery, or sheer subservience implicit in being lied to, the recipient of the lie states, in effect, that he is willing to barter these items for the truth." On the other hand, acceptance of the lie reassures the liar that he will not be punished, while reminding him of his dependence and subordination. "In this way, both parties gain a measure . . . of security." In Joseph Heller's novel *Something Happened*, the protagonist's boss makes it clear that he wants from his subordinates not "good work" but "spastic colitis and nervous exhaustion."

> God dammit, I want the people working for me to be worse off than I am, not better. That's the reason I pay you so well. I want to see you right on the verge. I want it right out in the open. I want to be able to hear it in a stuttering, flustered, tongue-tied voice. . . . Don't trust me. I don't trust flattery, loyalty, and sociability. I don't trust deference, respect, and cooperation. I trust fear.[20]

According to Jennings, the "loyalty ethic" has declined in American business among other reasons because loyalty can "be too easily simulated or feigned by those most desirous of winning."[21]

The argument that bureaucratic organizations devote more energy to the maintenance of hierarchical relations than to industrial efficiency gains strength from the consideration that modern capitalist production arose in the first place not because it was necessarily more efficient than other methods of organizing work but because it provided capitalists with greater profits and power. The case for the factory system, according to Stephen Marglin, rested not on its technological superiority over handicraft production but on the more effective control of the labor force it allowed the employer. In the words of Andrew Ure, the philosopher of manufactures, introduction of the factory system enabled the capitalist to "subdue the refractory tempers of work people."[22] As the hierarchical organization of work invades the managerial function itself, the office takes on the characteristics of the factory, and the enforcement of clearly demarcated lines of dominance and subordination within management takes on as much importance as the subordination of labor to management as a whole. In the "era of corporate mobility," however, the lines of superiority and subordination constantly fluctuate, and the successful bureaucrat survives not by appealing to the authority of his office but by establishing a pattern of upward movement, cultivating upwardly mobile superiors, and administering "homeopathic doses of humiliation" to those he leaves behind in his ascent to the top.[23]

The Art of Social Survival

The transformation of the myth of success—of the definition of success and of the qualities believed to promote it—is a long-term development arising not from particular historical events but from general changes in the structure of society: the shifting emphasis from capitalist production to consumption; the growth of large organizations and bureaucracies; the increasingly dangerous and warlike conditions of social life. More than twenty-five years have passed since David Riesman argued that the transition from the "invisible hand" to the "glad hand" marked a fundamental change in the organization of personality, from the inner-directed type dominant in the nineteenth century to the other-directed type of today. Other scholars at that time, when interest in culture and personality studies was stronger than it is now, proposed similar descriptions of the changing character structure of advanced capitalist society. William H. Whyte's "organization man," Erich Fromm's "market-oriented personality," Karen Horney's "neurotic personality of our time," and the studies of American national character by Margaret Mead and Geoffrey Gorer all captured essential aspects of the new man: his eagerness to get along well with others; his need to organize even his private life in accordance with the requirements of large organizations; his attempt to sell himself as if his own personality were a commodity with an assignable market value; his neurotic need for affection, reassurance, and oral gratification; the corruptibility of his values. In one respect, however, these studies of American culture and personality created a misleading impression of the changes that were taking place beneath what Riesman called the "bland surface of American sociability." The critics of the forties and fifties mistook this surface for the deeper reality.[24]

According to Erich Fromm, Americans had lost the capacity for spontaneous feeling, even for anger. One of "the essential aims of the educational process" was to eliminate antagonism, to cultivate a "commercialized friendliness." "If you do not smile you are judged lacking in a 'pleasing personality'—and you need a pleasing personality if you want to sell your services, whether as a waitress, a salesman, or a physician."[25] Like many social scientists, Fromm exaggerated the degree to which aggressive impulses can be socialized; he saw man as entirely a product of socialization, not as a creature of instinct whose partially repressed or sublimated drives always threaten to break out in all their original ferocity. The American cult of friendliness conceals but does not eradicate a murderous competition for goods and position; indeed this competition has grown more savage in an age of diminishing expectations.

In the fifties, affluence, leisure, and the "quality of life" loomed as major issues. The welfare state had allegedly eradicated poverty, gross economic inequalities, and the conflicts to which they formerly gave rise. The seeming triumphs of American capitalism left social critics little to worry about except the decline of individualism and the menace of conformity. Arthur Miller's Willy Loman, the salesman who wants no more out of life than to be "well liked," symbolized the issues that troubled the postwar period. In the seventies, a harsher time, it appears that the prostitute, not the salesman, best exemplifies the qualities indispensable to success in American society. She too sells herself for a living, but her seductiveness hardly signifies a wish to be well liked. She craves admiration but scorns those who provide it and thus derives little gratification from her social successes. She attempts to move others while remaining unmoved herself. The fact that she lives in a milieu of interpersonal relations does not make her a conformist or an "other-directed" type. She remains a loner, dependent on others only as a hawk depends on chickens. She exploits the ethic of pleasure that has replaced the ethic of achievement, but her career more than any other reminds us that contemporary hedonism, of which she is the supreme symbol, originates not in the pursuit of pleasure but in a war of all against all, in which even the most intimate encounters become a form of mutual exploitation.

It is not merely that pleasure, once it is defined as an end in itself, takes on the qualities of work, as Martha Wolfenstein observed in her essay on "fun morality"—that play is now "measured by standards of achievement previously applicable only to work."[26] The measurement of sexual "performance," the insistence that sexual satisfaction depends on proper "technique," and the widespread belief that it can be "achieved" only after coordinated effort, practice, and study all testify to the invasion of play by the rhetoric of achievement. But those who deplore the transformation of play into performance confine their attention to the surface of play, in this case to the surface of sexual encounters. Beneath the concern for performance lies a deeper determination to manipulate the feelings of others to your own advantage. The search for competitive advantage through emotional manipulation increasingly shapes not only personal relations but relations at work as well; it is for this reason that sociability can now function as an extension of work by other means. Personal life, no longer a refuge from deprivations suffered at work, has become as anarchical, as warlike, and as full of stress as the marketplace itself. The cocktail party reduces sociability to social combat. Experts write tactical manuals in the art of social survival, advising the status-seeking partygoer to take up a commanding position in the room, surround himself with a loyal band of retainers, and avoid turning his back on the field of battle.

The recent vogue of "assertiveness therapy," a counter-program designed to equip the patient with defenses against manipulation, appeals to the growing recognition that agility in interpersonal relations determines what looks on the surface like achievement. Assertiveness training seeks to rid the patient of "feelings of anxiety, ignorance, and guilt that . . . are used efficiently by other people to get us to do what they want." Other forms of game therapy alert patients to the "games people play" and thus attempt to promote "game-free intimacy."[27] The importance of such programs, however, lies not so much in their objectives as in the anxiety to which they appeal and the vision of reality that informs them—the perception that success depends on psychological manipulation and that all of life, even the ostensibly achievement-oriented realm of work, centers on the struggle for interpersonal advantage, the deadly game of intimidating friends and seducing people.

The Apotheosis of Individualism

The fear that haunted the social critics and theorists of the fifties—that rugged individualism had succumbed to conformity and "low-pressure sociability"—appears in retrospect to have been premature. In 1960, David Riesman complained that young people no longer had much social "presence," their education having provided them not with "a polished personality but [with] an affable, casual, adaptable one, suitable to the loose-jointed articulation and heavy job turnover in the expanding organizations of an affluent society."[28] It is true that "a present-oriented hedonism," as Riesman went on to argue, has replaced the work ethic "among the very classes which in the earlier stages of industrialization were oriented toward the future, toward distant goals and delayed gratification." But this hedonism is a fraud; the pursuit of pleasure disguises a struggle for power. Americans have not really become more sociable and cooperative, as the theorists of other-direction and conformity would like us to believe; they have merely become more adept at exploiting the conventions of interpersonal relations for their own benefit. Activities ostensibly undertaken purely for enjoyment often have the real object of doing others in. It is symptomatic of the underlying tenor of American life that vulgar terms for sexual intercourse also convey the sense of getting the better of someone, working him over, taking him in, imposing your will through guile, deception, or superior force. Verbs associated with sexual pleasure have acquired more than the usual overtones of violence and psychic exploitation. In the violent world of the ghetto, the language of which now pervades American society as a whole, the violence associated with sexual intercourse is directed with special intensity by men against women, specifically against their mothers. The language of ritualized aggression and abuse reminds those who use it that exploitation is the general rule and some form of dependence the common fate; that "the individual," in Lee Rainwater's words, "is not strong enough or adult enough to achieve his goal in a legitimate way, but is rather like a child, dependent on others who tolerate his childish maneuvers";[29] accordingly males, even adult males, often depend on women for support and nurture. Many of them have to pimp for a living, ingratiating themselves with a woman in order to pry money from her; sexual relations thus become manipulative and predatory. Satisfaction depends on taking what you want instead of waiting for what is rightfully yours to receive. All this enters everyday speech in language that connects sex with aggression and sexual aggression with highly ambivalent feelings about mothers.*

*In the late sixties, white radicals enthusiastically adopted the slogan, "Up against the Wall, Motherfucker!" But the term has long since lost its revolutionary associations, like other black idioms first popularized among whites by political radicals and spokesmen for the counterculture, and in slightly

In some ways middle-class society has become a pale copy of the black ghetto, as the appropriation of its language would lead us to believe. We do not need to minimize the poverty of the ghetto or the suffering inflicted by whites on blacks in order to see that the increasingly dangerous and unpredictable conditions of middle-class life have given rise to similar strategies for survival. Indeed the attraction of black culture for disaffected whites suggests that black culture now speaks to a general condition, the most important feature of which is a widespread loss of confidence in the future. The poor have always had to live for the present, but now a desperate concern for personal survival, sometimes disguised as hedonism, engulfs the middle class as well. Today almost everyone lives in a dangerous world from which there is little escape. International terrorism and blackmail, bombings, and hijackings arbitrarily affect the rich and poor alike. Crime, violence, and gang wars make cities unsafe and threaten to spread to the suburbs. Racial violence on the streets and in the schools creates an atmosphere of chronic tension and threatens to erupt at any time into full-scale racial conflict. Unemployment spreads from the poor to the white-collar class, while inflation eats away the savings of those who hoped to retire in comfort. Much of what is euphemistically known as the middle class, merely because it dresses up to go to work, is now reduced to proletarian conditions of existence. Many white-collar jobs require no more skill and pay even less than blue-collar jobs, conferring little status or security. The propaganda of death and destruction, emanating ceaselessly from the mass media, adds to the prevailing atmosphere of insecurity. Far-flung famines, earthquakes in remote regions, distant wars and uprisings attract the same attention as events closer to home. The impression of arbitrariness in the reporting of disaster reinforces the arbitrary quality of experience itself, and the absence of continuity in the coverage of events, as today's crisis yields to

---

expurgated form has become so acceptable that the term "mother" has everywhere become, even among teeny-boppers, a term of easygoing familiarity or contempt. Similarly the Rolling Stones and other exponents of hard or acid rock, who used the obscenity of the ghetto to convey a posture of militant alienation, have given way to groups that sing more sweetly, but still in ghetto accents, of a world where you get only what you're prepared to take. The pretense of revolutionary solidarity having evaporated, as the zonked-out lovefest of the "Woodstock Nation" deteriorated into the murderous chaos of Altamont, the underlying cynicism surfaces more clearly than ever. Every mother for himself!

a new and unrelated crisis tomorrow, adds to the sense of historical discontinuity—the sense of living in a world in which the past holds out no guidance to the present and the future has become completely unpredictable.

Older conceptions of success presupposed a world in rapid motion, in which fortunes were rapidly won and lost and new opportunities unfolded every day. Yet they also presupposed a certain stability, a future that bore some recognizable resemblance to the present and the past. The growth of bureaucracy, the cult of consumption with its immediate gratifications, but above all the severance of the sense of historical continuity have transformed the Protestant ethic while carrying the underlying principles of capitalist society to their logical conclusion. The pursuit of self-interest, formerly identified with the rational pursuit of gain and the accumulation of wealth, has become a search for pleasure and psychic survival. Social conditions now approximate the vision of republican society conceived by the Marquis de Sade at the very outset of the republican epoch. In many ways the most farsighted and certainly the most disturbing of the prophets of revolutionary individualism, Sade defended unlimited self-indulgence as the logical culmination of the revolution in property relations—the only way to attain revolutionary brotherhood in its purest form. By regressing in his writings to the most primitive level of fantasy, Sade uncannily glimpsed the whole subsequent development of personal life under capitalism, ending not in revolutionary brotherhood but in a society of siblings that has outlived and repudiated its revolutionary origins.

Sade imagined a sexual utopia in which everyone has the right to everyone else, where human beings, reduced to their sexual organs, become absolutely anonymous and interchangeable. His ideal society thus reaffirmed the capitalist principle that human beings are ultimately reducible to interchangeable objects. It also incorporated and carried to a surprising new conclusion Hobbes's discovery that the destruction of paternalism and the subordination of all social relations to the market had stripped away the remaining restraints and the mitigating illusions from the war of all against all. In the resulting state of organized anarchy, as Sade was the first to realize, pleasure becomes life's only business— pleasure, however, that is indistinguishable from rape, murder, unbridled aggression. In a society that has reduced reason to mere calculation, reason can impose no limits on the pursuit of pleasure—on the immediate gratification of every desire no matter how perverse, insane, criminal, or merely immoral. For the standards that would condemn crime or cruelty derive from religion, compassion, or the kind of reason that rejects purely instrumental applications; and none of these outmoded forms of thought or feeling has any logical place in a society based on commodity production. In his misogyny, Sade perceived that bourgeois enlightenment, carried to its logical conclusions, condemned even the sentimental cult of womanhood and the family, which the bourgeoisie itself had carried to unprecedented extremes.

At the same time, he saw that condemnation of "woman-worship" had to go hand in hand with a defense of woman's sexual rights—their right to dispose of their own bodies, as feminists would put it today. If the exercise of that right in Sade's utopia boils down to the duty to become an instrument of someone else's pleasure, it was not so much because Sade hated women as because he hated humanity. He perceived, more clearly than the feminists, that all freedoms under capitalism come in the end to the same thing, the same universal obligation to enjoy and be enjoyed. In the same breath, and without violating his own logic, Sade demanded for women the right "fully to satisfy all their desires" and "all parts of their bodies" and categorically stated that "all women must submit to our pleasure." Pure individualism thus issued in the most radical repudiation of individuality. "All men, all women resemble each other," according to Sade; and to those of his countrymen who would become republicans he adds the ominous warning: "Do not think you can make good republicans so long as you isolate in their families the children who should belong to the republic alone." The bourgeois defense of privacy culminates—not just in Sade's thought but in the history to come, so accurately foreshadowed in the very excess, madness, infantilism of his ideas—in the most thoroughgoing attack on privacy; the glorification of the individual, in his annihilation.[30]

NOTES

1. Robin Williams, *American Society* (New York, 1970), pp. 454–55.

2. Philip Rieff, *Freud: The Mind of the Moralist* (New York, 1961), p. 372.

3. Cotton Mather, *A Christian at His Calling* (1701), reprinted in *The American Gospel of Success*, ed. Moses Rischin (Chicago, 1965), pp. 23, 25, 28; John Cotton, "Christian Calling" (1664), reprinted in *The Puritans*, eds. Perry Miller and Thomas H. Johnson (New York, 1938), p. 324.

4. Max Weber, *The Protestant Ethic and the Spirit of Capitalism*, trans. Talcott Parsons (New York, 1958 [1904–5]), pp. 52–53. For another interpretation of the eighteenth-century meaning of self-improvement, more attentive to its nuances, see John G. Cawelti, *Apostles of the Self-Made Man* (Chicago, 1965), chap. 1.

5. P. T. Barnum, "The Art of Money-Getting," in *Gospel of Success*, ed. Rischin, pp. 47–66.

6. Quoted in Cawelti, *Apostles of the Self-Made Man*, p. 53.

7. Quoted in *The Self-Made Man in America: The Myth of Rags to Riches*, Irvin G. Wyllie (New York, 1966), p. 43.

8. James Freeman Clarke, *Self-Culture: Physical, Intellectual, Moral and Spiritual* (Boston, 1880), p. 266; unidentified industrialist quoted in *Self-Made Man*, Wyllie, p. 96. On self-culture, *see also* Cawelti, *Apostles of the Self-Made Man*, chap. 3.

9. Cawelti, *Apostles of the Self-Made Man*, pp. 171; 176–77; 182–83.

10. Dale Carnegie, quoted in ibid., p. 210.

11. Quoted in ibid., p. 211.

12. Robert L. Shook, *Winning Images* (New York, 1977), p. 22.

13. John McNaughton, quoted in *The Pentagon Papers*, Neil Sheehan et al. (New York, 1971), pp. 366, 442.

14. Daniel Boorstin, *The Image: A Guide to Pseudo-Events in America* (New York, 1961, new ed. 1972), p. 204.

15. Emerson Jennings, *Routes to the Executive Suite* (New York, 1971), pp. 29–30.

16. Pat Watters, *The Angry Middle-Aged Man* (New York, 1976), p. 24.

17. Jennings, *Routes to the Executive Suite*, pp. 12, 240.

18. O. William Battalia and John J. Tarraut, *The Corporate Eunuch* (New York, 1973), pp. 65, 71.

19. Thomas S. Szasz, *The Myth of Mental Illness* (New York, 1961), pp. 275–76.

20. Joseph Heller, *Something Happened* (New York, 1974), p. 414.

21. Jennings, *Routes to the Executive Suite*, p. 7.

22. Quoted in Stephen Marglin, "What Do Bosses Do?" *Review of Radical Political Economics* 6 (1974), pp. 60–112; 7 (1975), pp. 20–37.

23. Michael Maccoby, *The Gamesman: The New Corporate Leaders* (New York, 1976), p. 102.

24. See David Riesman et al., *The Lonely Crowd: A Study of the Changing American Character* (New Haven, 1950); William H. Whyte, Jr., *The Organization Man* (New York, 1956); Erich Fromm, *Escape from Freedom* (New York, 1941) and *Man for Himself* (New York, 1947); Karen Horney, *The Neurotic Personality of Our Time* (New

York, 1937); Margaret Mead, *And Keep Your Powder Dry* (New York, 1943); Geoffrey Gorer, *The American People: A Study in National Character* (New York, 1948); Allen Wheelis, *The Quest for Identity* (New York, 1958).

25. Fromm, *Escape from Freedom*, pp. 242–43.

26. Martha Wolfenstein, "Fun Morality" (1951), reprinted in *Childhood in Contemporary Cultures*, ed. Margaret Mead and Martha Wolfenstein (Chicago, 1955), pp. 168–76.

27. Manuel J. Smith, *When I Say No, I Feel Guilty* (New York, 1975), p. 22; Eric Berne, *Games People Play: The Psychology of Human Relationships* (New York, 1974).

28. David Riesman, Robert J. Potter, and Jeanne Watson, "Sociability, Permissiveness, and Equality," *Psychiatry* 23 (1960), pp. 334–36.

29. Lee Rainwater, *Behind Ghetto Walls: Black Families in a Federal Slum* (Chicago, 1970), pp. 388–89.

30. Sade, "On the Republican Utopia," *La Philosophia dams le Boudoir*, in *Oeuvres complèts du Marquis de Sade*, vol. 3 (Paris, 1966), pp. 504–6.

☆ • ☆ • ☆ • ☆ • ☆

With the exception of *The Lonely Crowd, The Culture of Narcissism* is the most complex modern work on American character and culture. This is not just because of its range (it has chapters on sports, schooling, and male-female relations) but because of the subtleties of its argument. More than any other thesis about American character, it constantly engages with other writers on the subject. Again and again Lasch says in effect: my argument may look like X's or Y's but really it's quite different.

And so it often is. Like other authors in this volume, Lasch declares that modern authority has become at once fuzzier and more insidious; but he finds a more destructive result. He agrees with Philip Slater (p. 201) that Americans have withdrawn from social responsibility, but he denies that the family is a fortress of privatism; on the contrary, its domain has been invaded by social experts. Margaret Mead, too, believed that American parents anxiously turned to professional advice-givers and their formulas, usually through the media; but Lasch characteristically put it the other way—that it was the experts who aggressively turned on the family.

Respecting as he did the disciplines of the traditional family, Lasch was not an obvious lefty. He disliked much that he saw in contemporary feminism, and his concern about "dependency" and the power of "bureaucracy" over the individual was an old, conservative American worry—even if he backed it up with chilling new psychological arguments. On the other hand, he attacked "capitalism" indiscriminately; he never explained its implied connection with the Holocaust, nuclear terror, or aggressive school counselors. In some places he seemed to confuse capitalism per se (a system of making and marketing for profit) with organized industrial society.

Lasch's book is like a gloomy Gothic cathedral, its stonework interconnected by wondrous tracery and flying buttresses. But does it rest on real earth? Did Lasch really believe that Americans were so sick and nasty? And if they were, how did he know that they had become *more* so?

Some testimony supports him—up to a point. As early as the 1950s, according to a survey by the anthropologist Clyde Kluckholn, a number of studies of American values agreed that Americans were losing the "Puritan ethic," putting more and more stress on "being and becoming" as opposed to "doing," and "present-time" as opposed to "future-time." They were getting more pessimistic while paying more attention to "psychological health."

All these things feature in Lasch's jeremiad, but they do not add up to narcissism. In 1983 a searching article by Jesse Battan on historical theories of narcissism argued that no real increase in it had taken place. More patients were now being diagnosed as narcissistic because more people were seeking psychiatric help and their problems were not easily classed with the 'old' disorders. 'Narcissistic personality' became a catchall category in which to put them. In fact, said Battan, Americans from the seventeenth century had been fascinated with "self-scrutiny, self-expression, and personal growth." At first this had taken religious forms, then economic, and more recently, psychological— hence the rising number of people seeking psychotherapy. This historical sequence is quite like Lasch's in the excerpt above, but Battan did not believe it led to narcissism. It has also been suggested that earlier types of American individualism were just as capable of encouraging narcissism by accentuating bodily prowess, attention-grabbing, and puffing out the self. A frontier tough like Wild Bill Hickok, who wore fancy gear and swaggered down a trail of bloody fights, seemed just as narcissistic as Lasch's modern managers.

In places, Lasch did back off a little from his general gloom and doom. His book's preface admits that "much could be written about

the signs of new life in the United States," as local groups of men and women get together to invent their own solutions, against the power of big business and government. Lasch says no more about that, but later in the book he suddenly concedes that "narcissistic disorders" and "narcissistic personalities" may not have increased. Narcissists, however, being well suited to bureaucratic intrigue and "the management of personal impressions," have obtained such prominent positions that they reinforce "narcissistic traits in everyone." Lasch does not explain the difference between people who merely have narcissistic traits and those with narcissistic personalities, and he doesn't say why the first group should grow but not the second. The whole thrust of his argument, stressing the deep pathological effects of modern family and social life, undercuts the proposition—he writes, indeed, of "the emergence of the narcissistic personality . . . as the typical form of character structure in a society that has lost its interest in the future."

Many of us, I imagine, know the 'liberal' parent who wraps an aggressive coolness in honeyed tones. This is very much the kind of parent described in Lasch's book. But how did Lasch know that teachers and professional counselors undermined such parents? Lasch's comments on the modern family were tenuous because he did not really get into evidence. Lasch was at heart a historian of ideas, not of social detail. *The Culture of Narcissism*, like its predecessor, *Haven in a Heartless World*, has much more information about social-science theories of the family than about family life itself.

The same applies to business. Lasch was no William Whyte (p. 70)—he gave no impression that he had studied business life firsthand. Instead he referred to other commentators on business culture and success. Historically, too, he gave little evidence for his claim that Americans were less competitive in the nineteenth century than in the twentieth. If language is anything to go by, it is worth noting that American slang in the nineteenth century crackled with competitiveness—'don't take his dust,' 'put the run on him,' 'put it too him,' and so on. The fact that success is now more apt to mean climbing a bureaucratic ladder—winning promotions—does not mean that nineteenth-century Americans had less desire in other ways to compete, stand out, surpass their fellows.

The main defect of Lasch's book is that he makes an extreme

pathology the kingpin of everything else, even U.S. foreign relations. As a result, he reads America in the worst possible light. His sections on feminism, for instance, stress only its most unpleasant effects on men and gender relations. If, however, we treat Lasch's American character as just *one* outcome of modern trends, he makes much more sense. Certainly he provides a better explanation of some of the 1980s' glitzy show-offs than David Riesman's theory of "other-direction." According to Riesman, "conspicuous consumption" was a thing of the past: Americans were becoming too conformist and unacquisitive to want to stand out dramatically or make everything their own. They consumed to be sociable, not to make a splash. No Trump Towers for them.

In later comments, Riesman conceded that other-direction, as he described it in 1950, had receded. By the 1980s he was agreeing with Lasch that more Americans had become aggressively egocentric—narcissistic too, though his explanation was not deeply psychoanalytic like Lasch's, and his historical thesis, his view of what had changed in America, was somewhat different as well.

Other writers, also, have suggested that the other-directed "organization man" is a dead or dying breed; that "unfriendly takeovers" and corporate cutbacks have produced an atmosphere of fear and suspicion in which executives try to get ahead through intrigue and showmanship (what the economic writer Robert Reich has called "the manipulation of symbols"). All this fits Lasch's picture of business life, though it does not necessarily support his theory of narcissism.

Lasch himself claimed that even the bland cooperator of the 1950s was threatened by ferocious feelings within (p. 280). Actually this is not far from a chapter in *The Lonely Crowd* where Riesman conjectured that some of his other-directed types might, in the future, give vent to their repressed aggression. They might, said Riesman, imitate their leaders whom they imagined to be more ruthless than they really were.

In the end, however, Lasch's work—like some other American-character studies—may be more valuable for what it says 'along the way' than for its basic theory of social character. His book may be respected less for what it says about narcissism than for picturing modern society as a "hall of mirrors," a circus of packaged and prerecorded experience where reality blurs into fakery. In 1962, the historian Daniel Boorstin had said much the same thing in his book, *The Image:* he called society a *"wall* of mirrors." Other writers, too, had discussed a loss of reality in a society of whirling messages and energetic poses. So Lasch's scenario was not as original as he suggested. Nevertheless he put it all together in a new and striking way.

DANIEL YANKELOVICH

Searching for
Self-Fulfillment

In the 1970s some leading market researchers moved beyond "demographics" to "psychographics." In classifying consumers, they no longer confined themselves to the old categories of region, income, education, age, family size, and so on; they also grouped consumers according to their "values and life-styles." In a way, these market analysts turned the tables on academic theorists of social character. As we have seen again and again in this volume, consumption and marketing have featured prominently in theories of modern American character. Now the marketers used ideas about American character to promote consumption.

After all this, it is not surprising that the president of a survey research firm should publish a major book on American attitudes and values. The author was Daniel Yankelovich (of Yankelovich, Skelly and White, Inc.) who had devised the "Yankelovich Monitor," a regular survey of the effects of social change on consumers. His book, published in 1981, was sonorously titled *New Rules: Searching for Self-Fulfillment in a World Turned Upside Down.*

By the 1980s other survey researchers, along with Yankelovich, had highlighted a set of young consumers who resisted the cruder blandishments of status and success and were more concerned with "inner growth." (The jargon often called them "inner-directed," a total misuse of David Riesman's label—see p. 50.) In most of the research these 'self-fulfillers' were just one of several consumer groups. For Yankelovich, however, they were the centerpiece in America's changing culture.

From the late 1960s to the early 1970s, Yankelovich had done several studies of "youth" (sixteen- to twenty-five-year-olds) in which he charted the rise of a new ethos—he called it "the New Values." The

New Values included a freer attitude to sex, less automatic obedience to institutions and authorities, more insistence that work should be satisfying, and a value on "self-fulfillment . . . in opposition to role obligations to others and [a] nose-to-the-grindstone quest for economic security." These values, said Yankelovich, had started on campus, but many of them were spreading to noncollege youth. But for college youth especially, the New Values meant rejecting the "bargain" of the 1950s in which people split themselves between the organization's demands at work and one's private self at home—now everything should express one, 'real self.'

Yankelovich's book, *New Rules,* expanded on these themes. Like David Riesman, Yankelovich claimed that values underwent a massive shift when a culture of scarcity became a culture of plenty—when people no longer felt they had to make sacrifices first to secure success and a decent life later. Unlike Riesman, however, Yankelovich placed the turning point in the generation that came of age in the 1960s (compare with Riesman, pp. 58–59). He also asserted that the new "psycho-culture," as he called it, had a momentum of its own; though it came out of economic change, it was not just a puppet of the economy. Therein lay a problem, for the search for self-fulfillment was often risky and expensive, and many searchers took a beating when the economy went sour in the 1970s.

Although Yankelovich saw some narcissism in the new ethos, he vehemently disagreed with Christopher Lasch (p. 242) that narcissistic egoism lay at the heart of it. In his view, the self-fulfillment drive had high potential for good as well as bad, and it was not confined to the Gucci-clad trendies that Tom Wolfe loved to write about. Yankelovich's survey data, fleshed out with interview-portraits of real men and women, showed the search for self-fulfillment reaching across class barriers, though it took different forms when it did so.

Writing at a time when the Moral Majority and other right-wing groups were helping elect Ronald Reagan to the White House, Yankelovich allowed for a puritan backlash against the self-fulfiller's permissiveness. At the same time he recognized that the new movement had its own spiritual force. Yankelovich himself had been trained in philosophy and psychology, and he had written in both fields. Reflecting this background, Yankelovich's introduction to *New Rules*—excerpted below—attaches much importance to what he calls the "sa-cred/expressive" part of life.

☆ • ☆ • ☆ • ☆ • ☆

Western literature and history are full of stories of individuals searching for self-fulfillment.* They seek it in many ways—in great deeds, money, love, fame, revolution, epic fornication, the quest for inner peace, sustained bursts of creativity or by simply wandering about. As backdrop to their adventures, one takes for granted the muted presence of the great mass of people routinely living their daily lives: busy with family, scrambling to make a living, going to church. What is extraordinary about the search for self-fulfillment in contemporary America is that it is not confined to a few bold spirits or a privileged class. Cross-section studies of Americans show unmistakably that the search for self-fulfillment is instead an outpouring of popular sentiment and experimentation, an authentic grass-roots phenomenon involving, in one way or another, perhaps as many as 80 percent of all adult Americans. It is as if tens of millions of people had decided simultaneously to conduct risky experiments in living, using the only materials that lay at hand—their own lives.

And the experiments *are* risky. Acting boldly in the name of their self-fulfillment, many people are startled to wake up one day and find themselves with a broken marriage, a wrong-headed career change or simply a muddled state of mind about what life choices to make. But despite many failures the experiments persist. There is something about our times that stimulates Americans to take big risks in pursuit of new conceptions of the good life.

Spontaneous transformations of life style are rare events, or so it would appear from history. Ordinarily, new cultural ideas enter our consciousness in prepackaged form: by the time we encounter them in "great books," the confusion and excitement and false starts that may have accompanied their beginnings have been tidied up. The history of ideas usually registers the views of small elites—leading philosophers, religious thinkers, scientists, artists and world statesmen whose thoughts are formulated with precision or eloquence. But every now and then a new way of conceiving life and its meaning arises spontaneously from the great mass of the population.

When this occurs we had better pay attention, for this kind of unorganized social movement can transform America and the world. But it is not easy to know what to pay attention to, for the true nature of the transformation remains hidden from view, its sheer diversity of expressions making it difficult to find a coherent pattern.

In the 1960s the search for self-fulfillment was largely confined to young Americans on the nation's campuses, and was masked by the political protests against the war in Southeast Asia. When the war ended in the early seventies, the campuses quieted and the challenge to traditional mores spread beyond college life to find a variety of expressions in the larger society—in the women's movement; in the consumer, environmental and quality-of-life movements ("small is beautiful"); in the emphasis on self-help, localism and participation; in the hospice movement; in the flood of books on cultivating the self; in the questioning of the scientific-technological world view; in greater acceptance of sexuality (nudity, sex outside of marriage, homosexuality and open eroticism of varied sorts); in a new preoccupation with the body and physical fitness; in a revival of interest in nature and the natural; and above all, in a search for the "full, rich life," ripe with leisure, new experience and enjoyment as a substitute for the orderly, work-centered ways of earlier decades.

Our surveys showed that new questions had arisen. Instead of asking, "Will I be able to make a good living?" "Will I be successful?" "Will I raise happy, healthy, successful children?"—the typical questions asked by average Americans in the 1950s and 1960s—Americans in the 1970s came to ponder more introspective matters. We asked, "How can I find self-fulfillment?" "What does personal success really mean?" "What kinds of commitments should I be making?" "What is worth sacrificing for?" "How can I grow?" "How can I best realize the commitment I have to develop myself?" and, by the start of the 1980s: "How can I prevent inflation from taking away the gains I have won and my chance to live the good life?"

In the sixties cross-section surveys showed that the shifts in culture barely touched the lives of the majority of Americans (a fact those enmeshed in the sixties "revolution" found difficult to comprehend). By the seventies, however, most Americans were involved in projects to prove

271

that life can be more than a grim economic chore. Americans from every walk of life were suddenly eager to give more meaning to their lives, to find fuller self-expression and to add a touch of adventure and grace to their lives and those of others. Where strict norms had prevailed in the fifties and sixties, now all was pluralism and freedom of choice: to marry or live together; to have children early or postpone them, perhaps forever; to come out of the closet or stay in; to keep the old job or return to school; to make commitments or hang loose; to change careers, spouses, houses, states of residence, states of mind.

In the 1970s all national surveys showed an increase in preoccupation with self. By the late seventies, my firm's studies showed more than seven out of ten Americans (72 percent) spending a great deal of time thinking about themselves and their inner lives—this in a nation once notorious for its impatience with inwardness. The rage for self-fulfillment, our surveys indicated, had now spread to virtually the entire U.S. population.

The search for self-fulfillment has developed into a prime source of energy in American culture, and like many vital things, it is sprawling, messy and unfinished; not good or bad, but good-and-bad. American society is probably freer, less fearful, less status-ridden, and more diverse and tolerant than ever before. But in our preoccupation with self-fulfillment we have also grown recklessly unrealistic in our demands on our institutions. And we are becoming less sensitive to the plight of the most vulnerable citizens in our economy, growing bored, for example, with the problems of race and unemployment that the nation had begun to address in earlier decades. At times our narrow self-concern threatens to get out of hand.

The life experiments of self-fulfillment seekers often collide violently with traditional rules, creating a national battle of moral norms. Millions of Americans are hungry to live their lives to the brim, determined to consume every dish on the smorgasbord of human experience. But their appetites have scandalized other millions, including groups such as the Moral Majority. It and other like-minded organizations have linked religious fundamentalism and political action to combat the moral evil of what they call "secular humanism," by which they mean social pluralism—that freedom to choose one's own life style within certain generous limits that identifies the dedicated seeker of self-fulfillment.

272

The Moral Majority strongly supports Senator Paul Laxalt's bill, the Family Protection Act. Among its thirty-eight proposals are: removing prayer in schools from the jurisdiction of the federal courts; giving parents the right to censor textbooks; giving local school boards the right to prevent boys and girls from participating in sports together; denying food stamps to college students who are "voluntarily unemployed"; excluding from child abuse laws all forms of corporal punishment; removing all tax advantages from cohabitation without marriage; and eliminating federal funds from any program that presents homosexuality as an "acceptable alternative life style."

When the values they cherish are challenged, people react passionately. Some Americans have come to hate the new morality associated with the search for self-fulfillment. Their reactions range from mere distaste for a self-indulgent generation to the judgment that the new life styles are morally evil and must be relentlessly crushed. The waves of emotion stirred by abortion, easier divorce, ERA, sex education, homosexuality and other developments the Moral Majority regards as anti-family, anti-American and anti-Christian show how deep-seated the issues are. For the rest of this century American culture will be a cockpit of conflict as political passions rise, single issue politics gain momentum, and new religious movements abound. The shifts in the plates of culture are creating deep fissures in our society.

Only if we find a pattern that unifies the astonishing variety of self-fulfillment experiments can we hope to fathom the significance of a phenomenon so diverse, so socially divisive and so morally ambiguous.

In seeking a pattern I have examined a vast array of survey findings, census data, economic information and life histories. From this jumble of information, a pattern has gradually taken shape, emerging in response to a few fruitful questions. The one question that proved most productive was the simplest: "What are the people pursuing their self-fulfillment actually looking for, and how are they going about finding it?" . . .

Confirmed seekers of self-fulfillment, often surprisingly vague and inarticulate, voiced their goal as a poignant and inchoate yearning to elevate what might be called the "sacred/expressive" aspects of their lives, and simultaneously, to downgrade the impersonal, manipulative aspects.

"Sacred," in this context, is not used in its strictly religious meaning. Though most familiar in religious thought, the idea of the sacred is also a sociological concept, used here in opposition not to the secular or profane as in religious belief, but to the instrumental. The distinction is an important one. We adopt an instrumental philosophy whenever we ask about something: what is it good for? From this perspective a tree is good for lumber, or to give shade, or to enhance the appearance of the landscape. A forest that no one harvests or sees is not good for anything. It is not valued in itself. From an instrumental perspective, a person is valued because he or she is a good worker, or provider, or sex object, or is useful in meeting one's needs in some other fashion. Everyone knows someone about whom you can say, "Oh, he's only interested in you if you can do something for him, otherwise you don't exist." This is an instrumental outlook. People and objects are sacred in the sociological sense when, apart from what instrumental use they serve, they are valued for themselves.

Our studies suggest that seekers of self-fulfillment are reassessing what is sacred and what is instrumental in American life. Should people in the workplace be exploited exclusively for instrumental purposes, or do they have intrinsic value as well? Should we value certain aspects of nature and society—a wilderness, a vanishing species, a primitive culture, old automobiles, old buildings—for themselves, apart from their instrumental value?

Some joggers maintain a purely instrumental attitude toward their running—it is a way to stimulate the cardiovascular system; but others come to regard their sweaty exertions as a "sacred" ritual. The cult of organic gardening develops a deep attachment to what is grown. For many Americans nature is a sacred object; for others art and human artifacts are too; still others endow sexuality or science or a region of the country or an ethnic link to one's roots with such meanings.

The domain of the "expressive" is also opposed to the instrumental. While instrumental actions are always a means to an end, what is expressive has value in its own right. Myths, art, poetry, monuments, storytelling, song, dance, customs, architecture, ritual, the harmonics of nature—all make expressive claims over and above any instrumental purpose they may serve. The idea of "style"—a decorator's style, styles in clothing, life styles—clearly connotes expressive values. Our daily living is drenched in expressive style: recent American visitors to China, for example, report a "color hunger" that manifests itself when Chinese audiences in a theater or puppet show grow wild with excitement when scenery and colorful costumes are presented. Except for young children's clothing, the Chinese were virtually deprived of color throughout their cultural revolution and the first few years following it. They now seize upon displays of colors as if they were gasping for air.

Seekers of self-fulfillment invest the best of their creativity in inventing expressive styles of living. For, at the heart of the self-fulfillment search, is the moral intuition that the very meaning of life resides in its sacred/expressive aspects, and that one must, therefore, fight to give these the importance they deserve.

From an historic perspective, the effort to keep the sacred/expressive side of life from being overwhelmed by the instrumental addresses a problem that has haunted Western civilization for centuries. Our advanced industrial society, for all its strengths, has long harbored a fundamental weakness: it has prodigiously generated goods and services, but has been seriously deficient in creating some of the basic conditions of human community. In some profound sense, all self-fulfillment experiments are struggling to overcome this weakness.

But average fulfillment seekers are not concerned with abstract historic issues; the arena within which they struggle is their everyday life. Their life experiments engage what we might call the "giving/getting compact"—the unwritten rules governing what we give in marriage, work, community and sacrifice for others, and what we expect in return. This giving/getting compact is almost never explicit. We take it so much for granted that we rarely see how extensive and powerful it is—until it begins to change. Indeed, so vital to American life are these unwritten rules that if we are truly launched on a cultural revolution the upheavals we encounter in the giving/getting compact are among the principal signs of its arrival.

The following comments are taken from my interviews with people between fifty-five and seventy years of age. In recalling their experiences in the early post–World War II decades, they hint at the terms of the giving/getting compact as it then prevailed:

"Even though we no longer had anything in common we stayed together. We didn't break up our marriage even when the children were grown."

————

"We lived on his salary even though I was making good money at the time. He said he would not feel right if we spent the money I earned for food and rent."

————

"I never felt I could do enough for my parents, especially my mother. She sacrificed a promising career as a singer to take care of us. I realize now that she must have been miserable most of the time. [Why?] Because she said so. She kept reminding us what she was giving up, but we didn't take her seriously."

————

"It never occurred to me not to have children. Now I realize I'd have felt less put upon if I had freely chosen that destiny and not had it chosen for me."

————

"I've worked hard all my life, and I've made a success out of it for myself and my family. We have a nice home. We have everything it takes to be comfortable. I've been able to send my kids to good schools, and my wife and I can afford to go anywhere we want. Yes, I have a real sense of accomplishment."

————

"Sure it was a rotten job. But what the hell. I made a good living, I took care of my wife and kids. What more do you expect?"

The old giving/getting compact might be paraphrased this way: "I give hard work, loyalty and steadfastness. I swallow my frustrations and suppress my impulse to do what I would enjoy, and do what is expected of me instead. I do not put myself first; I put the needs of others ahead of my own. I give a lot, but what I get in return is worth it. I receive an ever-growing standard of living, and a family life with a devoted spouse and decent kids. Our children will take care of us in our old age if we really need it, which thank goodness we will not. I have a nice home, a good job, the respect of my friends and neighbors; a sense of accomplishment at having made something of my life. Last but not least, as an American I am proud to be a citizen of the finest country in the world."

It is difficult to exaggerate how important this implicit contract has been in supporting the goals of American society in the post–World War II period. It lies at the heart of what we mean by the American dream. All the symbols of success and respectability in American society—the material goods; the opportunities to get ahead or have your children do so; the churches, graduations, promotions, celebrations—fit comfortably together as links in this social bond.

But now tens of millions of Americans have grown wary of demands for further sacrifices they believe may no longer be warranted. They want to modify the giving/getting compact in every one of its dimensions— family life, career, leisure, the meaning of success, relationships with other people and relations with themselves.

On traditional demands for material well-being seekers of self-fulfillment now impose new demands for intangibles—creativity, leisure, autonomy, pleasure, participation, community, adventure, vitality, stimulation, tender loving care. To the efficiency of technological society they wish to add joy of living. They seek to satisfy both the body *and* the spirit, which is asking a great deal from the human condition.

To many it is worth the try. Why, they argue, should we accept as inevitable that resourceful, highly educated people have to choose between the efficiency of technological society and quality of life? Why can we not have both? Are we to serve the machine, they ask, or is the machine to serve us? Must we accept poverty of spirit for wealth of goods? What meaning in life shall we seek beyond insuring economic security and creature comfort?

The predicaments of self-fulfillment seekers arise from the defective strategies they deploy to achieve these ambitious goals. These strategies are defective, first, in their economic premises. The typical self-fulfillment strategy presupposes that economic well-being is a virtual citizen's right, automatically guaranteed by both government and economy. A strategy built on the presumption of ever-expanding affluence is bound to run into trouble even in a country as abundant as our own.

The most serious defect, however, is psychological. People unwittingly bring a set of flawed psychological premises to their search for self-fulfillment, in particular the premise that the self is a hierarchy of inner needs, and self-fulfillment an inner journey to discover these. This premise is rarely examined, even though it leads people to defeat their own goals—and to end up isolated and anxious instead of fulfilled.

For example, among the married people I interviewed . . . those most devoted to their own self-fulfillment are having trouble in their marriages, as one might have predicted. Invariably, the trouble starts when one or both spouses abruptly introduces a change in the giving/getting compact. One or the other decides, for example, to take greater sexual license, or to press for a different division of effort in relation to work, home and children, or simply to become more self-assertive. Many couples take these changes in stride, but truly committed fulfillment seekers focus so sharply on their own needs that instead of achieving a more intimate, giving relationship, they grow further apart from each other. In looking to their own needs for fulfillment, they are caught in a debilitating contradiction: their goal is to expand their lives by reaching beyond the self, but the strategy they employ results in constricting their lives, drawing them inward toward an ever-narrowing, closed-off "I." People want to enlarge their choices, but by seeking to keep "all options open," actually diminish them.

Sensing this contradiction between their goals and strategies, and being aware of a change for the worse in economic conditions, what Americans most fear today is ending up empty-handed. Many of us suspect that at the very moment in our history when we are psychologically ready to satisfy our hunger for the best of the material and spiritual worlds, we may in fact be confronted with the worst of each. Americans fear we may have to endure, in exacerbated form, all of the familiar ills of advanced technological society—from high blood pressure and urban decay to the absence of community—and also to put up with an unstable economy and a lower standard of living.

———

Given this disparity between goals and means, what justifies the sanguine view . . . that the shifts in culture may help us cope with a turbulent world and thereby become part of the solution to our problems as well as part of their cause? Why should we not join those critics who dismiss the self-fulfillment phenomenon as narcissistic folly? What aspects of it are a source of strength rather than stress?

My relatively hopeful outlook grows from a conviction that out of the present disorder something vital and healthy is struggling to be born. From a multitude of life experiments Americans are learning bitter lessons. Many who started out with ill-conceived strategies are learning to correct them in the light of their experience. And, as Americans assimilate these lessons and adapt to new economic conditions, new rules are gradually starting to emerge. Along with self-absorbed strategies our surveys also show some fragmentary evidence of a growing concern with community and caring relationships (for example, over the past several years, the number of Americans engaged in activities to create closer bonds with neighbors, co-religionists, co-workers or others who form a community has grown by almost 50 percent). There is less talk than in earlier decades of status symbols (big homes, diamond rings, fur coats) and less comparing one's self to the neighbors. Young people speak more openly of their religious beliefs and their concern for the future. In my interviews, people express a longing for connectedness, commitment and creative expression.

From people's life experiments, a new social ethic is gradually starting to take shape. I call it an *ethic of commitment* to distinguish it from the traditional ethic of self-denial that underlies the old giving/ getting compact, and also from the ethic of duty to self that grows out of a defective strategy of self-fulfillment. It will take several years before this new ethic . . . emerges clearly from the confusions of the present.

It is on these embryonic beginnings that our hopes must rest, for without a new social ethic there is no assurance that the adaptive side of the self-fulfillment search will triumph. In our demand for greater fulfillment in a time of economic turbulence we have set in motion forces that can lead either to a higher stage of civilization or to disaster. Will we achieve a synthesis between traditional commitments and new forms of fulfillment to create a new direction for our society? Or will we indeed end up with the worst of two worlds—our society fragmented and anomic, the family a shambles, the work ethic collapsed, the economy uncompetitive, our morality flabby and self-centered, and with even less personal freedom than under the old order? If so, we enter a period of bitter, polarizing social conflict that will tear us apart, wreck our society and crush our spirit.

Clearly, the stakes are high. The outcome is uncertain. The prospects for success or failure are evenly balanced; or perhaps the odds are against us. The outcome depends in no small measure on how we define, approach and solve the predicaments associated with the search for self-fulfillment, . . . and how we nurture and develop the still embryonic ethic of commitment that may perhaps emerge.

☆ • ☆ • ☆ • ☆ • ☆

Yankelovich's main findings are in line with the research of Joseph Veroff and associates (p. 357). Comparing national samples from the late 1950s and late 1970s, Veroff and others found that Americans had become more interested in psychological fulfillment but were less communal: at least according to what they reported, they did slightly less social visiting and were much less involved in civic and voluntary associations. Yankelovich believed there had been an upturn in community involvement since the late 1970s, but there is little evidence on this either way. (Several American-character studies have mitigated a gloomy analysis by finding reasons to hope that things might be looking up.)

As a pollster, Yankelovich contributed an all-too-rare commodity to the study of American character—numbers! At one point in the book (not in the excerpt) he estimated that about 17 percent of employed Americans followed a "strong form" of the self-fulfillment ethic: for them, self-fulfillment was top priority ("I am my own work of art"). Yankelovich also gave a breakdown of the 17 percent: three-quarters, for example, were under thirty-five years old compared with half of the other people; and a half (but only half) had been to college compared with 35 percent of the others.

Most of Yankelovich's evidence came from what people *said* about themselves in questionnaires and interviews. What one says about oneself is not necessarily, of course, what one actually thinks and does. Over time, though, it is probably significant that more and more people should find it acceptable to endorse self-fulfillment when asked about their values. Unfortunately *New Rules* did not say exactly what questions were asked. The book sorely needs an appendix giving details of the questionnaires and interview methods.

Some of the book's chapters are built around individual people. Most of these case-portraits are quite persuasive: they are particularly good at showing the different routes of males and females to the same ethos. They do not, however, show trends over time. As far as one can tell, they were all done in the late 1970s. Yankelovich's *historical* argument, stressing the 1960s as the take-off point for self-fulfillment, depends on his survey statistics. And this means trouble for Yankelovich.

To show statistically that a big change occurred in the 1960s the author needs trend data going back *before* the 1960s. Yankelovich does cite a few polls from the 1930s, 1940s and 1950s, but these do not address the core of his proposition about what people want to live and work for. His own data on these attitudes only goes from the late 1960s to the late 1970s.

As a result, Yankelovich underestimates the vintage of what he finds. Had he read more history, he would have realized that the idea of self-engineering for happiness as well as success has been part of American individualism from at least the 1920s when psychoanalysis was popularized.

In other ways, too, Yankelovich exaggerated the newness of what he found. In a chapter called "Feliciano's Bicycle," he saw a Puerto Rican immigrant's passion for bicycle racing as part of the new self-fulfillment drive. He did not consider that this might not be so new: working-class men in dead-end jobs have often compensated by skilling themselves and making a mark in hobbies and sports, from carpentry to hunting.

In much of this Yankelovich ignored the survival of success-values *within* the drive for self-fulfillment. The fact that Americans had turned away from heavily chromed cars with tail fins—a shift that Yankelovich found significant—did not mean that new forms of self-expression were devoid of all status-display and materialism. Was the pleasure of owning a Jacuzzi or a customized van so different from the joys of an Olds 98? And could not the search for new 'experience' be a form of consumption too?

In 1974 the same report on youth by Yankelovich that showed a trend to the "New Values" also showed *rising* support for conventional goals such as job security, 'getting ahead,' and professional prestige. Yankelovich never fully dealt with this. Did the two trends represent two different groups, or were the self-fulfillers not as spiritual as Yankelovich had hoped? In *New Rules* seven years later, Yankelovich did recognize that conventional values of success and survival were still around, and that self-fulfillers had to make concessions to them. But he underestimated the way in which consumer values, status-seeking, and the quest for health and happiness all penetrated each other, and long had done so. *Feeling well* and *looking good* were part of the same tradition.

ROBERT N. BELLAH ET AL.

Individualism and Commitment in American Life

By the late 1980s, liberal academics and commentators were in full cry against what they saw as a 'decade of greed' and a new 'unconcerned' generation. In the middle of the decade, sociologist of religion Robert Bellah, aided by three other sociologists and a social philosopher, published a book that spoke to these criticisms. *Habits of the Heart: Individualism and Commitment in American Life* was not just about greed and selfishness; it described many different lives, but it did home in on two features of Reagan's America—self-serving individualism and the stresses of working in large organizations.

Habits of the Heart contains a long-term historical argument about the way American middle-class individualism has developed, but like Yankelovich's *New Rules* (excerpted above), it is largely built around case studies of individuals. The excerpt that follows is based on the opening case study of a San Jose business executive done by one of the authors, Ann Swidler. A Stanford sociologist, Swidler had written a sharp and searching book, *Organization Without Authority*, on the "free schools" that came out of 1960s radicalism. For Bellah's project she interviewed men and women from all over the United States who had settled in 'Silicon Valley.'

According to Bellah and others, American values had been shaped by four traditions. The two earliest traditions—puritan "biblical" and early "republican"—valued society as much as the individual. These two traditions still survived but two other traditions had become far more dominant—"utilitarian individualism" (success and self-interest) and "expressive individualism" (deep self-expression). Over time, both kinds of individualism had narrowed, giving less place to social commitment. When Americans did get together, they were apt to do so by splintering society (and the individual) into "lifestyle enclaves," clusters of people who smugly shared the same private tastes without interacting much.

In the twentieth century, utilitarian individualism often meant climbing a bureaucratic ladder, competing to get promoted yet yielding power to an engulfing organization. At the same time, both types of individualism—utilitarian and expressive—came together in the *therapeutic relationship*. In a society where more and more people managed others or provided advice and services, the therapeutic relationship became a model for many other relationships too. In therapy, two people met on unequal terms for particular payoffs (income and achievement for the therapist; health or relief for the client). Moral commitments to a given community or value system gave way to the question: what works best for you? Even churchgoers—in modern, liberalized religion—had often lost a strong framework of ethics.

Throughout American individualism, Bellah and others found

> the classic polarities . . . still operating: the deep desire for autonomy and self-reliance combined with an equally deep conviction that life has no meaning unless shared with others in the context of community; a commitment to the equal right to dignity of every individual combined with . . . inequality of reward which, when extreme, may deprive people of dignity; an insistence that life requires practical effectiveness and 'realism' combined with the feeling that compromise is ethically fatal. . . .
>
> We deeply feel the emptiness of a life without sustaining social commitments. Yet we are hesitant to articulate our sense that we need one another as much as we need to stand alone, for fear that if we did we would lose our independence altogether. (pp. 150–51)

Habits of the Heart was a culmination of Bellah's own search for unity and higher meaning in life, for beliefs that would unify the individual as well as society, that would make people feel more *complete*. As Bellah has described it, his life was a religious search for "wholeness," from a Presbyterian childhood to student Marxism to liberal humanism. Majoring in anthropology at Harvard, he was attracted to the "integrity" of Native American cultures in contrast to the "fragmentation" of modern American life. He wrote his honors thesis on *Apache Kinship Systems,* and it became his first book (published in 1952). Learning Japanese and Chinese, he then showed his interest in value systems by writing an important book on *Tokugawa Religion: The Values of Pre-Industrial Japan* (1957).

Bellah's writing also expresses a sense of loss—personal loss as well as loss in the society around him. He has written about the loss of his father when he was three; the loss of beckoning but restrictive dogmas (formal religion, then Marxism); America's loss of community; and the fear that America would lose the nobler side of its founding myths. Moving from Harvard to Berkeley in 1967, he had hopes of the youth movement: like Charles Reich (pp. 219–40), he believed it was finding a new, transcending vision, but he also saw the ease with which it "disintegrated into cultural nihilism."

In 1967 Bellah published an article on "Civil Religion in America." Written in the Vietnam War, it noted the biblical themes that ran through the rhetoric of America's leaders and the way they regarded the nation's past: "Chosen People," "Promised Land," "Sacrificial Death," "Rebirth," and so on. These themes, he said, were often used as a "cloak for petty interests and ugly passions," but they could also be used to help build a wider "world religion." Nine years later, in an essay on new forms of religion in America, he remained on the lookout for spiritual rebirth, but he also claimed that "utilitarian individualism" had corrupted biblical ideals. This message, elaborated in *Habits of the Heart,* comes through in the following excerpt on "Brian Palmer" (the name is a pseudonym). Palmer is a decent fellow but his life has no moral anchor, no set of fixed values beyond a simple 'live and let live.' He is not destructively aggressive—but something is missing.

☆ • ☆ • ☆ • ☆ • ☆

Living well is a challenge.* Brian Palmer, a successful businessman, lives in a comfortable San Jose suburb and works as a top-level manager in a large corporation. He is justifiably proud of his rapid rise in the corporation, but he is even prouder of the profound change he has made recently in his idea of success. "My value system," he says, "has changed a little bit as the result of a divorce and reexamining life values. Two years ago,

*"Individualism and Commitment," from *Habits of the Heart* by Robert Bellah, Richard Madsen, William M. Sullivan, Ann Swidler, and Stephen M. Tipton. Copyright © 1985. Reprinted by permission of the Regents of the University of California and the University of California Press.

confronted with the work load I have right now, I would stay in the office and work until midnight, come home, go to bed, get up at six, and go back in and work until midnight, until such time as it got done. Now I just kind of flip the bird and walk out. My family life is more important to me than that, and the work will wait, I have learned." A new marriage and a houseful of children have become the center of Brian's life. But such new values were won only after painful difficulties.

Now forty-one, his tall, lean body bursting with restless energy, Brian recalls a youth that included a fair amount of hell-raising, a lot of sex, and considerable devotion to making money. At twenty-four, he married. Shouldering the adult responsibilities of marriage and children became the guiding purpose of his life for the next few years.

Whether or not Brian felt his life was satisfying, he was deeply committed to succeeding at his career and family responsibilities. He held two full-time jobs to support his family, accepting apparently without complaint the loss of a youth in which, he himself reports, "the vast majority of my time from, say, the age of fifteen to twenty-two or twenty-three was devoted toward giving myself pleasure of one sort or another." Brian describes his reasons for working so hard after he married quite simply. "It seemed like the thing to do at the time," he says. "I couldn't stand not having enough money to get by on, and with my wife unable to contribute to the family income, it seemed like the thing to do. I guess self-reliance is one of the characteristics I have pretty high up in my value system. It was second nature. I didn't even question the thing. I just went out and did it." Brian and his wife came to share very little in their marriage, except, as he thought, good sex, children, and devotion to his career. With his wife's support, he decided to "test" himself "in the Big League," and he made it, although at great cost to his marriage and family life. "What was my concept of what constituted a reasonable relationship? I guess I felt an obligation to care for materially, provide for, a wife and my children, in a style to which I'd like to see them become accustomed. Providing for my family materially was important. Sharing wasn't important. Sharing of my time wasn't important. I put in extremely long hours, probably averaging sixty to sixty-five hours a week. I'd work almost every Saturday. Always in the office by 7:30. Rarely out of the office before 6:30 at night. Sometimes I'd work until 10:30 or 11. That was numero uno. But I compensated for that by saying, I have this nice car, this nice house, joined the Country Club. Now you have a place you can go, sit on your butt, drink, go into the pool. I'll pay the bills and I'll do my thing at work."

For Brian's wife, the compensations apparently weren't enough. After almost fifteen years of marriage, "One day I came home. In fact, our house was for sale, and we had an offer on the house. My wife said, 'Before you accept an offer, you should probably know that once we sell this house, we will live in different houses.' That was my official notification that she was planning to divorce me."

The divorce, "one of the two or three biggest surprises of my life," led Brian to reassess his life in fundamental ways and to explore the limits of the kind of success he had been pursuing. "I live by establishing plans. I had no plan for being single, and it gave me a lot of opportunity to think, and in the course of thinking, I read for the first time in many, many years. Got back into classical music for the first time since my college years. I went out and bought my first Bach album and a stereo to play it on. Mostly the thinking process of being alone and relating to my children."

When his children chose to live with him, Brian found himself forced to shift his sense of himself and his priorities in life. "I found that being a single parent is not all that it is cracked up to be. I found it an extremely humbling experience. Whereas I go into the office in the morning and I have a personal secretary and a staff of managers and a cast of hundreds working for me, I came home and just like every Tom, Dick, and Harry in the world, I'd clean up garbage after these three big boys of mine. I'd spend two hours preparing and cleaning up after dinner, doing laundry, folding clothes, sweeping the floor, and generally doing manual labor of the lowest form. But the fact that my boys chose to live with me was a very important thing to me. It made me feel that maybe I had been doing something right in the parenting department."

Although his wife had left him, and he later found out that she had been having an affair, Brian's period of reflection led him to rethink his role in the relationship. "Being a compulsive problem solver, I analyzed the failure. I don't like failure. I'm very competitive. I like to win. So I went back and reexamined where the thing broke down and found that I had contributed at least 50 percent and, depending on the vantage point, maybe 99 percent of the ultimate demise of the institution. Mostly it was asking myself the question of why am I behaving in such and such a way. Why am I doing this at work? Why was I doing this at home? The answer was that I was operating as if a certain value was of the utmost importance to me. Perhaps it was success. Perhaps it was fear of failure, but I was extremely success-oriented, to the point where everything would be sacrificed for the job, the career, the company. I said bullshit. That ain't the way it should be."

The revolution in Brian's thinking came from a reexamination of the true sources of joy and satisfaction in his life. And it is particularly in a marriage to a woman very different from his first wife that Brian has discovered a new sense of himself and a different understanding of what he wants out of life. He has a new sense of what love can be. "To be able to receive affection freely and give affection and to give of myself and know it is a totally reciprocal type of thing. There's just almost a psychologically buoyant feeling of being able to be so much more involved and sharing. Sharing experiences of goals, sharing of feelings, working together to solve problems, etc. My viewpoint of a true love, husband-and-wife type of relationship is one that is founded on mutual respect, admiration, affection, the ability to give and receive freely." His new wife, a divorcée his own age, brings four children to their marriage, added to Brian's own three. They have five children still living at home, and a sense of energy, mutual devotion, and commitment sufficient to make their family life a joy.

In many ways, Brian's is an individual success story. He has succeeded materially, and he has also taken hold of the opportunity to reach out beyond material success to a fuller sense of what he wants from life. Yet despite the personal triumph Brian's life represents, despite the fulfillment he seems to experience, there is still something uncertain, something poignantly unresolved about his story.

The difficulty becomes most evident when Brian tries to explain why it is that his current life is, in fact, better than his earlier life built around single-minded devotion to his career. His description of his reasons for changing his life and of his current happiness seems to come down mainly to a shift in his notions of what would make him happy. His new goal—devotion to marriage and children—seems as arbitrary and unexamined as his earlier pursuit of material success. Both are justified as idiosyncratic preference rather than as representing a larger sense of the purpose of life. Brian sees himself as consistently pursuing a utilitarian calculus—devotion to his own self-interest—except that there has been an almost inexplicable change in his personal preferences. In describing the reasons for this change, he begins, "Well, I think I just reestablished my priorities." He sometimes seems to reject his past life as wrong; but at other times, he seems to say he simply got bored with it. "That exclusive pursuit of success now seems to me not a good way to live. That's not the most important thing to me. I have demonstrated to myself, to my own satisfaction, that I can achieve about what I want to achieve. So the challenge of goal realization does not contain that mystique that it held for me at one time. I just have found that I get a lot of personal reward from being involved in the lives of my children."

American cultural traditions define personality, achievement, and the purpose of human life in ways that leave the individual suspended in glorious, but terrifying, isolation. These are limitations of our culture, of the categories and ways of thinking we have inherited, not limitations of individuals such as Brian who inhabit this culture. People frequently live out a fuller sense of purpose in life than they can justify in rational terms, as we see in Brian's case and many others.

Brian's restless energy, love of challenges, and appreciation of the good life are characteristic of much that is most vital in American culture. They are all qualities particularly well-suited to the hard-driving corporate world in which he works. When Brian describes how he has chosen to live, however, he keeps referring to "values" and "priorities" not justified by any wider framework of purpose or belief. What is good is what one finds rewarding. If one's preferences change, so does the nature of the good. Even the deepest ethical virtues are justified as matters of personal preference. Indeed, the ultimate ethical rule is simply that individuals should be able to pursue whatever they find rewarding, constrained only by the requirement that they not interfere with the "value systems" of others. "I guess I feel like everybody on this planet is entitled to have a little bit of space, and things that detract from other people's space are kind of bad," Brian observes. "One of the things that I use to characterize life in California, one of the things that makes California such a pleasant place to live, is people by and large aren't bothered by other people's value systems as long as they don't infringe upon your own. By and large, the rule of thumb out here is that if you've got the money, honey, you can do your thing as long as your thing doesn't destroy someone else's property, or interrupt their sleep, or bother their privacy, then that's fine. If you want to go in your house and smoke marijuana and shoot dope and get all screwed up, that's your business, but don't bring that out on the street, don't expose my children to it, just do your thing. That works out kind of neat."

In a world of potentially conflicting self-interests, no one can really say that one value system is better than another. Given such a world, Brian sets great store by one basic principle—the importance of honesty and communication. It is through communication that people have a chance to resolve their differences, since there is no larger moral ideal in terms of which conflicts can be resolved. "Communication is critical not only to a man-and-woman relationship, it is the essence of our being on this planet in my opinion. Given open communication and the ability to think problems out, most problems can be solved." Solving conflicts becomes a matter of technical problem solving, not moral decision. Lying, which would interfere in a critical way with the ability to communicate accurately and resolve interpersonal conflicts, is thus wrong, but, even here, wrongness is largely a matter of practicality—it doesn't pay. "The bottom line of my personal value system applies to the way I conduct business. My predecessor was characterized as a notorious, habitual, and compulsive liar, and that's a difficult act to follow. That's probably one of the reasons that led to his demise—that his lies were catching up with him and he left before the walls came tumbling down."

Not lying is one of the major things Brian wants to teach his children. "Why is integrity important and lying bad? I don't know. It just is. It's just so basic. I don't want to be bothered with challenging that. It's part of me. I don't know where it came from, but it's very important." Brian says "values" are important, and he stresses the importance of teaching them to his children. But apart from the injunction not to lie, he is vague about what those values are. "I guess a lot of them are Judeo-Christian ethics of modern society, that certain things are bad." Even the things that may be "absolutely wrong," such as killing, stealing, and lying, may just be matters of personal preference—or at least injunctions against them exist detached from any social or cultural base that could give them broader meaning.

290

Are there some things that are just absolutely wrong? "I don't think I would pontificate and say that I'm in a position to establish values for humanity in general, although I'm sufficiently conceited to say that if the rest of the world would live by my value system it would be a better place," Brian says. The justification he offers is simply, "I'm quite comfortable with my values." Yet values, in turn, continually slip back for Brian into a matter of personal preferences, and the only ethical problem is to make the decision that accords with one's preferences. His increased commitment to family and children rather than to material success seems strangely lacking in substantive justification. "I just find that I get more personal satisfaction from choosing course B over course A. It makes me feel better about myself. To participate in this union of chaos to try and mold something, this family situation—and maybe it's because of this bringing two families together—is a challenge. Believe me, this is a challenge. Maybe that's why it fascinates me. Maybe that's why it's important to me."

Despite the combination of tenderness and admiration he expresses for his wife, the genuine devotion he seems to feel for his children, and his own resilient self-confidence, Brian's justification of his life thus rests on a fragile foundation. Morally, his life appears much more coherent than when he was dominated by careerism, but, to hear him talk, even his deepest impulses of attachment to others are without any more solid foundation than his momentary desires. He lacks a language to explain what seem to be the real commitments that define his life, and to that extent the commitments themselves are precarious.

☆ • ☆ • ☆ • ☆ • ☆

Brian Palmer's shift from workaholic to family man, from 'success' to 'relationships,' enacts in one life what theorists of American character have often seen as a historical trend: the decline of the 'Protestant ethic' and the rise of various kinds of self-fulfillment. Palmer's first phase corresponded to what the authors called "utilitarian individualism"; his second phase, to "expressive individualism." In general, though, Bellah and others did not claim that the second type had *replaced* the first: both were in good supply and sometimes fused with each other. Bellah was more perceptive here than Daniel Yankelovich (pp. 268–82) who, like so many other writers on American character, exaggerated the decline of hard-driving ambition.

In their portrait of Brian Palmer, Bellah and others introduce an argument about values and *language* which they develop elsewhere in the book. Palmer's individualism, the authors say, inhibits him from *articulating* a set of values outside his preferences of the moment. Individualism, likewise, prevents Americans from using a language of community, of commitment to a world of others.

This stress on language, on a "vocabulary" of values, became an academic obsession in the 1970s and 1980s, and Bellah's use of it is not very persuasive. Bellah and others make much of the fact that Brian Palmer cannot or will not pronounce a universal morality. He finds it hard to say, for instance, why lying is wrong; he just feels it to be so. According to the authors, this shows that Palmer has no strong moral beliefs (though he does talk of "my value system"). It could simply be, however, that his beliefs are deeply implicit and assumed, a matter of deep feeling rather than academic theory. In any event, the book as a whole gives plenty of evidence that Americans have a vigorous language of community. 'Caring,' 'getting involved,' 'social bonds,' 'citizenship'—these and other such phrases are distinctively American and are the kind of language often quoted in the book and used by the authors themselves. The very tension between individualism and community in American culture makes many Americans more conscious of community and readier to talk about it.

As I have already suggested, Bellah's concern with community was part of his search for "wholeness"—it had a religious element which he shared with Margaret Mead, Charles Reich, and Daniel Yankelovich. At times, alas, his high purpose involved flabby writing. He sometimes seemed to assume that "commitment" to a value system was the same as commitment to community, and that commitment to community meant being democratic and living with different types and classes of people. It ain't necessarily so. You can have a strong value system that is not very communal, and you can be involved in a community of very similar people while not caring a fig for equality.

A redeeming feature of the book is a little "glossary" at the back that discusses the key concepts more rigorously than the main text does. Still, some of the book's message is stale news. Do we need to be told yet again that American individualism is antisocial, or that modern people suffer from a split between a career world of aggressive competition and a domestic world of love and caring? Both propositions are contentious without being new.

The book is fresher when it discusses issues of belief: how people hold whatever ethics they have. Despite their liberalism, however, Bellah and others seem to support old conservative charges, revived in the 1980s, that liberal permissiveness and social-science 'relativism' have eroded absolute standards of right and wrong. Instead of formal religion, they vaguely offer a democratic social philosophy as a basis for absolute values.

What in the end rescues the book is its case studies. Like Yankelovich, Bellah and others give a sense of real lives, each a variation on the book's main argument. Some of the people they portray are good, responsible citizens. It is not clear that other modern countries produce more of them.

American Values and Organized Crime: Suckers and Wiseguys

The last two books excerpted above—Yankelovich's *New Rules* and Bellah's *Habits of the Heart*—used individual case studies as a way of writing about American character; so did *Faces in the Crowd* (1951), David Riesman's sequel to *The Lonely Crowd*. This approach helps both the writer and the reader to guard against overgeneralizing about national trends.

Another way of doing this is to zero in on a *subculture*—the way of life of a specific set of people within the larger society—and ask to what extent they share or *don't* share what are often considered 'American' attitudes and values. In the late 1960s, for example, the Swedish anthropologist Ulf Hannerz studied different life-styles in a black ghetto in Washington, D.C., and asked how they related to "mainstream" values and culture. Again, in the 1970s and 1980s a series of lively books by John Shelton Reed explored the reality behind popular stereotypes of white southerners—male and female, and in different social classes too. Were southerners, he asked, a different breed? (Yes, to some extent, was the basic answer.)

The same question has been asked about America's lawbreakers. In character and values are they really 'deviant'? In the early 1960s (a boom time for theories of 'deviance') two distinguished criminologists—David Matza and Gresham Sykes—looked at the values of "juvenile delinquent" gang members and concluded that they overlapped those of middle- and upper-class Americans much more than was generally supposed.

In the following excerpt, the political scientist Peter Lupsha makes a similar claim about professional gangsters. The mobster, he says, often holds traditional American values but does not seek general respectability—instead, he wants "respect within his *borgata,* his 'family.' " Lupsha's thinking here was a reaction against a well-known article by Daniel Bell, "Crime as an American Way of Life: A Queer Ladder of Social Mobility" (1953). Like Lupsha, Bell noted the American-ness of many gangsters' values, but he made more of the ethnic factor and the blocking of opportunities. When Italian-Americans went into crime, they did so largely because other ethnic groups—especially Jews and Irish—had taken over the main immigrant routes into business and politics. For Italians, crime was a deviant ladder of mobility to a nondeviant goal: respectability in mainstream society. Lupsha disagreed with this, as his essay shows.

At the time of writing the essay, Lupsha was teaching at the University of New Mexico (where he was also faculty adviser to the Kali Club—Filipino knife and stick fighting under "nonlethal" conditions!). His route to studying criminals, however, started when he was a graduate student at Stanford. His Ph.D. dissertation—on patterns of politicking in city councils—was far from social character, but it tuned him to the way relationships are made and broken in small groups, and this counts for much in the study of organized crime.

☆ • ☆ • ☆ • ☆ • ☆

When we ask "What's American about American crime?" the answer is flashed for all of us (Americans) to see.* If we say "violent urban street crime," a host of modern American cultural images appears. A different set appears if we say "Jesse James," and a third set if we say "organized crime." This paper concentrates on the third set of images. . . .

The taproots of American culture are those Lockeian values embodied in the writings, declarations, and documents of the Founding Fathers

---

*"American Values and Organized Crime," by Peter A. Lupsha was first published in *The American Self: Myth, Ideology, and Popular Culture*, The University of New Mexico Press, ed. Sam B. Girgus. It is reprinted by permission of the author.

and their interpreters. These values are based in beliefs in individualism, property, or "materialism," competition, and freedom of action, or independence. From the interplay of these values come our perceptions of opportunity, democratic procedural equality, substantive equality, material success, acquisitiveness, and a belief in right vested in the individual rather than in the community.[1] As these values and ideas shape our political and economic system, so too, they shaped the development and evolution of organized crime in America.

Organized criminal groups have operated in the United States from its very beginnings.[2] Whenever there is an opportunity to enhance profit or create wealth, wherever there are imbalances in the market system or government has through its actions created scarcity and black markets, or wherever local culture and mores make for illicit actions or behaviors against which there are no universal taboos, enterprising individuals will take advantage of the opportunity, risking potential sanction in order to accrue windfall profits. Such fields of illicit action are limited only by culture, precedent, opportunity, and the swiftness and certainty of sanction. If large profits are easily available with relatively little risk, the potential for organized criminal entrepreneurship is enhanced. This point seems obvious enough, yet history and experience show that it has rarely been acted upon by designers of criminal justice systems, at least in the United States. The reason is not a failure of understanding; it is that such planning must operate within the cultural framework that allows the development of organized crime in the first place. Thus cultural and juridical treatment of symptoms, rather than causes, must be the rule; the opportunity for entrepreneurial and syndicated criminal enterprise remains.

America has always been a haven for the entrepreneurial endeavor of organized crime. John Hancock amassed his fortune financing smuggling operations that overcame the Crown's attempt at orderly regulation of West Indian commerce. Robert Morris and James Wilson, two of the important draftsmen of our Constitution, were, as a U.S. senator and associate justice of the Supreme Court respectively, involved with a number of prominent others in the famous Yazoo land fraud.

Land fraud and land speculation in America are older than our form of government. Such enterprise has been assisted, as Tocqueville noted, by the relative equality of condition in the United States, which "naturally urges men to embark on commercial and industrial pursuits, and . . . tends to increase and to distribute real property."[3] Americans have always been willing to opt for personal gain against the possibility of sanction and condemnation. The line between sharp practice and criminal act has always been a blurred one.

James Truslow Adams, of the illustrious Adams family, put it this way:

> Lawlessness has been and is one of the most distinctive American traits. . . . It is impossible to blame the situation on the "foreigners." The overwhelming mass of them were law-abiding in their own lands. If they become lawless here it must be largely due to the American atmosphere and conditions. There seems to me to be plenty of evidence to prove that the immigrants were made lawless by America, rather than America made lawless by them. If the general attitude towards law, if the laws themselves and their administration, were all as sound here as in the native lands of the immigrants, those newcomers would give no more trouble here than they did at home. This is not the case, and Americans themselves are, and most always have been, less law-abiding than the more civilized European nations.[4]

In America *caveat emptor*, let the buyer beware, was a ruling principle of commerce until this generation of consumers began to seek to restrain it. Our values and predisposition for material gain have always made the "Murphy game," "the pigeon drop," "three card Monte," and other ancient con games and swindles commonplace. P. T. Barnum's admonition "There's a sucker born every minute" rings as true today as it did a hundred years ago, as recent commodity and diamond investment swindles indicate. Indeed it is useful to examine the use and operation of the concept of "sucker" in our history and thought. This concept is an ingrained part of our nation, one of the most American things about American crime. It states, in part, that an avaricious individual, or just a naive and easily deceived one, is fair game for those who are sharper, quicker witted, or more worldly. All, in America, are at liberty to be suckers or swindlers.

As there are suckers, so there are "sharpies." Americans have always been willing to engage in sharp, often illegal, practice if the opportunity presents itself. We are told that the political epitaph of Boss Plunkett of Tammany Hall was, "I seen my opportunities, and I took 'em!"—an epitaph that is often seen not as a motto of avaricious behavior, or a violation of public role and trust, but simply as an example of living off politics as well as for it. In engaging in "white graft," Plunkett, Tweed, and other political bosses were simply combining "good business" with politics.

Tycoons like Cornelius "Let the public be damned" Vanderbilt, Andrew Carnegie, and John D. "The Lord gave me my money" Rockefeller, whom Theodore Roosevelt referred to as the "malefactors of great wealth," were not dismayed by the political bosses as long as they were not losing their share of what was there to be gained.[5] These captains of industry and politics were models for the street-gang immigrant kids who were to use the black market opportunity of Prohibition to accumulate capital and form the organizational connections that created modern organized crime in America.

Add to this the image of America as the land of opportunity, a land of milk and honey, where the streets were paved with gold. In such an early paradise, where the good things of life were for the taking, one would seem a fool to work long hours for low pay and slow advancement. America was a land of opportunity; its values prevented swift or easy punishment of those who interpreted liberty as a license to steal. The arrival of Prohibition simply added the hypocrisy of law, and its corruption, to this ethic, and it gave a certain veneer of legitimacy to the entrepreneurship of the bootlegger and rising organized gangster. Flowing alongside this social, economic, and political flotsam in our cultural stream was our concept of the "sucker."

A second aspect to the sucker concept must be mentioned here. This is the notion that one is a sucker if one who is outside the dominant value system, or social strata, lives by the values of that dominant system. This aspect of the concept is important because, along with freedom of individual choice, it lies behind much of the development of organized crime in America. In 1930 Courtney Terret published a novel about organized crime entitled *Only Saps Work*.[6] In the same period the celluloid mobsters of Hollywood—Edward G. Robinson, James Cagney, Humphrey Bogart—echoed this theme, as did the real-life gangster Charlie "Lucky" Luciano.

> A "crumb," according to Luciano, was one "who works and saves, and lays his money aside; who indulges in no extravagance." Luciano wanted "money to spend, beautiful women to enjoy, silk underclothes and places to go in style."[7]

Luciano had no intention of being a "crumb" or "sucker" or of participating in the "grind" of ordinary existence any more than his associates did. Vincent Teresa, a nonmember associate of the Patriarca Italian-American La Cosa Nostra (LCN) organized crime family, more recently repeated this theme:

> I knew that the only way I could live in the style I liked was by being a thief. It was easier than working for a living. The money rolled in. Sometimes it went out faster than I could steal it, but I liked the life. I liked the excitement. There was kind of a thrill to everything I did.[8]

A close study of Teresa's life suggests that these images of ease and excitement were mostly mythic, but there was more to it than that. Teresa continues:

> It's hard to explain, but there was a feeling of power being on the street with men that were always hustling, outfiguring the straights. It seemed that everyone I knew or grew up with was a thief of one kind or another. We were all living pretty good, spending high, dressing fine, hitting all the good spots. It was a helluva life.[9]

Now we have images of power, as well as excitement, in "conning" the modern version of the hard-working sucker. There is also the "high living" that Luciano referred to, as well as something else—the avoidance of a nine-to-five life at an ordinary job, the "grind." Teresa makes this explicit. He and an associate had opened a successful nightclub which Teresa wanted to burn down for the insurance money. His partner prevented him from doing so because the nightclub was making such a good profit. To Teresa, "The nightclub was making money, but it was strictly a grind, and who needs a grind when there is easy money to be made?"[10] Such statements by career professionals in syndicated crime tell us a lot, not only about crime in America but also about its roots in our cultural ideas about the "sucker."

Alongside the concept of the sucker, the willingness to engage in sharp practice, and visions of liberty and opportunity, stands the notion of material success. The organized criminal hungers for success while desperately seeking to avoid being a sucker. Wealth without work, however, is difficult to achieve. Thus the organized criminal seeks to place a veil of romance and myth over his activities to endow them with apparent ease and success so that he will not be thought of as society's fool.

The organized criminal must establish a code of conduct that permits success, or rationalizes success, without considering the successful criminal a "sucker." This is a paradox. If the "straight" world and work are the domain of suckers, then criminal actions—even failure, arrest, and imprisonment—must be endowed with ease, glamor, success, and correctness. This world view is accomplished in two ways, first, by the establishment of an internal personal code, a set of rules and ethics, which may seem perverse to the outside world, but which permits a sense of self-worth for the criminal, and second, by the establishment of an image of the outside world that considers suckers and straights as inherently corrupt, dishonest, and hypocritical. Paradoxically, this image suggests that the suckers lack the courage and grace to act on the insight that the world is a "con." They know that those with political and economic power get the good things of life, but because they are afraid, the suckers toil long and hard, accepting hardship, and deferring gratifications. Lucky Luciano summed it up like this:

> Everybody's got larceny in 'em, only most of 'em don't have the guts to do nothin' about it. That's the big difference between us and the guys who call themselves honest. We got the guts to do what they'd like to do only they're too scared to.[11]

This cynicism toward the outside world, plus a personal code of incorruptibility and loyalty to kin, peers, and criminal cohorts, permits the organized criminal to invert the mirror of reality and view his values as correct and society's as perverse.

"To be straight is to be a victim." So states a common La Cosa Nostra "borgata" expression. As Donald Cressey tells us about this code,

> A man who is committed to regular work and submission to duly con-stituted authority is a sucker. When one Cosa Nostra member intends to insult and cast aspersion on the competence of another, he is likely to say, sneeringly, "Why don't you go out and get a job?"[12]

To get a job requires education. During the first decade of this century, when young street hoodlums learned the habits and skills essen-tial for success during Prohibition, education was just beginning to "emerge as an increasing important qualification for employment." But as [Humbert] Nelli notes:

> To slum area youngsters like Salvatore Lucania (Charlie Lucky Luciano), John Torrio, and Alphonse Caponi (Al Capone), excitement and economic opportunity seemed to be out in the streets rather than in the classroom. As soon as they reached the legal withdrawal age of fourteen, they left school.[13]

According to Luciano, he knew "that school had nothing to teach him," but in the streets he saw "some people had money, some people didn't."

> When I looked around the neighborhood, I found out that the kids wasn't the only crooks. We were surrounded by crooks, and plenty of them was guys who were supposed to be legit, like the landlords and storekeepers and the politicians and cops on the beat. All of them was stealing from somebody.[14]

Here is a glimmer of that world view of society as corrupt emerging in the child, a view that was reinforced by Luciano's experiences in the Brooklyn Truancy School and Hampton Farms Penitentiary.[15] It is this world view that sets the organized criminal apart from his fellow street-gang members.

Nelli notes:

> Unlike most of their contemporaries, who also belonged to street gangs and were involved in occasional mischief-making, the criminals-in-the-making had little or nothing to do with legitimate labor, which they believed was

only for "suckers," men who worked long hours for low pay and lived in overcrowded tenements with their families.[16]

The picture painted here is rather different from the "queer ladder thesis" of crime as a method of upward mobility, which has been stressed by some sociologists.[17] Yes, some of these young immigrants chose careers in crime, but they did not act out of frustration, or any long struggle of being excluded from the political ladder, or because they were blocked from other avenues of career advancement. They turned to crime because they felt that the legitimate opportunity structures were for "suckers," and they were not going to be trapped in the nickel-and-dime world of ordinary work.

The young organized criminals of the Prohibition era saw themselves as the "wiseguys," a term still used in LCN circles to denote soldiers who appear to make an easy buck without working. These "wiseguys" could have economic mobility without ever climbing the status ladder. Their choice was an individual decision, reinforced by peers, experience, and a talent for violence. They were not more frustrated, nor more deprived (relatively or absolutely) than their classroom peers and fellow street-gang members who chose to be "straights" and suckers, following the legitimate socioeconomic ladder, narrow and crowded as it may have been.

To avoid becoming trapped as suckers in the grind of work and subservience to superiors, this alternative world view was created. As one was surrounded by crooks and hypocrites in the guise of legitimate businessmen and politicians, one could at least be honest with oneself, true to some personal code, and be an excellent thief. Luciano always said he needed nothing in writing because "his word was his bond." Luciano and the others had proved as street-gang kids that they had guts, courage, criminal skills, and a capacity for depersonalized violence, but they were also lucky. They arrived at adulthood just as the doors of criminal opportunity swung wide with Prohibition.

At the time of enactment of the legislation Lucky Luciano was twenty, Vito Genovese nineteen, Carlo Gambino seventeen, Al Capone eighteen, Thomas Lucchese eighteen, Joseph Profaci twenty, and Frank

Costello twenty-six. By the time Prohibition went into effect, 16 January 1920, other street-gang teen-agers were coming of age to make themselves a name in organized crime: Meyer Lansky, seventeen, Pete Licavoli, sixteen, Jerry Catena, seventeen, Joe Adonis, seventeen, and Albert Anastasia, fifteen. By March 1933, when the legislation repealing Prohibition was enacted, these teen-agers had grown to manhood and had capital, organizational skills, and influence. Thus the serendipity of Prohibition provided opportunity, capital, and organization to routinize organized crime. Prohibition and personal choice, not career blockage or frustration with the legitimate mobility paths, moved these small-time hoodlums into leadership positions in organized crime.

Another aspect of our cultural system reinforces and further legitimizes and justifies the perverse world view of the organized criminal. This is the relationship between politics and the public, particularly the political party nominating and financing system that maintained the urban political machine.

As [Francis] Ianni has succinctly put it,

> The corrupt political structures of the major American cities and organized crime have always enjoyed a symbiotic relationship in which success in one is dependent on the right connections in the other.[18]

To understand how this symbiosis raises the organized criminal to a superior personal status above politicians, one must recognize that the corruptor always feels superior to the corruptee. The politician who accepts "favors" and in return provides protection to the illegal enterprises of organized crime not only gives a living witness to the criminal's world view but also confirms for the organized criminal, in violating his oath of office, that a criminal's code is superior to society's.

In a *Chicago Tribune* interview in 1927 Al Capone put it this way:

> There is one thing that is worse than a crook and that's a crooked man in a big political job. A man who pretends he's enforcing the law and is really making dough out of somebody breaking it—a self-respecting hoodlum doesn't have any use for that kind of fellow—he buys them like he'd buy any other article necessary for his trade, but he hates them in his heart.[19]

Here is one of America's leading organized criminals stating his moral code, indicating his superiority over crooked politicians and his belief in fundamental American values which he himself does not follow. Above all, clearly contained in this statement is a disdain for another's hypocrisy and a lack of recognition of his own.

With their own world view, their blinders, their moral code, organized criminals are of American society but only tangentially part of it. The organized criminal's concern is for wealth and the good things of life that wealth can provide. Many sociologists feel that respectability is really what the organized criminal is striving for. [Daniel] Bell, [Francis] Ianni, and [Gus] Tyler all say this. These sociologists fail to realize that organized criminals are committed to their own moral code and world view and couldn't care less about respectability in mainstream terms. Respect and respectability in the larger society are unimportant because the organized criminal has rejected many if not most of the procedures on which mainstream values rest. Thus Daniel Bell is wrong when he implies that a desire for respectability led "the quondam racketeer" to provide "one of the major supports for a drive to win a political voice for Italians."[20]

Respectability was not what Costello, Lansky, and Luciano sought in political links to Al Smith, Franklin Roosevelt, Huey Long, Tammany leader James Hines, Mayor Jimmy Walker, and numerous judges and aldermen. They simply understood what Paul Kelly and Arnold Rothstein had understood before them, and what organized criminals understand today, that it helps to have friends in high places. Nelli notes that at the 1932 Democratic Party Convention Costello shared a suite with James Hines, a Smith supporter. Lucky Luciano shared one with Albert Marinelli, leader of the Second Assembly District in New York and a Roosevelt supporter. This arrangement was not based on some "quondam racketeer's" desire for respectability; it was business.

Nelli puts it this way:

> This sharing of quarters was of symbolic as well as practical significance for it demonstrated that criminal syndicate leaders from New York had achieved . . . power and influence equal to that of local party bosses.[21]

Bell himself notes that Tammany Hall had to turn to Costello and Luciano for support and funds, yet he overlooks the evidence in the court trial of James Hines, the resignation of Albert Marinelli, as well as Costello's movement of slot machines to Huey Long's Louisiana, calling them attempts at respectability when they were simply business trade-offs. Sounding the same note, Bell states:

> The early Italian gangsters were hoodlums—rough and unlettered and young (Al Capone was only twenty-nine at the height of his power). Those who survived learned to adapt. By now they are men of middle age or older. They learned to dress conservatively. Their homes are in respectable suburbs. They send their children to good schools and have sought to avoid publicity.[22]

Of course organized criminals buy homes in respectable suburbs and send their children to good schools. Such actions are common to anyone of affluence in our society, criminal or college professor. That they dress conservatively and avoid publicity likewise tells us nothing about either respectability or having left organized crime. Such comments focus on the trappings and appearance of a noncriminal life-style; they show nothing of the substance.

The organized criminal operates by a different standard . . . from that of the ordinary citizen seeking upward mobility and status within some dominant community. He seeks respect within his *borgata*, his "family," and not in that larger community which he mocks. Thus sociologists who point to the following as signs of mob desire for respectability can only be thought naive.

> Many of the top "crime" figures long ago had forsworn violence, and even their income, in large part, was derived from legitimate investments . . . or from such quasi-legitimate but socially acceptable sources as gambling casinos.[23]

The use of business "fronts" as laundries to wash illegally gained wealth and to create a basis for taxable income has been well documented.[24] The use of gambling casinos to skim millions of dollars in cash and as fronts for acts of corruption and blackmail is also well documented and is a common reason for organized crime's interest and hidden ownership in such enterprises.[25] Surely these facts suggest goals other than respectability.

What is American about American crime? Obviously, it is our values, their openness and pragmatism, our beliefs in competition, material success, individual action, freedom, and liberty. The openness of our values permits their reversal, which can be a very good and creative force, enhancing adaptability and change. As we have seen, it can also be a rather perverse one. Our values and the needs of our popular political institutions permit the creation of alternative ethical codes, and thus our values can be turned upside down.

Lucky Luciano, without fully being conscious of it, neatly captured both the possibilities and the paradox.

> I had Masseria and Maranzano knocked off to get to the top. What I did was illegal; I broke the law. [Franklin] Roosevelt had us and other guys like Hines and Walker sent to the can or squashed. What he did was legal. But the pattern was exactly the same; we was both shitass double-crossers, no matter how you look at it. Now, I don't say we elected Roosevelt, but we gave him a pretty good push. . . . I never knew that a guy who was gonna be President would stick a knife in your back when you wasn't looking. I never knew his word was no better than lots of rackets guys.[26]

Poor Luciano. He expected mainstream values to be different from his own chosen world view. In that, he failed to realize just how much a product of the American system he was.

NOTES

1. Gary Wills would agree on the values, but disagree with their Lockeian roots. He gives Francis Hutcheson credit for influencing Jefferson's thought. The authors of the Constitution, and Jefferson was not among them, were more influenced by Locke. See Gary Wills, *Inventing America* (New York, 1978).

2. Common definitions of organized crime run the gamut from New York District Attorney Frank Hogan's—"Organized crime is two or more persons engaged in criminal activities"—to the more recent: Organized crime includes any group of individuals whose primary activity involves violating criminal laws to seek illegal profits and power by engaging in racketeering activities and, when appropriate, engaging in intricate financial manipulations. Whatever the definition, organized crime has been part

of America since the first colonists realized how to take advantage of the Indians.

3. Alexis de Tocqueville, *Democracy in America* (Paris, 1840), vol. 2, p. 304 in the 1967 ed. (New York).

4. James Truslow Adams, *Our Business Civilization* (New York, 1929), cited in *Organized Crime in America*, Gus Tyler (Ann Arbor, 1962), p. 44.

5. See Arthur Schlesinger, *Paths to the Present* (New York, 1949); Max Lerner, *America as a Civilization* (New York, 1957); Wayne Moquin, ed., *The American Way of Crime* (New York, 1976).

6. This is a futuristic novel in which organized crime has gained control of government and much of industry. Courtney Terret, *Only Saps Work* (New York, 1930). The view that only suckers work is less discussed today but a 1942 sociology textbook gives this view as a prime cause of organized crime. See the "Something for Nothing Philosophy" in *The American Way of Life*, Harry E. Barnes and Oreen M. Ruedi (New York, 1942, new ed. 1950), pp. 827–29.

7. Humbert Nelli, *The Business of Crime* (New York, 1976), p. 106.

8. Vincent Teresa, *My Life in the Mafia* (Greenwich, Conn., 1973), p. 73.

9. Ibid.

10. Ibid., p. 111.

11. Martin A. Gosch and Richard Hammer, *The Last Testament of Lucky Luciano* (Boston, 1975), p. 37. This work was developed from interviews with Luciano in Italy a few years before his death.

12. Donald R. Cressey, *Theft of the Nation* (New York, 1969), pp. 177–78.

13. Nelli, *The Business of Crime*, p. 105.

14. Gosch and Hammer, *The Last Testament of Lucky Luciano*, p. 8.

15. Ibid., p. 16.

16. Nelli, *The Business of Crime*, p. 195.

17. Tyler, *Organized Crime in America*; Daniel Bell, "Crime as an American Way of Life," in *The End of Ideology*, ed. Daniel Bell (New York, 1960), pp. 127–50; Francis A. J. Ianni, *Ethnic Succession in Organized Crime* (Washington, D.C., 1973); Ianni, *A Family Business* (New York, 1972).

18. Francis A. J. Ianni, *The Black Mafia* (New York, 1974), p. 107.

19. *Chicago Tribune*, Dec. 6, 1927; reprinted in *The American Way of Crime*, ed. Moquin, p. 69.

20. Bell, "Crime as an American Way of Life," p. 143.

21. Nelli, *The Business of Crime*, p. 195.

22. Bell, "Crime as an American Way of Life," p. 147.

23. Ibid., p. 148.

24. See Melvin K. Bers, *The Penetration of Legitimate Business by Organized Crime* (Washington, D.C., 1970); Jonathan Kwitny, *Vicious Circles: The Mafia in the Marketplace* (New York, 1979); Annelise G. Anderson, *The Business of Organized Crime* (Stanford, Calif., 1979).

25. See Ed Reid and Ovid Demaris, *The Green Felt Jungle* (New York, 1963); Teresa, *My Life in the Mafia*; Gosch and Hammer, *The Last Testament of Lucky Luciano*; Hank Messick, *Lansky* (New York, 1974). Also 1,098 pages of affidavits of electronic surveil-

lance of the Kansas City, Nick Civella, LCN family, June 1979 (author's personal copy).

26. Gosch and Hammer, *The Last Testament of Lucky Luciano*, p. 167.

☆ • ☆ • ☆ • ☆ • ☆

Lupsha's piece is salutary. As I have already said, it approaches the issue of national character by looking at a particular subculture: it does not just generalize about 'Americans' or 'the American middle class.' At the same time Lupsha's description of "wiseguys" versus "suckers" challenges the common belief that a work ethic was central to American traditional values. From the early nineteenth century, indeed, many Americans have prized the fast route to success; if one can get to success and its kicks without much slogging, so much the better. In their study of youth gangs—p. 294 above—Matza and Sykes implied somewhat the same thing. Americans traditionally admire smart work and effective work, and lots of it, but only the more puritan have admired a nose to the grindstone for its own sake.

In discussing American values, Lupsha gives an interesting counterpoint to Robert Bellah and others in the preceding selection. What Lupsha calls "openness and pragmatism"—"our beliefs in competition, material success, individual freedom, and liberty"—Bellah calls a lack of commitment to *anything* except individual satisfaction and independence. But in the end they agree: American values are not very binding.

The main defect of Lupsha's essay is that he does not talk about ethnicity. He says nothing of the fact that most of the modern criminals he mentions have Italian names. In playing down the ethnic factor, Lupsha rejected a thesis put forward by Francis Ianni. Ianni argued that Sicilian codes of honor and family found new opportunities in America while adjusting in diverse ways to American culture. Lupsha's conclusion speaks in effect against this. Like Franklin Roosevelt, he said, Lucky Luciano did not pay much heed to personal ties (what some social scientists have seen as the familial, 'personalist' values of traditional Italy). Yet it is clear from Lupsha's concluding quotation that Luciano felt the moral claims of personal loyalty: "shitass doublecrossers" is the term he uses on himself and

Roosevelt. Lupsha does not mention this because he does not explicitly discuss Italian-American culture, even though he refers to *borgata*, a concept of 'family.' Whatever his position on the ethnic factor, Lupsha should have discussed it more openly—he might also have said more about contemporary criminals of other ethnic origins. In subsequent research, Lupsha has indeed stressed the undermining of 'Mafia' groups by other ethnics as well as the decline of 'family' ties among criminals.

The Control of Anger

In the 1980s several writers on American character tried a new approach. They concentrated on a particular value or emotional area that had not been squarely dealt with before, though each connected with the old topic of individualism.

The professional partnership of Carol Stearns, a psychiatrist, and Peter Stearns, a social historian, is a good example of the new approach. In an article titled "Emotionology" (1985), they apologized for coining an ugly bit of jargon but said it was needed. "Emotionology" meant studying how a society or group treated an emotion and what kind of expression it was allowed. In a way, emotionology was the study of "feelings about feelings." The Stearnses called for more work in this area, and they instanced the study of "anger control."

Their book *Anger*, published in 1986 and excerpted below, practiced what they had preached. From the seventeenth century, they said, ideas about the control of anger in America's "Protestant middle classes" had changed through four historical eras. The first two periods were general to the Western world, the second two more specifically American, though the authors did not say how Europe diverged. In the "pre-modern" seventeenth century, people did not worry much about anger itself. Controls applied to aggressive behavior, not the mood behind it.

In the second period, lasting from the early eighteenth century to the mid-nineteenth, anger control concentrated on the home, a haven to be defended. Children were often thought to be naturally free of anger. Men (more than women) might feel it but should curb it. In the third stage, stretching roughly from 1860 to 1940, Americans became more ambivalent to anger; they accepted it when diverted into safe channels such as athletics or reform movements. In the final phase, from World War II to the present, anger was subject to many controls. It was considered more natural than in the early nineteenth century, but it was also believed that hostile feelings should be *managed*. According to this approach—which started in the workplace and was then exported to family life—anger should be "talked out," trivialized, expressed in minor ways.

The Stearnses did not think this approach was very effective. Contemporary Americans, in their view, did not do as well as their combative forebears at the turn of the century in "channeling" anger. As a result, anger now found destructive outlets in random violence, lawsuits, and aggression against the self.

The Stearnses' four-stage chronology was not as crude as a brief summary makes it look. New ideas about anger affected different groups in different ways at different times and places. The sources of these ideas were equally varied: they ranged from religious and political beliefs to social and economic forces, as the excerpt below will explain.

The wide net cast by the Stearnses reflected their credentials. Carol Stearns has a Ph.D. in history as well as an M.D. At the time of cowriting the book she was a practicing psychiatrist; she also taught psychiatry at the University of Pittsburgh medical school. Her background enabled the book to start off by reviewing social-science theories of anger, including psychoanalysis—all of them are found wanting, largely because they neglected historical change.

Peter Stearns, history professor at Carnegie Mellon University, has published a stream of books and articles since the mid-1960s. His writing cuts a zigzag path from social history to national character. It is not at all an obvious path and needs some explanation.

Peter Stearns's main subject has been the history of western Europe from industrialization to the present—especially to World War I. Across this broad map his books have dealt with politics, social change, and culture, but his real specialty has been French industrial society and the French working class. Stearns's work made him a leader in what has been called 'history from the bottom up': a revolt against the focus on leaders and elites and formal institutions that dominated history-writing before the late 1960s. Stearns tried to understand the experience of ordinary, lower-class people. This led him, like some other social historians, into attitudes and outlooks—what in the trade was often called *mentalite*. For Stearns this meant writing about the social character of specific groups, especially that of the working class.

At the same time, Stearns discounted *national* character theories while showing that they fascinated him. He was particularly keen to debunk the notion that "French individualism" produced the "syndicalist" movement in French labor history. In a major article, "National Character and European Labor History" (1970), Stearns admitted that national differences, including national character, had had *some* effect on Western labor movements. He clearly enjoyed recounting the evidence for this, but he went on to argue that other factors were much more important. Essentially, he said, worker movements and attitudes were shaped by the stage of industrialization, the exact class of the workers (skilled versus unskilled), and the industry they were in. All these factors tended to cut across national boundaries.

Even here, though, Stearns was attracted to psychological arguments. He suggested that different industries attracted different personality types, even on the shop floor. Those industries where the workers and their leaders conformed to popular stereotypes of the national character and had most contact with the "national political culture" (French textiles, for example) were often assumed to be representative of *all* the nation's workers—which they were not. Stearns actually believed that a nation's elites were more apt than working-class people to have a common, 'national-character' outlook. This enabled him, in the book on anger, to make more of national character since the book concentrated on middle and upper-class attitudes.

The last book Peter Stearns wrote before *Anger* was *Be a Man! Males in Modern Society* (1979). It showed how the changing nature of an urban, industrial society affected the requirements of masculinity—what one had to do to "be a man"—in the working class and the middle class. As before, Stearns recognized some national differences; but he was more struck by what modern Western countries had in common.

This meant, however, that he was prepared to generalize even more widely than national-character studies do. *Be a Man!* also expressed Stearns's personal involvement in a subject closely related to anger and its control. In the book's introduction he told of his unease at the kinds of aggressiveness men often felt they had to show. Writing

a book about "men in modern society [was] an extraordinarily revealing path to male self-awareness."

☆ · ☆ · ☆ · ☆ · ☆

Anger at work has a history.* James Franklin, the eighteenth-century
Boston printer, indulged his temper freely against those in his employ,
with scant sign of compunction or restraint. His apprenticed younger
brother, Benjamin, though resentful of the resultant beatings and loud
arguments and most eager to escape the shop, saw nothing noteworthy or
unusual about James's emotional style, commenting only that his brother
was "passionate."

A foreman, interviewed a decade ago by Studs Terkel, sees himself
above all as a human relations expert, his own emotions geared toward
creating a friendly atmosphere. So thoroughly has he internalized his
mission that he deplores the occasional moodiness of his workers, not
because it hampers productivity, but because grumpiness is so distasteful
in itself: "If we could get everybody to feel great . . . ?" And a middle
manager with a similar emotional mission: "You have to keep peace with
people on all levels. Sometimes I get home worn to a frazzle over all this."[1]

Anger in marriage has a history too. Victorian thoughts: "I do not
see how it is possible to pass . . . 50 years of married life . . . and not,
sometimes, feel those risings of temper to which the best of manhood,
have, in general, been more or less subject. Nor can I say that I should
envy those, who were so indifferent—so wanting in sensibility—as never
to have a single feeling of displeasure towards each other"; "Tom was
spirited and quick tempered—great, lovinghearted men always are."[2]
And a thought from the 1940s: "Most bickering in marriage would stop
if husbands and wives would just be polite and 'behave like adults.' "[3]

Ideas about anger in marriage have changed, and sometimes real
people have been caught in the crunch of altered expectations. Consider
Ted, described in the popular series "Can This Marriage Be Saved?" in
the *Ladies Home Journal* of April 1965. The marriage counselor felt the
couple was in trouble, mostly because of the husband's angry ways. The

---

*"The Control of Anger," from *Anger: The Struggle for Emotional Control in America's History*
by Carol Zisowitz Stearns and Peter N. Stearns. Copyright © 1986 by Carol Zisowitz Stearns and
Peter N. Stearns. Reprinted by permission of the University of Chicago Press.

diagnosis—Ted had been raised by an old-fashioned father: "Although Ted decried his bad temper, he was secretly proud of it. He regarded his temper as a heritage from his father." As a child, Ted recalled smashing a plate over his brother's head to retaliate for a piece of stolen cake: "My mother was furious. My father was tickled, ignored her demands that I be punished, and took me downtown for ice cream." The counselor, understanding but not at all condoning the older approach, suggested that the unfortunate Ted was "what we call an 'angry' man" and that the marriage's only hope was for him to learn to take out his feelings on inanimate objects.[4]

Americans today worry about their emotions more than Ben Franklin's brother and his contemporaries, or indeed most Victorian husbands, ever did. And there is no emotion about which we fret, amid greater confusion, than anger. While our founding fathers felt relatively free to storm and rage when the mood seized them and even took temper to be a sign of manliness, we have become embarrassed by such displays today. Though our ancestors were certainly concerned about suppressing some behaviors that might result from anger, such as insubordination by servants or children, they saw no need to attack the emotional basis of those behaviors directly. Contemporary Americans have gone much further; they seek to regulate not only behavior but the feeling itself.

Indeed, during the past two hundred years, Americans have shifted in their methods of controlling social behavior toward greater reliance on direct manipulation of emotions and, particularly, of anger. This is not to argue that contemporary society imposes more social control than has been imposed in the past, for in part the effort to restrain anger replaces earlier forms of behavioral control, particularly tight, intimate community supervision. . . .

A history of the growing restraint of anger, as a significant theme in American history, may come as a surprise. Americans easily imagine themselves a rather angry people, heirs to a passionate past ranging from the righteous zeal of the Puritans who served a wrathful God, to Southern flashes of temper in defense of personal honor, through the quick-triggered Western frontiersmen with tempers to match. More recently, collective protest and widespread individual violence during the 1960s and early 1970s reminded us that our history has been peppered with angry acts of force, sometimes on the side of the law as well as against it.[5] Surely, major tides of American history have prepared us to be too angry rather than unusually restrained. A recent and well-received book on anger, playing to this theme, argued that anger has become a major American problem: not only has it become a national tradition, but contemporary therapeutic advice based on popularized-Freudian injunctions against the dangers of repression has also produced a dangerous penchant for letting angry feelings "hang out," regardless of the consequences.[6] It is easy to believe, in this context, that anger is wrecking our domestic lives as well as prompting some of the larger social tensions that concern us still. Even the august *New York Times* thunders against anger, as op-ed columnists excoriate anger as a danger to health—whether the emotion is expressed or not—and as a social menace, a "form of public littering."[7] Christopher Lasch, in his stinging indictment of contemporary culture, worries about the intense and unsocialized rage that shallow parental styles now produce among American children. A school official notes that "perhaps the emotion that causes the most problems, especially in the schools, is anger."[8]

But are we, indeed, as freely angry as we imagine ourselves? Studs Terkel's foremen are hardly quick-tempered gunslingers transported into the contemporary world of work. Rather they appear—correctly—more intensely concerned with repressing this emotion than many of their premodern antecedents were. Of course we can point to acts of anger in our past and in our present, and without question some of these cause legitimate dismay. But in the main Americans' worried preoccupation with anger is in fact a symptom of the national effort to repress and not the consequence of a particularly angry culture. We exaggerate our penchant for ventilating wrath in order to better prevent ourselves and others from recognizing how vigilant we are against the emotion. The myth of a blithely angry people is simply that—a myth, more useful in describing the way we were than the way we are today, and even then obscuring the long and complicated war against anger that many Americans have waged for a full two centuries. For at least a century past Americans have been characterized not by unusual readiness to express their tempers but by a complicated ambivalence that has focused on the need for control. Indeed, one reason for the popularity of cultural presentations of unfettered anger—the western or the street-tough detective, the athletic perform-ance in which the coach exhorts his charges to "get mad"—lies in their fantasy value, their escapist portrayal of freedom from real-world Ameri-can restraints. Some astute European observers, getting beneath surface stereotypes, have thus noted, not unusual American bluster, but a pecu-liar vulnerability to displays of anger on the part of others, a counterpart to the national desire for affectionate approval that may even affect the American style of diplomacy. . . .

Continuities

At this point—the mid-1980s—in a complex evolution of American atti-tudes toward anger, it is important to stress the fundamental continuities. Since the desire to recognize and control anger arose—perhaps within some families in the colonial period, somewhat more widely by the later eighteenth century—advice literature and other forms of exhortation, including both religious and behavioral science tracts, have pursued the goal of limiting the expression of anger with considerable dili-gence. . . .

Reflecting the long campaign against anger, Americans rated anger control as one of the most important personal characteristics in an exhaus-tive late 1970s survey of national attitudes. Ability to keep one's temper was one of the five most commonly mentioned strengths—"When I get into an argument with someone, I know how to calm things down quickly"—and, among these five, one of the most detailed, least home-spun-moralistic responses in the general category of personal strengths and weaknesses.[9] Thus has the prolonged battle to control anger borne fruit, not only in the goal of seeking internal restraint over anger and disapproving those who lack this restraint, but also in the intensity with which this goal is held.

Insistence on the durability of the basic campaign against an-ger . . . qualifies efforts to define a brand-new, late twentieth-century American character. While contemporary anger-control patterns do have some distinctive features, and possibly some ominous ones, they do not cast off entirely from previous modern patterns. Perhaps in other re-spects, also, contemporary character will prove to be a major variant on larger modern trends and not the entirely new animal that some critics have assumed. . . .

The movement to control anger responds fundamentally to several factors running through the American experience (and in many respects, doubtless, the modern Western experience) over the past two centuries. Three sets of factors are involved.

1. The initial tendency to focus the anger-control effort on the family (though with the family often assumed to provide a more general formation of character) related to some changes in the definition and valuation of family functions from the late seventeenth century on. Initially, these changes owed much to the new esteem for familial warmth generated by Protestantism and other ideological forces peculiar to that period. In a larger sense, however, the concentration on anger control was a response to the decline of traditional church and community supervision of behavior and the desire to replace this supervision with internalized restraints. In a society that was beginning to change rapidly, with the expansion of market economic relationships and the dislocations caused by population growth, internal control seemed essential if social and personal life were not to become completely random. The importance of anger control in defining a home environment separate from the buffetings of life in the marketplace was an extension of this felt need to inculcate personal emotional restraint. In the late eighteenth century and the early Victorian decades, of course, anger control was part of a broader pattern of internalized restraints. But anger control outlived this generalized campaign, remaining crucial in the development of personal mastery in a changing environment. More than other kinds of restraints, including sexual restraint, anger control has continued to be a vital tool in a society marked by a persistent need to deal with unpredictability and concourse with strangers in the absence of firm behavioral guidelines enforced by established community authorities. The growth of population and resultant crowding and particularly the experience of urbanization have provided consistent spurs to this emotional motif; unfettered anger became increasingly risky, as it had earlier, for example, in East Asian societies, where large numbers of people had to interact in a limited space.

2. Along with new needs for personal control came a culture that pressed increasingly for more democratic social behavior. From the Enlightenment on, and particularly in the United States, an egalitarian strain

has affected at least superficial social behavior. In the eighteenth century itself, new egalitarian ideals contributed to the new standards of behavior preached to family members.[10] The love-up, anger-down motif concentrated directly on relationships between husband and wife and between parents and children, which had once been hierarchical, with anger a major prerogative of superior place, but which now were supposed to become more reciprocal. Of course equality was not achieved, either in families or in the wider society, and this is one reason that the modern emotionology of anger has had incomplete effects. But the cultural strand of egalitarianism remained vibrant, never fully displaced. In the twentieth century, it spread beyond family to the workplace and to other public relationships. Formal hierarchy was replaced in part by greater negotiation among theoretical equals, which in turn involved more consideration for others, more patience—and less tolerated anger.[11] The reduction of hierarchy added a new unpredictability to human relationships—and then another need for personal self-control. A democratic culture thus extended its effect, but the factor itself was not new.

3. The economic basis for anger control in the initial phases of the modern emotionology is not entirely clear. Certainly, the rise of market relationships and the sense of nonfamily members as competitors helps explain the new focus on a warm, anger-free family.[12] But it is probable that market dealings encouraged anger control more directly as well, as the necessity of dealing with and pleasing strangers imposed new constraints. Certainly, the extension of wage labor created pressures for anger control in the proletarian segment of the population, though this same new hierarchy between employer and worker (or housewife and servant) created new possibilities for anger as well. In the twentieth century, the economic factor becomes clearer and more obviously important, in combination with the familial culture of anger control already established in the middle class and the pervasive egalitarian veneer in public relationships. With an increasingly intricate bureaucracy and then the expansion of people-dealing service occupations, the primacy of economic-organizational imperatives in restraining anger becomes increasingly patent. . . .[13]

Complexities

Continuity established, it is obvious that there have been important variations on the theme. The importance of major chronological periods in the campaign against anger must be emphasized. Each period, from the early Victorian through the turn of the century to the contemporary, tossed up a distinctive style of advice and suggested some distinctive behavior patterns. The final two periods, at least, also created a number of institutions designed in part to implement the prevailing views on anger, like the boxing enthusiasm encouraged by the idea of channeling or the various personnel and counseling programs set up to translate the more recent management ideal. Each period, finally, emphasized an emotionology focused on a particular range of behaviors and a new attempt to redefine home/work relationships. The early Victorians concentrated of course on the family and character development; the latter was intended, but without great specificity, to apply to nonfamily situations, though the assumption of a marked emotional and moral contrast between the home and the outside world rather limited the extension. During the turn-of-the-century period the home/work dichotomy was preserved, but with an explicit willingness to recommend the use of anger-based zeal in public situations. This emphasis shifted in turn toward the middle of the twentieth century, with the more explicit extension of anger-control goals and mechanisms to public, and, particularly, to work, life. . . .

Although the consistent effort to come to terms with the home/work problem was the most central thread defining our periodization, the larger periods also reflect shifts in the precise nature and balance of other factors determining the anger-control campaign. Democratic sentiment, for example, if of a somewhat patronizing sort, helped inspire the burst of reform activity around 1900, which in turn helped justify anger's utility in fueling moral outrage. Specific cultural factors also entered in: the idealistic optimism of mainstream religion for the early Victorians, social Darwinism for the emphasis on channeling, and various schools of behavioral science for the shift to the management approach. The effect of particular events, such as World War II, or of unusual currents in movements for private as opposed to public rights, as in the feminist periods of the early twentieth century and again the late 1960s and the early

1970s, left a mark on emotionology. The world war encouraged particular concern about aggression, which fit the larger period just beginning but produced a distinctive tone in the literature of the 1940s and 1950s. Feminist and, in the 1960s, other rights agitation produced some efforts to bend prevailing consensus toward a somewhat greater tolerance of personal anger, particularly in the marital advice literature.

The major periods are not simply analytical tools for understanding the complexities of change. They also organize important questions about effect. In particular, the abandonment of the channeling idea and its replacement with a more pervasive effort to manage anger leads inexorably to a fresh look at the widespread sense that some basic features of the American personality have been changing in recent decades. The continuity with earlier goals need not be neglected, but the potential gap between using the fighting instinct as goad for achievement and attempting to talk away any strong anger is so great that it demands recognition. . . .

The second complexity in the modern history of anger standards, in addition to tension between periods and continuities, involves the persistent sense of ambivalence. In various ways—and the variety depended heavily on the period involved—the American campaign against anger seemed to leave loopholes, seemed indeed to court tension between controlling the emotion and seeking ways to express it.

Certainly, American emotionology did not produce the kind of single-minded concentration on reducing anger that anthropologists have discovered in some smaller cultures or that may exist even in more complex civilizations such as that of China.[14] Perhaps no Western society can do so if only because of the proximity of earlier traditions of greater spontaneity. It is tempting, moreover, to suggest a peculiarly American ambivalence even within a common Western frame. Frontier values; the kind of emotional distinction suggested in seventeenth-century Massachusetts between family and community, with anger restrained in one and released in the other, against relative strangers; the sheer diversity of the ethnic as well as class and gender cultures that had to be considered even in mainstream emotionology—all of these might suggest a particularly American tension.[15] We cannot insist on this conclusion yet, save for the comparative evidence on distinctive American socialization patterns regarding anger during the early decades of the twentieth century.[16] Until comparable work is done on the emotionology and experience of anger in other Western societies, and such work is eminently desirable, the "distinctively American" impulse must not be pressed too far.

But that there was tension and ambivalence in the American approach to anger cannot be denied. The ambivalence showed in the home/ work dichotomy of the early Victorians, which reduced the explicit coverage of anger-control recommendations without formally diluting them. Ambivalence was of course built into the channeling ideas of the late nineteenth and early twentieth centuries, and it is hard to avoid the feeling, confirmed by the comparative child-rearing studies between 1920 and 1950, that channeling reflected a peculiarly happy American compromise in which anger could be attacked yet used. Ambivalence, though less enshrined by formal advice, showed also in the anger patterns of many American women, whose behavior as girls typically reflected a double emotional standard that did not, however, persist consistently into adulthood—with the result that many docile girls turned into morally indignant adult women, in the best traditions of male channeling advice, and many more turned into periodically angry wives. Even in the contemporary period, in which the anger-control campaign greatly expands its coverage and works for consistency in goal and method, ambivalence remains. If contemporary American values strive so vigorously for anger control—and in most ways they do—why the odd anomaly of the emotional context of many schools? The anomaly results in part, without question, from empirical problems, including the diversity of actual emotional approaches represented in student and teacher populations. Efforts have been made, at least in theory, to bring school approaches to anger in line with the general socialization approach. But the efforts have not only shattered when they run against empirical problems; they have not been massively promoted even in theory, as if Americans are still willing to see schools as places where older anger approaches can hold sway or teenagers as a group to which contemporary anger values cannot fully apply.

During each emotionological period, in other words, including to some extent the present period, Americans tolerated, and at points encouraged, some confusing signals about anger. The extent of the ambivalence varied with each period, and it has unquestionably been reduced—again at least in theory—in the most recent decades. But some sense remains that Americans, even in their formal standards, have combined

321

a desire to constrain anger with some notion that the emotion is too useful, or simply too inevitable, to push constraint to the maximum. . . .

The Problem of Outlets

> I watched the Steelers lose football games every way you could think of and I never bitched. And I ain't no gambler neither. Never bet a penny on a football game. I just used to go to old Forbes Field every Sunday when the Steelers were home and it just brought out a lot of emotion in me I couldn't get rid of no other way.

> Those are men. Giants. And they're down there strugglin' and sweatin' and bleedin' and doin' a little war right there between those chalk stripes on the grass and I just found out I could whoop and holler my guts out and nobody would think I was nuts. It didn't make no difference to anybody else what I was really hollering about. People around me were all hollering too. I mean, it really helps you, brother, to reach down to your toes and pull out a yell you been keepin' bottled up inside you for Christ knows how long.[17]

. . . The problem of outlets goes far back in the American past. John Demos described, though did not definitively prove, the use of anger against neighbors in Plymouth colony as a deliberate compensation for unusual attention to restraint of familial anger. During the Victorian period, when dominant emotionology hoped for a thorough restraint of anger based on good character, norms remained sufficiently novel in the actual experience of many families that the need for new outlets did not necessarily increase. Nevertheless, the recurrent fear that families were being used for the venting of anger developed but not expressed in the workplace suggests a new or increasingly important outlet that ran counter to public standards.

The idea of channeling fairly directly addressed the problem of outlets. In using sports to divert anger, and in developing new opportunities for spectatorship that may have vented anger as well through intense partisanship, the later nineteenth century developed a durable outlet for expressing anger and enthusiasm that could not be safely displayed in ordinary life. Historians have been inventive, in recent years, in developing reasons for the inclusion of the rise of modern sports in serious social and cultural history; at the risk of overburdening the categories of analysis, it seems obvious that emotional functions play a vital role in the origins and maintenance of sports interests. Protest also served as an anger outlet. This is not to argue that the need to vent anger caused protest or determined its incidence. But protest was an emotional expression, and protest ritual, the celebratory atmosphere of much protest, owed much to the need to find legitimate outlet for intense emotion. "You ought to be out raising hell," said an old woman to a crowd of Colorado miners in 1916. "This is the fighting age. Put on your fighting clothes." Feminists, temperance advocates, Progressive reformers, could also use the righteous cause to express anger that they tried to restrain in daily life. And the prerogative of anger was not one-sided. Employers, faced with insubordinate workers, often indulged their rage fully, and possibly they, too, drew some private pleasure from their outbursts.[18]

The problem of anger outlets for the late nineteenth and early twentieth centuries is not, to be sure, exhausted by the invocation of approved channels such as sports or even righteous indignation. The need to express anger may have been one of the ingredients of imperialist enthusiasm and other efforts to identify foreign enemies against whom unrestrained venom could be safely expressed. For women, certainly, despite the good causes that attracted some, the problem of safe outlets for anger was particularly acute. Many women doubtless found familial anger an essential escape valve, though it generated anxiety as well as relief. Others took out anger on servants and shopkeepers. Others displaced anger through hysteria and tears.

The rise of the managerial approach to anger, and its extension to the workplace, raised the problem of outlets to new levels, at least for men. The diminution of work-based protest was partly compensated, for some, by the rise of other protest outlets, including resurgent feminism, urban riots, single-issue political passions, and the youth movements of the 1960s. Yet Barrington Moore's sense of a decline in moral indignation, in recent decades, seems justified on the whole. Certainly, politics has declined as an opportunity for displays of passion, with declining voting levels and a tendency to downgrade the level and quality of vitriol in political rhetoric; symptomatically, a number of observers have noted the deterioration of the imaginativeness of insults exchanged in the halls of Congress.[19] Even youth movements reflected unusual ambivalence about using anger frankly, as they typically masked genuine rage with flowery invocations of love; this is one reason that radicals of an older tradition found their efforts wanting.[20] The question of outlets, endemic in the campaign against anger from its inception, takes on new contours in our own day.

Where can the contemporary American get mad? Are his or her opportunities adequate to the task? In sketching some lines of inquiry, we cannot pretend precision; nor are we claiming that the outlets are new to our own day (many are definitely not) or that their increased utilization is clearly measurable.

The importance of the family, and probably particularly the contemporary family, as an outlet has been a theme throughout our inquiry. Women may still require this outlet particularly, as they have been found particularly likely to initiate family conflict. Men's anger, in family settings, is more likely to be displayed in a disengaged grumpiness or attacks on material objects.[21]

An important subset of familial anger, measurably more intense in recent decades, is divorce itself as a ritual that legitimizes the expression of anger. As divorce has become both more common and more accepted, it clearly serves as one of the few occasions during which intense personal anger can be legitimately expressed and sympathetically listened to by friends and colleagues. This ritual ventilation, in a society that normally shuns the angry person or urges him to talk his anger out as quickly as possible, gives divorce—like protest in earlier decades—an important emotional function.

Outside the family, anger at strangers has also taken on new features. The rise of public canons of tolerance has reduced the acceptability of ritual attacks on large groups of strangers—particularly, identifiable minorities within our society, including groups once defined as deviant, but also foreign enemies to some extent. The tendency—admittedly not unqualified—to favor laid-back political styles, as opposed to the give-'em-hell rhetoric of earlier decades, both illustrates and furthers the decline of ritual outlet through identifying with angry attacks on others. But anger against unknown individuals has probably increased in importance. In rage (sometimes in the form of private cursing and shouting) against automobile drivers, sports fans, or service workers such as sales clerks and waiters, contemporary Americans may find an important safety valve. The need to vent anger against unknown strangers may also, by extension, help explain the otherwise puzzling twentieth-century increase in crimes of violence, including crimes against women, after several decades in which violent crime rates declined or stabilized. It may also help explain the popularity of media violence and our willingness, however reluctant, to tolerate its availability for young viewers. In various aspects of popular culture, we may implicitly recognize the need for some safe targets or symbols of violence since we seek to deny anger in so many daily interactions.

Are neighbors, also, still a semilegitimate outlet for anger, as they were in colonial society? The history of American neighborliness has yet to be written, but it would probably reveal a rise in superficial friendliness—the suburban veneer—in which anger was supposed to play no overt role. This trend, if substantiated, would simply fuel the need for targets among strangers, even targets who remain oblivious to the fury directed toward them from behind a steering wheel.

There is also anger in law. Americans, unusually litigious by tradition, have increasingly come to believe that the civil suit is a justifiable expression of anger. The establishment of small claims courts in most states during the 1920s and 1930s, justified by the need for consumer and labor protection, displays an interesting chronological correspondence to the development of the managerial approach toward anger that heightened the desirability of legitimate outlets.[22] Of course, lawsuits involve important factors other than emotions and probably even among emotions more commonly reflect greed than anger. Furthermore, the actual pattern of small claims court activity shows a dominance of organizational attacks on individuals, particularly for debt collection; only in a minority of cases have the courts allowed individuals to express anger at the wrongs done them by other people or by faceless corporations.[23] Yet there has remained some belief that the lawsuit gives the "little man" an opportunity to vent legitimate indignation.[24] Article titles on the American penchant for litigation, such as "So You're Mad Enough to Sue" and "Dial V for Vengeance," enhance this impression and may genuinely give contemporaries, even when not directly involved, some sense that appropriate emotional outlets do still exist.[25]

The search for outlets for anger helps describe some important trends in twentieth-century American life. Yet in another example of the pervasive American ambivalence about anger, many of the outlets have themselves become increasingly qualified. Sports still serve for emotional display. But the rise of largely noncompetitive, private sports such as jogging, often deliberately designed to drain emotional tensions without any direct manifestation as well as to promote physical health, suggests a growing aversion to the turn-of-the-century interest in using sports to channel anger without destroying it. Still more generally, the privatization of much American leisure—the tendency to do one's spectating at home, in front of the television—raises serious questions about the continued adequacy of sports enthusiasms as an anger outlet. Divorce continues to supply occasions for explosions of anger, but the spread of no-fault procedures qualifies the occasion, at least in theory, by reducing the extent to which the procedure pits the wronged against the villain. Other litigation, as an anger outlet, already limited in fact by the dominance of organizational suits and the drawn-out procedures, has shown interesting constraints. Here, too, a growing tendency to out-of-court settlement and formal, nonadversarial arbitration procedures demonstrates a public desire to reduce the opportunities for public displays of righteous anger. An interesting number of individual litigants—46 percent in a 1976 study—simply never show up for trial, finding the trial too much trouble or (most commonly) seeing the initiation of a suit as a sufficient way to let off steam.[26] "I was really angry. I'd been gypped and there was nothing I could do. I guess I knew that all along. I think that suing him made me feel better. I guess I did it just to let off steam."[27] Initial anger released, such plaintiffs often discovered an inability to sustain their anger. While this inability owed something to cumbersome procedures and the power of the opposition, it also reflected the entry of the dominant contemporary emotional style: force a person to repeat his grievance often enough, and he will retreat, embarrassed.

The effort to develop acceptable outlets for anger—acceptable because legitimate or private or both—forms an important thread in modern American history, particularly the history of the last half century. The campaign against anger may have reduced the emotion. It certainly reduced its normal, daily outlets or within the family made anger's expression increasingly uncomfortable. Compensations that did develop, such as sports, might be deeply cherished in part because of their emotional role, but they veered toward the peripheries of ordinary activity. Some of the outlets were themselves hedged by the spreading discomfort with anger, with an attempt even by the individuals directly involved to opt for unemotional mediation or to settle for brief and hollow display.

There remains, of course, a final outlet, aside from pathological cases in which anger is vented in violent crime, perhaps in part because of the absence of more general channels. Anger can be expressed against self. Many nineteenth-century women invalids used this option. A number of twentieth-century workers, both male and female, discuss the extent to which they are encouraged, and encourage themselves, to turn irritation at mistakes or frustrations against themselves. A study of patterns of violence in nineteenth-century Philadelphia finds that, while attacks on others decline per capita, suicidal attacks on self increase. The rise of the adolescent suicide rate might suggest, among other factors, a particular confusion and guilt about perceived anger and an inability to justify targeting the emotion against others. The anger-against-self theme must *not* be taken as a facile explanation of suicide rates or as an effort to see these rates as symbolic of larger social trends. But the tendency to use self as target for milder anger seems undeniable, as Americans (more indeed than Europeans) find it increasingly necessary to express discontent and frustration as psychic problems. . . .[28]

NOTES

1. Benjamin Franklin, *Autobiography* (New York, 1962), pp. 29–30; Studs Terkel, *Working* (New York, 1974), pp. 289ff.; William H. Whyte, Jr., *The Organization Man* (New York, 1956), p. 152.

2. William Alcott, *The Young Husband* (Boston, 1840), pp. 287ff.; *Peterson's Magazine* 47, no. 6 (1865), p. 405.

3. Paul Popenoe, *Marriage Before and After* (New York, 1943), pp. 210–17.

4. "Can This Marriage Be Saved?" *Ladies Home Journal* 4 (April 1965), p. 36.

5. Hugh D. Graham and Ted R. Gurr, *Violence in America: Historical and Comparative Perspective*, rev. ed. (Beverly Hills, Calif., 1979). On particularly American anxieties about the association between democracy and violence, see David Brion Davis, *Homicide in American Fiction, 1789–1860: A Study in Social Values* (Ithaca, N.Y., 1957), pp. 239ff., 312. For an interesting, though ahistorical, comment on stereotypical American aggressiveness, see Rupert Wilkinson, *American Tough: The Tough-Guy Tradition and American Character* (Westport, Conn., 1984).

6. Carole Tavris, *Anger: The Misunderstood Emotion* (New York, 1982).

7. "The Sixth Deadly Sin," *New York Times,* March 16, 1983.

8. Christopher Lasch, *Haven in a Heartless World: The Family Besieged* (New York, 1977); Ronald Tyrrell, Frederick McCarty, and Frank Johns, "The Many Faces of Anger," *Teacher* 94 (February 1977), p. 60.

9. Joseph Veroff, Elizabeth Douvan, and Richard A. Kulka, *The Inner American: A Self Portrait from 1957 to 1976* (New York, 1981), pp. 106–21.

10. Randolph Trumbach, *The Rise of the Egalitarian Family: Aristocratic Kinship and Domestic Relations in Eighteenth Century England* (New York, 1978).

11. Abram de Swaan, "The Politics of Agoraphobia: On Changes in Emotional and Relational Management," *Theory and Society* 10 (1981), pp. 373 and passim, Richard Sennett, *The Fall of Public Man: On the Social Psychology of Capitalism* (New York, 1978).

12. Benjamin Nelson, *The Idea of Usury* (Chicago, 1969), pp. 139–63.

13. de Swaan, "Politics of Agoraphobia," pp. 370–71.

14. Jean L. Briggs, *Never in Anger: Portrait of an Eskimo Family* (Cambridge, Mass., 1970); Jeffrey Gray, *The Psychology of Fear and Stress* (New York, 1971); Richard Solomon, *Mao's Political Revolution and the Chinese Political Culture* (Berkeley, Calif., 1971); William Goode, "The Theoretical Importance of Love," *American Sociological Review* 24 (1959), pp. 38–47.

15. Jerome Kagan, "The Child in the Family," in *The Family,* ed. A. S. Rossi, J. Kagan, and T. Hareven (New York, 1978), pp. 33–56.

16. Leigh Minturn and W. W. Lambert, *Mothers of Six Cultures* (New York, 1953); Robert B. Sears, Eleanor Maccoby, and Harry Levin, *Patterns of Child Rearing* (New York, 1957); Joel R. Davitz, *The Language of Emotion* (New York, 1969).

17. K. C. Constantine, *The Man Who Liked Slow Tomatoes* (New York, 1983), pp. 85–86.

18. *New York Times,* Oct. 6, 1916 (quoted in " 'You Are too Sentimental': Problems and Suggestions for a New Labor History," Lawrence T. McDonnell, *Journal of Social History* 17 [1984], pp. 629–54); and see Tamara K. Hareven and Randolph Langenbach, *Amoskeag: Life and Work in an American Factory City* (New York, 1978), on employer anger.

19. Benjamin Barber, *Strong Democracy: Participatory Politics for a New Age* (Berkeley, 1984).

20. Christopher Lasch, *Haven in a Heartless World: The Family Besieged* (New York, 1977); Barrington Moore, Jr., *Injustice: The Social Bases of Obedience and Revolt* (New York, 1978), pp. 500–502.

21. James R. Averill, *Anger and Aggression: An Essay on Emotion* (New York, 1982); Mirra Komarovsky, *Blue-Collar Marriage* (New York, 1964); Jean Baker Miller, "The Construction of Anger in Women and Men," Stone Center for Developmental Services and Studies, Work in Progress no. 83-01 (Wellesley, Mass., 1983).

22. Robert E. Veto, "Anger in American Litigation" (seminar paper, Carnegie-Mellon University, Department of History, 1984); James F. Corbetter, "Activities of Consumers' Organizations," *Law and Contemporary Problems* 1 (1933), p. 61.

23. Barbara Yngvesson and Patricia Hennessey, "Small Claims, Complex Disputes: A Review of the Small Claims Literature," *Law and Society Review* 10 (1975), p. 221; Craig Wanner, "The Public Ordering of Private Relations: Initiating Civil Cases in Urban Trial Courts," *Law and Society Review* 10 (1975), pp. 422–23; Jerold S. Auerbach, *Justice without Law?* (New York, 1983), pp. 13 and elsewhere.

24. Bruce J. Graham and John R. Snortum, "Small Claims Court—Where the Little Man Has His Day," *Judicature* 29 (1977), p. 267; Marc Galanter, "Why the 'Haves' Come Out Ahead: Speculations on the Limits of Legal Change," *Law and Society Review* 10 (1975), p. 108.

25. "So You're Mad Enough to Sue," *Changing Times* (Oct. 1953), pp. 25–31; "Dial V for Vengeance," *Newsweek* (Jan. 26, 1970), p. 63.

26. Austin Sarat, "Alternatives in Dispute Processing: Litigation in a Small Claims Court," *Law and Society Review* 11 (1976), p. 344.

27. Ibid., p. 346; see also Laura Nader, ed., *No Access to Law: Alternatives to the American Judicial System* (San Diego, 1980).

28. de Swaan, "Politics of Agoraphobia," pp. 373–85.

The Stearnses' bold attempt to divide history into different phases of "anger control" must be controversial. Historians often do not like this sort of classification: history, for them, is less tidy. The Stearnses' basic argument, nonetheless, has a lot to be said for it. As they more or less recognized, their discussion of the fourth (contemporary) phase fits David Riesman's theory of a shift in American culture to "other-directed" manipulation (see pp. 50–69). It also ties into the rise of the "therapeutic relationship" described by Robert Bellah and others (p. 284). Give or take a few years, the Stearnses make sense of the fact that the style of liberal reformers has on the whole become cooler, less full of righteous wrath, than it was at the turn of the century. (The acutely personal nature of the abortion issue makes that area an exception.) From the 1930s on, few public reformers have displayed the combative moralism of Teddy Roosevelt, Hiram Johnson, or 'Fighting Bob' La Follette. On the other hand, what of the movie hero who bides his time and then gives a magnificent dressing-down to an obnoxious boss or weak-kneed allies—a model of controlled but effectively *channeled* anger. This formula has survived well into our own time. Is it just a movie fantasy, compensating for what Americans usually do *not* do but want to?

The Stearnses did not discuss this kind of thing because their research material was quite restricted. Their evidence came mainly from "advice literature"—domestic manuals on how to be a good parent or spouse, and (in the twentieth century) management literature on how to deal with employees. The authors were quite aware of the limits of this evidence, and they supplemented it with some reading of diaries, children's stories, divorce reports, and so on. They were also conscious that their sources were mainly middle class and Protestant: different classes and ethnic groups might well have their own norms for controlling and showing anger. They did not explore the matter, but unlike some other theorists of American character, they did not assume that middle-class norms would simply percolate through society.

Despite their virtues, the authors did not always handle their evidence well. *Anger* lacks the crispness of Peter Stearns's writing on European history, and it is not above evasive argument. On page 327 in the excerpt above, what *do* the authors mean when they suggest a link between anger control and teenage suicides and then seem to deny it? On page 325, likewise, they hint in heavy language that the "establishment of small claims courts" reflected a new "managerial approach to anger"; they then explain away the connection by acknowledging other reasons for creating the courts. In fact they give no good reason for saying, as they do, that Americans have sued each other more in recent decades. It is sometimes supposed that Americans became more litigious in the 1970s, but the American Bar Association has data that refutes this. The Stearnses do not use ABA data or any other statistics on trends in lawsuits.

But the main defect of the book is its handling of anger itself. The Stearnses say little about different *kinds* of anger—the distinction, for example, between rancor and a quick flare-up. At times indeed, they are quite insensitive to shades of feeling. In quoting the Steelers fan in the above excerpt, they imply that anger was the only emotion he was talking about. Clearly this was not so.

Here as elsewhere, the authors concentrate too much on anger in isolation from other feelings. They do say that modern American taboos on anger contrast with a general trend to emotional expressiveness. But they do not say much about this: they don't really explore the relation of anger to the way other feelings are treated. This belies their book's subtitle, "The Struggle for Emotional Control in America's History," which promises to cover more emotions than anger. Like other works on American character, the Stearnses' book is simultaneously wide ranging and restricted.

Ideas and Their Background

T his bibliography does two things. It covers a stream of writing that bears on modern American character, and it gives an intellectual background of the main authors and their writing reprinted here. Most of it, therefore, is grouped under these writers. Inevitably there is some overlap between the different sections. Works mentioned more than once are cited in abbreviated form after the first reference. All authors cited here are in the index: italicized page numbers in the index refer to the bibliography.

Despite the length and range of this bibliography, it is based on a narrow definition of national character than other bibliographies of the subject: it is more apt to exclude general interpretations of American society and culture that do not focus much on personal attitudes. Recent examples, which might be considered 'outriggers' to the study of American character, include, e.g., Richard M. Merelman, *Making Something of Ourselves: On Culture and Politics in the United States* (Berkeley and Los Angeles, 1984); John G. Blair, *Modular America: Cross-Cultural Perspectives on the Emergence of an American Way* (Westport, Conn., 1988); Jean Baudrillard, *America*, trans. Chris Turner, (New York, 1988); and even the kinds of 'ethnography' found in *Symbolizing America,* ed. Hervé Varenne (Lincoln, Nebr., 1986).

I have also found no real place here for studies that simply list American tendencies without saying much about their causes, e.g., Robin Williams, *American Society: A Sociological Interpretation* (New York, 1951, rev. ed. 1960), chap. 11 ("Value Orientations . . ."). Less happily I omit some journalistic forays that are not deeply analytical but have brilliant touches—my favorite is Jane Walmsley, *Brit-Think Ameri-Think: A Transatlantic Survival Guide* (London, 1986), with cartoons by Gray Jolliffe, which I have given as a courtesy training kit to Study Abroad advisers on campuses across the United States.

I should warn that books with "American Character" in their titles are not necessarily useful on that subject. D. W. Brogan, *The American Character*

(New York, 1956; a revised ed. of *The American Problem*, London, 1944) is not primarily on American character though it has some sharp insights here and there. Norman Vincent Peale, with William Thomas Buckley, *The American Character* (Wynwood, N.Y., 1985) is glossy propaganda.

Even by my own standards, though, this bibliography is not exhaustive; it is not based on computer searches. In the meantime, as the British like to say, it is 'enough to be getting on with.'

Other Bibliographies on American Character

As mentioned above, these list some works that I would not class under 'American character.' Michael McGiffert, "Selected Writings on American National Character," *American Quarterly* 15 (Summer 1963 Supplement), pp. 271–88, is divided into "Culture and Personality," "National Character: Concepts and Methods," "American Character," and "The Uses of National Character Studies." McGiffert's sequel in *American Quarterly* 21 (Summer 1969) goes up to 1969 and is organized the same way. A long selection from both is in *The Character of Americans: A Book of Readings*, ed. by McGiffert, rev. ed. (Homewood, Ill., 1970), pp. 416–25. All three are annotated and indicate which works have further, useful bibliographies. A more recent bibliography is in "Introduction: The Search for American Character," by Luther S. Luedtke, in *Making America: The Society and Culture of the United States*, ed. by Luedtke (Washington, D.C., 1987).

A number of studies cited in this volume have useful references for further reading—especially Christopher Lasch's last three books (see pp. 358, 360).

Approaches to National Character

For basic definitions and conceptions of 'national character,' see Rupert Wilkinson, *The Pursuit of American Character* (New York, 1988), pp. 3–4; George De Vos, "National Character," in *International Encyclopaedia of the Social Sciences*, vol. 11 (New York, 1968), pp. 14–19; Daniel Bell, "National Character Revisited" (1968) in *The Winding Passage: Essays and Sociological Journeys*, ed. by Bell (New York, 1980). Bell discusses the interplay between different meanings of national character, style, imagery, and identity. On two national-character conceptions—'modal' and 'basic personality'—see also Anthony F. C. Wallace, *Culture and Personality* (New York, 1961, rev. ed. 1970), chap. 4; Wallace, "Individual Differences and Cultural Uniformities," *American Sociological Review* 17 (1952), pp. 747–50. None of these writers clearly point out that 'modal personality' (a statistical concept) does not depend on comparisons with other populations.

Graphic distinctions between *culture* per se and national or social character are in "England Your England," by George Orwell (1941) in *The Collected Essays, Journalism and Letters of George Orwell*, ed. by Sonia Orwell and Ian Angus, vol. 2 (London, 1970); and more explicitly in "National Character," by Margaret Mead, in *Anthropology Today*, ed. by A. L. Kroeber (Chicago, 1953), p. 643. See also Jay Mechling, "If They Can Build a Square Tomato: Notes toward a Holistic Approach to Regional Studies," in *Prospects: An Annual of American Cultural Studies*, ed. by Jack Salzman, vol. 4 (1979).

On the development of different approaches to national character by historians and social scientists up to the 1950s, see David M. Potter, *People of Plenty: Economic Abundance and the American Character* (Chicago, 1950), pt. 1 ("The Study of National Character"); Margaret Mead, "The Study of National Character" in *The Policy Sciences*, ed. by Daniel Lerner and Harold Lasswell (Stanford, 1951), which focuses more closely on anthropologists; David Riesman, "The Study of National Character" (1958) in *Abundance for What? and Other Essays*, by Riesman (New York, 1964); Alex Inkeles and Daniel J. Levinson, "National Character: The Study of Modal Personality and Sociocultural Systems," in *Handbook of Social Psychology*, ed. by Gardner Lindzey and Elliott Aronson, vol. 4 (Reading, Mass., 1968), chap. 34—their historical section is better than their section on definitions. See also Margaret M. Caffrey, *Ruth Benedict: Stranger in This Land* (Austin, Tex., 1989), esp. chaps. 9, 10, 12, 13; cf. Ruth Benedict, *Patterns of Culture* (Boston, 1934), esp. her last two chapters: she is hesitant to extend character generalizations across classes in large, modern societies.

All good discussions of the national-character concept address 'subcultural' differences—e.g., differences of class or region. Specific studies of American subcultures in relation to national character are noted on pp. 364–67. Studies of American women, gender, and masculinity are cited, p. 351.

In general, too, good discussions of the concept recognize its pitfalls, while dividing into those that essentially endorse it and those that find it false, useless, and/or pernicious. On both sides much of the writing combines sophisticated thinking with some non sequiturs and red herrings. Favorable assessments go back through M. Ginsberg, "National Character," *British Journal of Psychology* 32 (1942), pt. 3, pp. 185–205, to Ernest Barker, *National Character and the Factors in Its Formation* (London, 1927). Both minimize racial-biological factors without wholly excluding them. Subsequent reviews of the field— favorable without being uncritical—include Maurice L. Farber, "The Problem of National Character: A Methodological Analysis," *Journal of Psychology* 30 (1950), pp. 307–16; H. C. J. Duiksher and N. H. Fridja, *National Character and*

National Stereotypes (Amsterdam, 1960); Don Martindale, *American Social Structure: Historical Antecedents and Contemporary Analysis* (New York, 1960), chap. 1; Washington Platt, *National Character in Action—Intelligence Factors in Foreign Relations* (New Brunswick, N.J., 1961); Walter P. Metzger, "Generalizations about National Character," in *Generalization in the Writing of History*, ed. by Louis Gottschalk (Chicago, 1963); and Gordon DiRenzo, "Theoretical and Methodological Perspectives on the Study of Social Character" in *We, the People: American Character and Social Change*, ed. by DiRenzo (Westport, 1977). Metzger, above, distinguishes the "Freudian model" from a "dramaturgical model" of national character.

Unfavorable assessments of national character as a general idea and as a research concept include Hamilton Fyfe, *The Illusion of National Character* (London, 1940), written from an antinationalist position; Alfred R. Lindesmith and Anselm L. Strauss, "A Critique of Culture-Personality Writings," *American Sociological Review* 15 (1950), pp. 587–600; David E. Stannard, "American Historians and the Idea of National Character," *American Quarterly* 23 (May 1971), pp. 202–20, reflecting attacks at the time on ideas of national 'consensus.' A recurring issue is whether national or social character has much continuity, a cultural momentum independent of immediate circumstances. See also Robert Colls and Philip Dodd, eds., *Englishness: Politics and Culture 1880–1920* (London, 1986) which tends, like Fyfe above, to see 'national character' as a stereotype politically imposed on diverse categories and classes of people. Cf. Theodore Zeldin, "Ourselves, as We See Us," *Times Literary Supplement* (London, Dec. 31, 1982), p. 1435.

Questions of evidence and research methods in studying national character recur throughout this volume. A good place to begin is Mead, "National Character" (1953). On comparative and statistical surveys, see pp. 349, 361–62. For differing views of popular literature and 'popular culture' as evidence, see Bruce Kuklick, "Myth and Symbol in American Studies," *American Quarterly* 24 (1972), pp. 435–50; Rupert Wilkinson, *American Tough: The Tough-Guy Tradition and American Character*, appendix (Westport, Conn., 1986); the pioneering study by Janice A. Radway, *Reading the Romance: Women, Patriarchy, and Popular Literature* (Chapel Hill, N.C., 1984); Elizabeth Long, *The American Dream and the Popular Novel* (Boston, 1985), chaps. 1, 2, 6, 7. In *Movies: A Psychological Study*, by Martha Wolfenstein and Nathan Leites (New York, 1950; with new 1977 preface) the methodological discussion is better than its actual comparison of American, British, and French movies. Cf. Richard Maltby, *"Film Noir:* The Politics of the Maladjusted Text," *Journal of American Studies* 18 (1984), pp. 49–71. For discussion and demonstration of other kinds of visual evidence, see Gregory Bateson and Margaret Mead, *Balinese Character: A Photographic Analysis* (New York, 1942); John A. Kouwenhoven, *The Beer Can by the Highway: Essays on What's 'American' about America* (New York, 1961); Wilkinson, *American Tough*, new Foreword and photo essays in the 1988 Harper ed.; and the use of art in Simon Schama, *The Embarrassment of Riches: An Interpretation of Dutch Culture in the Golden Age* (New York, 1987), with further discussion (including group differences and historical change) in Peter Burke's long review in the *London Review of Books* 9 (Nov. 12, 1987) and Jonathan Israel and Schama's exchange in the *Times Literary Supplement* (London, Nov. 20–26 and Dec. 4–10, 1987).

American Background

A number of cultural and intellectual histories give background to modern writing on American character and discuss some of that writing. They include Douglas Tallack, *Twentieth-Century America: The Intellectual and Cultural Context* (New York, 1991), which is influenced by 'post-modernist' literary-cultural theory; Christopher Brookeman, *American Culture and Society since the 1930s* (London, 1984), organized around major interpreters of the culture; Richard H. Pells, *The Liberal Mind in a Conservative Age: American Intellectuals in the 1940s and 1950s* (New York, 1985); Paul Blumberg, *Inequality in an Age of Decline* (New York, 1980), chaps. 1, 5, 6; Barbara Ehrenreich, *The Hearts of Men: American Dreams and the Flight from Commitment* (New York, 1983), a 'genderized' argument; and Long, *American Dream and the Popular Novel* (1985) on changing values in best-selling fiction between 1945 and 1975. Long's chapter 6 ("The Social Critics") is a fresh and trenchant discussion of some leading critics of American culture and character since World War II, analyzing their biases and shifts of perspective. Cf. Mark Krupnick, *Lionel Trilling and the Fate of Cultural Criticism* (Evanston, Ill., 1986), pp. 1–6. William Chafe, *The Unfinished Journey: America since World War II* (New York, 1986), gives a relevant history of the period, esp. in chaps. 5, 14, 15.

Only two book-length studies have provided a systematic history of writing on American character: Thomas L. Hartshorne, *The Distorted Image: Changing Conceptions of the American Character since Turner* (Cleveland, 1968), which goes to the 1950s; and Wilkinson, *Pursuit of American Character* (1988), which mainly covers the 1940s to 1980s. Wilkinson, "American Character Revisited," *Journal of American Studies* 17 (1983), pp. 165–87, analyzes the same period of writing in a different way. Clyde Kluckholn, ". . . Discernible Shifts in American Values during the Past Generation?" in *The American Style: Essays in Values and Performance*, ed. by Elting E. Morison (New York, 1948), reviews and summarizes studies in the 1940s and 1950s. Luedtke, "Search for American Character" (1987), reviews different strands in American-character studies, mainly from the 1930s, but neglects much of their critical thrust. On the jeremiad tradition in popular interpretations of America, see Denis Wrong, "The Paperbacking of the American Mind," *New York*

Times Book Review (Apr. 17, 1988); cf. Robert Reich, "Great Exhortations," *New York Times Book Review* (Jan. 3, 1988).

Hartshorne's book (above) explicitly excludes foreign commentators, so it needs to be supplemented with, e.g., *America through British Eyes*, ed. by Allan Nevins (New York, 1948), an anthology covering 1798 to 1940; see also many of the notes following Lipset's essay, pp. 129–31, and the bibliography in "Search for American Character," by Luedtke (1987), pp. 29–30. The epilogue to Roger Thompson, *The Golden Door: A History of the U.S.A. (1606–1945)* (London, 1969) starts with a hilarious and witty collection of postwar British anti-American stereotypes and then notes that many of these were what foreign observers were picturing in the nineteenth century. On continuity and change, going well back into American history, see also Lee Coleman, "What is American? A Study of Alleged American Traits," *Social Forces* 19 (1941), pp. 429–99, and Gabriel A. Almond, *The American People and Foreign Policy* (New York, 1950), chap. 3 ("American Character and Foreign Policy").

Both Coleman and Almond note that pairs of opposite traits have sometimes been attributed to American character. For differing views of this question of duality, see Cora DuBois, "The Dominant Value Profile of American Culture," *American Anthropologist* 57 (1955), pp. 192–99; Richard Hofstadter, "Commentary . . . Have There Been Discernable Shifts in American Values During the Past Generation?," in *American Style*, ed. by Morison (1958); John Higham, "The Cult of the American Consensus," *Commentary* 59 (1959), pp. 93–100; Michael Kammen, *People of Paradox: An Enquiry Concerning the Origins of American Civilization* (1972); cf. *The Contrapuntal Civilization: Essays toward a New Understanding of the American Experience*, ed. by Kammen (New York, 1971); Wilkinson, *American Tough* (1984), chap. 1. See also references in "American Character," by Wilkinson (1983), p. 174.

No one has written a full history of comments on American character before the 1890s, but cf. Perry Miller, *Nature's Nation* (Cambridge, Mass., 1967), chap. 1; John P. McWilliams, Jr., *Hawthorne, Melville and the American Character: A Looking-Glass Business* (Cambridge, U.K., 1984), Preface, Introd., Conclusion; and William R. Taylor, *Cavalier and Yankee: The Old South and American National Character* (Cambridge, Mass., 1961), esp. Introd., on the literature of American character and regional stereotypes before the Civil War. For three key, nineteenth-century writers, see J. Hector St. John Crèvecoeur, *Letters from an American Farmer* (London, 1782), written in the 1770s, possibly before the Revolution; Alexis de Tocqueville, *Democracy in America*, 2 vols. (Paris and London, 1835, 1840); Frederick Jackson Turner, esp. his papers/essays of 1893 and 1903 reprinted in Turner, *The Frontier in American History* (New York, 1920), chaps. 1, 9. On Tocqueville, see Abraham S. Eisenstadt, ed., *Reconsidering Tocqueville's* Democracy in America (New Brunswick, N.J., 1988), though several contributors exaggerate the difference between the book's two volumes. Cf. James Bryce, *The American Commonwealth*, 2 vols. (New York, 1894, 1895), which addresses many of Tocqueville's concerns while attending more to regional and class differences.

In the 1920s, several writers anticipated later discussions of conformity: see George Nathan and H. L. Mencken, *The American Credo: A Contribution toward the Interpretation of the American Mind* (New York, 1920); Hilaire Belloc, *The Contrast* (London, 1923), chap. 3; Sinclair Lewis's novel *Babbitt* (New York, 1922); and the great Dutch historian Johan Huizinga's *Man and the Masses in America* (1920) and *Life and Thought in America* (1926), reprinted in *America*, by Huizinga, (New York, 1972).

On 'mass society' in the ideas of the 'Frankfurt School' and others from before the 1940s, see Brookeman, *American Culture* (1984), esp. chaps. 5, 8; H. Stuart Hughes, *The Sea Change: The Migration of Social Thought, 1930–1965* (New York, 1975); Leon Bramson, *The Political Context of Sociology* (Princeton, 1961), esp. chaps. 2, 3, 5, 6; and Martin Jay, *The Dialectical Imagination: A History of the Frankfurt School and the Institute of Social Research, 1923–50* (London, 1973). Daniel Bell, "America as a Mass Society: A Critique" (1955) in *The End of Ideology*, by Bell (Cambridge, Mass., 1960) analyzes and criticizes different meanings of "mass society."

For views that stress Cold War influences on American-character writing more than I do (pp. 5–7), see Hartshorne, *Distorted Image* (1968), chap. 8; and the essay by Jackson Lears in *Recasting America: Culture and Politics in the Age of Cold War*, ed. by Lary May (Chicago, 1989); cf. the essay by Terence Ball, ibid. Stephen J. Whitfield, *A Critical American: The Politics of Dwight Macdonald* (Hamden, Conn., 1984) gives some political background; see also Allen F. Davis, "The Politics of American Studies," *American Quarterly* 42 (1990), pp. 353–74. A survival, or revival, of popular social-class criticism in the Cold War is *The Status Seekers: An Exploration of Class Behavior in America*, by Vance Packard (New York, 1959). For a rare 'Cold War' statement by a writer on American character, see Kouwenhoven, *Beer Can by the Highway* (1960), p. 219. Much of the Walgreen-Chicago story (p. 7n) is in *Unseasonable Truths: The Life of Robert Maynard Hutchins*, by Harry S. Ashmore (Boston, 1989), pp. 129–32; the rest is in the University of Chicago Library Special Collection. Cf. Ellen W. Schrecker, *No Ivory Tower: McCarthyism and the Universities* (New York, 1986).

World War II and Margaret Mead

Philip Gleason, "World War II and the Development of American Studies," *American Quarterly* 36 (1984), pp. 343–58, shows the wartime convergence of social-science studies of national character with democratic thought in the humanities. Another strand was the British and American study of fascism and personality going back to Harold Lasswell, "The Psychology of Hitlerism," *Political Quarterly* 4 (1933), pp. 373–84. Postwar products included Henry V. Dicks, "Personality Traits and National Socialist Ideology," *Human Relations* 3 (1950), pp. 111–53, and T. W. Adorno et al., *The Authoritarian Personality* (New York, 1950), a famous spinoff from the 'Frankfurt School.'

On anthropologists and national character in the war, see John W. Dower, *War Without Mercy: Race and Power in the Pacific War* (New York, 1986), chap. 6; Sheila K. Johnson, *American Attitudes toward Japan, 1941–1975* (Washington, D.C., 1975), pp. 1–7 and Conclusion, which rejects 'national character' less than the author thinks; and Margaret Mead, "Anthropological Contributions to National Policies . . ." in *The Uses of Anthropology*, ed. by Walter Goldschmidt (Washington, D.C., 1979).

Margaret Mead, *And Keep Your Powder Dry: An Anthropologist Looks at America* (New York, 1942) was shrewdly reviewed by her fellow anthropologists, Florence and Clyde Kluckholn, in *American Anthropologist* 45 (1943), pp. 622–24. Mead said more about peer groups ("age mates") in "Principles of Morale Building," by Gregory Bateson and M. Mead, *Journal of Educational Sociology* 15 (1941), pp. 206–20. *Powder Dry's* British Penguin edition was titled *The American Character* (Harmondsworth, 1944). In 1943, the U.S. Office of War Information enabled Mead to join her husband Gregory Bateson in England by sending her there as an expert on courtship patterns!—GIs and British women were misreading each other's signals. One result was a pamphlet by Mead, *The American Troops and the British* (London, 1944). Cf. her BBC talk, "Why We Americans Talk Big," *Listener* 30 (Oct. 28, 1943), p. 494. Outside the social sciences, too, World War II produced comparisons of American character with that of allies and enemies: e.g., Chester Wilmot, *The Struggle for Europe*, Reprint Society ed. (London, 1954), pp. 476–77, 515–17. Another aspect of Mead's wartime thinking was her internationalism; cf. Wendell Willkie, *One World* (New York, 1943).

On Mead's intellectual background and her path to wartime anthropology, see Rupert Wilkinson, "Journeys to American Character: Margaret Mead, David Potter and David Riesman," in *American Studies: Essays in Honour of Marcus Cunliffe*, ed. by Brian Holden Reid and John White (London, 1991), which also gives extensive references to writing on and by her, including her early pieces on America. It notes various tensions in her thought, including a dialectic between psychoanalysis and anthropology, and a contradiction between her perceptions of consumer diversity and standardization. Cf. Mead, *Blackberry Winter: My Earlier Years* (New York, 1972); Jane Howard, *Margaret Mead: A Life* (New York, 1984); Christopher Lasch, *Haven in a Heartless World: The Family Besieged* (New York, 1977), chap. 4 on Mead and others; and Caffrey, *Ruth Benedict* (1989) on Mead's great mentor and intimate.

For early influences on Mead, see also C. G. Seligman, "Anthropology and Psychology: A Study of Some Points of Contact," *Journal of the Royal Anthropological Institute* 54 (1924), pp. 13–46; and Franz Boas, *The Mind of Primitive Man* (New York, 1911). Cf. Richard Handlin, "Boasian Anthropology and the Critique of American Culture," *American Quarterly* 42 (June 1990), pp. 252–73. Mead's first book in her stream of writing on Polynesians (and American Indians) was *Coming of Age in Samoa: A Psychological Study of Primitive Youth for Western Civilization* (New York, 1928).

Mead's early interest in the immigrant factor in American culture was reflected in her article, "Group Intelligence Tests and Linguistic Disability among Italian Children," *School and Society* 25 (1927), pp. 465–68, based on her 1924 M.A. thesis. Some of her ideas can be read as a revision of Marcus Hansen, *The Problem of the Third Generation Immigrant* (Rock Island, Ill., 1938), though she does not mention him in *Powder Dry*. Cf. Hansen, *The Immigrant in American History* (Cambridge, Mass., 1940), esp. chaps. 4, 5. Donald Weber, "Reconsidering the Hansen Thesis: Generational Metaphors and American Ethnic Studies," *American Quarterly* 43 (1991), pp. 320–32, gives a guide to criticisms and appeals of the "Hansen thesis."

In the early postwar period, Mead's influence was reflected in *The American People: A Study in National Character*, by Geoffrey Gorer (New York, 1948) and in *Childhood and Society*, by Erik H. Erikson (New York, 1950), chap. 8 ("Reflections on the American Identity"). Erikson was a leader in studies of feelings about personal identity, a field that paralleled the growth of national-character studies. See Philip Gleason, "Identifying Identity: A Semantic History," *Journal of American History* 69 (1983), pp. 910–31. Allen Wheelis, *The Quest for Identity* (New York, 1958), and Hendrik R. Ruitenbeck, *The Individual and the Crowd: A Study of Identity in America* (New York, 1964), make somewhat shaky bridges between Erikson's ideas and those of David Riesman.

An update on Mead's picture of achievement-pressures on American children is *Miseducation: Preschoolers at Risk*, by David Elkind (New York, 1987).

Ralph Barton Perry and "Collective Individualism"

"The American Cast of Mind," Perry's chapter in his book, *Characteristically American* (New York, 1949), is one of several studies of American character in the 1940s that appear to be influenced by the rise of big organizations—including government—in the New Deal and World War II. All deal in different ways with tradition and modernity. A forebear of these was Robert S. Lynd, *Knowledge for What? The Place of Social Science in American Culture* (Princeton, 1939), chap. 3 ("The Pattern of American Culture"), a development from Robert S. and Helen Merrell Lynd, *Middletown in Transition: A Study in Cultural Conflicts* (New York, 1937). In the 1940s, cf. Arthur M. Schlesinger, Sr., "What Then Is the American, This New Man?" (1942–43), and "Biography of a Nation of Joiners" (1944–45) in *Paths to the Present*, by Schlesinger (New York, 1949); Ray R. Grinker and John P. Spiegel, *Men under Stress* (New York, 1945), chap. 20; Gardner Murphy, *Personality: A Biosocial Approach to Origins and Structure* (New York, 1947), esp. pp. 832–41; and Harold J. Laski, *The American Democracy* (London, 1949), esp. chaps. 1, 2, and pp. 714–20.

Perry's portraits of William James and Josiah Royce which preview his two sides of American character are in *In the Spirit of William James*, by Perry (New Haven, Conn., 1938), chap. 1. It undertakes the social-cooperative side of James's thought: cf. James, "The Moral Equivalent of War" (1910) in *Essays on Faith and Morals*, by James (New York, 1943). Perry's own internationalist idealism was expressed in the war in *Our Side Is Right* (Cambridge, Mass., 1942), which is much less nationalistic than the title sounds; and *One World in the Making* (New York, 1945). On America's puritan heritage and its modern connections, see Perry, *Puritanism and Democracy* (New York, 1944).

With regard to Perry's remarks on immigrant selection—what kind of people came—the biggest debate about migrant motives and attitudes has focused on early New England. Cf. Virginia DeJohn Anderson, "Migrants and Motives: Religion and the Settlement of New England, 1630–1640," *New England Quarterly* 58 (1985), pp. 339–83, with rejoinders by Robert Charles Anderson, David Grayson Allen, and Virginia Anderson again in *New England Quarterly* 59 (1986), pp. 406–24; Andrew Delbano, *The Puritan Ideal* (Cambridge, Mass., 1989); Roger Thompson, "Early Modern Migration," *Journal of American Studies* 25 (1991), pp. 61–69. On types and groups of migrants, see also T. H. Breen and Stephen Foster, "Moving to the New World: The Character of Early Massachusetts Immigration" (1973) in *Puritans and Adventurers*, by Breen (New York, 1980); and Roger Thompson, *Mobility, Migration and Modernization: East Anglian Founders of New England* (provisional title, forthcoming). Even if economic individualism was not important among early New England immigrants, it was more so further south. Perry's stress on the British origins of American culture is taken even further in David Hackett Fischer's recent book, *Albion's Seed: Four British Folkways in America* (New York, 1989). John Higham, *Send These to Me: Jews and Other Immigrants in Urban America* (New York, 1975) makes more of America's unusual ethnic mix, which Perry also recognized.

Perry's claim that American character has affected U.S. foreign policy is supported by Almond, *American People and Foreign Policy* (1950), and Stanley Hoffman, *Gulliver's Troubles, or the Setting of American Foreign Policy* (New York, 1968), esp. pp. 176–94.

David Riesman and The Lonely Crowd

David Riesman, with Nathan Glazer and Reuel Denney, *The Lonely Crowd: A Study of the Changing American Character* (New Haven, Conn., 1950) was followed by Riesman with Glazer, *Faces in the Crowd: Individual Studies in Character and Politics* (New Haven, 1952); see also Riesman, "Listening to Popular Music" (1950) in *Individualism Reconsidered and Other Essays*, by Riesman (New York, 1954). The prefaces to various editions of *The Lonely Crowd* (called *LC* below) and *Faces in the Crowd* give illuminating comments and afterthoughts on the work and its background. Riesman, "The Saving Remnant" (1949) in *Individualism Reconsidered*, by Riesman (1954) is a preliminary statement of the *LC* thesis but has some interesting differences from it. For Riesman's view of the Cold War climate just after *LC* was published, cf. "Individualism Reconsidered" (1951) and "Some Observations on Intellectual Freedom" (1953, with 1954 "Postscript"), ibid.

Wilkinson, "Journeys to American Character" (1991) explores Riesman's background and path to *LC* and gives many references to relevant writing by Riesman and others. Herbert Gans et al., eds., *On the Making of Americans: Essays in Honor of David Riesman* (Philadelphia, 1979) has a fairly comprehensive bibliography of Riesman's prolific publications (mainly essays) to 1978. It also contains a chapter by Joseph Featherstone, "John Dewey and David Riesman: From the Lost Individual to the Lonely Crowd." On the nature of Riesman's mind and writing, see Eric Larrabee, "David Riesman and His Readers," in *Culture and Social Character: The Work of David Riesman Reviewed*, ed. by Seymour Martin Lipset and Leo Lowenthal (New York, 1961); Lionel Trilling, "Two Notes on David Riesman" (1954) in *A Gathering of Fugitives*, by Trilling (New York, 1956); Bennett M. Berger, "David Riesman" (1965) in *Looking for America: Essays on Youth, Suburbia, and Other American Obsessions*, by Berger (Englewood Cliffs, N.J., 1971), pp. 319–21. See also Norman Mailer, "David Riesman Reconsidered" (1954) in *Advertisements for Myself*, by Mailer (New York, 1959), which makes a powerful criticism of Riesman; and Herbert Aptheker, "The Cadillac Credo of David Riesman," in *History and Reality*, by Aptheker (New York, 1955), which partly misreads him. Cf. Riesman, "Politics" in *Faces in the Crowd*, by Riesman with Glazer (1952), chap. 2.

For precursors and inspirations of *LC*, see that book's notes, p. 65 (nn. 4 and 5); also Max Weber, *The Protestant Ethic and the Spirit of Capitalism* (New York, 1930; orig. pub. in German, 1904–05); Erich Fromm, *Escape from Freedom* (New York, 1941); Arnold W. Green, "Why Americans Feel Insecure," *Commentary* 6 (July 19, 1948), pp. 18–28, which implicitly connects some of Margaret Mead's ideas to those of Riesman. Also Leo Lowenthal, "Biographies in Popular Magazines," in *Radio Research 1942–43*, ed. by Paul Lazarsfeld and Frank Stanton (New York, 1944), criticized by Fred I. Greenstein, "New Light on Changing American Values: A Forgotten Body of Survey Data," *Social Forces* 42 (1964), pp. 441–50.

An influence on Nathan Glazer was the study of Madagascar by Abram Kardiner and Ralph Linton in *The Individual and His Society: The Psychodynamics of a Primitive Social Organization* (New York, 1939), by Abram Kardiner, esp. chaps. 7, 8—a rare mixture of economic history with the anthropology of 'culture and personality.' Like *LC* later, it distinguished a "scarcity culture" from a nonscarcity culture and looked at change from one to the other. (In *LC*, anthropology itself appears most obviously in the book's chapter contrasting two American Indian cultures in comparison with American character. At one point Riesman had thought of calling the book "The Continental Pueblo.")

The initial concerns and ideas that governed the *LC* research are stated in Riesman's important memo to C. Wright Mills, "A Suggestion for Coding the Intensive White Collar Interviews," Mills Papers (University of Texas Library, Austin, Feb. 5, 1948); "Research News" column, *International Journal of Public Opinion and Attitude Research* 2 (1948), p. 305; Riesman and Glazer, "Social Structure, Character Structure and Opinion," ibid. (1949), pp. 512–17; and Riesman and Glazer, "The Meaning of Opinion" (1949) in *Individualism*, by Riesman (1954). Some of their data was used rather differently by C. Wright Mills, *White Collar: The American Middle Classes* (New York, 1951). Cf. Richard Gillam, "*White Collar* from Start to Finish," *Theory and Society* 10 (1981), pp. 1–30.

Wilkinson, "Journeys" (1991) says more about *LC*'s two-edged relation to the Frankfurt School and to the sociology of group opinion. It refers to some other key studies that addressed or used both approaches. Cf. Bramson, *Political Context of Sociology* (1961), chap. 5, and David Riesman with Evelyn T. Riesman, "Movies and Audiences" (1952) in *Individualism*, by Riesman (1954).

Some of the commentary on *LC* was collected by Lipset and Lowenthal, eds., *Culture and Social Character* (1961). It included the extensive psychological study by Elaine Graham Sofer, "Inner-Direction, Other-Direction, and Autonomy: A Study of College Students," which used questionnaires and other, subtler psychological tests including Rorschach. Sofer's results suggested, among other things, that people who scored very high on 'other-direction' tended to have a weak sense of self which made them other-dependent rather than highly *aware* of others.

For a lucid view of other-directed behavior as *role-playing*, and the question of how far the roles are embedded in personality, see Metzger, "Generalizations about National Character" (1963), pp. 90ff. Cf. Sheldon L. Messinger and Burton R. Clark, "Individual Character and Social Constraint" in *Culture and Social Character*, ed. by Lipset and Lowenthal (1961); Fromm, *Escape from Freedom*, Routledge ed. (titled *The Fear of Freedom*) (1960), pp.

168ff; Robert Jungk, *Tomorrow is Already Here: Scenes from a Man-made World* (London, 1954), pp. 201–202; Michael Moffatt, *Coming of Age in New Jersey: College and American Culture* (New Brunswick, N.J., 1989), pp. 40–45.

For general historical criticisms of the *LC* thesis, see Lipset, "A Changing American Character?" (pp. 98–133); and Carl N. Degler, "The Sociologist as Historian: Riesman's *The Lonely Crowd,*" *American Quarterly* 15 (1963), pp. 483–97, rebutted by Cushing Strout in *American Quarterly* 16 (1964), pp. 100–102. Hartshorne, *Distorted Image* (1968), chap. 9, reprinted in *Character of Americans,* ed. by McGiffert (1970), defends *LC* against Lipset and Degler. For nineteenth-century perspectives, see also Lawrence Frederick Kohl, *The Politics of Individualism: Parties and the American Character* (New York, 1989); Karen Haltunen, *Confidence Men and Painted Women: A Study of Middle-Class Culture in America, 1830–1870* (New Haven, 1982), esp. pp. 34–35, 201–203; Sally Foreman Griffith, *Home Town News: William Allen White and the* Emporia Gazette (New York, 1989), e.g., pp. 30–31; Booker T. Washington, *Up From Slavery* (1901) in *Three Negro Classics,* ed. by John Hope Franklin (New York, 1965), pp. 75–76; and Michael Moffatt, *The Rutgers Picture Book: An Illustrated History of Student Life in the Changing College and University* (New Brunswick, N.J., 1985), e.g., pp. 52–53, on peer groups and authority figures.

Some historical studies of attitudes to consumption and leisure are relevant to *LC.* They include Neil McKendrick et al., *The Birth of a Consumer Society: The Commercialization of Eighteenth-Century England* (London, 1982); Rosalind Williams, *Dream Worlds: Mass Consumption in Late-Nineteenth-Century France* (Berkeley and Los Angeles, 1982); Daniel Horowitz, *The Morality of Spending: Attitudes toward the Consumer Society in America, 1875–1940* (Baltimore, 1985), which reaches back much earlier than 1875 and has an extensive bibliography; Richard Wightman Fox and T. J. Jackson Lears, eds., *The Culture of Consumption: Critical Essays in American History 1880–1980* (New York, 1983); Thorstein Veblen, *The Theory of the Leisure Class* (New York, 1899); Simon N. Patten, *The New Basis of Civilization* (New York, 1907); Patten, "The Standardization of Family Life," *Annals of the American Academy of Political and Social Science* 48 (1913), pp. 81–90; Daniel M. Fox, *The Discovery of Abundance: Simon N. Patten and the Transformation of Social Theory* (Ithaca, N.Y., 1967); Daniel T. Rodgers, *The Work Ethic in Industrializing America 1850–1920* (Chicago, 1974), chap. 4 ("Play, Repose, and Plenty"); Robert S. Lynd with Alice C. Hanson, "The People as Consumers," in U.S. President's Research Committee on Social Trends, *Recent Social Trends,* vol. 2 (New York, 1933), chap. 17 on trends to the 1920s; Lizabeth Cohen, "Encountering Mass Culture at the Grass Roots: The Experience of Chicago Workers in the 1920s," *American Quarterly* 41 (1989), pp. 6–33. On World War II's empowering of a new "teen culture"—Riesman's adolescent "peer groups"—see Steven Mintz and Susan Kellog, *Domestic Revo-*

lutions: A Social History of American Family Life (New York, 1988), pp. 166–67.

Some assessments of *LC*'s historical arguments have examined trends in popular-advice literature and children's readers. They include Richard DeCharms and Gerald H. Moeller, "Values Expressed in American Children's Readers: 1800–1950," *Journal of Abnormal and Social Psychology* 64 (1962), pp. 136ff, which also looks at rates of patents issued as an index against which to compare "achievement imagery"; Forrest J. Berghorn and Geoffrey H. Steere, "Are American Values Changing?" *American Quarterly* 18 (1964), pp. 52–61, which also compared questionnaire responses from school students and their parents as a (dubious) measure of historical change; and Marshall Graney, "Role Models in Children's Readers," *School Review* 85 (1977), pp. 247–63. Cf. Martha Wolfenstein, "The Emergence of Fun Morality," *Journal of Social Issues* 7 (1951), pp. 15–23, which studied infant-care bulletins, 1914–45; among other things, it illuminated *LC*'s other-directed character by suggesting that "gratification" had been extended into all of life but was thereby diluted. See also Warren Susman, " 'Personality' and the Making of Twentieth-Century Culture" (1977) in *New Directions in American Intellectual History*, ed. by John Higham and Paul Conkin (Baltimore, 1979)—very 'Riesman' but shamefully does not mention him. An engaging piece of front-porch 'fieldwork' on *LC* is Gregory Stone's study of Halloween (pp. 88–96).

Studies of advertising that bear on *LC*'s claims include Sanford M. Dornbusch and Lauren C. Hickman, "Other-Directedness in Consumer-Goods Advertising: A Test of Riesman's Historical Theory," *Social Forces* 38 (1959), pp. 99–102, based on the *Ladies Home Journal*, 1890–1956; Nicholas Somers, "A Comparative Study of Advertising as a Reflection of American Society in the Twenties," undergraduate Extended Essay (American Studies, Sussex University, 1970), based on the *Saturday Evening Post* in 1905 and 1925; and Roland Marchand, *Advertising the American Dream: Making Way for Modernity, 1920–1940* (Berkeley and Los Angeles, 1985).

Fictional suggestions of other-direction, or its prototypes, can be found, e.g., in *Ragged Dick*, by Horatio Alger (Boston, 1869); Henry James, *The Bostonians* (London, 1886); Theodore Dreiser, *Sister Carrie* (New York, 1900); Edith Wharton, *The House of Mirth* (New York, 1905); Saul Bellow, *The Victim* (New York, 1947); Ella Leffland, *Rumors of Peace*, Harper Colophon paperback ed. (New York, 1985), pp. 287–89, 301 (based on a World War II girlhood). Cf. Rachel Bowlby, *Just Looking: Consumer Culture in Dreiser, Gissing and Zola* (New York, 1985).

William H. Whyte, Jr., and Corporate-Suburban Life

In addition to its sections on corporation and suburban culture, *The Organization Man,* by Whyte (New York, 1956) has chapters on scientists and foundations, a superbly written chapter on attitudes to Herman Wouk, *The Caine Mutiny* (New York, 1951), and a sabotaging appendix, "How to Cheat on Personality Tests." The book is a development from Whyte and the editors of *Fortune—Is Anybody Listening? How and Why U.S. Business Fumbles When It Talks with Human Beings* (New York, 1952), with brilliant sociological cartoons by Robert Osborne. See also Whyte, "How Hard Do Executives Work?" in *The Executive Life,* by *Fortune* eds. (New York, 1956).

Current Biography (Princeton, 1959), pp. 482–83, gives a background to Whyte and *The Organization Man.* Pells, *Liberal Mind in a Conservative Age* (1985), chap. 4, gives cultural and political background; its discussion of other writers includes David Riesman, and it shows that Daniel Bell had a minor key of radical criticism somewhat like Whyte's. Cf. Bell, "Work and Its Discontents" (1947, rev. ed. 1956) in *The End of Ideology,* ed. by Bell (Cambridge, Mass., 1962). Whyte's use of the phrase "Protestant ethic" comes ultimately from Weber, *Protestant Ethic and the Spirit of Capitalism* (1904–1905, trans. 1930).

Some assessments of Riesman's historical argument, cited in the section above, are explicitly applied to Whyte's too. In line with his thesis, Carol Zisowitz Stearns and Peter N. Stearns, *Anger: The Struggle for Emotional Control* (Chicago, 1986), chap. 5, gives evidence that manipulation (or just plain 'good management') has replaced barking and bullying as prescribed managerial behavior.

Whyte's own survey supported his proposition that organization-man conformity correlated with size of organization: *Organization Man,* Simon and Schuster Clarion ed. (1972), pp. 76–77. Survey research by Melvin L. Kohn, "Bureaucratic Man," *American Sociological Review* 36 (1971), pp. 461–74, found the opposite. Wilkinson, *Pursuit of American Character* (1988), pp. 42, 125 (n. 6), discusses the two studies' different criteria and the possibility of change between their two eras. (Whyte's study actually compared college seniors headed for different sizes of organization.)

In decades since the 1950s, some commentary on executive character that stresses a variety of other types besides Whyte's or claims it is disappearing still concurs that it dominated at the time he wrote. See Michael Maccoby, *The Gamesman: The New Corporate Leaders* (New York, 1976), which may overgeneralize from high-tech executives; and Amanda Bennett, *The Death of the Organization Man* (New York, 1990), whose interview research found the patient going strong well into the 1970s. For an earlier sense of alternatives, see Walter Guzzardi, "The Young Executive" series of articles, *Fortune* (June, July, Sept., Oct. 1964). Max Lerner, *America as a Civilization,* vol. 2 (New

York, 1957), chap. 9 ("Varieties of American Character"), sec. 4, defined a range of middle-class types, formed mainly in response to bureaucracy, marketing, and a fragmented, mass society—several of them overlapped Whyte's conformer. Sloan Wilson's novel, *The Man in the Gray Flannel Suit* (New York, 1955), is often considered a close fictional parallel of Whyte's book, but although it values a good family life in the suburbs, most of its leading characters are explicitly *anti*–organization man.

Whyte's chapters on the Park Forest suburb mount a sophisticated discussion (see esp. chap. 26), though in a session held by Whyte and David Riesman with Park Foresters afterward, many of them said that Whyte had distorted their attitudes (DR letter to RW, Nov. 14, 1983). For various views of suburban character and stereotypes in the 1950s and 1960s, see Riesman, "The Suburban Dislocation" (1957) and "Flight and Search in the New Suburbs" (1959) in *Abundance for What?* by Riesman (1964); also "The Found Generation" (1956), ibid.; William A. Dobriner, ed., *The Suburban Community* (New York, 1958), chaps. by Sylvia Feis Flava and Ernest R. Mowrer; Bennett M. Berger, "The Myth of Suburbia" (1961) and "Suburbs, Subcultures and Styles of Life" (1965) in *Looking for America*, by Berger (1971); Berger, *Working-Class Suburb: A Study of Auto Workers in Suburbia* (Berkeley, 1960); Scott Donaldson, *The Suburban Myth* (New York, 1969); Pells, *Liberal Mind in a Conservative Age* (1985), pp. 196–200. On changes since that time, see the cogent article by Nicholas Lemann, "Stressed Out in Suburbia," *Atlantic* (Nov. 1989).

On the relation between community and conformity, Whyte and Erich Fromm conducted a distended debate, citing each other: Whyte, "The Transients" article series, *Fortune* (May, June, July, Aug. 1953); Fromm, *The Sane Society,* 1963, Routledge paperback ed. (New York, 1955), pp. 110–21, 154–63, 283ff., 306ff.; Whyte, *Organization Man,* (1956), Simon and Schuster Clarion ed. (1972), pp. 361–62; Peter Biskind, *Seeing Is Believing: How Hollywood Taught Us to Stop Worrying and Love the Bomb* (New York, 1983) explores subtle and unsubtle endorsements of conformity in movies of the 1950s; his concluding chapter is on "coming apart"—to the right and left—in movies of the 1960s.

Gregory P. Stone and the Meaning of Masks

Stone, "Halloween and the Mass Child," *American Quarterly* 11 (1959), pp. 373–79, was reprinted in *The American Culture: Approaches to the Study of the United States,* ed. by Hennig Cohen (Boston, 1968). The reprint carried a brief "afternote" that cited support from two other studies and a news item; it also told most of Howard Becker's story (pp. 96–97) but literally watered it down—in fact, the water pistol carried *ink!* Dave Barry's funny piece, "It

Wouldn't Be Halloween If the Eyeholes Lined Up," *International Herald Tribune* (Oct. 26, 1988; syndicated, Knight-Riddler newspapers) mainly supports Stone, but not entirely.

In essentially supporting Riesman's *Lonely Crowd* thesis, Stone's essay had some similarities with Don Martindale's *Community, Character and Civilization: Studies in Social Behaviorism* (New York, 1963), pt. 4, chaps. 8, 9, which saw a "Yankee" type giving way to one more attuned to the consumer technology of the "packaged suburb."

Stone's historical thinking about children, play, and costume drew from Philippe Ariès, *Centuries of Childhood: A Social History of Family Life* (Paris, 1960; London, 1962)—cited elsewhere in Stone's writing—as well as *The Lonely Crowd.* In his own field of "symbolic interaction," Stone acknowledged the influence of the sociologists Herbert Blumer and G. H. Mead. His own writing in this field includes Stone and William H. Form, *The Local Community Shopping Market: A Study of the Social and Psychological Contexts of Shopping* (East Lansing, Mich., 1957); Stone, "Clothing and Social Relations: A Study of Appearance in the Context of Community Life" (doct. diss., Sociology Dept., Chicago, 1959); Stone, "Appearance and the Self," in *Human Behavior and Social Processes,* ed. by Arnold M. Rose (Boston, 1962), chap. 5; Stone, "Clothing," *Encyclopaedia International,* vol. 4 (New York, 1963), pp. 505–509; and several chapters in *Social Psychology through Symbolic Interaction,* ed. by Stone and Harvey Faberman, 2d ed. (New York, 1981). In Arnold Rose's book just cited, Rose starts with a summary of the main tenets of "symbolic interaction theory." On status signals through appearance, cf. Vance Packard, *Status Seekers* (1959).

Seymour Martin Lipset and International Comparisons

Lipset's essay, "A Changing American Character?" is from his book, *The First New Nation: The United States in Historical and Comparative Perspective* (New York, 1963), chap. 3. The book's 1979 Norton edition has a new and long, updating introduction. The full book notes to Lipset's essay on American character contain many historical and sociological commentaries. An earlier version of the essay appeared in *Culture and Social Character,* ed. by Lipset and Lowenthal (1961).

The essay was written as a qualified rebuttal to Riesman, *Lonely Crowd* (1950), and Whyte, *Organization Man* (1956), and also to 'materialist' explanations of history in Marxism. In the book's original introduction citing Friedrich Engels *against* purely economic explanations of behavior, he quoted Engels, *Socialism, Utopian and Scientific,* Kerr ed. (Chicago, 1912), pp. 37–43.

Lipset's autobiographical essay, "Socialism and Sociology" in *Sociological Self-Images,* ed. by Irving Louis Horowitz (Beverly Hills, Calif., 1969), pp.

145–76, explores some of the personal, political, and intellectual background of his writing; it is a fascinating narrative. His early thinking about political parties and authoritarian leadership was influenced by the more pessimistic Robert Michels, *Political Parties: A Sociological Study of the Oligarchic Tendencies of Modern Democracy* (New York, 1915). Cf. Lipset et al., *Union Democracy: The Internal Politics of the International Typographical Union* (Glencoe, Ill., 1956). His interest in the social-psychological bases of political movements emerged in several essays in *Political Man: The Social Bases of Politics*, by Lipset (New York, 1960); two chapters in *The Radical Right*, ed. by Daniel Bell (New York, 1963), including a 1955 essay; and later, Lipset and Earl Raab, *The Politics of Unreason: Right-Wing Extremism in America 1790–1970* (New York, 1970).

As I suggested in my comments on Lipset's essay (pp. 131–33), he brought together two strands of thought about conformity in America. The first, stressing status-conformity ('I want to be like you'), appeared in some of the sparkling, knockabout prose of Nathan and Mencken, *American Credo* (1920); more briefly in *The American: The Making of a New Man*, by James Truslow Adams (New York, 1943), p. 374, which also anticipated some of Riesman's "inside-dopester"; and in "American Core Value and National Character," by Francis L. K. Hsu, in *Psychological Anthropology*, ed. by Hsu (Homewood, Ill., 1961), chap. 7, reprinted in *Character of Americans*, ed. by McGiffert (1970). The second strand, stressing a 'get on the team' pressure, is in "American Cast of Mind," by Perry (1949), excerpted pp. 33–47; and Laski, *American Democracy* (1949). At the end of his American-character essay, Lipset quotes the proposition by Kluckhohn, "American Values" (1958), that external conformity can free a person for personal fulfillment and development. This echoes Sinclair Lewis, *Babbitt* (1920), in which the radical Seneca Doane distinguishes between "standardized" behavior that "leaves me more time and money to be individual in"—a pattern just as common in England—and "standardization of thought." See pp. 84–85 in the 1961 Signet ed. My student Iain Wilson points out to me that the Kluckhohn-Lipset proposition is close to the ideal of "Autonomy" in Riesman's *Lonely Crowd*.

Lipset's longtime interest in comparing the United States, and its relative lack of socialism, with other industrial democracies is reflected in Lipset's book on the Canadian CCF Party, *Agrarian Socialism: The Cooperative Commonwealth Federation in Saskatchewan* (Berkeley and Los Angeles, 1950); Lipset and Reinhard Bendix, *Social Mobility in Industrial Society* (Berkeley and Los Angeles, 1959), esp. chap. 3 ("Ideological Equalitarianism and Social Mobility in the United States"); Lipset, *First New Nation* (1963), pt. 3; and Lipset, *The Continental Divide: The Values and Institutions of the United States and Canada* (Toronto, 1989; New York, 1990), which explains more explicitly than *First New Nation* why Canada has more socialism *and*, in a sense, more conservatism. Lipset's 'exceptionalist' stress on an American 'non-feudal' past (exaggerated in some views) owes something to Louis Hartz, *The Liberal Tradition in America: An Interpretation of American Thought since the Revolution* (New York, 1955). Cf. Hartz et al., *The Founding of New Societies: Studies in the History of the United States, Latin America, South Africa, Canada and Australia* (New York, 1964).

Statistical, comparative-attitude surveys that bear on American character—some of them mentioned by Lipset—includes Maurice L. Farber, "English and Americans: A Study in National Character," *Journal of Psychology* 32 (1951), pp. 241–49; Farber, "English and Americans: Values in the Socialization Process," ibid. 36 (1953), pp. 243–50; David C. McClelland, *The Achieving Society* (Princeton, 1961); McClelland, *The Roots of Consciousness* (Princeton, 1964); Gabriel A. Almond and Sidney Verba, *The Civic Culture: Political Attitudes and Democracy in Five Nations* (Princeton, 1963); George Katona et al., *Aspirations and Affluence: Comparative Studies in the United States and Western Europe* (New York, 1971); Alan J. Stern and Donald H. Searing, "The Stratification Beliefs of English and American Adolescents," *British Journal of Political Science* 6 (1976), pp. 177–203; Ronald Inglehart, *The Silent Revolution: Changing Values and Political Styles among Western Publics* (Princeton, 1977); Geert Hofstede, *Culture's Consequences: International Differences in Work-Related Values* (Beverly Hills, Calif., 1981); James Q. Wilson, *Bureaucracy: What Government Agencies Do and Why They Do It* (New York, 1989), chap. 16 ("National Differences"). See also Alex Inkeles, "Continuity and Change in the American National Character" in *The Third Century: America as a Post-Industrial Society,* ed. by Lipset (Stanford, Calif., 1979), which discusses a number of international comparisons.

Some of the statistical studies cited above are of two countries; others are of a number of industrial democracies; still others include a larger range of societies. None of them makes a clear-cut statement on American character tendencies; not all give causal explanations; and they vary in rigor and depth. But here and there one can glean important findings, especially on individualism and attitudes to social involvement.

Nonquantitative comparisons include Daniel Snowman, *Britain and America: An Interpretation of British and American Culture, 1945–1975* (New York, 1977; British title, *Kissing Cousins*), which makes unusual bridges between earlier and later writers in this period; Wilkinson, *American Tough* (1984), pp. 110–18, which compares five traditions of personal strength; and John Harmon McElroy, *Finding Freedom: America's Distinctive Cultural Formation* (Carbondale, Ill., 1989), a historical comparison with Canada and Latin America. See also Martin Green, *A Mirror for Anglo-Saxons: A Discovery of America, a Rediscovery of England* (New York, 1957), a semiautobiographical musing, quite good on subcultural variations. On British individualism and other foreign points of reference, see also p. 352.

David M. Potter: *From the American South to American Individualism*

(These references and comments predate the opening of the Potter Papers at Stanford University Library, due in 1991.)

Wilkinson, "Journeys to American Character" (1991) says more about Potter's mind and background; it argues that Potter's ambivalent involvement with the study of American character went through four phases. It also gives extensive references to writing on and by Potter, including economic history. For a comprehensive list of his publications (he died in 1971), see Potter, *Freedom and Its Limitations in American Life*, essays ed. by Don E. Fehrenbacher (Stanford, 1976), bibliog. by George Harmon Knowles (incl. major reviews of Potter's books). Many of his essays are collected in Potter, *The South and the Sectional Conflict* (Baton Rouge, La., 1968) and *History and American Society: Essays of David M. Potter*, ed. by Fehrenbacher (New York, 1973).

Both of Potter's two history books on the North-South conflict discuss whether cultural attitudes were important. See Potter, *Lincoln and His Party in the Secession Crisis* (New Haven, Conn., 1942), esp. 1962 Preface, and *The Impending Crisis, 1848–1861,* completed and ed. by Don E. Fehrenbacher (New York, 1976), esp. pp. 44–48. Writing on the South by others who may have influenced his social-character ideas includes John Dollard, *Caste and Class in a Southern Town* (New Haven, 1937); W. J. Cash, *The Mind of the South* (New York, 1941); and Liston Pope, *Millhands and Preachers: A Study of Gastonia* (New Haven, 1942). Some of his later thinking about American character was previewed by his long, factual introduction to *Trail to California: The Overland Journal of Vincent Geiger and Wakeman Bryarly*, ed. by Potter (New Haven, 1945), discussed by Wilkinson, "Journeys" (1991).

Potter, *People of Plenty: Economic Abundance and the American Character* (Chicago, 1954) derives from six Walgreen Foundation lectures prepared in the summer and fall of 1950 and given the same year at the University of Chicago. Part 1 of the book includes a rather forced attempt to incorporate into his theory of American abundance the ideas of Karen Horney, *The Neurotic Personality of Our Time* (New York, 1937); Mead, *And Keep Your Powder Dry* (1942); and Riesman et al., *Lonely Crowd* (1950). Potter's book has received extended criticism from Stannard, "American Historians and the Idea of National Character" (1971), and Robert M. Collins, "David Potter's *People of Plenty* and the Recycling of Consensus History," *Reviews in American History* 16 (1988), pp. 321–335. On the matter of its Cold War background, cf. Potter, "The Marshall Plan and American Foreign Policy," *Current Affairs* (London, Feb. 21, 1948), esp. p. 6; *People of Plenty*, pp. 117ff. and chap. 6. A subsequent article by Potter, "The American Economic System" in *An Outline of Man's Knowledge of the Modern World*, ed. by Lyman Bryson (New

York, 1960) was reprinted as a pamphlet by the U.S. Information Service (London, n.d.).

In a long, 1968 interview with the historian John A. Garraty, Potter reflected on *People of Plenty,* including its relation to previous work by American historians and the experience of poverty amid affluence in America. See the abridged interview in *Interpreting American History: Conversations with Historians,* ed. by Garraty (New York, 1970); original interview by Garraty, "David M. Potter: Interpreting American History" (Oral History Dept., Butler Library, Columbia University, deposited Dec. 1968). Potter's discussion of historians included Frederick Jackson Turner: see p. 11. From an economist's standpoint, some implicit support for *People of Plenty's* historical argument is given by Gavin Wright, "The Origins of American Industrial Success, 1879–1940," *American Economic Review* 90 (1990), pp. 651–68.

For other views of abundance and American character developed in the 1950s, see John A. Kouwenhoven, "The Beer Can by the Highway" (1957, rev. ed. 1959) in *Beer Can,* ed. by Kouwenhoven (1961); Vance Packard, *The Waste Makers* (New York, 1960), chap. 20 ("The Changing American Character"). *People of Plenty,* chap. 4, argues that American-type social mobility undermines security of status and belonging. Wilkinson, "Journeys" (1990) suggests that Potter's southern background may have sharpened his sense of this. It is also reminiscent of Charles Dickens's ideas about mobility: see esp. *Great Expectations* (London, 1861), chap. 8.

Potter, "American Women and the American Character," *Stetson University Bulletin* 62 (Jan. 1962), pp. 1–22, was given as a Stetson University lecture in 1959. It is reprinted in *Character of Americans,* ed. by McGiffert (1970); Potter, *History and American Society* (1973); and John A. Hague, ed., *American Character and Culture in a Changing World* (Westport, Conn., 1979), which also contains the criticism by Alice Kessler-Harris, "American Women and the American Character: A Feminist Perspective." Potter's essay was published just before Betty Friedan, *The Feminine Mystique* (New York, 1963), and after some studies of American females featuring 'Moms' and sexuality: cf. Philip Wylie, *Generation of Vipers* (New York, 1942); Gorer, *American People* (1948); Margaret Mead, *Male and Female: A Study of the Sexes in a Changing World* (New York, 1949), pt. 4; Erikson, *Childhood and Society* (1950), chap. 8, sec. on " 'Mom.' " See also Hans D. Sebald, *Momism: The Silent Disease of America* (Chicago, 1976).

Sara M. Evans, *Born for Liberty: A History of Women in America* (New York, 1989), chaps. 11, 12, is informative and concise on crosscurrents affecting American women in the 1950s and 1960s. Ruth Sidel, *On Her Own: Growing Up in the Shadow of the American Dream* (New York, 1990) is in some respects an update of Potter's essay, discussing different mixtures of domesticity, career individualism, and community service. It focuses on adolescents and young women and finds three kinds of aspiration (or lack of). Like Potter, it attends to themes in advertising; cf. Vance Packard, *The Hidden Persuaders* (New York, 1957).

On traditions and shifts in American individualism, see Potter, "The Quest for the National Character" in *The Reconstruction of American History*, ed. by John Higham (New York, 1962), reprinted in *Character of Americans*, ed. by McGiffert (1970), and Potter, *History and American Society* (1973); see also Potter, "American Individualism in the Twentieth Century," rev. ed. (1965) in *Innocence and Power: Individualism in Twentieth-Century America*, ed. by Gordon Mills (Austin, Tex., 1965), reprinted in *History and American Society*, by Potter (1973). See other essays, ibid. and in *Freedom and Its Limitations*, by Potter (1976).

The French comparison in Potter's essay on "American Individualism" (cited above) gets some support from Bernard Poli's nicely written article, "The Hero in France and in America," *Journal of American Studies* 2 (1968), pp. 225–38, though Poli chiefly concentrates on characters in major fiction. Potter's own interest in foreign comparisons shows up in, e.g., "The Lincoln Theme and American National Historiography" (1947) and "The Civil War in the History of the World" (1968) in *South and the Sectional Conflict*, by Potter (1968); *People of Plenty* (1954), chap. 3; and "Canadian Views of the United States as a Reflex of Canadian Values" in *Canada Views the United States: Nineteenth-Century Political Attitudes*, ed. by S. F. Wise and Robert Craig Brown (Seattle, 1967).

In view of this interest in foreign comparisons, Potter's essay on "American Individualism" might have referred to portraits of British character, many of which also feature types of individualism. Cf. C. F. G. Masterman, *The Condition of England* (London, 1909); Henry L. Stuart, "As an Englishman Sees It," in *Civilization in the United States*, ed. by Harold L. Stearns (New York, 1922); Salvador de Madariaga, *Englishmen, Frenchmen, Spaniards* (London, 1928); Odette Keun, *I Discover the English* (London, 1934), remarkably frank sexually for the period; Orwell, "England Your England" (1941); Ginsberg, "National Character" (1942); Ernest Barker, ed., *The Character of England* (London, 1947), chaps. by Richard Law, I. J. Pittman, and Barker; Virginia Cowles, *No Cause for Alarm: A Study of Trends in England Today* (London, 1949); Farber's two articles titled "English and Americans" (1951, 1953); Geoffrey Gorer, *Exploring English Character* (London, 1955). In a later period, see the Anglo-American comparisons in Quentin Anderson's philosophical discussion of individualism, "John Dewey's American Democrat," *Daedalus* 108 (1979), pp. 145–59.

Potter's writing did not show the artistic eye for the symbolic detail of a Margaret Mead or David Riesman—in that sense he was less *literary* than them—yet he made more use of literary commentators in and around American Studies. See esp. Henry Nash Smith, *Virgin Land: The American West as Symbol and Myth* (Cambridge, Mass., 1950); Leslie Fiedler, *An End of Inno-*

cence (Boston, 1965); Fiedler, *Love and Death in the American Novel* (New York, 1960); and Dwight Macdonald, *Against the American Grain* (New York, 1962). A later literary work on American and modern individualism is *The Law of the Heart: Individualism and the Modern Self*, by Sam B. Girgus (Austin, Tex., 1979).

George W. Pierson and "The Moving American"

Pierson's four main articles on movement, migration, and mobility in relation to American culture and character are "The Moving American," *Yale Review* 44 (Autumn 1954), pp. 99–111; " 'The M-Factor' in American History," *American Quarterly* 14 (Summer 1962 Supplement), pp. 275–89; "Under a Wandering Star," *Virginia Quarterly Review* 39 (Autumn 1963), pp. 621–38; and " 'A Restless Temper . . . ,' " *American Historical Review* 69 (July 1964), pp. 969–89. These and other essays, variously revised, are in *The Moving American*, by Pierson (New York, 1973). "Goin' Some" (1964), one of the book's other pieces, has better examples of American slang than "The "M-Factor" does. Pierson added more notes to the book—these and his acknowledgments say more than most authors' do about the sources and development of his ideas. His 'coda,' quoted in my commentary (p. 200), is from a letter, GWP to RW, Nov. 9, 1988.

Pierson, "Henry Nash Smith," *American Scholar* 57 (1988), pp. 158–59, is informative on his own American Studies background at Yale while criticizing the literary-based "Garden" concept of the West in Smith's *Virgin Land* (1950). Pierson much admired the ideas of his senior colleague at Yale, Ralph H. Gabriel: see Gabriel, *The Course of American Democratic Thought* (New York, 1940). On the transplanting of cultures, and the question of regional culture, character, and stereotyping, see Pierson, "The Obstinate Concept of New England: A Study in Denudation," *New England Quarterly* 28 (1955), pp. 3–17, written as usual with great zest. An early influence here was Dixon Ryan Fox, *Ideas in Motion* (New York, 1935).

Pierson, *Tocqueville and Beaumont in America* (Cambridge, Mass., 1938), abridged by D. C. Lunt as *Tocqueville in America* (New York, 1959), contains excellent writing on Alex de Tocqueville's mind and background as well as his U.S. travels and the resulting book, Tocqueville, *Democracy in America* (2 vols., 1835, 1840). On the frontier factor, see Pierson, "The Frontier and Frontiersmen of Turner's Essays," *Pennsylvania Magazine of History and Biography* 64 (1940), abridged in *The Frontier Thesis*, ed. by Ray Allen Billington (New York, 1966); and Pierson, "The Frontier and American Institutions: A Criticism of the Turner Theory" (1942) in *The Turner Thesis Concerning the Role of the Frontier in American History*, ed. by George Rogers Taylor (Boston, 1956). Some of Pierson's revision of Turner's thesis was quite like that of

Hansen, *Immigrant in American History* (1940); and his ideas converged with those of Everett S. Lee, "The Turner Thesis Re-examined" (1961) in *Frontier Thesis*, ed. by Billington (1966): Lee stressed movement too.

Other modern theories of American character that highlight immigration and/or movement include Mead (pp. 15–29); Perry (pp. 33–47); Erikson, "American Identity" (1950) on a dual "cultivation of the sedentary and migratory . . ."; Kouwenhoven, *Beer Can by the Highway* (1961); Philip Slater (pp. 201–216); and McElroy, *Finding Freedom* (1989), which is actually better and fresher on historical geography than on immigration and values. In a more journalistic vein, see Ted Morgan, *On Becoming American* (Boston, 1976); Henry Fairlie, "Why I Love America," *New Republic* (July 4, 1983), pp. 13–17; and James Fallows, *More Like Us: Making America Great Again* (Boston, 1989), esp. introd. Vance Packard gives an unfavorable view of American movement in *A Nation of Strangers* (New York, 1972); it mainly concentrates on executive-class moving about and it does not say much about social character. A new literary perspective on the importance of how early immigrants wrote about America is Stephen Fender, *Sea Changes: British Emigration and American Literature* (Cambridge, UK, 1992).

Pierson's comments on mobility and the destruction of the environment suggest the influence of Rachel Carson, *The Silent Spring* (Boston, 1962). His belief that selective migration from the ghetto added to ghetto blight has received recent support from Nicholas Lemann's two Chicago articles on "The Origins of the Underclass," *Atlantic* (June 1986; July 1986). Still, Pierson's generally upbeat picture of American motives for moving needs to be set alongside studies of the migrating poor. Recent studies of two great movements of the poor in this century are *Land of Hope: Chicago, Black Southerners and the Great Migration,* by James R. Grossman (Chicago, 1989), and James N. Gregory, *American Exodus: The Dustbowl Migration and Okie Culture in California* (New York, 1989). Gregory notes that many of the 'Okies' came from towns and cities. Cf. John Steinbeck, *The Grapes of Wrath* (New York, 1939); Warren French, ed., *Companion to* The Grapes of Wrath (New York, 1963).

Philip E. Slater and "The Pursuit of Loneliness"

Slater, *The Pursuit of Loneliness: American Culture at the Breaking Point* (Boston, 1970), has chapters on family and sexual relationships and a tortuous psychology of American technological violence. Part of its first chapter addresses Whyte's *Organization Man* (1956) and the individualist ideal in "Individualism Reconsidered," by Riesman (1951). Slater revised and expanded his book in a 1976 edition. See also Slater, *Wealth Addiction* (New York, 1980).

Slater's path to these books is marked by some earlier writing: Robert

Bales and Slater, "Role Differentiation in Small Groups," in *Family, Socialization and Interaction Processes*, by Talcott Parsons et al. (Glencoe, Ill., 1955), chap. 5; Warren G. Bennis and Slater, *The Temporary Society* (New York, 1968); Slater, *The Glory of Hera: Greek Mythology and the Greek Family* (Boston, 1968).

Slater's writing in the late 1960s reflected the concern of intellectuals about violence in America. McGiffert, ed., *Character of Americans*, rev. ed. (1970) contained a collection of comments on the question, "Is America by Nature a Violent Society?" from the *New York Times Magazine* (Apr. 1968) and an excerpt from *Black Rage*, by William H. Grier and Price M. Cobbs (New York, 1968). But only some of the former, esp. David Riesman's comment, really touched on national character. For more on national character, written in the same climate, see Ronald Segal, *The Americans: A Conflict of Creed and Reality* (New York, 1968): his tone and position is quite like Slater's.

Slater's suggestion that respectable citizens attacked 'delinquents' as a way of battening down their own delinquent feelings was hypothetically supported, long before he wrote, by G. H. Mead, "The Psychology of Punishment," *American Journal of Sociology* 23 (1918), pp. 577–602—a psychological version of some of the ideas of Emile Durkheim. On contradictory feelings about social justice and obedience in the late 1960s, cf. Robert Coles, *The Middle Americans* (Boston, 1970), with evocative photos by Jon Erikson.

Kenneth T. Jackson, *Crabgrass Frontier: The Suburbanization of the United States* (New York, 1985), writes of the "loss of community" in a technological suburbia—his views here are quite like Slater's but more qualified. David M. Potter, "The Roots of American Alienation" (1963) in *History and American Society*, by Potter (1973) supplies a bridge between older ideas of modern isolation and newer interpretations more specific to America.

Charles Reich: Toward a New "Consciousness"

Reich, *The Greening of America* (New York, 1970), was preceded by Reich's long article, "The Greening of America," *New Yorker* (Sept. 26, 1970) which summarized the book but rather highlighted the institutional nature of "the corporate state" (the world of Consciousness II). Reich's autobiography, *The Sorcerer of Bolinas Reef* (New York, 1976), gives much background; so does his entry in *Current Biography*, rev. ed. (Princeton, 1972), pp. 362–64. Reich's law articles that led up to *Greening* are: "The New Property," *Yale Law Journal* 73 (1964), pp. 733–87; "Toward the Humanistic Study of Law," ibid. 74 (1965), pp. 1402–1408; "The Law of the Planned Society," ibid. 75 (1966), pp. 1227–70.

Greening's acknowledgments page lists twenty-two books which, Reich says, are only "a few of the most important [of his] written sources." Ideologically they range from Karl Marx, *The Economic and Philosophic Manuscripts of 1844* (London, 1968), through Jacques Ellul, *The Technological Society* (London, 1965), to the free-market argument of Friedrich A. Hayek, *The Road to Serfdom* (London, 1944). They include history, economics, sociology, and literary studies of American romanticism; two black writers (Malcolm X and Eldridge Cleaver); and novels by Ken Kesey, Norman Mailer, and Tom Wolfe. Of particular importance, it seems, were John Kenneth Galbraith, *The New Industrial State* (Boston, 1967), and Herbert Marcuse, *One-Dimensional Man* (Boston, 1964); also perhaps Marcuse, *Eros and Civilization* (Boston, 1955). On youth and the counterculture itself, Reich drew some information and ideas from Kenneth Keniston, *Young Radicals* (New York, 1968); he also cites Keniston, *The Uncommitted* (New York, 1965).

Reich's critique of "Consciousness II" America has some similarities with a founding document of the New Left, the "Port Huron Statement," issued by Students for a Democratic Society (SDS) and mainly written by Tom Hayden. It is reprinted in, e.g., *The Sixties Papers*, ed. by Judith Clavier Albert and Stewart Edward Albert (New York, 1984), pp. 176–96. The term "military-industrial complex," often quoted by opponents of 'technocracy' and the Vietnam War in the 1960s and 1970s, was coined by Dwight D. Eisenhower, "Farewell Address to the Nation" (Jan. 17, 1961): excerpted with comment in *The Military and American Society*, ed. by Stephen Ambrose and James Alden Barber (New York, 1972). On images of the Kennedy-type professional (a "Consciousness II" variant), see Rupert Wilkinson, "Connections with Toughness: The Novels of Eugene Burdick," *Journal of American Studies* 11 (1977), pp. 223–39.

On the history and different meanings of Reich's "false consciousness" concept, see Guenter Lewy, *False Consciousness: An Essay on Mystification* (New Brunswick, N.J., 1982), which traces it back to Engels and Marx. Cf. Marcuse's two books cited above; Fromm, *Escape from Freedom* (1941), chap. 5 and Appendix; Jules Henry's book on American character, *Culture Against Man* (New York, 1963); and Wilkinson, "Journeys to American Character" (1990), which compares Fromm's views with David Riesman's and gives more references. Cf. Riesman, "The Cash Customer," *Common Sense* 11 (1942), pp. 183–85. For a different approach to the social self, see Erving Goffman, *The Presentation of Self in Everyday Life* (New York, 1959).

Richard King, *The Party of Eros: Radical Social Thought and the Realm of Freedom* (Chapel Hill, N.C., 1972), tries to fit Reich into a tradition of sexual radicalism, but his comments on Reich and precursors are not narrowly confined to this theme. He also comments on Philip Slater (pp. 203–16), but his remarks here are less valid. On religious aspects of Reich's outlook, cf. William G. McLoughlin, *Revivals, Awakenings and Reform: An Essay on Religion and Social Change in America, 1607–1977* (Chicago, 1978), chap. 6.

Philip Nobile, ed., *The Con III Controversy: The Critics Look at* The

Greening of America (New York, 1971) includes a large number of distinguished commentators: some of them discuss the book's impact as well as its content. See esp. the fairly favorable comment by Max Ways, from a *Fortune* editorial, and a feminist criticism by Nancy McWilliams. A number of Nobile's authors saw *Greening* as a restricted elite view. See also the critique and background by Paul Wachtel, *The Poverty of Affluence: A Psychological Portrait of the American Way of Life* (New York, 1983), pp. 114–21. Barbara Ehrenreich's feminist criticism of male liberation in *Hearts of Men* (1983) has much to say about Reich but exaggerates his support for "consumerist" values. Richard F. Hamilton and James D. Wright, *The State of the Masses* (New York, 1986) starts with a criticism of *Greening* and uses survey data to refute the idea of a trend to "Consciousness III." They don't, however, do much tapping for the kinds of hopes and personal attitudes that Reich wrote about.

The theory of modern change in Ralph Turner, "The Real Self: From Institution to Impulse," *American Journal of Sociology* 81 (1976), pp. 989–1015, and trend data in Joseph Veroff et al., *The Inner American: A Self-Portrait from 1957 to 1976* (New York, 1981) give a kind of support to Reich's picture of a shift from "Consciousness II" toward "Consciousness III." Cf. Daniel Bell, *The Cultural Contradictions of Capitalism* (New York, 1976), based on essays going back to the early 1960s, with a summarizing, long foreword in the 1978 Basic Books paperback ed. Rather like Jack Kramer in Nobile's book above, Bell sees an emerging pattern in which people are "straight by day and swingers by night."

Reich's vision of "Consciousness III" has some similarity with Alvin Toffler, *The Third Wave* (New York, 1984). And if one extends his "Consciousness II" phase much further back in history and looks at it in gender terms, one gets close to the position of Susan Griffin's imaginative, whackily-written book, *Woman and Nature: The Roaring Inside* (New York, 1980). For Griffin, the quantifying, classifying control of nature is a historic male aggression against the female spirit. Reich's model of "Consciousness III," however, does leave a place for technology. For one story of what happened to a Reichian, techno-hippie dream, see Frank Rose, *West of Eden: The End of Innocence at Apple Computer* (New York, 1989).

Christopher Lasch and the 'New' Egoism

From the early 1970s to the early 1980s, assessments of the 'awareness movement' more or less expanded into a general critique of 'egocentrism' and narcissism in American character, or American upper-middle–class character. To a varying extent the trends were seen to be reaching through the 'modern world,' not just America. See, e.g., Henry Malcolm, *Generation of Narcissus*

(Boston, 1971); Tom Wolfe's essays and cartoons in *Mauve Gloves and Madmen, Clutter and Vine* (New York, 1976), esp. "The Perfect Crime" (1973) and "The Me Decade and the Third Great Awakening" (1976); Hans J. Morgenthau and Ethel Person, "The Roots of Narcissism," *Partisan Review* 45 (1978), pp. 337–47; Peter Marin, "The New Narcissism," *Harper's Magazine* 251 (Oct. 1985), pp. 45–46. Cf. the fictionalized narrative of Marin County, Calif., by Cyra McFadden, *The Serial* (New York, 1977). Theories of a new egoism not so centered on the awareness movement include Arnold Rogow, *The Dying Light: A Searching Look at America Today* (New York, 1975); a richer analysis by David Riesman, "Egocentrism: Is the American Character Changing?" *Encounter* (Aug.–Sept. 1980), pp. 19–28; and Marvin Harris, "Why It's Not the Same Old America," *Psychology Today* (Aug. 1981).

Christopher Lasch, *The Culture of Narcissism: American Life in an Age of Diminishing Expectations* (New York, 1979), fits into this writing, though it also connects with earlier writers (see below). See also its sequel, *The Minimal Self: Psychic Survival in Troubled Times* (New York, 1984), which makes more of doomsday and existential fears. The texts and notes of both books discuss many similar works and explain Lasch's differences with them.

Several books in the early 1980s quarreled with Lasch's stress on narcissism while sharing his view that Americans had become riveted on their psyches. See, e.g., Daniel Yankelovich, *New Rules: Searching for Self-Fulfillment in a World Turned Upside Down* (New York, 1981), pp. 34–36; Wachtel, *Poverty of Affluence* (1983), chap. 10. Stearns, *Anger* (1986), pp. 186, 283 (n. 66), disagreed on more technical grounds with Lasch's application of "narcissism" to modern young Americans. Peter Clecak, *America's Quest for the Ideal Self: Dissent and Fulfillment in the 60s and 70s* (New York, 1983), opposed Lasch and said that cultural critics had exaggerated the selfish, uncommunal nature of the search for psychic self-fulfillment. Cf. Marilyn Ferguson, *The Aquarian Conspiracy: Personal and Social Transformation in the 1980s* (Los Angeles, 1981). Richard Crockatt's lucid review essay on Clecak in *Over Here,* no. 1 (Nottingham, U.K., Spring 1984), pp. 18–22, explores the differences between Lasch and Clecak and their traditions.

One of the best essays on Lasch—and much more—is "The 'New' Narcissism in 20th-Century America," by Jesse Battan, *Journal of Social History* 17 (1983), pp. 199–220. In criticizing Lasch's historical theory of narcissism, Battan discusses a large number of writers and gives notes on even more—precursors of Lasch, critics of Lasch, contemporary theorists of American character and culture, and clinical writers on narcissism. She also contrasts late nineteenth-century fears of "neurasthenia" with late twentieth-century concerns about narcissism. On Lasch's book as history, see also Kenneth Lynn's critical review in *The Air-Line to Seattle: Studies in Literary and Historical Writing about America* (Chicago, 1983), chap. 16, reprinted from *Commentary* (Apr. 1979). For suggestions that American narcissism is not new to this century, see Tocqueville, *Democracy in America*, Vintage ed. (1954), I, pp. 53, 104; McWilliams, *Hawthorne . . . Looking-Glass Business* (1984); Wilkinson, *American Tough* (1986), pp. 13–14, 118–19.

As my commentary on Lasch observes (pp. 263–67), some of the trends perceived by Lasch, other than narcissism itself, were noted by Kluckhohn, "Shifts in American Values?" (1958), and Daniel Boorstin, *The Image, or What Happened to the American Dream* (New York, 1962), reissued with the subtitle *A Guide to Pseudo-events in America* (1964). Lasch's picture of a distrustful and fearful middle class, who want to have it all now, gets some support from Barbara Ehrenreich, *Fear of Falling: The Inner Life of the Middle Class* (New York, 1989). Like her *Hearts of Men*, however, it gives too little evidence for stressing, as it does, a middle-class dislike and fear of the working class. Helen Lefkowitz Horowitz, *Campus Life: Undergraduate Cultures from the End of the Eighteenth Century to the Present* (Chicago, 1987), pp. 255, 265ff., provides better quoted evidence of a fearful materialism. Michael Lewis, *The Culture of Inequality* (Amherst, 1978) does not use a clinical concept of narcissism but argues that American success-beliefs cause people to compensate in various ways for feeling failures. On fear and manipulation in corporation life, see Bennett, *Death of the Organization Man* (1990), and Robert B. Reich, *The Next American Frontier* (New York, 1983), chap. 8 ("Paper Entrepreneurialism"). However, John Taylor, *Circus of Ambition: The Culture of Wealth and Power in the Eighties* (New York, 1989), tells a story of voracious optimism rather than the underlying pessimism stressed by Lasch; and Herbert J. Gans, *Middle American Individualism: The Future of Liberal Democracy* (New York, 1988), pp. 104ff., denied that "middle Americans" *in general* had become greedier or more hedonist than they had in the past. On another front, though, Rodney A. Smolla, *Suing the Press* (New York, 1987) includes a kind of narcissism in explaining why Americans, or at least prominent Americans, seem to sue for defamation more than they used to.

In the literary realm, Wendy Lesser, "Autobiography and the 'I' of the Beholder," *New York Times Book Review* (Nov. 27, 1988), implicitly suggests that narcissism shapes American, not British, autobiography. In fiction, upper-class prototypes can be found in F. Scott Fitzgerald, *The Beautiful and Damned* (New York, 1922) and *The Great Gatsby* (New York, 1926). See also Joseph Heller, *Catch 22* (New York, 1961), whose Colonel Cathcart is a destructive version of David Riesman's "other-direction" mixed with narcissism: see chap. 19. Riesman, *Lonely Crowd* (1950) imagined an outcome quite like this (end of chap. 11). See also Norman Mailer, "The White Negro: Superficial Reflections on the Hipster" (1957) in *Advertisements for Myself*, by Mailer (1968), pp. 269–89; and Tom Wolfe, *The Bonfire of the Vanities* (New York, 1987), though Wolfe's Sherman McCoy does not have the deep vengefulness of a Lasch character. He does have some similarities with the real-life portrait in "Financing the American Dream," by Douglas Kennedy, *Indepen-*

dent Magazine (London, April 21, 1990), p. 16, though Kennedy presents his own ideas—not just Lasch's or Wolfe's—about the American cultural background. A recent report of a counter-trend, away from the selfish-yuppie stereotype, is Sherry Buchanan, "Dropping off the Track into a 'Helping' Career?" *International Herald Tribune* (Mar. 22, 1990), Business/Finance section.

For the personal and intellectual background of Lasch's ideas, see *Current Biography Yearbook* (Princeton, 1985), pp. 250–53. In "A Symposium: Christopher Lasch and the Culture of Narcissism," *Salmagundi*, no. 46 (Fall, 1979), pp. 194–202, Lasch's own comments start with his book's relation to his earlier writing and to "a tradition of social criticism . . . of Herbert Marcuse, Max Horkheimer, the early Erich Fromm, and before them Marx and Freud. . . ." See other contributors in the same issue; also Bernard Siegel, "The Agony of Christopher Lasch," *Reviews in American History* 8 (1980), pp. 285–95, whose critique includes an interesting argument that Lasch's treatment of other thinkers puts him in the same fix as the modern Americans he describes. At a British conference, Lasch later said that he was not just describing Americans; another panelist disagreed. See the discussion between Lasch and Michael Rustin in *Capitalism and Infancy: Essays on Psychoanalysis and Politics,* ed. by Barry Richards (London, 1984), section on "Family and Authority."

Key writing by Lasch that led to *Culture of Narcissism* includes *The New Radicalism in America 1889–1963: The Intellectual as a Social Type* (New York, 1965); *The Agony of the American Left* (New York, 1969); and *Haven in a Heartless World: The Family Besieged* (New York, 1977). A later article by Lasch, "Making America Feel Good about Itself," *New Statesman* (London, Aug. 29, 1986) stresses his belief in the *un*-conservative, disintegrating nature of modern capitalism. His view ties into various 'post-modernist' theories of literary-cultural critics. A place to begin is with Fredric Jameson, "Postmodernism, or the Cultural Logic of Late Capitalism," *New Left Review*, No. 146 (July–Aug. 1984), pp. 53–92.

Daniel Yankelovich: "Searching for Self-Fulfillment"

In *New Rules: Searching for Self-Fulfillment in a World Turned Upside Down* (New York, 1981), Yankelovich said he was looking at a changing American "psycho-culture," not American "social character" which he associated with much slower-changing values. Both, he believed, existed. In my terms, however, he was still writing about American social character.

New Rules was preceded by a long article excerpting and summarizing the book: Yankelovich, "New Rules in American Life," *Psychology Today* (Apr. 1981), pp. 35ff. See also Yankelovich, "The Work Ethic is Underemployed," *Psychology Today* (May 1982), pp. 5–8. Yankelovich's psychological and philosophical interests were reflected in the book he wrote with the philosopher William Barrett, *Ego and Instinct: Psychoanalysis and the Science of Man* (New York, 1969).

James Atlas, "Beyond Demographics," *Atlantic Monthly* (Oct. 1984), pp. 49–58, is informative on the "psycho-graphic" ("life-style" and social character) approach to market research including some of Yankelovich's work. Cf. Garry Trudeau's "Doonesbury" strip (syndicated Mar. 21, 22, 1985). A leader in the field was the Values and Lifestyles Program ("VALS") at Stanford Research Institute (not part of Stanford University) which produced a book by its director, Arnold Mitchell, *The Nine American Lifestyles: Who We Are and Where We're Going* (New York, 1983). The book included international comparisons but the researchers made a hash of it: they really altered their typology in different countries. A more sophisticated development is Young and Rubicam's "4C" program ("Cross Cultural Consumer Characterization"), but its reports are not published on the open market. See also Michael J. Weiss, *The Clustering of America* (New York, 1989), on the values and life-styles of forty "neighborhood types"—it has a chapter on "The Myth of the Average American," but the book is mainly on specific consumer behavior. On a more general plane, *America in Perspective: Major Trends in the United States through the 1980s* (Boston, 1986), by the British research firm, Oxford Analytica, started as a limited-release document for corporate clients; it includes some social-character data on changing attitudes to work, leisure, the future, and so on.

Mitchell's work on VALS, cited above, drew on A. A. Maslow's theory of a human "hierarchy of needs." In *New Rules*, Yankelovich accepted the theory to some degree but believed that the idea of scaling the hierarchy was a bad philosophy of life. *New Rules* came out of Yankelovich's studies of youth, dating from 1967. His culminating report in the series was *The New Morality: A Profile of America's Youth in the 70s* (New York, 1974). For a qualifying perspective on his conclusions, see American Council of Education, *Norms for Entering Freshmen* (Washington, D.C., annual) which shows changes in the way freshmen at various types of college rank different life "objectives." See esp. the series 1967–73. See also Horowitz, *Campus Life* (1987), chap. 11; John Brooks, "The New Snobbery: How to Show Off in America," *Atlantic Monthly* 247 (Jan. 1981), pp. 37–48; and Brooks, *Showing Off in America: From Conspicuous Consumption to Parody Display* (Boston, 1981). Unlike Yankelovich, they stress career ambition and materialism in the 1970s. At one point in his *Psychology Today* article, cited above, Yankelovich himself used an image that implied that self-fulfillers were like consumers: in their philosophy, psychological "needs" resembled the cubes of an icetray, each to be filled to the brim. But he did not stress this consumer analogy.

Yankelovich's idea of what might be called a 'post-materialist' age is opposed by Hamilton and Wright, *State of the Masses* (1986), but their survey data does not do much to address his core arguments. Yankelovich gets some support from data in Veroff et al., *Inner American* (1981). Carin Rubinstein, "The Revolution Within," *Psychology Today* (Aug. 1981), pp. 78, 80, gives a useful summary of this big, dense book. Its data, though, only goes back to 1957. Other studies have suggested that value shifts toward psychological self-fulfillment started somewhat earlier, and in older generations too, than Yankelovich's key young generation of the 1960s. Cf. Long, *American Dream and the Popular Novel* (1985); and Ehrenreich, *Hearts of Men* (1983), who sees the shift as a male one. On Yankelovich's side, Mintz and Kellog, *Domestic Revolutions* (1988), chap. 10, locates a shift in family values, including a new ethic of self-fulfillment, in the 1960s. Psychologists, they suggest, prepared the ground in the 1950s with new theories of 'self-actualization' and so on, but they did not really affect family structure until later.

One question in all this is whether the latter-day quest for self-fulfillment was psychologically wider and deeper than the hedonist, antirepressive movements earlier in the century. Cf. William E. Leuchtenburg, *The Perils of Prosperity, 1914–32* (Chicago, 1958), pp. 162–66; Grace Adams, "The Rise and Fall of Psychology," *Atlantic Monthly* 153 (Jan. 1934), pp. 82–92, which analyzes trends in magazine topics; and Elaine Tyler May, *Great Expectations: Marriage and Divorce in Post-Victorian America* (Chicago, 1980).

In a social and philosophical vein, Clecak, *America's Quest for the Ideal Self* (1983), pp. 152–55, agreed with much of what Yankelovich reported but assessed it more favorably than either he or Ehrenreich (above) did.

Robert N. Bellah: The Loss of "Commitment"

Robert N. Bellah, Richard Madsen, William M. Sullivan, Ann Swidler, and Steven M. Tipton, *Habits of the Heart* (Berkeley and Los Angeles, 1985) is based on "fieldwork" (interviews and observations) done from 1979 to 1984 in seven places, *four* of them in California. The others were a town near Boston; Philadelphia; and "a major Southern city." Ann Swidler, who did the San Jose study reported in the excerpt, had written *Organization Without Authority: Dilemmas of Social Organization in Free Schools* (Cambridge, Mass., 1980), which developed its topic into major questions of social change.

Bellah coordinated the research projects and produced the final draft of the book. He gives a personal, political, and intellectual background of his writing in the autobiographical introduction to *Beyond Belief: Essays on Religion in a Post-Traditional World*, by Bellah (New York, 1970). See also Schreker, *No Ivory Tower* (1986), pp. 262–63. Key writing by Bellah that led to *Habits of the Heart*—all connecting with it in various ways—included *Apache Kinship Systems* (Cambridge, Mass., 1952); *Tokugawa Religion: The*

Values of Pre-Industrial Japan (Glencoe, Ill., 1957); *Beyond Belief* (1970); and the preface and his two chapters in *The New Religious Consciousness*, ed. by Charles Y. Glock and Bellah (Berkeley and Los Angeles, 1976). Also "Civil Religion in America," *Daedalus* 96 (Winter 1976), pp. 1–21, which Bellah expanded into a book, *The Broken Covenant: American Civil Religion in Time of Trial* (New York, 1975).

For background on Bellah's concern with the *language* of individualism versus social bonds, see Rupert Wilkinson, "Language: The Sources of a Modern Obsession," *Encounter* (May 1982). An important forerunner of some of Bellah's thinking was Philip Rieff, *The Triumph of the Therapeutic* (New York, 1966). Clecak, *America's Quest* (1983), pp. 232–35, gives a helpful and relevant summary of this highly theoretical book (which is also addressed by Christopher Lasch, pp. 243ff). A more right-wing attack on relativism in American values is Allan Bloom, *The Closing of the American Mind* (New York, 1987). Variations on Bellah's theme include Louise Bernikow, "Alone: Yearning for Companionship in America," *New York Times Magazine* (Aug. 15, 1982), which quotes Bellah among others; and the concluding argument in *The Good Life: The Meaning of Success for the American Middle Class*, by Loren Baritiz (New York, 1989), chap. 6—much of the book is a loose and biased pastiche of American twentieth-century history.

On the other side, amid a flurry of newspaper articles implicitly agreeing with Bellah (or seeing the situation as worse), an article by T. R. Reid argued that Americans had retained and revived commitments to traditional values and community service: Reid, "Mom and Apple Pie: American Values Hold Firm," *Washington Post Service/Int. Herald Tribune* (Dec. 15, 1989). Two years before, Robert S. McElvaine had said much the same thing and put a liberal cast on it: he found signs of a new liberal concern for community. See McElvaine, *The End of the Conservative Era: Liberalism after Reagan* (New York, 1987), chaps. 8, 9. In regard to workers, Rick Fantasia has shown they can still form militant communities: Fantasia, *Cultures of Solidarity: Consciousness, Action, and Contemporary American Workers* (Berkeley and Los Angeles, 1988). And in the 1970s, Carol Stack observed communities of mutual help among poor black women: Stack, *All Our Kin: Strategies for Survival in a Black Community* (New York, 1974). Bellah et al., it is true, explicitly concentrated their studies on "white, middle-class Americans" but they also declared that "everyone in America thinks largely in middle-class categories" (p. ix). Whether right or wrong, their statement meant that lower-class studies were relevant to their argument.

Peter A. Lupsha and the Question of Subcultures

Lupsha, "American Values and Organized Crime: Suckers and Wise-guys"—reprinted here with slight abridgments—was originally published in *The American Self: Myth, Ideology, and Popular Culture*, ed. by Sam B. Girgus (Albuquerque, 1981), chap. 9. Lupsha's work on the nature and control of crime came out of research in local politics and decision making: see Heinz Eulau and Lupsha, "Decisional Structures and Coalition Formation . . ." in *Lawmakers in a Changing World*, ed. by Elke Frank (Englewood Cliffs, N.J., 1966). On his subsequent research, see Selwyn Raab's article on the "Mafia" in *New York Times* (Oct. 23, 1990).

Lupsha's essay was in part a response to Daniel Bell's "Crime as an American Way of Life: A Queer Ladder of Social Mobility" (1953) in *The End of Ideology*, by Bell (Cambridge, Mass., 1962), and some writing by Francis A. J. Ianni, esp. Ianni with Elizabeth Reuss Ianni, *A Family Business: Kingship and Social Control in Organized Crime* (New York, 1972). The arguments of all three are illuminated by Robert K. Merton's distinction between deviant means and deviant goals: see the typology of social types in his classic essay, "Social Structure and Anomie" (1949) in *Social Theory and Social Structure*, by Merton (New York, 1957, 1967).

As I said in the introduction to Lupsha's essay, his discussion of tradi-tional, mainstream values in professional crime is quite like that of David Matza and Gresham M. Sykes on youth gangs, "Juvenile Delinquency and Subterranean Values," *American Sociological Review* 26 (1961), pp. 711–19. Such gangs, they say, select out and stress some of the more *sub rosa* values of respectable elites. See their text and notes for related debates in criminology at the time. See also Ulf Hannerz, *Soulside: Inquiries into Ghetto Culture and Community* (New York, 1969), esp. chaps. 2, 9—based on a study done in Washington, D.C., that explored the relationship of "mainstream" culture to a black "ghetto" culture and different "life-style" types within it. Wilkinson, *American Tough* (1984), pp. 85–87, draws on the theoretical discussion in both these studies in developing a concept of "parallel idiom" and "cooption and feedback" between minority groups and middle-class elites: cf. Dick Hebdige, *Subculture: The Meaning of Style* (London, 1979).

For other, theoretical views of culture/subculture and elites/minorities that connect with national-character issues, see Elizabeth Fox-Genovese, "Be-tween Individualism and Fragmentation: American Culture and the New Literary Studies of Race and Gender," *American Quarterly* 42 (Mar. 1990), pp. 7–34; and T. H. Breen's essay on seventeenth-century Virginians, "Looking Out for Number One" (1979) in *Puritans and Adventurers*, by Breen (1980), incl. p. 299, n. 2. Breen cites anthropological writing on "dominant and variant value systems." As Walter Metzger has suggested in "Generalizations about National Character" (1963), one way of approaching it is to build up comparisons of equivalent subcultures in several countries. A good start here is Lynn Payer, *Medicine and Culture: Varieties of Treatment in the United States, England, West Germany, and France* (New York, 1988), which includes national attitudes as one factor in the differences between the various nations' doctors and medical practices.

This bibliography cannot begin to cover studies of social character based on specific American groups and subcultures. What it can do is to cite some of the studies that, directly or indirectly, address the main question here: Do differences of group and subculture within the United States invalidate or merely modify the idea of a national character? Many kinds of subculture are relevant; they might even, for example, include the *generation* group. See Wade Green on "the so-called Silent Generation," born in the 1930s, in the *New York Times* (Jan. 5, 1990), and David Riesman, "The Found Generation" (1956) in *Abundance for What?* by Riesman (1964); but cf. Joseph Adelson, "What Generation Gap?" *New York Times Magazine* (Jan. 18, 1970), reprinted in *Character of Americans*, ed. by McGiffert (1970), which is also a data-backed warning against overgeneralizing from elite youth.

The following notes concentrate mainly on region (especially the South) and class. On region, see John Gillin, "National and Regional Cultural Values in the United States," *Social Forces* 34 (1955), pp. 107–13. For decades it has been said that media, national brands, migration, and so on are 'homogenizing' the nation, but some census and survey data has shown no weakening of regional differences in behavior; and a study by Evon Z. Vogt found that when a population from a particular "subcultural" background migrated across the country, it retained its traditional "variant" on American culture. See Vogt, "American Subcultural Continua as Exemplified by the Mormons and Texans," *American Anthropologist* 57 (1955), pp. 1163–72. On regions, ethnic groups, national character, and so on, a supporter of the 'homogenizing' thesis is Martindale, *Community, Character and Civilization* (1963). So was David M. Potter with regard to the South vis-à-vis Americans in general: see Potter, "An Appraisal of Fifteen Years of the *Journal of Southern History*," *Journal of Southern History* 16 (1950), pp. 25–32; and "On Understanding the South" (1964) in *South and the Sectional Conflict*, by Potter (1968).

For differing views on the question of a distinctive southern character (or characters), past and present, cf. ibid; C. Vann Woodward, *The Burden of Southern History*, Vintage paperback ed. (1960) (Baton Rouge, La., 1950), pp. 16–24, 36–37, 168–69; Howard Zinn, *The Southern Mystique* (New York, 1964); and a series of books by John Shelton Reed which range from lively essays to survey statistics and discuss gender, class, and the operation of stereotypes. See Reed, *The Enduring South: Subcultural Persistence in Mass Society* (Lexington, Mass., 1972) with a good and relevant bibliography; *One South: An Ethnic Approach to Regional Culture* (Baton Rouge, 1982), esp. chap. 13; *Southerners: The Social Psychology of Sectionalism* (Chapel Hill, N.C.,

1983); and *Southern Folk Plain and Fancy: Native White Social Types* (Athens, Ga., 1986). See also Michael O'Brien, *Rethinking the South: Essays in Intellectual History* (Baltimore, 1988); and Cherry Good, "The Southern Lady, or the Art of Dissembling," *Journal of American Studies* 23 (1989), pp. 72–77, which includes its own interview results, has an extensive bibliography, and attends to different levels of the ideal and the real.

A brilliant piece, truly 'American Studies,' which combines aspects of region and class, is "The Manassa Mauler and the Fighting Marine: An Interpretation of the Dempsey-Tunney Fights," by Elliott J. Gorn, *Journal of American Studies* 19 (1985), pp. 27–47. Gorn argues that each boxer symbolized an ethos with distinctive American roots. On the question of class differences in basic attitudes and values, cf. Clyde and Florence Kluckholn, "American Culture: Generalized Orientations and Class Patterns" in *Conflicts of Power in Modern Culture*, ed. by Lyman Bryson (New York, 1947); Florence Rockwood Kluckholn, "Dominant and Substitute Profiles of Cultural Orientations: . . . Social Stratification," *Social Forces* 28 (1950), pp. 376–93; Herbert Hyman, "The Value Systems of Different Classes" (1953) in *Class, Status and Power,* ed. by Richard Bendix and S. M. Lipset (New York, 1953, rev. ed. 1966), pp. 488–89, which sometimes confuses values with realistic appraisals of opportunities; Ely Chinoy, *Automobile Workers and the American Dream* (Boston, 1955); Donald G. McKinley, *Social Class and Family Life* (New York, 1964), which cites and argues with earlier studies; Bennett M. Berger, "Suburbs, Subcultures and Styles of Life" (1965) in *Looking for America,* by Berger (1971); Richard F. Hamilton, *Class and Politics in the United States* (New York, 1972), esp. chap. 11; and David M. Schneider and Raymond T. Smith, *Class Differences and Sex Roles in American Kinship and Family Structure* (Englewood Cliffs, N.J., 1973). On theories of class and ethnic "homogenization" in mid–twentieth-century consumer culture, see Gary Gerstle, *Working-Class Americanism: The Politics of Labor in a Textile City, 1914–1960* (Cambridge, U.K., and New York, 1989), pp. 2–3.

In *Blue-Collar Aristocrats: Life-Styles at a Working Class Tavern* (Madison, Wis., 1975), E. E. LeMasters claimed that working-class wives had more 'middle-class' attitudes to child-rearing than working-class husbands, due in part at least to their different exposure to mass media. David Halle, too, suggested that the wives of the New Jersey male chemical workers he studied were quite 'middle-class' in attitude as they tended to have white-collar jobs. Halle's excellent book, *America's Working Man: Work, Home, and Politics among Blue-Collar Property Owners* (Chicago, 1984), has an extensive bibliography and is especially relevant because it argues that the men simultaneously held three different group identities and ideologies; only one of the three was really a 'working-class' consciousness.

In a more celebratory vein, Michael Novak has tried to fit the national-character idea into America's cultural pluralism by claiming that Americans have evolved a "pluralistic personality," a new and unique character type, adept at relating to different groups and cultural traditions, and able to select its own mixtures from them. See Novak, "Pluralism: A Humanistic Perspective" in *Harvard Encyclopaedia of American Ethnic Groups*, ed. by Stephan Thernstrom (Cambridge, Mass., 1980), pp. 776–78 (section on "The Pluralistic Personality"). Cf. Herbert J. Gans, "Symbolic Ethnicity: The Future of Ethnic Groups and Cultures in America" in *On the Making of Americans*, ed. by Gans et al. (1979).

Finally, elites too can be subcultures. In *The Way of the Wasp: How It Made America and How It Can Save It, So to Speak* (New York, 1991) esp. ch. 3, Richard Brookhiser superficially delineates the character of what is still often considered America's dominant group, as an influential subculture in decline but worthy of recovery.

Peter N. Stearns and "Emotionology"

Carol Zisowitz Stearns and Peter N. Stearns defined "emotionology" and staked out the field in their article, "Emotionology: Clarifying the History of Emotions and Emotional Standards," *American Historical Review* 90 (1985), pp. 813–36. They defined the field more briefly in the introduction to their book, *Anger: The Struggle for Emotional Control in America's History* (Chicago, 1986), and they went on to co-edit *Emotion and Social Change: Toward a New Psychohistory* (New York, 1988). (*Anger* was Carol Stearns's first book; hence the focus of this bibliography is on Peter Stearns's writing.)

As a scholar of European social history, Peter Stearns had already grappled with issues about national character in his article, "National Character and European Labor History," *Journal of Social History* 4 (Winter 1970–71), pp. 95–124, reprinted in *Workers in the Industrial Revolution: Recent Studies of Labor in the United States and Europe*, ed. by Stearns and Daniel J. Walkowitz (New Brunswick, N.J., 1974). Other relevant writing by Stearns includes *Revolutionary Syndicalism and French Labor: A Cause without Rebels* (New Brunswick, N.J., 1971), which questioned the importance of national character in the movement; Harvey Mitchell and Stearns, *Workers and Protest: The European Labor Movement, the Working Classes, and the Origins of Social Democracy* (Itasca, Ill., 1971), a book of essays in which Stearns argued against his co-author's stress on national differences; *Paths to Authority: The Middle Class and the Industrial Labor Force in France, 1820–48* (Urbana, Ill., 1978), which discussed middle-class varieties of attitude and behavior among "industrialists"; and *Old Age in European Society: The Case of France* (London, 1977), esp. chap. 2, which made some comparisons with American attitudes. See also Stearns, *Be a Man! Males in Modern Society* (New York, 1979), which generalized about definitions of masculinity in Western society on the basis of class rather than nation (without being Marxist).

Stearns's approach to masculinity can be compared with more American-focused studies: e.g., Myron Brenton, *The American Male* (New York, 1966); Lucy Komisar, "Violence and the Masculine Mystique," *Washington Monthly* (July 1970), pp. 39–48; Marc Feigen Fasteau, *The Male Machine* (New York, 1975); Mark Gerzon, *A Choice of Heroes: The Changing Faces of American Manhood* (Boston, 1982), which is more superficial than Ehrenreich's closely argued, if somewhat distorted, *Hearts of Men* (1983). See also Paul Gardner's British view, *Nice Guys Finish Last: Sport and American Life* (London, 1974). From the early 1970s, most writing on masculinity has been influenced to a varying degree by feminism and 'men's liberation,' the movement to 'free' men from a need to dominate, compete, and curb their feelings. Earlier commentaries on American masculinity made more of reactions against 'Momism.' See, e.g., Gorer, *American People* (1948); also two studies not ostensibly confined to the United States: Talcott Parsons, "Certain Primary Sources and Patterns of Aggression in the Social Structure of the Western World," *Psychiatry* 10 (1947), pp. 167–81; Jackson Toby, "Violence and the Masculine Ideal," *Annals of the American Academy of Political and Social Science* 364 (1966), pp. 19ff.

Wilkinson, *American Tough* (1984), on conceptions of toughness in American history and culture, tries to go beyond the subject of masculinity, but the photo essays in the 1986 Harper paperback ed. give more suggestions of American *female* tough modes than the main text does. See also David Bertelson, *Snowflakes and Snowdrifts: Individualism and Sexuality in America* (Lanham, Md., 1986), whose theories are not confined to one gender or to heterosexuality; it has an extensive bibliography. For historical background, see John D'Emilio and Estelle B. Freedman, *Intimate Matters: A History of Sexuality in America* (New York, 1988).

Like the Stearnses' book on anger, some of this writing was an attempt to get a new purchase on American character by concentrating on an emotional area or type of attitude not fully dealt with before. Joseph Epstein, *Ambition: The Secret Passion* (New York, 1980) is an example of this. Americans, he said, still showed ambition, but from the early 1900s it had become more defensive, more challenged by other values. His evidence was largely literary, but his book reflected the fears of various pundits at the time that Americans had lost confidence, competence, and vigor. As usual, writing about American character told a tale of contemporary intellectual moods.

Index of Names

Page numbers in **boldface** refer to major excerpts and accompanying introductions and commentaries. Page numbers in *italic* refer to the bibliography.

Index

Index